Implementing Cisco IP Switched Networks (SWITCH) Foundation Learning Guide

Richard Froom, CCIE No. 5102

Balaji Sivasubramanian

Erum Frahim, CCIE No. 7549

Cisco Press

800 East 96th Street

Indianapolis, IN 46240

Implementing Cisco IP Switched Networks (SWITCH) Foundation Learning Guide

Richard Froom, CCIE No. 5102

Balaji Sivasubramanian

Erum Frahim, CCIE No. 7549

Copyright© 2010 Cisco Systems, Inc.

Published by:
Cisco Press
800 East 96th Street
Indianapolis, IN 46240 USA

Printed in the United States of America

Third Printing: February 2011

Library of Congress Cataloging-in-Publication data is on file.

ISBN-13: 978-1-58705-884-4

ISBN-10: 1-58705-884-7

Warning and Disclaimer

This book is designed to provide information about the Implementing Cisco IP Switched Networks (SWITCH) course in preparation for taking the SWITCH 642-813 exam. Every effort has been made to make this book as complete and as accurate as possible, but no warranty or fitness is implied.

The information is provided on an "as is" basis. The authors, Cisco Press, and Cisco Systems, Inc. shall have neither liability nor responsibility to any person or entity with respect to any loss or damages arising from the information contained in this book or from the use of the discs or programs that may accompany it.

The opinions expressed in this book belong to the author and are not necessarily those of Cisco Systems, Inc.

Trademark Acknowledgments

All terms mentioned in this book that are known to be trademarks or service marks have been appropriately capitalized. Cisco Press or Cisco Systems, Inc., cannot attest to the accuracy of this information. Use of a term in this book should not be regarded as affecting the validity of any trademark or service mark.

Corporate and Government Sales

The publisher offers excellent discounts on this book when ordered in quantity for bulk purchases or special sales, which may include electronic versions and/or custom covers and content particular to your business, training goals, marketing focus, and branding interests. For more information, please contact: **U.S. Corporate and Government Sales**   1-800-382-3419   corpsales@pearsontechgroup.com

For sales outside the United States, please contact: **International Sales**   international@pearsoned.com

Feedback Information

At Cisco Press, our goal is to create in-depth technical books of the highest quality and value. Each book is crafted with care and precision, undergoing rigorous development that involves the unique expertise of members from the professional technical community.

Readers' feedback is a natural continuation of this process. If you have any comments regarding how we could improve the quality of this book, or otherwise alter it to better suit your needs, you can contact us through e-mail at feedback@ciscopress.com. Please make sure to include the book title and ISBN in your message.

We greatly appreciate your assistance.

Publisher: Paul Boger

Associate Publisher: Dave Dusthimer

Executive Editor: Mary Beth Ray

Managing Editor: Sandra Schroeder

Development Editor: Andrew Cupp

Senior Project Editor: Tonya Simpson

Editorial Assistant: Vanessa Evans

Book Designer: Louisa Adair

Cover Designer: Sandra Schroeder

Composition: Mark Shirar

Indexer: Tim Wright

Cisco Representative: Erik Ullanderson

Cisco Press Program Manager: Anand Sundaram

Technical Editors: Geoff Tagg, Sonya Coker, Jeremy Creech, Rick Graziani, David Kotfila, Wayne Lewis, Jim Lorenz, Snezhy Neshkova, Allan Reid, Bob Vachon

Copy Editor: Apostrophe Editing Services

Proofreader: Sheri Cain

Americas Headquarters	Asia Pacific Headquarters	Europe Headquarters
Cisco Systems, Inc.	Cisco Systems (USA) Pte. Ltd.	Cisco Systems International BV
San Jose, CA	Singapore	Amsterdam, The Netherlands

Cisco has more than 200 offices worldwide. Addresses, phone numbers, and fax numbers are listed on the Cisco Website at **www.cisco.com/go/offices.**

About the Authors

Richard E. Froom, CCIE No. 5102, attended Clemson University where he majored in computer engineering. While attending Clemson, Richard held positions at different times for the university network team, IBM, and Scientific Research Corporation. After graduation, Richard joined Cisco. Richard's first role within Cisco was as a TAC engineer supporting Cisco Catalyst switches. After several years in the TAC, Richard moved into a testing role supporting Cisco MDS and SAN technologies. In 2009, Richard moved into the Enhanced Customer Aligned Testing Services (ECATS) organization within Cisco as a test manager of a team focused on testing customer deployments of UCS and Nexus.

Balaji Sivasubramanian is a product line manager in the Cloud Services and Switching Technology Group focusing on upcoming products in the cloud services and Data Center virtualization area. Before this role, Balaji was a senior product manager for the Catalyst 6500 switches product line, where he successfully launched the Virtual Switching System (VSS) technology worldwide. He started his Cisco career in Cisco Technical Assistant Center working in the LAN switching products and technologies. Balaji has been a speaker at various industry events such as Cisco Live and VMworld. Balaji has a Master of Science degree in computer engineering from the University of Arizona and a Bachelor of Engineering degree in electrical and electronics from the College of Engineering, Guindy, Anna University (India).

Erum Frahim, CCIE No. 7549, is a technical leader working for Enhanced Customer Aligned Testing Services (ECATS) at Cisco. In her current role, Erum is leading efforts to test Datacenter solutions for several Cisco high-profile customers. Prior to this, Erum managed the Nexus platform escalation group and served as a team lead for Datacenter SAN Test lab under the Cisco Datacenter Business Unit. Erum joined Cisco in 2000 as a technical support engineer. Erum has a Master of Science degree in electrical engineering from Illinois Institute of Technology and also holds a Bachelor of Engineering degree from NED University, Karachi Pakistan. Erum also authors articles in *Certification* Magazine and Cisco.com.

About the Technical Reviewers

Geoff Tagg runs a small U.K. networking company and has worked in the networking industry for nearly 30 years. Before that, he had 15 years of experience with systems programming and management on a wide variety of installations. Geoff has clients ranging from small local businesses to large multinationals and has combined implementation with training for most of his working life. Geoff's main specialties are routing, switching, and networked storage. He lives in Oxford, England, with his wife, Christine, and family and is a visiting professor at nearby Oxford Brookes University.

Sonya Coker has worked in the Cisco Networking Academy program since 1999 when she started a local academy. She has taught student and instructor classes locally and internationally in topics ranging from IT Essentials to CCNP. As a member of the Cisco Networking Academy development team she has provided subject matter expertise on new courses and course revisions.

Jeremy Creech is a learning and development manager for Cisco with more than 13 years experience in researching, implementing, and managing data and voice networks. Currently, he is a curriculum development manager for the Cisco Networking Academy

Program leveraging his experience as the content development manager for CCNP Certification exams. He has recently completed curriculum development initiatives for ROUTE, SWITCH, TSHOOT, and CCNA Security.

Rick Graziani teaches computer science and computer networking courses at Cabrillo College in Aptos, California. Rick has worked and taught in the computer networking and information technology field for almost 30 years. Prior to teaching Rick worked in IT for various companies including Santa Cruz Operation, Tandem Computers, and Lockheed Missiles and Space Corporation. He holds a Master of Arts degree in computer science and systems theory from California State University Monterey Bay. Rick also does consulting work for Cisco and other companies. When Rick is not working, he is most likely surfing. Rick is an avid surfer who enjoys surfing at his favorite Santa Cruz breaks.

David Kotfila, CCNA, CCDA, CCNP, CCDP, CCSP, CCVP, CCAI, teaches in the computer science department at Rensselaer Polytechnic Institute, Troy, New York. More than 550 of his students have received their CCNA, 200 have received their CCNP, and 14 have received their CCIE. David likes to spend time with his wife Kate, his daughter Charis, and his son Chris. David enjoys hiking, kayaking, and reading.

Dr. Wayne Lewis has been a faculty member at Honolulu Community College since receiving a Ph.D. in math from the University of Hawaii at Manoa in 1992, specializing in finite rank torsion-free modules over a Dedekind domain. Since 1992, he served as a math instructor, as the state school-to-work coordinator, and as the legal main contact for the Cisco Academy Training Center (CATC). Dr. Lewis manages the CATC for CCNA, CCNP, and Security, based at Honolulu Community College, which serves Cisco Academies at universities, colleges, and high schools in Hawaii, Guam, and American Samoa. Since 1998, he has taught routing, multilayer switching, remote access, troubleshooting, network security, and wireless networking to instructors from universities, colleges, and high schools in Australia, Britain, Canada, Central America, China, Germany, Hong Kong, Hungary, Indonesia, Italy, Japan, Korea, Mexico, Poland, Singapore, Sweden, Taiwan, and South America both onsite and at Honolulu Community College.

Jim Lorenz is an instructor and curriculum developer for the Cisco Networking Academy Program. Jim has co-authored Lab Companions for the CCNA courses and the textbooks for the Fundamentals of UNIX course. He has more than 25 years of experience in information systems, ranging from programming and database administration to network design and project management. Jim has developed and taught computer and networking courses for both public and private institutions. As the Cisco Academy Manager at Chandler-Gilbert College in Arizona, he was instrumental in starting the Information Technology Institute (ITI) and developed a number of certificates and degree programs. Jim co-authored the CCNA Discovery online academy courses, *Networking for Home and Small Businesses* and *Introducing Routing and Switching in the Enterprise*, with Allan Reid. Most recently, he developed the hands-on labs for the CCNA Security course and the CCNPv6 Troubleshooting course.

Snezhy Neshkova, CCIE No. 11931, has been a Cisco Certified Internetwork Expert since 2003. She has more than 20 years of networking experience, including IT field services and support, management of information systems, and all aspects of networking education. Snezhy has developed and taught CCNA and CCNP networking courses to instructors from universities, colleges, and high schools in Canada, the United States, and Europe. Snezhy's passion is to empower students to become successful and compassionate lifelong learners. Snezhy holds a Master of Science degree in computer science from Technical University, Sofia.

Allan Reid, CCNA, CCNA-W, CCDA, CCNP, CCDP, CCAI, MLS, is a professor in information and communications engineering technology and the lead instructor at the Centennial College CATC in Toronto, Canada. He has developed and taught networking courses for both private and public organizations and has been instrumental in the development and implementation of numerous certificate, diploma, and degree programs in networking. Outside his academic responsibilities, Allan has been active in the computer and networking fields for more than 25 years and is currently a principal in a company specializing in the design, management, and security of network solutions for small and medium-sized companies. Allan is a curriculum and assessment developer for the Cisco Networking Academy Program and has authored several Cisco Press titles.

Bob Vachon, CCNP, CCNA-S, CCAI, is a professor in the computer systems technology program at Cambrian College and has more than 20 years of experience in the networking field. In 2001 he began collaborating with the Cisco Networking Academy on various curriculum development projects including CCNA, CCNA Security, and CCNP courses. For 3 years Bob was also part of an elite team authoring CCNP certification exam questions. In 2007, Bob co-authored the Cisco Press book *CCNA Exploration: Accessing the WAN*.

Dedications

This book is dedicated to my wife Beth and my son Nathan. I appreciate their support for the extra time that went into completing this book. —Richard

This book is dedicated to my wife Swapna, who has been very supportive and encouraging in me writing this book. —Balaji

This book is dedicated to my husband Faraz and my dearest daughter Alisha, who were very supportive as I wrote this book. I would like to say extra thanks to my mom and grandmother for remembering me in their prayers. I would also like to dedicate this book to my niece and nephew Shayan and Shiza and a very new member Zayan, who are the love of my life, and finally, my siblings, sister-in-law, and father, who are always there to help me out in any situation. —Erum

Acknowledgments

Richard: I'd like to give special recognition to the entire Cisco Press team for the patience and support in producing this title.

Balaji: I would like to acknowledge Mary Beth and Andrew from the Cisco Press team for their patience and support during the development of the book.

Erum: I would like to give my thanks to Cisco Press—especially to Mary Beth for being understanding during the development of the book. In addition, I would like to acknowledge all the reviewers who helped make the book more valuable.

Contents at a Glance

Contents

Icons Used in This Book

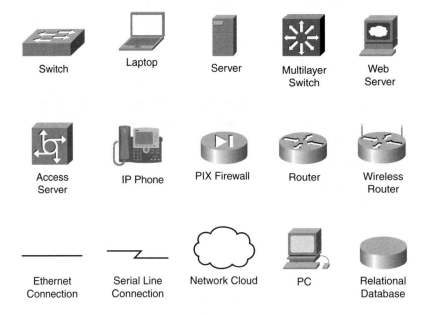

Command Syntax Conventions

The conventions used to present command syntax in this book are the same conventions used in the IOS Command Reference. The Command Reference describes these conventions as follows:

- **Boldface** indicates commands and keywords that are entered literally as shown. In actual configuration examples and output (not general command syntax), boldface indicates commands that are manually input by the user (such as a **show** command).

- *Italic* indicates arguments for which you supply actual values.

- Vertical bars (|) separate alternative, mutually exclusive elements.

- Square brackets ([ ]) indicate an optional element.

- Braces ({ }) indicate a required choice.

- Braces within brackets ([{ }]) indicate a required choice within an optional element.

Introduction

Over the past several years, switching has evolved from simple Layer 3 switches to switches supporting Layer 4 through Layer 7 features, such as server load balancing, URL inspection, firewalls, VPNs, access-based control, and so on, with large port densities. The multilayer switch has become an all-in-one component of the network infrastructure. As a result of this evolution, enterprise and service providers are deploying multilayer switches in place of multiple network components, such as routers and network appliances. Switching is no longer a part of the network infrastructure; it is now *the* network infrastructure, with wireless as the latest evolution.

As enterprises, service providers, and even consumers deploy multilayer switching, the need for experienced and knowledgeable professionals to design, configure, and support the multilayer switched networks has grown significantly. CCNP and CCDP certifications offer the ability for network professionals to prove their competency.

CCNP and CCDP are more than résumé keywords. Individuals who complete the CCNP and CCDP certifications truly prove their experience, knowledge, and competency in networking technologies. A CCNP certification demonstrates an individual's ability to install, configure, and operate LAN, WAN, and dial access services for midsize to large networks deploying multiple protocols. A CCDP certification demonstrates an individual's ability to design high-performance, scalable, and highly available routed and switched networks involving LAN, WAN, wireless, and dial access services.

Both the CCNP and CCDP certification tracks require you to pass the SWITCH 642-813 exam. For the most up-to-date information about Cisco certifications, visit the following website: www.cisco.com/web/learning/le3/learning_career_certifications_and_learning_paths_home.html.

Objectives and Methods

This book's content is based on the Cisco SWITCH course that has recently been introduced as part of the CCNP curriculum; it provides knowledge and examples in the area of implementing Cisco switched networks. It is assumed that the reader possesses as much Cisco background as is covered in the Cisco ROUTE and TSHOOT courses. The content of this book is enough to prepare the reader for the SWITCH exam, too. Note that the e-learning content of the Cisco SWITCH course has been integrated into this book.

To accomplish these tasks, this text includes in-depth theoretical explanations of SWITCH topics and provides illustrative design and configuration examples. The theoretical explanations of SWITCH topics include background information, standards references, and document listings from Cisco.com. This book goes beyond just presenting the necessary information found on the certification exam and in the SWITCH course. This book attempts to present topics, theory, and examples in such a way that you truly understand the topics that are necessary to build multilayer switched networks in today's demanding networks. The examples and questions found in the chapters of this book make you contemplate and apply concepts found in each chapter. The goal is to have you understand the topics and then apply your understanding when you attempt the certification exam or take the SWITCH course.

Chapter review questions help readers evaluate how well they absorbed the chapter content. The questions are also an excellent supplement for exam preparation.

Who Should Read This Book?

Those individuals who want to learn about modern switching techniques and want to see several relevant examples will find this book very useful. This book is most suitable for those who have some prior routing and switching knowledge but would like to learn or enhance their switching skill set. Readers who want to pass the Cisco SWITCH exam can find all the content they need to successfully do so in this book. The Cisco Networking Academy CCNP SWITCH course students use this book as their official book.

Cisco Certifications and Exams

Cisco offers four levels of routing and switching certification, each with an increasing level of proficiency: Entry, Associate, Professional, and Expert. These are commonly known by their acronyms CCENT (Cisco Certified Entry Networking Technician), CCNA (Cisco Certified Network Associate), CCNP (Cisco Certified Network Professional), and CCIE (Cisco Certified Internetworking Expert). There are others, too, but this book focuses on the certifications for enterprise networks.

For the CCNP certification, you must pass exams on a series of CCNP topics, including the SWITCH, ROUTE, and TSHOOT exams. For most exams, Cisco does not publish the scores needed for passing. You need to take the exam to find that out for yourself.

To see the most current requirements for the CCNP certification, go to Cisco.com and click **Training and Events**. There you can find out other exam details such as exam topics and how to register for an exam.

The strategy you use to prepare for the SWITCH exam might differ slightly from strategies used by other readers, mainly based on the skills, knowledge, and experience you have already obtained. For instance, if you have attended the SWITCH course, you might take a different approach than someone who learned switching through on-the-job training. Regardless of the strategy you use or the background you have, this book helps you get to the point where you can pass the exam with the least amount of time required.

How This Book Is Organized

This book is organized such that the fundamentals of multilayer switched network design are covered in the first chapters. Thereafter, the book continues with a discussion of implementation of the design features such as VLAN, Spanning Tree, and inter-VLAN routing in the multilayer switched environment. This book is organized as follows:

- **Chapter 1, "Analyzing the Cisco Enterprise Campus Architecture"**—This chapter opens with a brief introution to Cisco campus network architectures and designs. The chapter continues with a brief review of switching terminology for campus networks, followed by an introduction to Cisco switches. The chapter then continues with a of discussion of campus design fundamentals. Lastly, the chapter closes by introducing the PPDIOO Lifecycle Approach to Network Design and Implementation.

- **Chapter 2, "Implementing VLANs in Campus Networks"**—This chapter covers implemenation of virtual LANs (VLAN) in a given campus network, including discussions on private VLANs, VTP, and 802.1Q trunking. In addition, this chapter covers implementation of EtherChannel in an enterpruse network.

- **Chapter 3, "Implementing Spanning Tree"**—This chapter discusses the various Spanning Tree protocols, such as PVRST+ and MST, with overview and configuration samples. This chapter also continues the discussion with advanced Cisco STP enhancements and spanning-tree troubleshooting methodology.

- **Chapter 4, "Implementing Inter-VLAN Routing"**—This chapter transitions into discussing Layer 3 switching by covering inter-VLAN routing. The chapter then continues with the discussion on Dynamic Host Configuration Protocol (DHCP). In addition, it discusses Cisco Express Forwarding (CEF)–based multilayer switching.

- **Chapter 5, "Implementing High Availability and Redundancy in a Campus Network"**—This chapter covers the introduction to high availability in campus networks, followed by methodology on how to build resilient networks. This chapter continues to describe the tools available to monitor high availability such as SNMP and IP Service Level Agreement (SLA). This chapter concludes with available high availability options for switch supervisor engine and gateway redundancy protocols such as Hot Standby Router Protocol (HSRP), Virtual Router Redundancy Protocol (VRRP), and Gateway Load Balancing Protocol (GLBP).

- **Chapter 6, "Securing the Campus Infrastructure"**—This chapter covers the potential campus security risks and how to mitigate them through features such as DCHP snooping, Dynamic ARP Inspection (DAI), and IP Source Guard. The chapter then continues to cover how to secure the switch device, and troubleshooting tools and techniques such as Switched Port Analyzer (SPAN) and Remote SPAN.

- **Chapter 7, "Preparing the Campus Infrastructure for Advanced Services"**—This chapter discusses the application of advanced services to Cisco switches. The three main services discussed in this chapter are IP telephony (voice), video, and wireless. Moreover, because these advanced services require additional switch features for implementation, topics such as QoS and IP multicast are also discussed.

- **Appendix A, "Answers to Chapter Review Questions"**—This appendix provides answers for the review questions that appear at the end of each chapter.

Chapter 1

Analyzing the Cisco Enterprise Campus Architecture

This chapter covers the following topics:

- Introduction to Enterprise Campus Network Design

- Enterprise Campus Design

- PPDIOO Lifecycle Approach to Network Design and Implementation

Over the last half century, businesses have achieved improving levels of productivity and competitive advantages through the use of communication and computing technology. The enterprise campus network has evolved over the last 20 years to become a key element in this business computing and communication infrastructure. The interrelated evolution of business and communications technology is not slowing, and the environment is currently undergoing another stage of evolution. The complexity of business and network requirements creates an environment where a fixed model no longer completely describes the set of capabilities and services that comprise the enterprise campus network today.

Nevertheless, designing an enterprise campus network is no different than designing any large, complex system—such as a piece of software or even something as sophisticated as the international space station. The use of a guiding set of fundamental engineering principles serves to ensure that the campus design provides for the balance of availability, security, flexibility, and manageability required to meet current and future business and technological needs. This chapter introduces you to the concepts of enterprise campus designs, along with an implementation process that can ensure a successful campus network deployment.

Introduction to Enterprise Campus Network Design

Cisco has several different design models to abstract and modularize the enterprise network. However, for the content in this book the enterprise network is broken down into the following sections:

- Core Backbone

- Campus

- Data Center

- Branch/WAN

- Internet Edge

Figure 1-1 illustrates at a high level a sample view of the enterprise network.

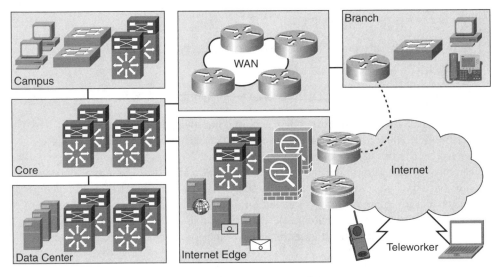

Figure 1-1 *High-Level View of the Enterprise Network*

The campus, as a part of the enterprise network, is generally understood as that portion of the computing infrastructure that provides access to network communication services and resources to end users and devices spread over a single geographic location. It might span a single floor, a building, or even a large group of buildings spread over an extended geographic area. Some networks have a single campus that also acts as the core or backbone of the network and provides interconnectivity between other portions of the overall network. The campus core can often interconnect the campus access, the data center, and WAN portions of the network. In the largest enterprises, there might be multiple campus sites distributed worldwide with each providing both end-user access and local backbone connectivity. Figure 1-1 depicts the campus and the campus core as separate functional areas. Physically, the campus core is generally self contained. The campus itself may be physically spread out through an enterprise to reduce the cost of cabling. For example, it might be less expensive to aggregate switches for end-user connectivity in wiring closets dispersed throughout the enterprise.

The data center, as a part of the enterprise network, is generally understood to be a facility used to house computing systems and associated components. Examples of computing systems are servers that house mail, database, or market data applications. Historically, the data center was referred to as the server farm. Computing systems in the data center are generally used to provide services to users in the campus, such as algorithmic market data. Data center technologies are evolving quickly and imploring new technologies centered on virtualization. Nonetheless, this book focuses exclusively on the campus network of the enterprise network; consult Cisco.com for additional details about the Cisco data center architectures and technologies.

Note   The campus section of the enterprise network is generally understood as that portion of the computing infrastructure that provides access to network communication services and resources to end users and devices spread over a single geographic location.

The data center module of the enterprise network is generally understood to be a facility used to house computing systems and associated components.

Note   For the remainder of this text, the term *enterprise campus network* is referred to as simply *campus network*. The remainder of this text implies that all *campus* references are related to enterprise networks.

The branch/WAN portion of the enterprise network contains the routers, switches, and so on to interconnect a main office to branch offices and interconnect multiple main sites. Keep in mind, many large enterprises are composed of multiple campuses and data centers that interconnect. Often in large enterprise networks, connecting multiple enterprise data centers requires additional routing features and higher bandwidth links to interconnect remote sites. As such, Cisco designs now partition these designs into a grouping known as Data Center Interconnect (DCI). Branch/WAN and DCI are both out of scope of CCNP SWITCH and this book.

Internet Edge is the portion of the enterprise network that encompasses the routers, switches, firewalls, and network devices that interconnect the enterprise network to the Internet. This section includes technology necessary to connect telecommuters from the Internet to services in the enterprise. Generally, the Internet Edge focuses heavily on network security because it connects the private enterprise to the public domain. Nonetheless, the topic of the Internet Edge as part of the enterprise network is outside the scope of this text and CCNP SWITCH.

Tip   The terms *design* and *architecture* are used loosely in most published texts. In this text, the term *architecture* implies a model. Consequently, the term *design* implies the actual network topology designed by a person or persons.

In review, the enterprise network is composed of four distinct areas: core backbone, campus, data center, branch/WAN, and Internet edge. These areas can have subcomponents, and additional areas can be defined in other publications or design documents. For the purpose of CCNP SWITCH and this text, focus is only the campus section of the enterprise network. The next section discusses regulatory standards that drive enterprise networks designs and models holistically, especially the data center. This section defines early information that needs gathering before designing a campus network.

Regulatory Standards Driving Enterprise Architectures

Many regulatory standards drive enterprise architectures. Although most of these regulatory standards focus on data and information, they nonetheless drive network architectures. For example, to ensure that data is as safe as the Health Insurance Portability and Accountability Act (HIPAA) specifies, integrated security infrastructures are becoming paramount. Furthermore, the Sarbanes-Oxley Act, which specifies legal standards for maintaining the integrity of financial data, requires public companies to have multiple redundant data centers with synchronous, real-time copies of financial data.

Because the purpose of this book is to focus on campus design applied to switching, additional detailed coverage of regulatory compliance with respect to design is not covered. Nevertheless, regulatory standards are important concepts for data centers, disaster recovery, and business continuance. In designing any campus network, you need to review any regulatory standards applicable to your business prior to beginning your design. Feel free to review the following regulatory compliance standards as additional reading:

- Sarbanes-Oxley (http://www.sarbanes-oxley.com)

- HIPAA (http://www.hippa.com)

- SEC 17a-4, "Records to Be Preserved by Certain Exchange Members, Brokers and Dealers"

Moreover, the preceding list is not an exhaustive list of regulatory standards but instead a list of starting points for reviewing compliance standards. If regulatory compliance is applicable to your enterprise, consult internally within your organization for further information about regulatory compliance before embarking on designing an enterprise network. The next section describes the motivation behind sound campus designs.

Campus Designs

Properly designed campus architectures yield networks that are module, resilient, and flexible. In other words, properly designed campus architectures save time and money, make IT engineers' jobs easier, and significantly increase business productivity.

To restate, adhering to design best-practices and design principles yield networks with the following characteristics:

- **Modular:** Campus network designs that are modular easily support growth and change. By using building blocks, also referred to as pods or modules, scaling the network is eased by adding new modules instead of complete redesigns.

- **Resilient:** Campus network designs deploying best practices and proper high-availability (HA) characteristics have uptime of near 100 percent. Campus networks deployed by financial services might lose millions of dollars in revenue from a simple 1-second network outage.

- **Flexibility:** Change in business is a guarantee for any enterprise. As such, these business changes drive campus network requirements to adapt quickly. Following campus network designs yields faster and easier changes.

The next section of this text describes legacy campus designs that lead to current generation campus designs published today. This information is useful as it sets the ground work for applying current generation designs.

Legacy Campus Designs

Legacy campus designs were originally based on a simple flat Layer-2 topology with a router-on-a-stick. The concept of *router-on-a-stick* defines a router connecting multiple LAN segments and routing between them, a legacy method of routing in campus networks.

Nevertheless, simple flat networks have many inherit limitations. Layer 2 networks are limited and do not achieve the following characteristics:

- Scalability

- Security

- Modularity

- Flexibility

- Resiliency

- High Availability

A later section, "Layer 2 Switching In-Depth" provides additional information about the limitations of Layer 2 networks.

One of the original benefits of Layer 2 switching, and building Layer 2 networks, was speed. However, with the advent of high-speed switching hardware found on Cisco Catalyst and Nexus switches, Layer 3 switching performance is now equal to Layer 2 switching performance. As such, Layer 3 switching is now being deployed at scale. Examples of Cisco switches that are capable of equal Layer 2 and Layer 3 switching performance are the Catalyst 3000, 4000, and 6500 family of switches and the Nexus 7000 family of switches.

Note   With current-generation Cisco switches, Layer 3 switching performance is equal to Layer 2 switching performance in terms of throughput.

Note   The Nexus families of switches are relatively new switches targeted for deployment in the data center. As such, these switches support high bandwidth in hundreds of gigabits per second. In addition, Nexus switches optionally offer low-latency switching for market data applications, Fibre Channel over Ethernet (FCOE), and advanced high-availability features. Unfortunately, because Nexus switches are targeted for data centers, they lack some features found in Catalyst switches, such as support for inline power for IP phones.

Since Layer 3 switching performance of Cisco switches allowed for scaled networks, hierarchical designs for campus networks were developed to handle this scale effectively. The next section introduces, briefly, the hierarchical concepts in the campus. These concepts are discussed in more detail in later sections; however, a brief discussion of these topics is needed before discussing additional campus designs concepts.

Hierarchical Models for Campus Design

Consider the Open System Interconnection (OSI) reference model, which is a layered model for understanding and implementing computer communications. By using layers, the OSI model simplifies the task required for two computers to communicate.

Cisco campus designs also use layers to simplify the architectures. Each layer can be focused on specific functions, thereby enabling the networking designer to choose the right systems and features for the layer. This model provides a modular framework that enables flexibility in network design and facilitates implementation and troubleshooting. The Cisco Campus Architecture fundamentally divides networks or their modular blocks into the following access, distribution, and core layers with associated characteristics:

- **Access layer:** Used to grant the user, server, or edge device access to the network. In a campus design, the access layer generally incorporates switches with ports that provide connectivity to workstations, servers, printers, wireless access points, and so on. In the WAN environment, the access layer for telecommuters or remote sites might provide access to the corporate network across a WAN technology. The access layer is the most feature-rich section of the campus network because it is a best practice to apply features as close to the edge as possible. These features that include security, access control, filters, management, and so on are covered in later chapters.

■ **Distribution layer:** Aggregates the wiring closets, using switches to segment work-groups and isolate network problems in a campus environment. Similarly, the distribution layer aggregates WAN connections at the edge of the campus and provides a level of security. Often, the distribution layer acts as a service and control boundary between the access and core layers.

■ **Core layer (also referred to as the backbone):** A high-speed backbone, designed to switch packets as fast as possible. In current generation campus designs, the core backbone connects other switches a minimum of 10 Gigabit Ethernet. Because the core is critical for connectivity, it must provide a high level of availability and adapt to changes quickly. This layer's design also provides for scalability and fast convergence

This hierarchical model is not new and has been consistent for campus architectures for some time. In review, the hierarchical model is advantageous over nonhierarchical modes for the following reasons:

■ Provides modularity

■ Easier to understand

■ Increases flexibility

■ Eases growth and scalability

■ Provides for network predictability

■ Reduces troubleshooting complexity

Figure 1-2 illustrates the hierarchical model at a high level as applied to a modeled campus network design.

The next section discusses background information on Cisco switches and begins the discussion of the role of Cisco switches in campus network design.

Impact of Multilayer Switches on Network Design

Understanding Ethernet switching is a prerequisite to building a campus network. As such, the next section reviews Layer 2 and Layer 3 terminology and concepts before discussing enterprise campus designs in subsequent sections. A subset of the material presented is a review of CCNA material.

Ethernet Switching Review

Product marketing in the networking technology field uses many terms to describe product capabilities. In many situations, product marketing stretches the use of technology terms to distinguish products among multiple vendors. One such case is the terminology of Layers 2, 3, 4, and 7 switching. These terms are generally exaggerated in the network-ing technology field and need careful review.

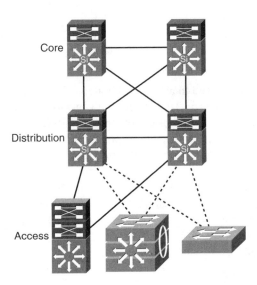

Figure 1-2   *High-Level Example of the Hierarchical Model as Applied to a Campus Network*

The Layers 2, 3, 4, and 7 switching terminology correlates switching features to the OSI reference model. Figure 1-3 illustrates the OSI reference model and its relationship to pro-tocols and network hardware.

The next section provides a CCNA review of Layer 2 switching. Although this section is a review, it is a critical subject for later chapters.

Layer 2 Switching

Product marketing labeling a Cisco switch as either as a Layer 2 or as a Layer 3 switching is no longer black and white because the terminology is not consistent with product capabilities. In review, Layer 2 switches are capable of switching packets based only on MAC addresses. Layer 2 switches increase network bandwidth and port density without much complexity. The term *Layer 2 switching* implies that frames forwarded by the switch are not modified in any way; however, Layer 2 switches such as the Catalyst 2960 are capable of a few Layer 3 features, such as classifying packets for quality of service (QoS) and network access control based on IP address. An example of QoS marking at Layer 4 is marking the differentiated services code point (DSCP) bits in the IP header based on the TCP port number in the TCP header. Do not be concerned with understand-ing the QoS technology at this point as highlighted in the proceeding sentence in this chapter; this terminology is covered in more detail in later chapters. To restate, Layer 2-only switches are not capable of routing frames based on IP address and are limited to forwarding frames only based on MAC address. Nonetheless, Layer 2 switches might support features that read Layer 3 information of a frame for specific features.

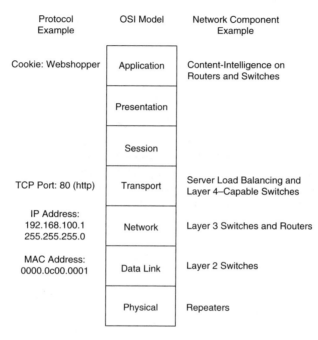

Figure 1-3 *OSI Layer Relationship to Protocols and Networking Hardware*

Legacy Layer 2 switches are limited in network scalability due to many factors. Consequently, all network devices on a legacy Layer 2 switch must reside on the same subnet and, as a result, exchange broadcast packets for address resolution purposes. Network devices grouped together to exchange broadcast packets constitute a broadcast domain. Layer 2 switches flood unknown unicast, multicast, and broadcast traffic throughout the entire broadcast domain. As a result, all network devices in the broadcast domain process all flooded traffic. As the size of the broadcast domain grows, its network devices become overwhelmed by the task of processing this unnecessary traffic. This caveat prevents network topologies from growing to more than a few legacy Layer 2 switches. Lack of QoS and security features are other features that can prevent the use of low-end Layer 2 switches in campus networks and data centers.

However, all current and most legacy Cisco Catalyst switches support virtual LANs (VLAN), which segment traffic into separate broadcast domains and, as a result, IP subnets. VLANs overcome several of the limitations of the basic Layer 2 networks, as discussed in the previous paragraph. This book discusses VLANs in more detail in the next chapter.

Figure 1-4 illustrates an example of a Layer 2 switch with workstations attached. Because the switch is only capable of MAC address forwarding, the workstations must reside on the same subnet to communicate.

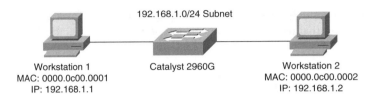

Figure 1-4   *Layer 2 Switching*

Layer 3 Switching

Layer 3 switches include Layer 3 routing capabilities. Many of the current-generation Catalyst Layer 3 switches can use routing protocols such as BGP, RIP, OSPF, and EIGRP to make optimal forwarding decisions. A few Cisco switches that support routing protocols do not support BGP because they do not have the memory necessary for large routing tables. These routing protocols are reviewed in later chapters. Figure 1-5 illustrates a Layer 3 switch with several workstations attached. In this example, the Layer 3 switch routes packets between the two subnets.

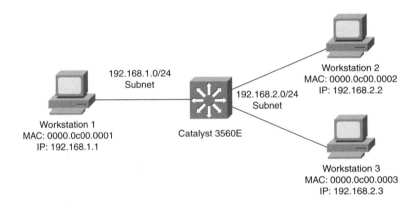

Figure 1-5   *Layer 3 Switching*

Note   Layer 2 switching:

- Switching based on MAC address
- Restricts scalability to a few switches in a domain
- May support Layer 3 features for QoS or access-control

Layer 3 switching:

- Switching based on IP address
- Interoperates with Layer 2 features
- Enables highly scalable designs

Layer 4 and Layer 7 Switching

Layers 4 and 7 switching terminology is not as straightforward as Layers 2 and 3 switching terminology. Layer 4 switching implies switching based on protocol sessions. In other words, Layer 4 switching uses not only source and destination IP addresses in switching decisions, but also IP session information contained in the TCP and User Datagram Protocol (UDP) portions of the packet. The most common method of distinguishing traffic with Layer 4 switching is to use the TCP and UDP port numbers. Server load balancing, a Layer 4 to Layer 7 switching feature, can use TCP information such as TCP SYN, FIN, and RST to make forwarding decisions. (Refer to RFC 793 for explanations of TCP SYN, FIN, and RST.) As a result, Layer 4 switches can distinguish different types of IP traffic flows, such as differentiating the FTP, Network Time Protocol (NTP), HTTP, Secure HTTP (S-HTTP), and Secure Shell (SSH) traffic.

Layer 7 switching is switching based on application information. Layer 7 switching capability implies content-intelligence. Content-intelligence with respect to web browsing implies features such as inspection of URLs, cookies, host headers, and so on. Content-intelligence with respect to VoIP can include distinguishing call destinations such as local or long distance.

Table 1-1 summarizes the layers of the OSI model with their respective protocol data units (PDU), which represent the data exchanged at each layer. Note the difference between frames and packets and their associated OSI level. The table also contains a column illustrating sample device types operating at the specified layer.

Table 1-1 *PDU and Sample Device Relationship to the OSI Model*

OSI Level	OSI Layer	PDU Type	Device Example	Address
1	Physical	Electrical signals	Repeater, transceiver	None
2	Data link	Frames	Switches	MAC address
3	Network	Packet	Router, multilayer switches	IP address
4	Transport	TCP or UDP data segments	Multilayer switch load balancing based on TCP port number	TCP or UDP port numbering
7	Application	Embedded application information in data payload	Multilayer switch using Network-Based Application Recognition (NBAR) to permit or deny traffic based on data passed by an application	Embedded information in data payload

Layer 2 Switching In-Depth

Layer 2 switching is also referred to as hardware-based bridging. In a Layer 2-only switch, ASICs handle frame forwarding. Moreover, Layer 2 switches deliver the ability to increase bandwidth to the wiring closet without adding unnecessary complexity to the network. At Layer 2, no modification is required to the frame content when going between Layer 1 interfaces, such as Fast Ethernet to 10 Gigabit Ethernet.

In review, the network design properties of current-generation Layer 2 switches include the following:

- Designed for near wire-speed performance

- Built using high-speed, specialized ASICs

- Switches at low latency

- Scalable to a several switch topology without a router or Layer 3 switch

- Supports Layer 3 functionality such as Internet Group Management Protocol (IGMP) snooping and QoS marking

- Offers limited scalability in large networks without Layer 3 boundaries

Layer 3 Switching In-Depth

Layer 3 switching is hardware-based routing. Layer 3 switches overcome the inadequacies of Layer 2 scalability by providing routing domains. The packet forwarding in Layer 3 switches is handled by ASICs and other specialized circuitry. A Layer 3 switch performs everything on a packet that a traditional router does, including the following:

- Determines the forwarding path based on Layer 3 information

- Validates the integrity of the Layer 3 packet header via the Layer 3 checksum

- Verifies and decrements packet Time-To-Live (TTL) expiration

- Rewrites the source and destination MAC address during IP rewrites

- Updates Layer 2 CRC during Layer 3 rewrite

- Processes and responds to any option information in the packet such as the Internet Control Message Protocol (ICMP) record

- Updates forwarding statistics for network management applications

- Applies security controls and classification of service if required

Layer 3 routing requires the ability of packet rewriting. Packet rewriting occurs on any routed boundary. Figure 1-6 illustrates the basic packet rewriting requirements of Layer 3 routing in an example in which two workstations are communicating using ICMP.

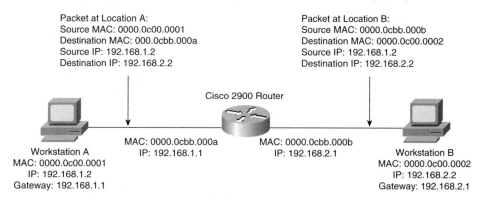

Figure 1-6   *Layer 3 Packet Rewriting*

Address Resolution Protocol (ARP) plays an important role in Layer 3 packet rewriting. When Workstation A in Figure 1-6 sends five ICMP echo requests to Workstation B, the following events occur (assuming all the devices in this example have yet to communicate, use static addressing versus DHCP, and there is no event to trigger a gratuitous ARP):

1. Workstation A sends an ARP request for its default gateway. Workstation A sends this ARP to obtain the MAC address of the default gateway. Without knowing the MAC address of the default gateway, Workstation A cannot send any traffic outside the local subnet. Note that, in this example, Workstation A's default gateway is the Cisco 2900 router with two Ethernet interfaces.

2. The default gateway, the Cisco 2900, responds to the ARP request with an ARP reply, sent to the unicast MAC address and IP address of Workstation A, indicating the default gateway's MAC address. The default gateway also adds an ARP entry for Workstation A in its ARP table upon receiving the ARP request.

3. Workstation A sends the first ICMP echo request to the destination IP address of Workstation B with a destination MAC address of the default gateway.

4. The router receives the ICMP echo request and determines the shortest path to the destination IP address.

5. Because the default gateway does not have an ARP entry for the destination IP address, Workstation B, the default gateway drops the first ICMP echo request from Workstation A. The default gateway drops packets in the absence of ARP entries to

avoid storing packets that are destined for devices without ARP entries as defined by the original RFCs governing ARP.

6. The default gateway sends an ARP request to Workstation B to get Workstation B's MAC address.

7. Upon receiving the ARP request, Workstation B sends an ARP response with its MAC address.

8. By this time, Workstation A is sending a second ICMP echo request to the destination IP of Workstation B via its default gateway.

9. Upon receipt of the second ICMP echo request, the default gateway now has an ARP entry for Workstation B. The default gateway in turn rewrites the source MAC address to itself and the destination MAC to Workstation B's MAC address, and then forwards the frame to Workstation B.

10. Workstation B receives the ICMP echo request and sends an ICMP echo reply to the IP address of Workstation A with the destination MAC address of the default gateway.

Figure 1-6 illustrates the Layer 2 and Layer 3 rewriting at different places along the path between Workstation A and B. This figure and example illustrate the fundamental operation of Layer 3 routing and switching.

The primary difference between the packet-forwarding operation of a router and Layer 3 switching is the physical implementation. Layer 3 switches use different hardware components and have greater port density than traditional routers.

These concepts of Layer 2 switching, Layer 3 forwarding, and Layer 3 switching are applied in a single platform: the multilayer switch. Because it is designed to handle high-performance LAN traffic, a Layer 3 switch is locatable when there is a need for a router and a switch within the network, cost effectively replacing the traditional router and router-on-a-stick designs of the past.

Understanding Multilayer Switching

Multilayer switching combines Layer 2 switching and Layer 3 routing functionality. Generally, the networking field uses the terms Layer 3 switch and multilayer switch interchangeably to describe a switch that is capable of Layer 2 and Layer 3 switching. In specific terms, multilayer switches move campus traffic at wire speed while satisfying Layer 3 connectivity requirements. This combination not only solves throughput problems but also helps to remove the conditions under which Layer 3 bottlenecks form. Moreover, multilayer switches support many other Layer 2 and Layer 3 features besides routing and switching. For example, many multilayer switches support QoS marking. Combining both Layer 2 and Layer 3 functionality and features allows for ease of deployment and simplified network topologies.

Moreover, Layer 3 switches limit the scale of spanning tree by segmenting Layer 2, which eases network complexity. In addition, Layer 3 routing protocols enable load-balancing, fast convergence, scalability, and control compared to traditional Layer 2 features.

In review, multilayer switching is a marketing term used to refer to any Cisco switch capable of Layer 2 switching and Layer 3 routing. From a design perspective, all enterprise campus designs include multilayer switches in some aspect, most likely in the core or distribution layers. Moreover, some campus designs are evolving to include an option for designing Layer 3 switching all the way to the access layer with a future option of supporting Layer 3 network ports on each individual access port. Over the next few years, the trend in the campus is to move to a pure Layer 3 environment consisting of inexpensive Layer 3 switches.

Note   The remainder of this text uses the term *multilayer switch* and *Layer 3 switch* interchangeably.

Introduction to Cisco Switches

Cisco has a plethora of Layer 2 and Layer 3 switch models. For brevity, this section highlights a few popular models used in the campus, core backbone, and data center. For a complete list of Cisco switches, consult product documentation at Cisco.com.

Cisco Catalyst 6500 Family of Switches

The Cisco Catalyst 6500 family of switches are the most popular switches Cisco ever produced. They are found in a wide variety of installs not only including campus, data center, and backbone, but also found in deployment of services, WAN, branch, and so on in both enterprise and service provider networks. For the purpose of CCNP SWITCH and the scope of this book, the Cisco Catalyst 6500 family of switches are summarized as follows:

- Scalable modular switch up to 13 slots

- Supports up to 16 10-Gigabit Ethernet interfaces per slot in an over-subscription model

- Up to 80 Gbps of bandwidth per slot in current generation hardware

- Supports Cisco IOS with a plethora of Layer 2 and Layer 3 switching features

- Optionally supports up to Layer 7 features with specialized modules

- Integrated redundant and high-available power supplies, fans, and supervisor engineers

- Supports Layer 3 Non-Stop Forwarding (NSF) whereby routing peers are maintained during a supervisor switchover.

- Backward capability and investment protection have lead to a long life cycle

Cisco Catalyst 4500 Family of Switches

The Cisco Catalyst 4500 family of switches is a vastly popular modular switch found in many campus networks at the distribution layer or in collapsed core networks of small to medium-sized networks. Collapsed core designs combine the core and distribution layers into a single area. The Catalyst 4500 is one step down from the Catalyst 6500 but does support a wide array of Layer 2 and Layer 3 features. In summary, the Cisco Catalyst 4500 family of switches are summarized as follows:

- Scalable module switch with up to 10 slots

- Supports multiple 10 Gigabit Ethernet interfaces per slot

- Supports Cisco IOS

- Supports both Layer 2 switching and Layer 3 switching

- Optionally supports integrated redundant and high-available power supplies and su-pervisor engines

Cisco Catalyst 4948G, 3750, and 3560 Family of Switches

The Cisco Catalyst 4948G, 3750, and 3560 family of switches are popular switches used in campus networks for fixed-port scenarios, most often the access layer. These switches are summarized as follows:

- Available in a variety of fixed port configurations with up to 48 1-Gbps access layer ports and 4 10-Gigabit Ethernet interfaces for uplinks to distribution layer

- Supports Cisco IOS

- Supports both Layer 2 and Layer 3 switching

- Not architected with redundant hardware

Cisco Catalyst 2000 Family of Switches

The Cisco Catalyst 2000 family of switches are Layer 2-only switches capable of few Layer 3 features aside from Layer 3 routing. These features are often found in the access layer in campus networks. These switches are summarized as follows:

- Available in a variety of fixed port configurations with up to 48 1-Gbps access layer ports and multiple 10-Gigabit Ethernet uplinks

- Supports Cisco IOS

- Supports only Layer 2 switching

- Not architected with redundant hardware

Nexus 7000 Family of Switches

The Nexus 7000 family of switches are the Cisco premier data center switches. The prod-uct launch in 2008; and thus, the Nexus 7000 software does not support all the features of Cisco IOS yet. Nonetheless, the Nexus 7000 is summarized as follows:

- Modular switch with up to 18 slots

- Supports up to 230 Gbps per slot

- Supports Nexus OS (NX-OS)

- 10-slot chassis is built on front-to-back airflow

- Supports redundant supervisor engines, fans, and power supplies

Nexus 5000 and 2000 Family of Switches

The Nexus 5000 and 2000 family of switches are low-latency switches designed for deployment in the access layer of the data center. These switches are Layer 2-only switches today but support cut-through switching for low latency. The Nexus 5000 switches are designed for 10-Gigabit Ethernet applications and also support Fibre Channel over Ethernet (FCOE).

Hardware and Software-Switching Terminology

This book refers to the terms hardware-switching and software-switching regularly throughout the text. The industry term *hardware-switching* refers to the act of processing packets at any Layers 2 through 7, via specialized hardware components referred to as application-specific integrated circuits (ASIC). ASICs can generally reach throughput at wire speed without performance degradation for advanced features such as QoS marking, ACL processing, or IP rewriting.

Note   Other terms used to describe hardware-switching are in-hardware, using ASICs, and hardware-based. These terms are used interchangeably throughout the text. Multilayer switching (MLS) is another term commonly used to describe hardware-switching. The term MLS can be confusing; for example, with the Catalyst 5500, the term MLS described a legacy hardware-switching method and feature. With today's terminology, MLS describes the capability to route and switch frames at line-rate (the speed of all ports sending traffic at the same time, full-duplex, at the maximum speed of the interface) with advanced features such as Network Address Translation (NAT), QoS, access controls, and so on using ASICs.

Switching and routing traffic via hardware-switching is considerably faster than the traditional software-switching of frames via a CPU. Many ASICs, especially ASICs for Layer 3 routing, use specialized memory referred to as ternary content addressable memory (TCAM) along with packet-matching algorithms to achieve high performance, whereas CPUs simply use higher processing rates to achieve greater degrees of performance. Generally, ASICs can achieve higher performance and availability than CPUs. In addition, ASICs scale easily in switching architecture, whereas CPUs do not. ASICs integrate not only on Supervisor Engines, but also on individual line modules of Catalyst switches to hardware-switch packets in a distributed manner.

ASICs do have memory limitations. For example, the Catalyst 6500 family of switches can accommodate ACLs with a larger number of entries compared to the Catalyst 3560E family of switches due to the larger ASIC memory on the Catalyst 6500 family of switches. Generally, the size of the ASIC memory is relative to the cost and application of the switch. Furthermore, ASICs do not support all the features of the traditional Cisco IOS. For instance, the Catalyst 6500 family of switches with a Supervisor Engine 720 and an MSFC3 (Multilayer Switch Feature Card) must software-switch all packets requiring Network Address Translation (NAT) without the use of specialized line modules. As products continue to evolve and memory becomes cheaper, ASICs gain additional memory and feature support.

For the purpose of CCNP SWITCH and campus network design, the concepts in this section are overly simplified. Use the content in this section as information for sections that refer to the terminology. The next section changes scope from switching hardware and technology to campus network types.

Campus Network Traffic Types

Campus designs are significantly tied to network size. However, traffic patterns and traffic types through each layer hold significant importance on how to shape a campus design. Each type of traffic represents specific needs in terms of bandwidth and flow patterns. Table 1-2 lists several different types of traffic that might exist on a campus network. As such, indentifying traffic flows, types, and patterns is a prerequisite to designing a campus network.

Table 1-2 highlights common traffic types with a description, common flow patterns, and a denotation of bandwidth (BW). The BW column highlights on a scale of low to very high the common rate of traffic for the corresponding traffic type for comparison purposes. Note: This table illustrates common traffic types and common characteristics; it is not uncommon to find scenarios of atypical traffic types.

For the purpose of enterprise campus design, note the traffic types in your network, particularly multicast traffic. Multicast traffic for servers-centric applications is generally restricted to the data center; however, whatever multicast traffics spans into the campus needs to be accounted for because it can significantly drive campus design. The next sections delve into several types of applications in more detail and their traffic flow characteristics.

Note   IP multicast traffic requirements in the campus need careful review prior to any campus network design because of its high-bandwidth requirements.

Figure 1-7 illustrates a sample enterprise network with several traffic patterns highlighted as dotted lines to represent possible interconnects that might experience heavy traffic utilization.

Table 1-2 *Common Traffic Types*

Traffic Type	Description	Traffic Flow	BW
Network Management	Many different types of network management traffic may be present on the network. Examples include bridge protocol data units (BPDU), Cisco Discovery Protocol (CDP) updates, Simple Network Management Protocol (SNMP), Secure Shell (SSH), and Remote Monitoring (RMON) traffic. Some designers assign a separate VLAN to the task of carrying certain types of network management traffic to make network troubleshooting easier.	Traffic is found flowing in all layers.	Low
Voice (IP Telephony)	There are two types of voice traffic: signaling information between the end devices (for example, IP phones and soft switches, such as Cisco CallManager) and the data packets of the voice conversation itself. Often, the data to and from IP phones is configured on a separate VLAN for voice traffic because the designer wants to apply QoS measures to give high priority to voice traffic.	Traffic generally moves from access layer to servers in core layer or data center.	Low
IP Multicast	IP multicast traffic is sent from a particular source address to group MAC addresses. Examples of applications that generate this type of traffic are video such as IP/TV broadcasts and market data applications used to configure analysis trading market activities. Multicast traffic can produce a large amount of data streaming across the network. Switches need to be configured to keep this traffic from flooding to devices that have not requested it, and routers need to ensure that multicast traffic is forwarded to the network areas where it is requested.	Market data applications are usually contained within the data center. Other traffic such as IP/TV and user data flows from access layer to core layers and to the data center.	Very High

continues

Table 1-2 *Common Traffic Types (continued)*

Traffic Type	Description	Traffic Flow	BW
Normal Data	This is typical application traffic related to file and print services, email, Internet browsing, database access, and other shared network applications. You may need to treat this data the same or in different ways in different parts of the network, based on the volume of each type. Examples of this type of traffic are Server Message Block, Netware Core Protocol (NCP), Simple Mail Transfer Protocol (SMTP), Structured Query Language (SQL), and HTTP.	Traffic usually flows from the access layer to core layer and to the data center.	Low to Mid
Scavenger class	Scavenger class includes all traffic with protocols or patterns that exceed their normal data flows. It is used to protect the network from exceptional traffic flows that might be the result of malicious programs executing on end-system PCs. Scavenger class is also used for less than best-effort type traffic, such as peer-to-peer traffic.	Traffic patterns vary.	Mid to High

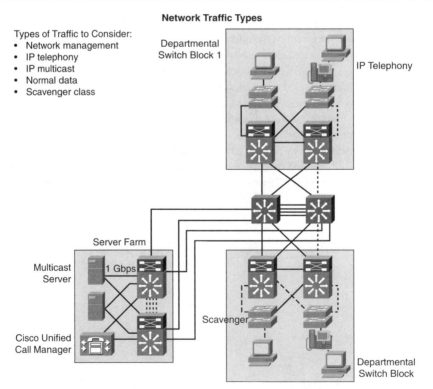

Figure 1-7 *Network Traffic Types*

Peer-to-Peer Applications

Some traffic flows are based on a peer-to-peer model, where traffic flows between end-points that may be far from each other. Peer-to-peer applications include applications where the majority of network traffic passes from one end device, such as a PC or IP phone, to another through the organizational network. (See Figure 1-8.) Some traffic flows are not sensitive to bandwidth and delay issues, whereas some others require real-time interaction between peer devices. Typical peer-to-peer applications include the following:

- **Instant messaging:** Two peers establish communication between two end systems. When the connection is established, the conversation is direct.

- **File sharing:** Some operating systems or applications require direct access to data on other workstations. Fortunately, most enterprises are banning such applications because they lack centralized or network-administered security.

- **IP phone calls:** The network requirements of IP phone calls are strict because of the need for QoS treatment to minimize jitter.

- **Video conference systems:** The network requirements of video conferencing are demanding because of the bandwidth consumption and class of service (CoS) requirements.

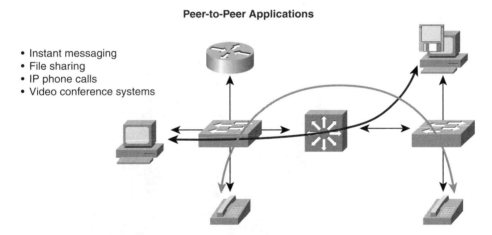

Peer-to-Peer Applications

- Instant messaging
- File sharing
- IP phone calls
- Video conference systems

Figure 1-8   *High-Level Peer-to-Peer Application*

Client/Server Applications

Many enterprise traffic flows are based on a client/server model, where connections to the server might become bottlenecks. Network bandwidth used to be costly, but today, it is cost-effective compared to the application requirements. For example, the cost of Gigabit Ethernet and 10 Gigabit is advantageous compared to application bandwidth requirements that rarely exceed 1 Gigabit Ethernet. Moreover, because the switch delay is insignificant for most client/server applications with high-performance Layer 3 switches, locating the servers centrally rather than in the workgroup is technically feasible and reduces support costs. Latency is extremely important to financial and market data applications, such as 29 West and Tibco. For situations in which the lowest latency is necessary, Cisco offers low-latency modules for the Nexus 7000 family of switches and the Nexus 5000 and 2000 that are low-latency for all variants. For the purpose of this book and CCNP SWITCH, the important take-away is that data center applications for financials and market trade can require a low latency switch, such as the Nexus 5000 family of switches.

Figure 1-9 depicts, at a high level, client/server application traffic flow.

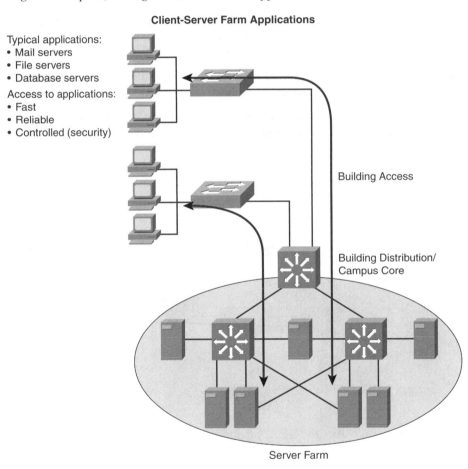

Figure 1-9   *Client/Server Traffic Flow*

In large enterprises, the application traffic might cross more than one wiring closet or LAN to access applications to a server group in a data center. Client-server farm applications apply the 20/80 rule, in which only 20 percent of the traffic remains on the local LAN segment, and 80 percent leaves the segment to reach centralized servers, the Internet, and so on. Client-server farm applications include the following:

- Organizational mail servers

- Common file servers

- Common database servers for organizational applications such as human resource, inventory, or sales applications

Users of large enterprises require fast, reliable, and controlled access to critical applications. For example, traders need access to trading applications anytime with good response times to be competitive with other traders. To fulfill these demands and keep administrative costs low, the solution is to place the servers in a common server farm in a data center. The use of server farms in data centers requires a network infrastructure that is highly resilient and redundant and that provides adequate throughput. Typically, high-end LAN switches with the fastest LAN technologies, such as 10 Gigabit Ethernet, are deployed. For Cisco switches, the current trend is to deploy Nexus switches while the campus deploys Catalyst switches. The use of the Catalyst switches in the campus and Nexus in the data center is a market transition from earlier models that used Catalyst switches throughout the enterprise. At the time of publication, Nexus switches do not run the traditional Cisco IOS found on Cisco routers and switch. Instead, these switches run Nexus OS (NX-OS), which was derived from SAN-OS found on the Cisco MDS SAN platforms.

Nexus switches have a higher cost than Catalyst switches and do not support telephony, inline power, firewall, or load-balancing services, and so on. However, Nexus switches do support higher throughput, lower latency, high-availability, and high-density 10-Gigabit Ethernet suited for data center environments. A later section details the Cisco switches with more information.

Client-Enterprise Edge Applications

Client-enterprise edge applications use servers on the enterprise edge to exchange data between the organization and its public servers. Examples of these applications include external mail servers and public web servers.

The most important communication issues between the campus network and the enterprise edge are security and high availability. An application that is installed on the enterprise edge might be crucial to organizational process flow; therefore, outages can result in increased process cost.

The organizations that support their partnerships through e-commerce applications also place their e-commerce servers in the enterprise edge. Communications with the servers located on the campus network are vital because of two-way data replication. As a result, high redundancy and resiliency of the network are important requirements for these applications.

Figure 1-10 illustrates traffic flow for a sample client-enterprise edge application with connections through the Internet.

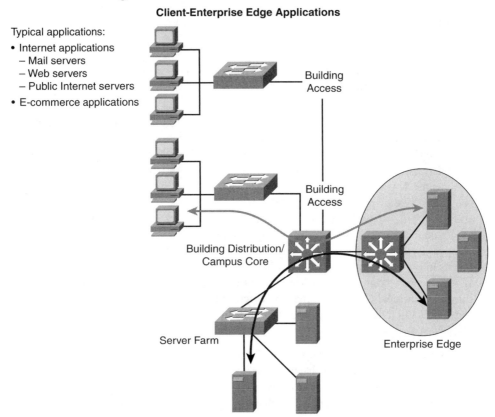

Figure 1-10 *Client-Enterprise Edge Application Traffic Flow*

Recall from earlier sections that the client-enterprise edge applications in Figure 1-10 pass traffic through the Internet edge portion of the Enterprise network.

In review, understanding traffic flow and patterns of an enterprise are necessary prior to designing a campus network. This traffic flow and pattern ultimately shapes scale, features, and use of Cisco switches in the campus network. Before further discussion on designing campus networks, the next section highlights two Cisco network architecture models that are useful in understanding all the elements that make a successful network deployment.

Overview of the SONA and Borderless Networks

Proper network architecture helps ensure that business strategies and IT investments are aligned. As the backbone for IT communications, the network element of enterprise architecture is increasingly critical. Service-Oriented Network Architecture (SONA) is the Cisco architectural approach to designing advanced network capabilities.

Figure 1-11 illustrates SONA pictorially from a marketing perspective.

Overview of Cisco SONA

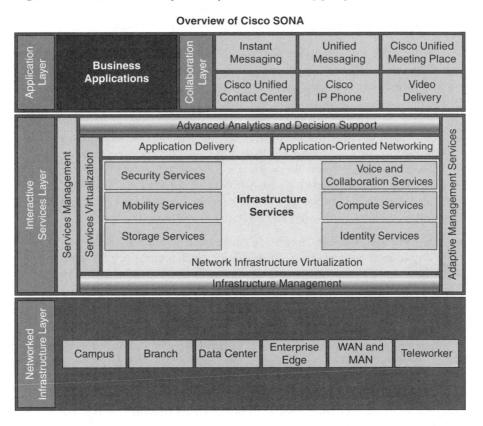

Figure 1-11   *SONA Overview*

SONA provides guidance, best practices, and blueprints for connecting network services and applications to enable business solutions. The SONA framework illustrates the concept that the network is the common element that connects and enables all components of the IT infrastructure. SONA outlines these three layers of intelligence in the enterprise network:

■   **The Networked Infrastructure Layer:** Where all the IT resources are interconnected across a converged network foundation. The IT resources include servers, storage, and clients. The network infrastructure layer represents how these resources exist in different places in the network, including the campus, branch, data center, WAN, metropolitan-area network (MAN), and telecommuter. The objective for customers in this layer is to have anywhere and anytime connectivity.

- **The Interactive Services Layer:** Enables efficient allocation of resources to applications and business processes delivered through the networked infrastructure.

- **The Application Layer:** Includes business applications and collaboration applications. The objective for customers in this layer is to meet business requirements and achieve efficiencies by leveraging the interactive services layer.

The common thread that links the layers is SONA embeds application-level intelligence into the network infrastructure elements so that the network can recognize and better support applications and services.

Deploying a campus design based on the Cisco SONA framework yields several benefits:

- **Convergence, virtualization, intelligence, security, and integration in all areas of the network infrastructure:** The Cisco converged network encompasses all IT technologies, including computing, data, voice, video, and storage. The entire network now provides more intelligence for delivering all applications, including voice and video. Employees are more productive because they can use a consistent set of Unified Communications tools from almost anywhere in the world.

- **Cost savings:** With the Cisco SONA model, the network offers the power and flexibility to implement new applications easily, which reduces development and implementation costs. Common network services are used on an as-needed basis by voice, data, and video applications.

- **Increased productivity:** Collaboration services and product features enable employees to share multiple information types on a rich-media conferencing system. For example, agents in contact centers can share a Web browser with a customer during a voice call to speed up problem resolution and increase customer knowledge using a tool such as Cisco WebEX. Collaboration has enabled contact center agents to reduce the average time spent on each call, yet receive higher customer satisfaction ratings. Another example is cost saving associated with hosting virtual meetings using Cisco WebEx.

- **Faster deployment of new services and applications:** Organizations can better deploy services for interactive communications through virtualization of storage, cloud computing, and other network resources. Automated processes for provisioning, monitoring, managing, and upgrading voice products and services help Cisco IT achieve greater network reliability and maximize the use of IT resources. Cloud computing is the next wave of new technology to be utilized in enterprise environments.

- **Enhanced business processes:** With the SONA, IT departments can better support and enhance business processes and resilience through integrated applications and intelligent network services. Examples include change-control processes that enable 99.999 percent of network uptimes.

Keep in mind, SONA is strictly a model to guide network designs. When designing the campus portion of the enterprise network, you need to understand SONA only from a high level as most of the focus of the campus design is centered on features and functions of Cisco switching.

Cisco.com contains additional information and readings on SONA for persons seeking more details.

In October 2009, Cisco launched a new enterprise architecture called Borderless Networks. As with SONA, the model behind Borderless Networks enables businesses to transcend borders, access resources anywhere, embrace business productivity, and lower business and IT costs. One enhancement added to Borderless Networks over SONA is that the framework focuses more on growing enterprises into global companies, noted in the term "borderless." In terms of CCNP SWITCH, focus on a high-level understanding of SONA because Borderless Networks is a new framework. Consult Cisco.com for additional information on Borderless Networks.

In review, SONA and Borderless Networks are marketing architectures that form high-level frameworks for designing networks. For the purpose of designing a campus network, focus on terms from building requirements around traffic flow, scale, and general requirements. The next section applies a life-cycle approach to campus design and delves into more specific details about the campus designs.

Enterprise Campus Design

The next subsections detail key enterprise campus design concepts. The access, distribution, and core layers introduced earlier in this chapter are expanded on with applied examples. Later subsections of this chapter define a model for implementing and operating a network.

The tasks of implementing and operating a network are two components of the Cisco Lifecycle model. In this model, the life of the network and its components are taught with a structural angle, starting from the preparation of the network design to the optimization of the implemented network. This structured approach is key to ensure that the network always meets the requirements of the end users. This section describes the Cisco Lifecycle approach and its impact on network implementation.

The enterprise campus architecture can be applied at the campus scale, or at the building scale, to allow flexibility in network design and facilitate ease of implementation and troubleshooting. When applied to a building, the Cisco Campus Architecture naturally divides networks into the building access, building distribution, and building core layers, as follows:

■   **Building access layer:** This layer is used to grant user access to network devices. In a network campus, the building access layer generally incorporates switched LAN devices with ports that provide connectivity to workstations and servers. In the WAN environment, the building access layer at remote sites can provide access to the corporate network across WAN technology.

- **Building distribution layer:** Aggregates the wiring closets and uses switches to segment workgroups and isolate network problems.

- **Building core layer:** Also known as the campus backbone, this is a high-speed backbone designed to switch packets as fast as possible. Because the core is critical for connectivity, it must provide a high level of availability and adapt to changes quickly.

Figure 1-12 illustrates a sample enterprise network topology that spans multiple buildings.

The enterprise campus architecture divides the enterprise network into physical, logical, and functional areas. These areas enable network designers and engineers to associate specific network functionality on equipment based upon its placement and function in the model.

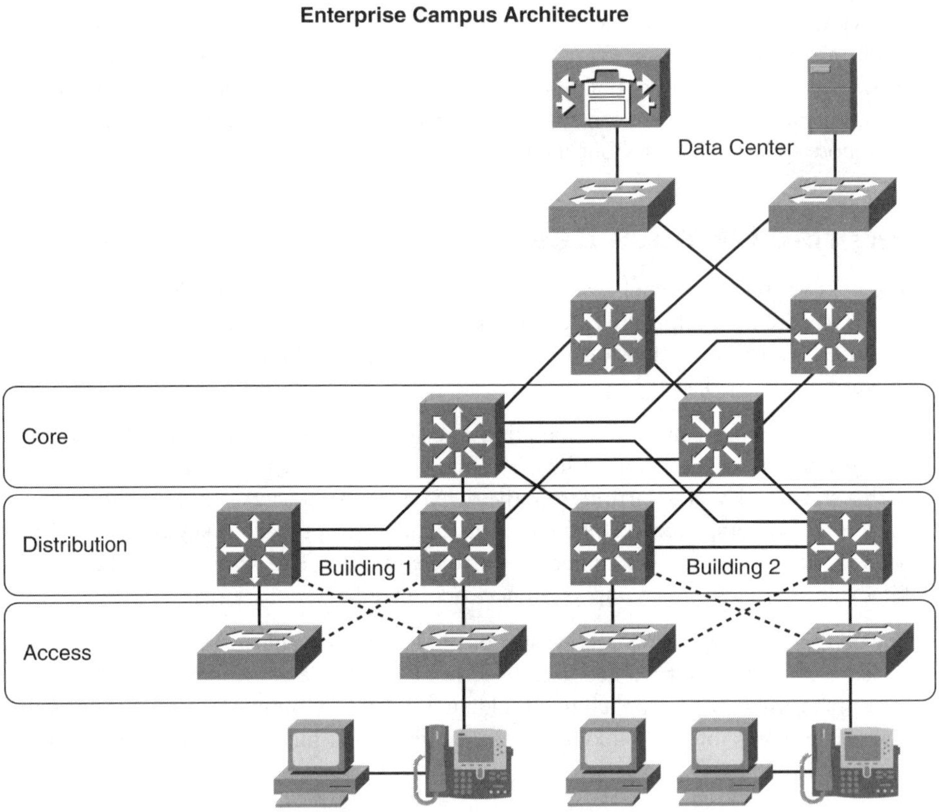

Enterprise Campus Architecture

Figure 1-12   *Enterprise Network with Applied Hierarchical Design*

Access Layer In-Depth

The building access layer aggregates end users and provides uplinks to the distribution layer. With the proper use of Cisco switches, the access layer may contain the following benefits:

■ **High availability:** The access layer is supported by many hardware and software features. System-level redundancy using redundant supervisor engines and redundant power supplies for critical user groups is an available option within the Cisco switch portfolio. Moreover, additional software features of Cisco switches offer access to default gateway redundancy using dual connections from access switches to redundant distribution layer switches that use first-hop redundancy protocols (FHRP) such as the hot standby routing protocol (HSRP). Of note, FHRP and HSRP features are supported only on Layer 3 switches; Layer 2 switches do not participate in HSRP and FHRP and forwarding respective frames.

■ **Convergence:** Cisco switches deployed in an access layer optionally support inline Power over Ethernet (PoE) for IP telephony and wireless access points, enabling customers to converge voice onto their data network and providing roaming WLAN access for users.

■ **Security:** Cisco switches used in an access layer optionally provide services for additional security against unauthorized access to the network through the use of tools such as port security, DHCP snooping, Dynamic Address Resolution Protocol (ARP) Inspection, and IP Source Guard. These features are discussed in later chapters of this book.

Figure 1-13 illustrates the use of access layer deploying redundant upstream connections to the distribution layer.

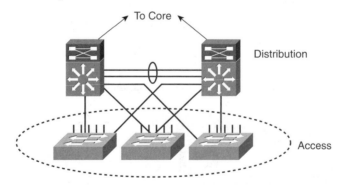

Figure 1-13 *Access Layer Depicting Two Upstream Connections*

Distribution Layer

Availability, fast path recovery, load balancing, and QoS are the important considerations at the distribution layer. High availability is typically provided through dual paths from the distribution layer to the core, and from the access layer to the distribution layer. Layer 3 equal-cost load sharing enables both uplinks from the distribution to the core layer to be utilized.

The distribution layer is the place where routing and packet manipulation are performed and can be a routing boundary between the access and core layers. The distribution layer represents a redistribution point between routing domains or the demarcation between static and dynamic routing protocols. The distribution layer performs tasks such as controlled-routing decision making and filtering to implement policy-based connectivity and QoS. To improve routing protocol performance further, the distribution layer summarizes routes from the access layer. For some networks, the distribution layer offers a default route to access layer routers and runs dynamic routing protocols when communicating with core routers.

The distribution layer uses a combination of Layer 2 and multilayer switching to segment workgroups and isolate network problems, preventing them from affecting the core layer. The distribution layer is commonly used to terminate VLANs from access layer switches. The distribution layer connects network services to the access layer and implements policies for QoS, security, traffic loading, and routing. The distribution layer provides default gateway redundancy by using an FHRP such as HSRP, Gateway Load Balancing Protocol (GLBP), or Virtual Router Redundancy Protocol (VRRP) to allow for the failure or removal of one of the distribution nodes without affecting endpoint connectivity to the default gateway.

In review, the distribution layer provides the following enhancements to the campus network design:

- Aggregates access layer switches

- Segments the access layer for simplicity

- Summarizes routing to access layer

- Always dual-connected to upstream core layer

- Optionally applies packet filtering, security features, and QoS features

Figure 1-14 illustrates the distribution layer interconnecting several access layer switches.

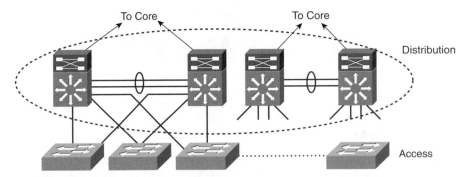

Figure 1-14 *Distribution Layer Interconnecting the Access Layer*

Core Layer

The core layer is the backbone for campus connectivity and is the aggregation point for the other layers and modules in the enterprise network. The core must provide a high level of redundancy and adapt to changes quickly. Core devices are most reliable when they can accommodate failures by rerouting traffic and can respond quickly to changes in the network topology. The core devices must be able to implement scalable protocols and technologies, alternative paths, and load balancing. The core layer helps in scalability during future growth.

The core should be a high-speed, Layer 3 switching environment utilizing hardware-accelerated services in terms of 10 Gigabit Ethernet. For fast convergence around a link or node failure, the core uses redundant point-to-point Layer 3 interconnections in the core because this design yields the fastest and most deterministic convergence results. The core layer should not perform any packet manipulation in software, such as checking access-lists and filtering, which would slow down the switching of packets. Catalyst and Nexus switches support access lists and filtering without effecting switching performance by supporting these features in the hardware switch path.

Figure 1-15 depicts the core layer aggregating multiple distribution layer switches and subsequently access layer switches.

In review, the core layer provides the following functions to the campus and enterprise network:

- Aggregates multiple distribution switches in the distribution layer with the remainder of the enterprise network

- Provides the aggregation points with redundancy through fast convergence and high availability

- Designed to scale as the distribution and consequently the access layer scale with future growth

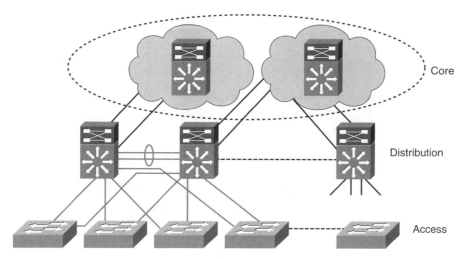

Figure 1-15 *Core Layer Aggregating Distribution and Access Layers*

The Need for a Core Layer

Without a core layer, the distribution layer switches need to be fully meshed. This design is difficult to scale and increases the cabling requirements because each new building distribution switch needs full-mesh connectivity to all the distribution switches. This full-mesh connectivity requires a significant amount of cabling for each distribution switch. The routing complexity of a full-mesh design also increases as you add new neighbors.

In Figure 1-16, the distribution module in the second building of two interconnected switches requires four additional links for full-mesh connectivity to the first module. A third distribution module to support the third building would require eight additional links to support connections to all the distribution switches, or a total of 12 links. A fourth module supporting the fourth building would require 12 new links for a total of 24 links between the distribution switches. Four distribution modules impose eight interior gateway protocol (IGP) neighbors on each distribution switch.

As a recommended practice, deploy a dedicated campus core layer to connect three or more physical segments, such as building in the enterprise campus or four or more pairs of building distribution switches in a large campus. The campus core helps make scaling the network easier when using Cisco switches with the following properties:

- 10-Gigabit and 1-Gigabit density to scale

- Seamless data, voice, and video integration

- LAN convergence optionally with additional WAN and MAN convergence

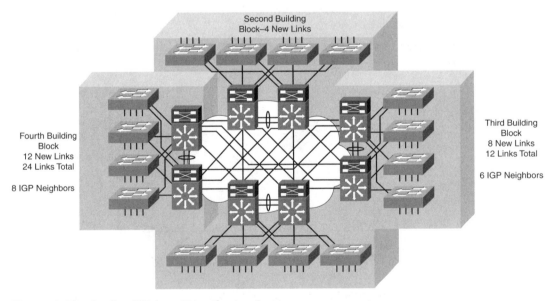

Figure 1-16 *Scaling Without Distribution Layer*

Campus Core Layer as the Enterprise Network Backbone

The core layer is the backbone for campus connectivity and optionally the aggregation point for the other layers and modules in the enterprise campus architecture. The core provides a high level of redundancy and can adapt to changes quickly. Core devices are most reliable when they can accommodate failures by rerouting traffic and can respond quickly to changes in the network topology. The core devices implement scalable protocols and technologies, alternative paths, and load balancing. The core layer helps in scalability during future growth. The core layer simplifies the organization of network device interconnections. This simplification also reduces the complexity of routing between physical segments such as floors and between buildings.

Figure 1-17 illustrates the core layer as a backbone interconnecting the data center and Internet edge portions of the enterprise network. Beyond its logical position in the enterprise network architecture, the core layer constituents and functions depend on the size and type of the network. Not all campus implementations require a campus core. Optionally, campus designs can combine the core and distribution layer functions at the distribution layer for a smaller topology. The next section discusses one such example.

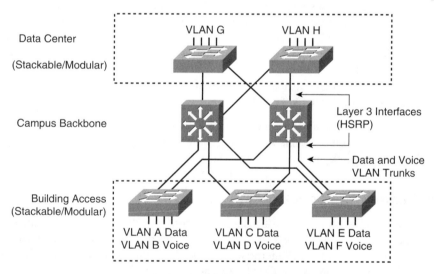

Figure 1-17 *Core Layer as Interconnect for Other Modules of Enterprise Network*

Small Campus Network Example

A small campus network or large branch network is defined as a network of fewer than 200 end devices, whereas the network servers and workstations might be physically connected to the same wiring closet. Switches in small campus network design might not require high-end switching performance or future scaling capability.

In many cases with a network of less than 200 end devices, the core and distribution layers can be combined into a single layer. This design limits scale to a few access layer switches for cost purposes. Low-end multilayer switches such as the Cisco Catalyst 3560E optionally provide routing services closer to the end user when there are multiple VLANs. For a small office, one low-end multilayer switch such as the Cisco Catalyst 2960G might support the Layer 2 LAN access requirements for the entire office, whereas a router such as the Cisco 1900 or 2900 might interconnect the office to the branch/WAN portion of a larger enterprise network.

Figure 1-17 depicts a sample small campus network with campus backbone that interconnects the data center. In this example, the backbone could be deployed with Catalyst 3560E switches, and the access layer and data center could utilize the Catalyst 2960G switches with limited future scalability and limited high availability.

Medium Campus Network Example

For a medium-sized campus with 200 to 1000 end devices, the network infrastructure is typically using access layer switches with uplinks to the distribution multilayer switches that can support the performance requirements of a medium-sized campus network. If redundancy is required, you can attach redundant multilayer switches to the building access switches to provide full link redundancy. In the medium-sized campus network, it is best practice to use at least a Catalyst 4500 series or Catalyst 6500 family of switches because they offer high availability, security, and performance characteristics not found in the Catalyst 3000 and 2000 family of switches.

Figure 1-18 shows a sample medium campus network topology. The example depicts physical distribution segments as buildings. However, physical distribution segments might be floors, racks, and so on.

Large Campus Network Design

Large campus networks are any installation of more than 2000 end users. Because there is no upper bound to the size of a large campus, the design might incorporate many scaling technologies throughout the enterprise. Specifically, in the campus network, the designs generally adhere to the access, distribution, and core layers discussed in earlier sections. Figure 1-17 illustrates a sample large campus network scaled for size in this publication.

Large campus networks strictly follow Cisco best practices for design. The best practices listed in this chapter, such as following the hierarchical model, deploying Layer 3 switches, and utilizing the Catalyst 6500 and Nexus 7000 switches in the design, scratch only the surface of features required to support such a scale. Many of these features are still used in small and medium-sized campus networks but not to the scale of large campus networks.

Moreover, because large campus networks require more persons to design, implement, and maintain the environment, the distribution of work is generally segmented. The sections of the enterprise network previously mentioned in this chapter, campus, data

center, branch/WAN and Internet edge, are the first-level division of work among network engineers in large campus networks. Later chapters discuss many of the features
that might be optionally for smaller campuses that become requirements for larger
networks. In addition, large campus networks require a sound design and implementation plans. Design and implementation plans are discussed in upcoming sections of this
chapter.

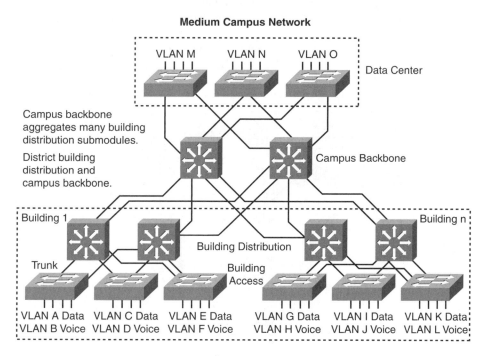

Figure 1-18 *Sample Medium Campus Network Topology*

Data Center Infrastructure

The data center design as part of the enterprise network is based on a layered approach
to improve scalability, performance, flexibility, resiliency, and maintenance. There are
three layers of the data center design:

■ **Core layer:** Provides a high-speed packet switching backplane for all flows going in
and out of the data center.

■ **Aggregation layer:** Provides important functions, such as service module integration, Layer 2 domain definitions, spanning tree processing, and default gateway
redundancy.

■ **Access layer:** Connects servers physically to the network.

Multitier HTTP-based applications supporting web, application, and database tiers of servers dominate the multitier data center model. The access layer network infrastructure can support both Layer 2 and Layer 3 topologies, and Layer 2 adjacency requirements fulfilling the various server broadcast domain or administrative requirements. Layer 2 in the access layer is more prevalent in the data center because some applications support low-latency via Layer 2 domains. Most servers in the data center consist of single and dual attached one rack unit (RU) servers, blade servers with integrated switches, blade servers with pass-through cabling, clustered servers, and mainframes with a mix of oversubscription requirements. Figure 1-19 illustrates a sample data center topology at a high level.

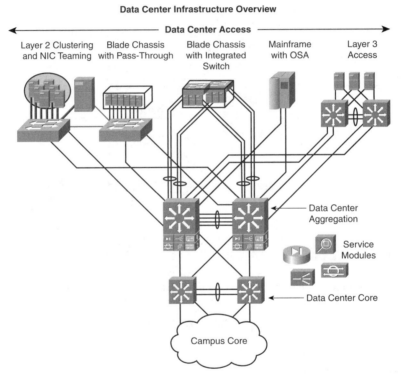

Figure 1-19   *Data Center Topology*

Multiple aggregation modules in the aggregation layer support connectivity scaling from the access layer. The aggregation layer supports integrated service modules providing services such as security, load balancing, content switching, firewall, SSL offload, intrusion detection, and network analysis.

As previously noted, this book focuses on the campus network design of the enterprise network exclusive to data center design. However, most of the topics present in this text overlap with topics applicable to data center design, such as the use of VLANs. Data center designs differ in approach and requirements. For the purpose of CCNP SWITCH, focus primarily on campus network design concepts.

The next section discusses a lifecycle approach to network design. This section does not cover specific campus or switching technologies but rather a best-practice approach to design. Some readers might opt to skip this section because of its lack of technical content; however, it is an important section for CCNP SWITCH and practical deployments.

PPDIOO Lifecycle Approach to Network Design and Implementation

PPDIOO stands for Prepare, Plan, Design, Implement, Operate, and Optimize. PPDIOO is a Cisco methodology that defines the continuous life-cycle of services required for a network.

PPDIOO Phases

The PPDIOO phases are as follows:

- **Prepare:** Involves establishing the organizational requirements, developing a network strategy, and proposing a high-level conceptual architecture identifying technologies that can best support the architecture. The prepare phase can establish a financial justification for network strategy by assessing the business case for the proposed architecture.

- **Plan:** Involves identifying initial network requirements based on goals, facilities, user needs, and so on. The plan phase involves characterizing sites and assessing any existing networks and performing a gap analysis to determine whether the existing system infrastructure, sites, and the operational environment can support the proposed system. A project plan is useful for helping manage the tasks, responsibilities, critical milestones, and resources required to implement changes to the network. The project plan should align with the scope, cost, and resource parameters established in the original business requirements.

- **Design:** The initial requirements that were derived in the planning phase drive the activities of the network design specialists. The network design specification is a comprehensive detailed design that meets current business and technical requirements, and incorporates specifications to support availability, reliability, security, scalability, and performance. The design specification is the basis for the implementation activities.

- **Implement:** The network is built or additional components are incorporated according to the design specifications, with the goal of integrating devices without disrupting the existing network or creating points of vulnerability.

- **Operate:** Operation is the final test of the appropriateness of the design. The operational phase involves maintaining network health through day-to-day operations, including maintaining high availability and reducing expenses. The fault detection, correction, and performance monitoring that occur in daily operations provide the initial data for the optimization phase.

- **Optimize:** Involves proactive management of the network. The goal of proactive management is to identify and resolve issues before they affect the organization. Reactive fault detection and correction (troubleshooting) is needed when proactive management cannot predict and mitigate failures. In the PPDIOO process, the optimization phase can prompt a network redesign if too many network problems and errors arise, if performance does not meet expectations, or if new applications are identified to support organizational and technical requirements.

Note Although design is listed as one of the six PPDIOO phases, some design elements can be present in all the other phases. Moreover, use the six PPDIOO phases as a model or framework; it is not necessary to use it exclusively as defined.

Benefits of a Lifecycle Approach

The network lifecycle approach provides several key benefits aside from keeping the design process organized. The main documented reasons for applying a lifecycle approach to campus design are as follows:

- Lowering the total cost of network ownership
- Increasing network availability
- Improving business agility
- Speeding access to applications and services

The total cost of network ownership is especially important into today's business climate. Lower costs associated with IT expenses are being aggressively assessed by enterprise executives. Nevertheless, a proper network lifecycle approach aids in lowering costs by these actions:

- Identifying and validating technology requirements
- Planning for infrastructure changes and resource requirements
- Developing a sound network design aligned with technical requirements and business goals
- Accelerating successful implementation
- Improving the efficiency of your network and of the staff supporting it
- Reducing operating expenses by improving the efficiency of operational processes and tools

Network availability has always been a top priority of enterprises. However, network downtime can result in a loss of revenue. Examples of where downtime could cause loss of revenue is with network outages that prevent market trading during a surprise interest rate cut or the inability to process credit card transactions on black Friday, the shopping day following Thanksgiving. The network lifecycle improves high availability of networks by these actions:

- Assessing the network's security state and its capability to support the proposed design

- Specifying the correct set of hardware and software releases, and keeping them operational and current

- Producing a sound operations design and validating network operations

- Staging and testing the proposed system before deployment

- Improving staff skills

- Proactively monitoring the system and assessing availability trends and alerts

- Proactively identifying security breaches and defining remediation plans

Enterprises need to react quickly to changes in the economy. Enterprises that execute quickly gain competitive advantages over other businesses. Nevertheless, the network lifecycle gains business agility by the following actions:

- Establishing business requirements and technology strategies

- Readying sites to support the system that you want to implement

- Integrating technical requirements and business goals into a detailed design and demonstrating that the network is functioning as specified

- Expertly installing, configuring, and integrating system components

- Continually enhancing performance

Accessibility to network applications and services is critical to a productive environment. As such, the network lifecycle accelerates access to network applications and services by the following actions:

- Assessing and improving operational preparedness to support current and planned network technologies and services

- Improving service-delivery efficiency and effectiveness by increasing availability, resource capacity, and performance

- Improving the availability, reliability, and stability of the network and the applications running on it

- Managing and resolving problems affecting your system and keeping software applications current

Note The content of this book focuses on the prepare phase, plan phase, and design phases of the PPDIOO process as applied to building an enterprise campus network.

Planning a Network Implementation

The more detailed the implementation plan documentation is, the more likely the implementation will be a success. Although complex implementation steps usually require the designer to carry out the implementation, other staff members can complete well-documented detailed implementation steps without the direct involvement of the designer. In practical terms, most large enterprise design engineers rarely perform the hands-on steps of deploying the new design. Instead, network operations or implementation engineers are often the persons deploying a new design based on an implementation plan.

Moreover, when implementing a design, you must consider the possibility of a failure, even after a successful pilot or prototype network test. You need a well-defined, but simple, process test at every step and a procedure to revert to the original setup in case there is a problem.

Note   It is best-practice to lay out implementation steps in a tabular form and review those steps with your peers

Implementation Components

Implementation of a network design consists of several phases (install hardware, configure systems, launch into production, and so on). Each phase consists of several steps, and each step should contain, but be not limited to, the following documentation:

■   Description of the step

■   Reference to design documents

■   Detailed implementation guidelines

■   Detailed roll-back guidelines in case of failure

■   Estimated time needed for implementation

Summary Implementation Plan

Table 1-3 provides an example of an implementation plan for migrating users to new campus switches. Implementations can vary significantly between enterprises. The look and feel of your actual implementation plan can vary to meet the requirements of your organization.

Each step for each phase in the implementation phase is described briefly, with references to the detailed implementation plan for further details. The detailed implementation plan section should describe the precise steps necessary to complete the phase.

Table 1-3   *Sample Summary Implementation Plan*

Phase	Date, Time	Description	Implementation Details	Completed
Phase 3	12/26/2010 1:00 a.m. EST	Installs new campus switches	Section 6.2.3	Yes
Step 1		Installs new modules in campus backbone to support new campus switches	Section 6.2.3.1	Yes
Step 2		Interconnects new campus switches to new modules in campus backbone	Section 6.2.3.2	Yes
Step 3		Verifies cabling	Section 6.2.3.3	
Step 4		Verifies that interconnects have links on respective switches	Section 6.2.3.4	
Phase 4	12/27/2010 1:00 a.m. EST	Configures new campus switches and new modules in campus backbone	Section 6.2.4.1	
Step 1		Loads standard configuration file into switches for network management, switch access, and so on	Section 6.2.4.2	
Step 2		Configures Layer 3 interfaces for IP address and routing configuration on new modules in campus backbone	Section 6.2.4.3	
Step 3		Configures Layer 3 interfaces for IP address and routing info on new campus switches	Section 6.2.4.4	
Step 4		Configures Layer 2 features such as VLAN, STP, and QoS on new campus switches	Section 6.2.4.5	

continues

Table 1-3   *Sample Summary Implementation Plan (continued)*

Phase	Date, Time	Description	Implementation Details	Completed
Step 5		Tests access layer ports on new campus switches by piloting access for a few enterprise applications	Section 6.2.4.6	
Phase 5	12/28/2010 1:00 a.m. EST	Production implementation	Section 6.2.5	
Step 1		Migrate users to new campus switches	Section 6.2.5.1	
Step 2		Verifies migrated workstations can access enterprise applications	Section 6.2.5.2	

Detailed Implementation Plan

A detailed implementation plan describes the exact steps necessary to complete the implementation phase. It is necessary to includes steps to verify and check the work of the engineers implementing the plan. The following list illustrates a sample network implementation plan:

Section 6.2.4.6, "Configure Layer 2 features such as VLAN, STP, and QoS on new campus switches"

- Number of switches involved: 8

- Refer to Section 1.1 for physical port mapping to VLAN

- Use configuration template from Section 4.2.3 for VLAN configuration

- Refer to Section 1.2 for physical port mapping to spanning-tree configuration

- Use configuration template from Section 4.2.4 for spanning-tree configuration

- Refer to Section 1.3 for physical port mapping to QoS configuration

- Use configuration template from Section 4.2.5 for QoS configuration

- Estimate configuration time to be 30 minutes per switch

- Verify configuration preferable by another engineer

This section highlighted the key concepts around PPDIOO. Although this topic is not a technical one, the best practices highlighted will go a long way with any network design and implementation plan. Poor plans will always yield poor results. Today's networks are too critical for business operations not to plan effectively. As such, reviewing and utilizing the Cisco Lifecycle will increase the likelihood of any network implementation.

Summary

Evolutionary changes are occurring within the campus network. One example is the migration from a traditional/Layer 2 access-switch design (with its requirement to span VLANs and subnets across multiple access switches) to a virtual switch-based design. Another is the movement from a design with subnets contained within a single access switch to the routed-access design. This evolvement requires careful planning and deployments. Hierarchical design requirements along with other best practices are detailed throughout the remainder of this book to ensure a successful network.

As the network evolves, new capabilities are added, such as virtualization of services or mobility. The motivations for introducing these capabilities to the campus design are many. The increase in security risks, the need for a more flexible infrastructure, and the change in application data flows have all driven the need for a more capable architecture. However, implementing the increasingly complex set of business-driven capabilities and services in the campus architecture can be challenging if done in a piece meal fashion. Any successful architecture must be based on a foundation of solid design theory and principles. For any enterprise business involved in the design and operation of a campus network, the adoption of an integrated approach based on solid systems design principles, is a key to success.

Review Questions

Use the questions here to review what you learned in this chapter. The correct answers are found in Appendix A, "Answers to Chapter Review Questions."

1. The following statement describes which part of the enterprise network that is understood as the portion of the network infrastructure that provides access to services and resources to end users and devices that are spread over a single geographic location?

    a. Campus

    b. Data center

    c. Branch/WAN

    d. Internet Edge

2. The following statement describes which part of the enterprise network that is generally understood to be the facility used to house computing systems and associated components and was original referred to as the server farm?

   a. Campus

   b. Data center

   c. Branch/WAN

   d. Internet Edge

3. This area of the enterprise network was originally referred to as the server farm.

   a. Campus

   b. Data center

   c. Branch/WAN

   d. Internet Edge

4. Which of the following are characteristics of a properly designed campus network?

   a. Modular

   b. Flexible

   c. Scalable

   d. Highly available

5. Layer 2 networks were originally built to handle the performance requirements of LAN interconnectivity, whereas Layer 3 routers could not accommodate multiple interfaces running at near wire-rate speed. Today, Layer 3 campus LAN networks can achieve the same performance of Layer 2 campus LAN networks due to the following technology change:

   a. Layer 3 switches are now built using specialized components that enable similar performance for both Layer 2 and Layer 3 switching.

   b. Layer 3 switches can generally switch packets faster than Layer 2 switches.

   c. Layer 3 switches are now built using multiple virtual routers enabling higher speed interfaces.

6. Why are Layer 2 domains popular in data center designs?

   a. Data centers do not require the same scalability as the campus network.

   b. Data centers do not require fast convergence.

   c. Data centers place heavier emphasis on low-latency, whereas some applications operate at Layer 2 in an effort to reduce Layer 3 protocol overhead.

   d. Data centers switches such as the Nexus 7000 are Layer 2-only switches.

7. In the content of CCNP SWITCH and this book, what number of end devices or users quantifies as a small campus network?

   a. Up to 200 users

   b. Up to 2000 users

   c. Between 500 to 2500 users

   d. Between 1000 to 10,000 users

8. In the context of CCNP SWITCH and this book, what number of end devices or user quantifies a medium-sized campus network?

   a. A message digest encrypted with the sender's private key

   b. Up to 200 users

   c. Up to 2000 users

   d. Between 500 to 2500 users

   e. Between 1000 to 10,000 users

9. Why are hierarchical designs used with layers as an approach to network design?

   a. Simplification of large-scale designs.

   b. Reduce complexity of troubleshooting analysis.

   c. Reduce costs by 50 percent compared to flat network designs.

   d. Packets that move faster through layered networks reduce latency for applications.

10. Which of the following is not a Layer 2 switching feature? You might need to consult later chapters for guidance in answering this question; there might be more than one answer.

   a. Forwarding based upon the destination MAC address

   b. Optionally supports frame classification and quality of service

   c. IP routing

   d. Segmenting a network into multiple broadcast domains using VLANs

   e. Optionally applies network access security

11. Which of the following switches support(s) IP routing?

   a. Catalyst 6500

   b. Catalyst 4500

   c. Catalyst 3750, 3560E

   d. Catalyst 2960G

   e. Nexus 7000

   f. Nexus 5000

12. Which of the following switches support(s) highly available power via integrated redundant power?

    a. Catalyst 6500

    b. Catalyst 4500

    c. Catalyst 3750, 3560E

    d. Catalyst 2960G

    e. Nexus 7000

    f. Nexus 5000

13. Which of the following switches support(s) redundant supervisor/routing engines?

    a. Catalyst 6500

    b. Catalyst 4500

    c. Catalyst 3750, 3560E

    d. Catalyst 2960G

    e. Nexus 7000

    f. Nexus 5000

14. Which of the following switches use(s) a modular architecture for additional scalability and future growth?

    a. Catalyst 6500

    b. Catalyst 4500

    c. Catalyst 3750, 3560E

    d. Catalyst 2960G

    e. Nexus 7000

    f. Nexus 5000

15. Which of the following traffic generally utilizes more network bandwidth than other traffic types?

    a. IP telephony

    b. Web traffic

    c. Network Management

    d. Apple iPhone on Wi-Fi campus network

    e. IP multicast

16. Which of the following are examples of peer-to-peer applications?

   a. Video conferencing

   b. IP phone calls

   c. Workstation-to-workstation file sharing

   d. Web-based database application

   e. Inventory management tool

17. Which of the following are examples of client-server applications?

   a. Human resources user tool

   b. Company wiki

   c. Workstation-to-workstation file sharing

   d. Web-based database application

   e. Apple iTunes media sharing

18. A small-sized campus network might combine which two layers of the hierarchical model?

   a. Access and distribution

   b. Access and core

   c. Core and distribution

19. In a large-sized enterprise network, which defined layer usually interconnects the data center, campus, Internet edge, and branch/WAN sections.

   a. Specialized access layer

   b. Four fully meshed distribution layers

   c. Core backbone

20. Which layer of the campus network are Layer 2 switches most likely to be found in a medium-sized campus network if at all?

   a. Core layer

   b. Distribution layer

   c. Access layer

21. SONA is an architectural framework that guides the evolution of _____?

   a. Enterprise networks to integrated applications

   b. Enterprise networks to a more intelligent infrastructure

   c. Commercial networks to intelligent network services

    d. Enterprise networks to intelligent network services

    e. Commercial networks to a more intelligent infrastructure

22. SONA Which are the three layers of SONA?

    a. Integrated applications layer

    b. Application layer

    c. Interactive services layer

    d. Intelligent services layer

    e. Networked infrastructure layer

    f. Integrated transport layer

23. Which of the following best describe the core layer as applied to the campus network?

    a. A fast, scalable, and high-available Layer 2 network that interconnects the different physical segments such as buildings of a campus

    b. A point to multipoint link between the headquarters and the branches, usually based on a push technology

    c. A fast, scalable, and high-available Layer 3 network that interconnects the different physical segments such as buildings of a campus

    d. The physical connections between devices, also known as the physical layer

24. Which of the following best describes the relationship between the data center and the campus backbone?

    a. The campus backbone interconnects the data center to the campus core layer.

    b. The data center devices physically connect directly to the Enterprise Distribution Layer switches.

    c. The data center devices physically connect to access switches.

    d. The data center devices connection model is different from the Layer 3 model used for the rest of the enterprise network

25. List the phases of the Cisco Lifecycle approach in the correct order.

    a. Propose

    b. Implement

    c. Plan

    d. Optimize

    e. Prepare

    f. Inquire

g. Design

h. Document

i. Operate

26. Which three are considered to be technical goals of the Cisco Lifecycle approach?

a. Improving security

b. Simplifying network management

c. Increasing competitiveness

d. Improving reliability

e. Increasing revenue

f. Improving customer support

27. When implementing multiple complex components, which of the following is the most-efficient approach per the PPDIOO model?

a. Implement each component one after the other, test to verify at each step.

b. Implement all components simultaneously for efficiency reasons.

c. Implement all components on a per physical location approach.

Chapter 2

Implementing VLANs in Campus Networks

This chapter covers the following topics:

- Implementing VLAN Technologies in a Campus Network

- Implementing Trunking in Cisco Campus Network

- VLAN Trunking Protocol

- Private VLANs

- Configuring Link Aggregation with EtherChannel

This chapter reviews the purpose of VLANs and describes how VLAN implementation can simplify network management and troubleshooting, and can improve network performance. It reviews the end-to-end VLAN architecture where VLANs span switches and local VLANs connected via Layer 3 switching used in the Campus Enterprise Architecture. In addition to this, trunking and VLAN Trunking Protocol (VTP) that are also the significant features of deploying VLANs are discussed.

This chapter addresses how design considerations determine which VLANs span all the switches in a network and which VLANs remain local to a switch block. The configuration components of this chapter describe how individual switch ports can carry traffic for one or more VLANs, depending on their configuration as access or trunk ports. In addition, this chapter explains both why and how VLAN implementation occurs in an enterprise network.

In some scenarios, devices must belong to the same VLAN but still be prevented from communicating with one another. A specific feature, private VLANs, is useful for fine-tuning which devices can be reached by all VLAN members and which devices should be isolated. This chapter also describes how to use and configure private VLANs.

Finally, when several physical links connect the same devices, network designers can create a specific configuration to join those physical links in a common virtual connection using EtherChanneling. This chapter also explains the various possible technologies available to configure EtherChannel.

This chapter covers the following topics:

- Given a large enterprise network, design, plan, and implement VLANs based on business and technical requirements and constraints.

- Given a large enterprise network design, plan, implement and verify trunking based on business and technical requirements and constraints.

- Design, plan, and implement and verify VTP based on business and technical requirements and constraints.

- Plan, implement, and verify private VLANs.

- Plan, implement, and verify EtherChannel in a Layer 2 topology based on business and technical requirements and constraints.

Implementing VLAN Technologies in a Campus Network

A VLAN is a logical group of end devices with a common set of requirements independent of their physical location, as shown in Figure 2-1, in which sales, human resources, and engineering are three different VLANs spread across all three floors.

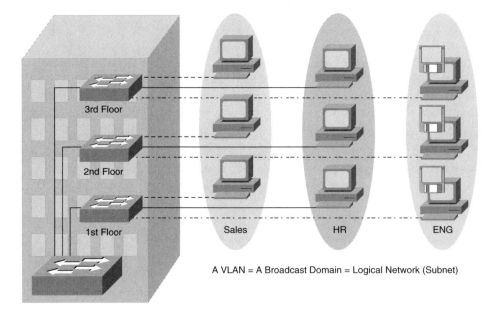

Figure 2-1   *VLAN Overview*

Although switches do not propagate Layer 2 broadcasts between VLANs, VLANs can exist anywhere in the switch network. Because a VLAN is a single broadcast domain, campus design best practices recommend mapping a VLAN generally to one IP subnet. To communicate between VLANs, packets need to pass through a router or Layer 3 device.

Generally, a port carries traffic only for the single VLAN. For a VLAN to span multiple switches, Catalyst switches use trunks. A trunk carries traffic for multiple VLANs by using Inter-Switch Link (ISL) encapsulation or IEEE 802.1Q. This chapter discusses trunking in more detail in later sections. Because VLANs are an important aspect of any campus design, almost all Cisco devices support VLANs and trunking.

Note   Most of the Cisco products support only 802.1Q trunking because 802.1Q is the industry standard. This book focuses only on 802.1Q.

When a network architect hands off a design, you need to create an implementation plan based on the knowledge of VLANs and trunks.

This section discusses in detail how to plan, implement, and verify VLAN technologies and address schemes to meet the given business and technical requirements and constraints. This ability includes being able to meet these objectives:

■   Describe the different VLAN segmentation models.

■   Discuss VLAN implementation in a hierarchical network.

■   Given an enterprise VLAN network design, describe the information needed to create an implementation plan and the choices that need to be made and analyze the consequences of those choices.

■   Discuss best practices for VLAN implementation.

■   Given an enterprise VLAN network design, configure, verify, and troubleshoot VLANs.

VLAN Segmentation Model

Larger, flat networks generally consist of many end devices in which broadcasts and unknown unicast packets are flooded on all ports in the network One advantage of using VLANs is the capability to segment the Layer 2 broadcast domain. All devices in a VLAN are members of the same broadcast domain. If an end device transmits a Layer 2 broadcast, all other members of the VLAN receive the broadcast. Switches filter the broadcast from all the ports or devices that are not part of the same VLAN.

In a campus design, a network administrator can design a campus network with one of two models: end-to-end VLANs or local VLANs. Business and technical requirements, past experience, and political motivations can influence the design chosen. Choosing the right model initially can help create a solid foundation upon which to grow the business. Each model has its own advantages and disadvantages. When configuring a switch for an

existing network, try to determine which model is used so that you can understand the
logic behind each switch configuration and position in the infrastructure.

End-to-End VLAN

The term end-to-end VLAN refers to a single VLAN that is associated with switch ports
widely dispersed throughout an enterprise network on multiple switches. A Layer 2
switched campus network carries traffic for this VLAN throughout the network, as
shown in Figure 2-2 where VLANs 1, 2 and 3 are spread across all three switches.

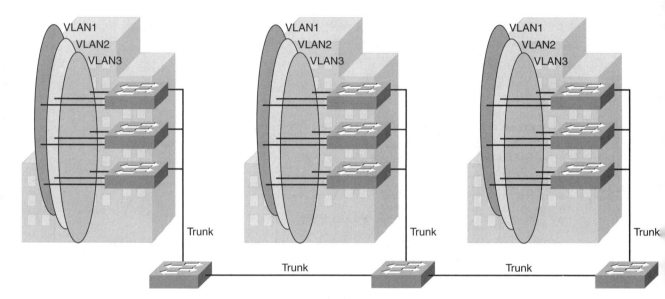

Figure 2-2   *End-to-End VLANs*

If more than one VLAN in a network is operating in the end-to-end mode, special links
(Layer 2 trunks) are required between switches to carry the traffic of all the different
VLANs.

An end-to-end VLAN model has the following characteristics:

- Each VLAN is dispersed geographically throughout the network.

- Users are grouped into each VLAN regardless of the physical location.

- As a user moves throughout a campus, the VLAN membership of that user remains
  the same, regardless of the physical switch to which this user attaches.

- Users are typically associated with a given VLAN for network management reasons.
  This is why they are kept in the same VLAN, therefore the same group, as they move
  through the campus.

- All devices on a given VLAN typically have addresses on the same IP subnet.

- Switches commonly operate in a server/client VTP mode.

Local VLAN

The Campus Enterprise Architecture is based on the local VLAN model. In a local VLAN model, all users of a set of geographically common switches are grouped into a single VLAN, regardless of the organizational function of those users. Local VLANs are generally confined to a wiring closet, as shown in Figure 2-3, that VLANs are local to one access switch and trunking to the distribution switch. If users move from one location to another in the campus, their connection changes to the new VLAN at the new physical location.

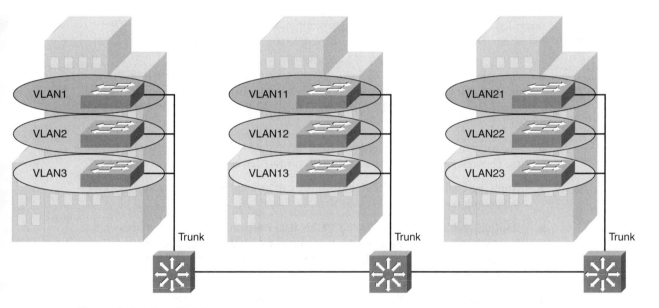

Figure 2-3 *Local VLANs*

In the local VLAN model, Layer 2 switching is implemented at the access level and routing is implemented at the distribution and core level, as shown in Figure 2-3, to enable users to maintain access to the resources they need.

The following are some local VLAN characteristics and user guidelines:

- The network administrator should create local VLANs with physical boundaries in mind rather than the job functions of the users on the end devices.

- Generally, local VLANs exist between the access and distribution levels.

- Traffic from a local VLAN is routed at the distribution and core levels to reach destinations on other networks.

■ Configure the VTP mode in transparent mode because VLANs on a given access switch should not be advertised to all other switches in the network, nor do they need to be manually created in any other switch's VLAN database.

■ A network that consists entirely of local VLANs can benefit from increased convergence times offered via routing protocols, instead of a spanning tree for Layer 2 networks. It is usually recommended to have one to three VLANs per access layer switches.

Comparison of End-to-End VLANs and Local VLANs

This subsection describes the benefits and drawbacks of local VLANs versus end-to-end VLANs.

Because a VLAN usually represents a Layer 3 segment, each end-to-end VLAN enables a single Layer 3 segment to be dispersed geographically throughout the network. The following could be some of the reasons for implementing the end-to-end design:

■ **Grouping users:** Users can be grouped on a common IP segment, even though they are geographically dispersed. Recently the trend has been moving toward virtualization. Solutions such as VMWARE need end-to-end VLANs to be spread across segments of the campus.

■ **Security:** A VLAN can contain resources that should not be accessible to all users on the network, or there might be a reason to confine certain traffic to a particular VLAN.

■ **Applying quality of service (QoS):** Traffic can be a higher or lower access priority to network resources from a given VLAN.

■ **Routing avoidance:** If much of the VLAN user traffic is destined for devices on that same VLAN, and routing to those devices is not desirable, users can access resources on their VLAN without their traffic being routed off the VLAN, even though the traffic might traverse multiple switches.

■ **Special purpose VLAN:** Sometimes a VLAN is provisioned to carry a single type of traffic that must be dispersed throughout the campus (for example, multicast, voice, or visitor VLANs).

■ **Poor design:** For no clear purpose, users are placed in VLANs that span the campus or even span WANs. Sometimes when a network is already configured and running, organizations are hesitant to improve the design because of downtime or other political reasons.

Following are some items that the network admin should consider when implementing end-to-end VLANs:

■ Switch ports are provisioned for each user and associated with a given VLAN. Because users on an end-to-end VLAN can be anywhere in the network, all switches must be aware of that VLAN. This means that all switches carrying traffic for end-to-end VLANs are required to have those specific VLANs defined in each switch's VLAN database.

■ Also, flooded traffic for the VLAN is, by default, passed to every switch even if it does not currently have any active ports in the particular end-to-end VLAN.

■ Finally, troubleshooting devices on a campus with end-to-end VLANs can be challenging because the traffic for a single VLAN can traverse multiple switches in a large area of the campus, and that can easily cause potential spanning-tree problems.

Mapping VLANs to a Hierarchical Network

In the past, network designers have attempted to implement the 80/20 rule when designing networks. The rule was based on the observation that, in general, 80 percent of the traffic on a network segment was passed between local devices, and only 20 percent of the traffic was destined for remote network segments. Therefore, network architecture used to prefer end-to-end VLANs. To avoid the complications of end-to-end VLANs, designers now consolidate servers in central locations on the network and provide access to external resources, such as the Internet, through one or two paths on the network because the bulk of traffic now traverses a number of segments. Therefore, the paradigm now is closer to a 20/80 proportion, in which the greater flow of traffic leaves the local segment, so local VLANs have become more efficient.

In addition, the concept of end-to-end VLANs was attractive when IP address configuration was a manually administered and burdensome process; therefore, anything that reduced this burden as users moved between networks was an improvement. However, given the ubiquity of DHCP, the process of configuring an IP address at each desktop is no longer a significant issue. As a result, there are few benefits to extending a VLAN throughout an enterprise; for example, if there are some clustering and other requirements.

Local VLANs are part of the enterprise campus architecture design, as shown in Figure 2-4, in which VLANs used at the access layer should extend no further than their associated distribution switch. For example VLANs 1, 10 and VLANs 2, 20 are confined to only a local access switch. Traffic is routed from the local VLAN as it is passed from the distribution layer into the core. It is usually recommended to have two to three VLANs per access block rather than span all the VLANs across all access blocks. This design can mitigate Layer 2 troubleshooting issues that occur when a single VLAN traverses the switches throughout a campus network. In addition, because STP is configured for redundancy, the switch limits the STP to only the access and distribution switches that help to reduce the network complexity in times of failure.

Implementing the enterprise campus architecture design using local VLANs provides the following benefits:

■ **Deterministic traffic flow:** The simple layout provides a predictable Layer 2 and Layer 3 traffic path. If a failure occurs that was not mitigated by the redundancy features, the simplicity of the model facilitates expedient problem isolation and resolution within the switch block.

- **Active redundant paths:** When implementing Per VLAN Spanning Tree (PVST) or Multiple Spanning Tree Protocol (MSTP) because there is no loop, all links can be used to make use of the redundant paths.

- **High availability:** Redundant paths exist at all infrastructure levels. Local VLAN traffic on access switches can be passed to the building distribution switches across an alternative Layer 2 path if a primary path failure occurs. Router redundancy protocols can provide failover if the default gateway for the access VLAN fails. When both the Spanning Tree Protocol (STP) instance and VLAN are confined to a specific access and distribution block, Layer 2 and Layer 3 redundancy measures and protocols can be configured to failover in a coordinated manner.

- **Finite failure domain:** If VLANs are local to a switch block, and the number of devices on each VLAN is kept small, failures at Layer 2 are confined to a small subset of users.

- **Scalable design:** Following the enterprise campus architecture design, new access switches can be easily incorporated, and new submodules can be added when necessary.

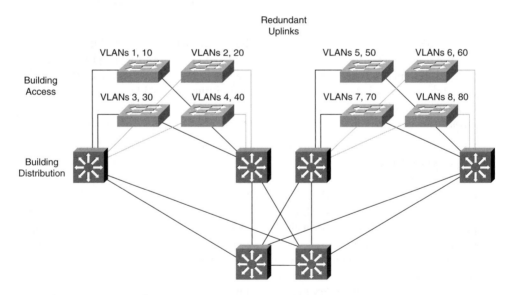

Figure 2-4   *VLAN Implementation in Campus Architecture Design*

Planning VLAN Implementation

The type of VLAN module used in the network affects how the implementation and verification plan is developed and executed. In this section, we focus only on implementing the Layer 2 end-to-end VLAN model. In later sections, we focus on the local VLAN model used by the campus enterprise architecture.

This section describes the steps necessary to create a plan for the implementation of VLANs in a campus environment. In general, planning end-to-end VLAN implementation involves the following tasks:

Step 1.   Understand the existing network flow. Unless you design the network, designers usually present the network infrastructure VLAN layout with defined groups. These groups usually represent subnets and associated VLANs. It is important to collect the VLAN numbers, names, purposes, and associate VLAN to the IP mapping scheme.

Step 2.   When you have the VLAN list, document which part of the campus needs what VLANs. This determines the traffic flow between switches and which VLANs should be present in which switches.

Step 3.   VLANs are commonly assigned statically on a port basis. Some network implementations use a different method based, for example, on dot1x authentication. The configuration tasks depend on the assignment method. You also need to know what you should do with unused ports on a switch. Should they be left to their default configuration, assigned to an unused VLAN for security purposes, or assigned to a default VLAN?

Note   This book focuses only on configuring VLANs statically.

Step 4.   After you gather all the information about VLANs, the next important step is trunk configuration. If there is inter-switch communication, trunks will be required. Regarding trunk configuration, you need to know where the trunks should be placed. Should all VLANs be allowed on these trunks? And what should the native VLAN be?

Step 5.   VTP can help simplify VLAN configuration and pruning. You should also know whether it is useful in the current network case. For VTP implementation, you need to gather where it should be implemented. Which switch should be the server, which should be clients, and which (if any)should be transparent?

Note   VTP is discussed in more detail later in this chapter.

Step 6.   Most important to all, create a test plan to implement the VLANs and verify whether it suits the traffic flow requirements and future growth.

Best Practices for VLAN Design

Usually, network designers design and implement the VLANs and their components depending on the business needs and requirements, but this section provides general best practices for implementing VLAN in a campus network.

Following are some of the practices for VLAN design:

■ For the Local VLANs model, it is usually recommended to have only one to three VLANs per access module and, as discussed, limit those VLANs to a couple of access switches and the distribution switches.

■ Avoid using VLAN 1 as the "blackhole" for all unused ports. Use any other VLAN except 1 to assign all the unused ports to it.

■ Try to always have separate voice VLANs, data VLANs, management VLANs, native VLANs, blackhole VLANs, and default VLANs (VLAN 1).

■ In the local VLANs model, avoid VTP; it is feasible to use manually allowed VLANs in a network on trunks.

■ For trunk ports, turn off DTP and configure it manually. Use IEEE 802.1Q rather than ISL because it has better support for QoS and is a standard protocol.

■ Manually configure access ports that are not specifically intended for a trunk link.

■ Prevent all data traffic from VLAN 1; only permit control protocols to run on VLAN 1 (DTP, VTP, STP BPDUs, PAgP, LACP, CDP, and such.).

■ Avoid using Telnet because of security risks; enable SSH support on management VLANs.

Configuring VLANs

All Cisco Catalyst switches support VLANs. That said, each Cisco Catalyst switch supports a different number of VLANs, with high-end Cisco Catalyst switches supporting as many as 4096 VLANs. Table 2-1 notes the maximum number of VLANs supported by each model of Catalyst switch.

VLAN Ranges

Cisco Catalyst switches support up to 4096 VLANs depending on the platform and software version. Table 2-2 illustrates the VLAN division for Cisco Catalyst switches.

Note   The Catalyst 2950 and 2955 support as many as 64 VLANs with the Standard Software image, and up to 250 VLANs with the Enhanced Software image. Cisco Catalyst switches do not support VLANs 1002 through 1005; these are reserved for Token Ring and FDDI VLANs. Furthermore, the Catalyst 4500 and 6500 families of switches do not support VLANs 1006 through 1024. In addition, several families of switches support more VLANs than the number of spanning-tree instances. For example, the Cisco Catalyst 2970 supports 1005 VLANs but only 128 spanning-tree instances. For information on the number of supported spanning-tree instances, refer to the Cisco Product Technical Documentation.

Table 2-1   *VLAN Support Matrix for Catalyst Switches*

Type of Switch	Maximum No. of VLANs	VLAN ID Range
Catalyst 2940	4	1–1005
Catalyst 2950/2955	250	1–4094
Catalyst 2960	255	1–4094
Catalyst 2970/3550/3560/3750	1005	1–4094
Catalyst 2848G/2980G/4000/4500	4094	1–4094
Catalyst 6500	4094	1–4094

Table 2-2   *VLAN Ranges*

VLAN Range	Range	Usage	Propagated via VTP
0, 4095	Reserved	For system use only. You cannot see or use these VLANs.	—
1	Normal	Cisco default. You can use this VLAN, but you cannot delete it.	Yes
2–1001	Normal	For Ethernet VLANs. You can create, use, and delete these VLANs.	Yes
1002–1005	Normal	Cisco defaults for FDDI and Token Ring. You cannot delete VLANs 1002–1005.	Yes
1006–1024	Reserved	For system use only. You cannot see or use these VLANS.	—
1025–4094	Extended	For Ethernet VLANs only.	Not supported in VTP versions 1 and 2. The switch must be in VTP transparent mode to configure extended-range VLANS. Only supported in version 3.

To create a new VLAN in global configuration mode, follow these steps:

Step 1.   Enter global configuration mode:

```
Switch# configure terminal
```

Step 2.   Create a new VLAN with a particular ID number:

```
Switch(config)# vlan vlan-id
```

Step 3.   (Optional.) Name the VLAN:

```
Switch(config-vlan)# name vlan-name
```

Example 2-1 shows how to configure a VLAN in global configuration mode.

Example 2-1   *Creating a VLAN in Global Configuration Mode in Cisco IOS*

```
Switch# configure terminal
Switch(config)# vlan 5
Switch(config-vlan)# name Engineering
Switch(config-vlan)# exit
```

To delete a VLAN in global configuration mode, follow these steps:

Step 1.   Enter global configuration mode:

```
Switch# configure terminal
```

Step 2.   Delete the VLAN by referencing its ID number:

```
Switch(config)# no vlan vlan-id
```

Note   After a VLAN is deleted, the access ports that belong to that VLAN move into the inactive state until the ports are moved to another VLAN. As a security measure, ports in the inactive state do not forward traffic.

Example 2-2 shows deletion of a VLAN in global configuration mode.

Example 2-2   *Deleting a VLAN in Global Configuration Mode*

```
Switch# configure terminal
Switch(config)# no vlan 3
Switch(config)# end
```

To assign a switch port to a previously created VLAN, follow these steps:

Step 1.   From global configuration mode, enter the configuration mode for the particular port you want to add to the VLAN:

    Switch(config)# **interface** *interface_id*

Step 2.   Specify the port as an access port:

    Switch(config-if)# **switchport mode access**
    Switch(config-if)# **switchport host**

> **Note**   The **switchport host** command effectively configures a port for a host device, such as a workstation or server. This feature is a macro for enabling Spanning Tree PortFast and disabling EtherChanneling on a per-port basis. These features are discussed in later chapters.
>
> The **switchport mode access** command is needed so that the interface doesn't attempt to negotiate trunking.

Step 3.   Remove or place the port in a particular VLAN:

    Switch(config-if)# [**no**] **switchport access vlan** *vlan-id*

Example 2-3 illustrates configuration of an interface as an access port in VLAN 200.

Example 2-3   *Assigning an Access Port to a VLAN*

```
Switch# configure terminal
Enter configuration commands, one per line. End with CNTL/Z.
Switch(config)# interface FastEthernet 5/6
Switch(config-if)# description PC A
Switch(config-if)# switchport
Switch(config-if)# switchport host
Switch(config-if)# switchport mode access
Switch(config-if)# switchport access vlan 200
Switch(configif)# no shutdown
Switch(config-if)# end
```

> **Note**   Use the **switchport** command with no keywords to configure interfaces as Layer 2 interfaces on Layer 3 switches. After configuring the interface as a Layer 2 interface, use additional **switchport** commands with keywords to configure Layer 2 properties, such as access VLANs or trunking.

Verifying the VLAN Configuration

As previously discussed, after you configure the VLANs, one of the important step of PPDIOO is to able to verify the configuration. To verify the VLAN configuration of a Catalyst switch, use **show** commands. The **show vlan** command from privileged EXEC mode displays information about a particular VLAN. Table 2-3 documents the fields displayed by the **show vlan** command.

Table 2-3   show vlan *Field Descriptions*

Field	Description
VLAN	VLAN number
Name	Name, if configured, of the VLAN
Status	Status of the VLAN (active or suspended)
Ports	Ports that belong to the VLAN
Type	Media type of the VLAN
SAID	Security association ID value for the VLAN
MTU	Maximum transmission unit size for the VLAN
Parent	Parent VLAN, if one exists
RingNo	Ring number for the VLAN, if applicable
BridgNo	Bridge number for the VLAN, if applicable
Stp	Spanning Tree Protocol type used on the VLAN
BrdgMode	Bridging mode for this VLAN
Trans1	Translation bridge 1
Trans2	Translation bridge 2
AREHops	Maximum number of hops for All-Routes Explorer frames
STEHops	Maximum number of hops for Spanning Tree Explorer frames

Note   PPDIOO stands for Prepare, Plan, Design, Implement, Operate, and Optimize. In this chapter, our focus is also to follow the model to design the VLAN implementation in a campus architecture. PPDIOO is discussed in detailed in Chapter 1, "Analyzing the Cisco Enterprise Campus Architecture."

Example 2-4 displays information about a VLAN identified by number in Cisco IOS.

Example 2-4   *Displaying Information About a VLAN by Number in Cisco IOS*

```
Switch# show vlan id 3
VLAN Name                             Status    Ports
---- -------------------------------- --------- -------------------------------
3    VLAN0003                         active
VLAN Type  SAID       MTU   Parent RingNo BridgeNo Stp  BrdgMode Trans1 Trans2
---- ----- ---------- ----- ------ ------ -------- ---- -------- ------ ------
3    enet  100003     1500  -      -      -        -    -        0      0
------- --------- ----------------- -----------------------------------------
```

Example 2-5 displays information about a VLAN identified by name in Cisco IOS.

Example 2-5   *Displaying Information About a VLAN by Name in Cisco IOS*

```
Switch# show vlan name VLAN0003
VLAN Name                             Status    Ports
---- -------------------------------- --------- --------------------
3    VLAN0003                         active

VLAN Type  SAID       MTU   Parent RingNo BridgeNo Stp  Trans1 Trans2
---- ----- ---------- ----- ------ ------ -------- ---- ------ ------
3    enet  100003     1500  -      -      -        -    0      0
```

To display the current configuration of a particular interface, use the **show running-config interface** *interface_type slot/port* command. To display detailed information about a specific switch port, use the **show interfaces** command. The command **show interface** *interface_type slot/port* with the switchport keyword displays not only a switch port's characteristics but also private VLAN and trunking information. The **show-mac address-table interface** *interface_type slot/port* command displays the MAC address table information for the specified interface in specific VLANs. During troubleshooting, this command is helpful in determining whether the attached devices are sending packets to the correct VLAN.

Example 2-6 displays the configuration of a particular interface. Example 2-6 shows that the interface Ethernet 5/6 is configured with the VLAN 200 and in an access mode so that the port doesn't negotiate for trunking.

Example 2-6   *Displaying Information About the Interface Config*

```
Switch# show running-config interface FastEthernet 5/6
Building configuration...
!
Current configuration :33 bytes
interface FastEthernet 5/6
switchport access vlan 200
switchport mode access
switchport host
end
```

Example 2-7 displays detailed switch port information as the port VLAN and operation modes. As shown in Example 2-7, the fastethernet port 4/1 is configured as the switch-port port means Layer 2 port, working as an access port in VLAN 2.

Example 2-7   *Displaying Detailed Switch Port Information*

```
BXB-6500-10:8A# show interfaces FastEthernet 4/1 switchport
Name: Fa4/1
Switchport: Enabled
Administrative Mode: static access
Operational Mode: static access
Administrative Trunking Encapsulation: negotiate
Operational Trunking Encapsulation: native
Negotiation of Trunking: Off
Access Mode VLAN: 2 (VLAN0002)
Trunking Native Mode VLAN: 1 (default)
Voice VLAN: none
Administrative private-vlan host-association: none
Administrative private-vlan mapping: none
Administrative private-vlan trunk native VLAN: none
Administrative private-vlan trunk encapsulation: dot1q
Administrative private-vlan trunk normal VLANs: none
Administrative private-vlan trunk private VLANs: none
Operational private-vlan: none
Trunking VLANs Enabled: ALL
Pruning VLANs Enabled: 2-1001
Capture Mode Disabled
Capture VLANs Allowed: ALL

Voice VLAN: none (Inactive)
Appliance trust: none
```

Example 2-8 displays the MAC address table information for a specific interface in VLAN 1.

Example 2-8   *Displaying MAC Address Table Information*

```
Switch# show mac-address-table interface GigabitEthernet 0/1 vlan 1
          Mac Address Table
-------------------------------------------
Vlan    Mac Address      Type       Ports
----    -----------      ----       -----
   1    0008.2199.2bc1   DYNAMIC    Gi0/1
Total Mac Addresses for this criterion: 1
```

Troubleshooting VLANs

When troubleshooting problems related to VLANs, always review the following items:

- Physical connections

- Switch configuration

- VLAN configuration

Figure 2-5 shows, at a high level, VLAN problems that can occur on a switch.

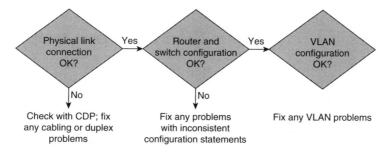

Figure 2-5   *Troubleshooting VLAN Problems*

The following sections cover several common VLAN issues and the action plan to troubleshoot these issues.

Troubleshooting Slow Throughput

To troubleshoot slow-throughput issues within the same VLAN, perform the following steps:

Step 1.   A point-to-point switch link consists of two ports where the problem may exist on either side of a link. Make sure the speed and duplex settings are consistent on both link partners.

Step 2.   Using **show interface** commands, check to see what types of errors exist on the suspected interfaces. Combinations of frame check sequence (FCS) errors, alignment errors, and runts generally point to a duplex mismatch; auto-negotiation is the usual culprit, but it could also be a mismatched manual setting.

Step 3.   Determine which Layer 2 path the packet is taking if there are redundant paths using spanning tree. For additional information on troubleshooting Spanning Tree Protocol (STP), read Chapter 3, "Implementing Spanning Tree."

If you see from the output of the **show interface** command that the number of collisions is increasing rapidly, the problem might be an oversubscribed half-duplex link, faulty hardware, a bad cable, or a duplex mismatch.

Troubleshooting Communication Issues

When one device cannot communicate with another device within a VLAN, troubleshoot the problem by doing the following:

■   Ensure that the VLAN membership of the switch ports is correct by using the **show interface, show mac,** and **show running** commands, as discussed in the previous "Verifying VLAN" section.

■   Make sure the switch ports are up and connected using the **show interface** command. Try to reset the port by using the **shut** and **no shut** commands under the switch interface.

Implementing Trunking in Cisco Campus Network

Trunks carry the traffic for multiple VLANs across a single physical link (multiplexing). Trunking is used to extend Layer 2 operations across an entire network, such as end-to-end VLANs, as shown in Figure 2-6. The host in VLAN 2 can communicate with the host in VLAN 2 in the other switch over the single trunk link, the same as a host in VLAN 1 can communicate with a host in another switch in VLAN 1.

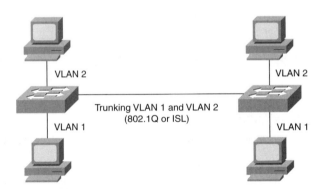

Figure 2-6   *VLAN Trunking*

To allow a switchport that connect two switches to carry more than one VLAN, it must be configure as a trunk. If frames from a single VLAN traverse a trunk link, a trunking protocol must mark the frame to identify its associated VLAN as the frame is placed onto the trunk link. The receiving switch then knows the frame's VLAN origin and can process the frame accordingly. On the receiving switch, the VLAN ID (VID) is removed when the frame is forwarded onto an access link associated with its VLAN.

When configuring an 802.1Q trunk, a matching native VLAN must be defined on each end of the trunk link. A trunk link is inherently associated with tagging each frame with a VID. The purpose of the native VLAN is to enable frames that are not tagged with a VID to traverse the trunk link. Native VLAN is discussed in more detail in a later part of this section.

The following sections discuss trunking implementation, configuration, and trouble-shooting in a multilayer switched network in more detail, including coverage of the following topics:

- Trunking protocols

- Understanding DTP

- Best practices for trunking

- Configuring 802.1Q Trunking in Cisco IOS

- Verifying trunking configurations

- Troubleshooting trunking

Trunking Protocols

This subsection covers the following two trunking protocols in more detail:

- **Inter-Switch Link (ISL):** A Cisco proprietary trunking encapsulation

- **IEEE 802.1Q:** An industry-standard trunking method

Because ISL protocol is almost obsolete, this book focuses only on 802.1Q. Figure 2-7 depicts how ISL encapsulates the normal Ethernet frame. Currently, all Catalyst switches support 802.1Q tagging for multiplexing traffic from multiple VLANs onto a single physical link.

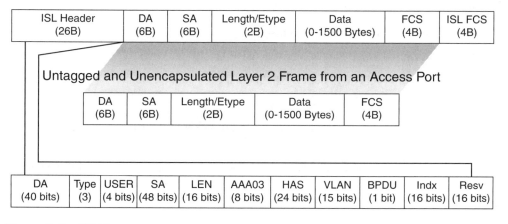

Figure 2-7   *ISL Frame*

IEEE 802.1Q trunk links employ the tagging mechanism to carry frames for multiple VLANs, in which each frame is tagged to identify the VLAN to which the frame belongs.

The IEEE 802.1Q/802.1p standard provides the following inherent architectural advantages over ISL:

- 802.1Q has smaller frame overhead than ISL. As a result, 802.1Q is more efficient than ISL, especially in the case of small frames. 802.1Q overhead is 4 bytes, whereas ISL is 30 bytes.

- 802.1Q is a widely supported industry-standard protocol.

- 802.1Q has the support for 802.1p fields for QoS.

Figure 2-8 describes the 802.1Q frame.

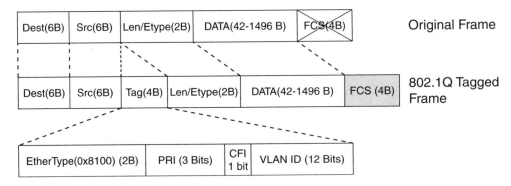

Figure 2-8 *802.1Q Frame*

The 802.1Q Ethernet frame header contains the following fields:

- **Dest:** Destination MAC address (6 bytes)

- **Src:** Source MAC address (6 bytes)

- **Tag:** Inserted 802.1Q tag (4 bytes, detailed here):

  - **EtherType(TPID):** Set to 0x8100 to specify that the 802.1Q tag follows.

  - **PRI:** 3-bit 802.1p priority field.

  - **CFI:** Canonical Format Identifier; is always set to 0 for Ethernet switches and to 1 for Token Ring-type networks.

  - **VLAN ID:** 12-bit VLAN field. Of the 4096 possible VLAN IDs, the maximum number of possible VLAN configurations is 4094. A VLAN ID of 0 indicates priority frames, and value 4095 (FFF) is reserved. CFI, PRI, and VLAN ID are represented as Tag Control information (TCI) fields.

- **Len/Etype:** 2-byte field specifying length (802.3) or type (Ethernet II).

- **Data:** Data itself.

- **FCS:** Frame check sequence (4 bytes).

IEEE 802.1Q uses an internal tagging mechanism that modifies the original frame (as shown by the "X" over FCS in the original frame in Figure 2-8), recalculates the CRC value for the entire frame with the tag, and inserts the new CRC value in a new FCS. ISL, in comparison, wraps the original frame and adds a second FCS that is built only on the header information but does not modify the original frame FCS.

IEEE 802.1p redefined the three most significant bits in the 802.1Q tag to allow for prioritization of the Layer 2 frame.

If a non-802.1Q-enabled device or an access port receives an 802.1Q frame, the tag data is ignored and the packet is switched at Layer 2 as a standard Ethernet frame. This allows for the placement of Layer 2 intermediate devices, such as unmanaged switches or bridges, along the 802.1Q trunk path. To process an 802.1Q tagged frame, a device must enable a maximum transmission unit (MTU) of 1522 or higher.

Baby giants are frames that are larger than the standard MTU of 1500 bytes but less than 2000 bytes. Because ISL and 802.1Q tagged frames increase the MTU beyond 1500 bytes, switches consider both frames as baby giants. ISL-encapsulated packets over Ethernet have an MTU of 1548 bytes, whereas 802.1Q has an MTU of 1522 bytes.

Understanding Native VLAN in 802.1Q Trunking

802.1Q trunks define a native VLAN for frames that are not tagged by default. Switches transmit any Layer 2 frames from a native VLAN on the trunk port untagged, as shown in Figure 2-9. The receiving switch forwards all untagged packets to its native VLAN. The native VLAN is the default VLAN configuration of the port. When the port is not trunking, the access VLAN configuration defines the native VLAN. In the case of Cisco switches, the default native VLAN is VLAN 1, and you can configure any other VLAN as the native VLAN.

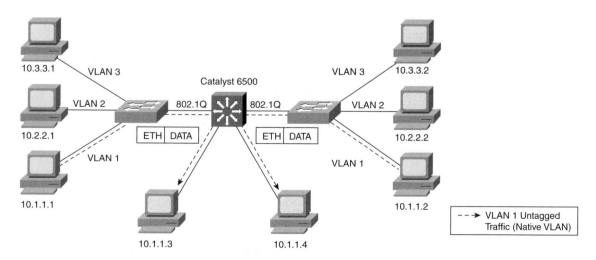

Figure 2-9 *Native VLAN*

It is important that the 802.1Q trunk port between two devices have the same native VLAN configuration on both sides of the link. If there is a native VLAN mismatch on an 802.1Q link, CDP (if used and functioning) issues a Native VLAN Mismatch error. On select versions of Cisco IOS Software, CDP might not be transmitted or will be automatically turned off if VLAN1 is disabled on the trunk.

In addition, if there is a native VLAN mismatch on either side of an 802.1Q link, Layer 2 loops might occur because VLAN1 STP bridge protocol data units (BPDU) are sent to the IEEE STP MAC address (0180.c200.0000) untagged.

Understanding DTP

All recent Cisco Catalyst switches, except for the Catalyst 2900XL and 3500XL, use a Cisco proprietary point-to-point protocol called Dynamic Trunking Protocol (DTP) on trunk ports to negotiate the trunking state. DTP negotiates the operational mode of directly connected switch ports to a trunk port and selects an appropriate trunking protocol. Negotiating trunking is a recommended practice in multilayer switched networks because it avoids network issues resulting from trunking misconfigurations for initial configuration, but best practice is when the network is stable, change to permanent trunk.

Cisco Trunking Modes and Methods

Table 2-4 describes the different trunking modes supported by Cisco switches.

Table 2-4 *Trunking Modes*

Mode in Cisco IOS	Function
Access	Puts the interface into permanent nontrunking mode and negotiates to convert the link into a nontrunk link. The interface becomes a nontrunk interface even if the neighboring interface does not agree to the change.
Trunk	Puts the interface into permanent trunking mode and negotiates to convert the link into a trunk link. The interface becomes a trunk interface even if the neighboring interface does not agree to the change.
Nonegotiate	Puts the interface into permanent trunking mode but prevents the interface from generating DTP frames. You must configure the neighboring interface manually as a trunk interface to establish a trunk link. Use this mode when connecting to a device that does not support DTP.
Dynamic desirable	Makes the interface actively attempt to convert the link to a trunk link. The interface becomes a trunk interface if the neighboring interface is set to trunk, desirable, or auto mode.
Dynamic auto	Makes the interface willing to convert the link to a trunk link. The interface becomes a trunk interface if the neighboring interface is set to trunk or desirable mode. This is the default mode for all Ethernet interfaces in Cisco IOS.

Note   The Cisco Catalyst 4000 and 4500 switches run Cisco IOS or Cisco CatOS depending on the Supervisor Engine model. The Supervisor Engines for the Catalyst 4000 and 4500 do not support ISL encapsulation on a per-port basis. Refer to the product documentation on Cisco.com for more details.

Figure 2-10 shows the combination of DTP modes between the two links. Combination of DTP modes can either make the port as an access port or trunk port.

	Dynamic Auto	Dynamic Desirable	Trunk	Access
Dynamic Auto	Access	Trunk	Trunk	Access
Dynamic Desirable	Trunk	Trunk	Trunk	Access
Trunk	Trunk	Trunk	Trunk	Limited Connectivity
Access	Access	Access	Limited Connectivity	Access

Figure 2-10   *DTP Modes Configuration*

VLAN Ranges and Mappings

ISL supports VLAN numbers in the range of 1 to 1005, whereas 802.1Q VLAN numbers are in the range of 1 to 4094. The default behavior of VLAN trunks is to permit all normal- and extended-range VLANs across the link if it is an 802.1Q interface and to permit normal VLANs in the case of an ISL interface.

Best Practices for Trunking

In a hierarchical design, access layer switches connect to distribution layer switches. This is where the trunks are implementing, as illustrated in Figure 2-11, where the links from each access switch to the distribution switches are the trunks links because they must carry two VLANs from each switch. Links between distribution and core layers are usually Layer 3. Also, usually to avoid spanning-tree problems, it is recommended not to link the two distribution switches as Layer 2 trunk links or have no link between them. In this way, the access layer switches are configured as a spanning-tree, loop-free V topology if one distribution link fails, using the HSRP or VRRP protocols for creating a virtual default-gateway. Spanning tree, HSRP, and VRRP are discussed more in later chapters.

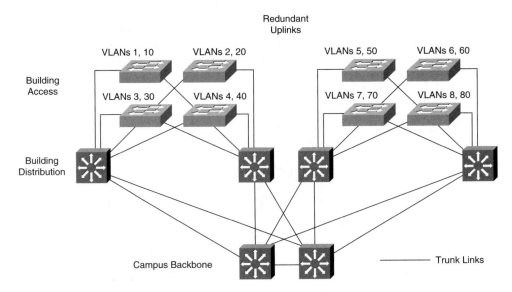

Figure 2-11   *Trunk Implementations*

DTP is useful when the status of the switch on the other end of the link is uncertain or might be changing over time. When the link is to be set to trunk in a stable manner, changing both ends to trunk nonegotiate accelerates the convergence time, saving up to two seconds upon boot time. We recommend this mode on stable links between switches that are part of the same core infrastructure.

On trunk links, it is recommended to manually prune the VLANs that are not used. You can use VTP pruning if VTP is in use, but manual pruning (using a switchport trunk allowed VLAN) is a secure way of allowing only those VLANs that are expected and allowed on the link. In addition to this, it is also a good practice to have an unused VLAN as a native VLAN on the trunk links to prevent DTP spoofing.

If trunking is not used on a port, you can disable it with the interface level command **switchport host**. This command is a macro that sets the port to access mode (switchport mode access) and enables portfast.

Configuring 802.1Q Trunking

To configure a switch port as an 802.1Q trunking port in Cisco IOS, use the following commands:

Step 1.   Enter the interface configuration mode:

```
Switch(config)# interface {FastEthernet | GigabitEthernet} slot/port
```

Step 2.   Select the encapsulation type:

```
Switch(config-if)# switchport trunk encapsulation {isl | dot1q |
    negotiate}
```

Step 3.   Configure the interface as a Layer 2 trunk:

```
Switch(config-if)# switchport mode {dynamic {auto | desirable} | trunk}
```

Step 4.   Specify the native VLAN:

```
Switch(config-if)# switchport trunk native vlan vlan-id
```

Step 5.   Configure the allowable VLANs for this trunk:

```
Switch(config-if)# switchport trunk allowed vlan {add | except | all |
    remove} vlan-id[,vlan-id[,vlan-id[,...]]]
```

Note   With Cisco IOS Software Release 12.1(13)E and later, VLAN IDs might be in the range of 1 to 4094, except in the case of reserved VLANs. With Cisco IOS Release 12.1(11b)E or later, you can remove VLAN 1 from a trunk port. Even after removing VLAN 1 from a trunk, the trunk interface continues to send and receive management traffic. For example, CDP, VTP, Port Aggregation Protocol (PAgP), and DTP all use VLAN 1, regardless of the existence of VLAN 1 on the port.

Example 2-9 shows the configuration of interface Fast Ethernet 5/8 for 802.1Q trunking in the desirable mode and allowing only VLANs 1 through 100 on the trunk.

Example 2-9   *Configuring a Port for 802.1Q Trunking in Cisco IOS*

```
Switch# configure terminal
Enter configuration commands, one per line. End with CNTL/Z.
Switch(config)# interface FastEthernet 5/8
Switch(config-if)# switchport trunk encapsulation dot1q
Switch(config-if)# switchport mode dynamic desirable
Switch(config-if)# switchport trunk allowed vlan 1-100
Switch(config-if)# no shutdown
Switch(config-if)# end
```

Verifying Trunking Configurations

To verify the trunk configuration in Cisco IOS, use the commands in Table 2-5.

Table 2-5 *Cisco IOS Commands to Verify Trunk Configuration*

Command	Notes
show running-config *interface _id*	Displays the running configuration of the interface
show interfaces *interface_id* switchport	Displays the switch port configuration of the interface
show interfaces *interface_id* trunk	Displays the trunk configuration of the interface

Example 2-10 displays port configuration for trunking.

Example 2-10   *Displaying Port Information for Trunkiing*

```
Switch# show running-config interface FastEthernet 5/8
Building configuration...
Current configuration:
!
interface FastEthernet5/8
switchport mode dynamic desirable
switchport trunk encapsulation dot1q
end
```

Example 2-11 displays switchport information about interface FastEthernet 5/8, which is operating as an 802.1Q trunk.

Example 2-11   *Displaying Switchport Information for Trunking*

```
Switch# show interfaces FastEthernet 5/8 switchport
Name: Fa5/8
Switchport: Enabled
Administrative Mode: dynamic desirable
Operational Mode: trunk
Administrative Trunking Encapsulation: negotiate
Operational Trunking Encapsulation: dot1q
Negotiation of Trunking: Enabled
Access Mode VLAN: 1 (default)
Trunking Native Mode VLAN: 1 (default)
Trunking VLANs Enabled: ALL
Pruning VLANs Enabled: 2-1001
```

Example 2-12 displays trunk information for a particular port.

Example 2-12   *Displaying Trunk Information for a Particular Port*

```
Switch# show interfaces FastEthernet 5/8 trunk


Port        Mode            Encapsulation   Status        Native vlan
Fa5/8       desirable       n-802.1q        trunking      1


Port        Vlans allowed on trunk
Fa5/8       1-1005


Port        Vlans allowed and active in management domain
Fa5/8       1-6,10,20,50,100,152,200,300,303-305,349-351,400,500,521,524,570,801-8
            02,850,917,999,1002-1005


Port        Vlans in spanning tree forwarding state and not pruned
Fa5/8       1-6,10,20,50,100,152,200,300,303-305,349-351,400,500,521,524,570,801-8
            02,850,917,999,1002-1005
```

Troubleshooting Trunking

To troubleshoot a problem with a trunk port, verify that the following configurations are correct:

- Interface modes

- Native VLAN

- Encapsulation types

A common problem with VLANs is where a device cannot establish a connection across a trunk link. Suggested solutions to the problem are as follows:

- Ensure that the Layer 2 interface mode configured on both ends of the link is valid. The trunk mode should be trunk or desirable for at least one side of the trunk. Use the **show interface** *interface_id* **trunk** command in Cisco IOS to verify the configuration.

- Ensure that the trunk encapsulation type configured on both ends of the link is valid and compatible.

- On IEEE 802.1Q trunks, make sure that the native VLAN is the same on both ends of the trunk.

- When using DTP, ensure that both ends of the link are in the same VTP domain.

VLAN Trunking Protocol

VTP is a protocol that is used to distribute and synchronize information about VLAN databases configured throughout a switched network. VTP minimizes misconfigurations and configuration inconsistencies that might result in various problems, such as duplicate VLAN names, incorrect VLAN-type specifications, and security violations. Switches transmit VTP messages only on 802.1Q or ISL trunks. Cisco switches transmit VTP summary advertisements over the management VLAN (VLAN 1 by default) using a Layer 2 multicast frame every 5 minutes. VTP packets are sent to the destination MAC address 01-00-0C-CC-CC-CC with a logical link control (LLC) code of Subnetwork Access Protocol (SNAP) (AAAA) and a type of 2003 (in the SNAP header).

VTP is a Layer 2 messaging protocol that maintains VLAN configuration consistency by managing the additions, deletions, and name changes of VLANs within a VTP domain.

A VTP domain is one switch or several interconnected switches that share the same VTP environment. Catalyst switches support only a single VTP domain per switch.

By default, a Catalyst switch is in the no-management-domain state until it receives an advertisement for a VTP domain over a trunk link or until a VTP configuration is applied, as shown in Figure 2-12.

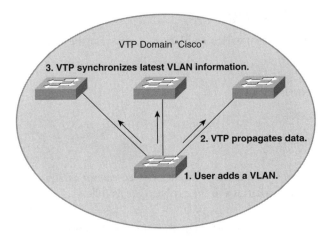

Figure 2-12   *VTP Protocol*

Configurations made to a single VTP server propagate across trunk links to all connected switches in the network in the following manner:

Step 1.   An administrator adds a new VLAN definition.

Step 2.   VTP propagates the VLAN information to all switches in the VTP domain.

Step 3.   Each switch synchronizes its configuration to incorporate the new VLAN data.

VTP operates in one of the following modes: server mode, client mode, transparent mode, or off mode. The default VTP mode is server mode, but Catalyst switches do not propagate VTP information out trunk interfaces until a management domain name is specified or learned.

Table 2-6 describes the features of the VTP client, server, transparent, and off modes.

Table 2-6   *VTP Modes of Operation*

VTP Mode	Feature
Client	Cannot create, change, or delete VLANs on command-line interface (CLI). Forwards advertisements to other switches. Synchronizes VLAN configuration with latest information received from other switches in the management domain. Does not save VLAN configuration in nonvolatile RAM (NVRAM).
Server	Creates, modifies, and deletes VLANs. Sends and forwards advertisements to other switches. Synchronizes VLAN configuration with latest information received from other switches in the management domain. Saves VLAN configuration in NVRAM.
Transparent	Creates, deletes, and modifies VLANs only on the local switch. Forwards VTP advertisements received from other switches in the same management domain. Does not synchronize its VLAN configuration with information received from other switches in the management domain. Saves VLAN configuration in NVRAM.

Note   In VTP version 3, there is a concept of a primary server and a secondary server. VTP version 3 is not the scope of this book; please refer to documents on Cisco.com.

A device that receives VTP summary advertisements checks various parameters before incorporating the received VLAN information. First, the management domain name and password in the advertisement must match those configured in the local switch. Next, if the configuration revision number indicates that the message was created after the configuration currently in use, the switch incorporates the advertised VLAN information if the switch is a VTP server or client.

One of the most critical components of VTP is the configuration revision number. Each time a VTP server modifies its VLAN information, it increments the configuration revision number by 1. It then sends out a VTP subnet advertisement with the new configuration revision number. If the configuration revision number that is advertised is higher than the number stored on the other switches in the VTP domain, the rest of the switches in the domain overwrite their VLAN configurations with the new information advertised, as shown in Figure 2-13.

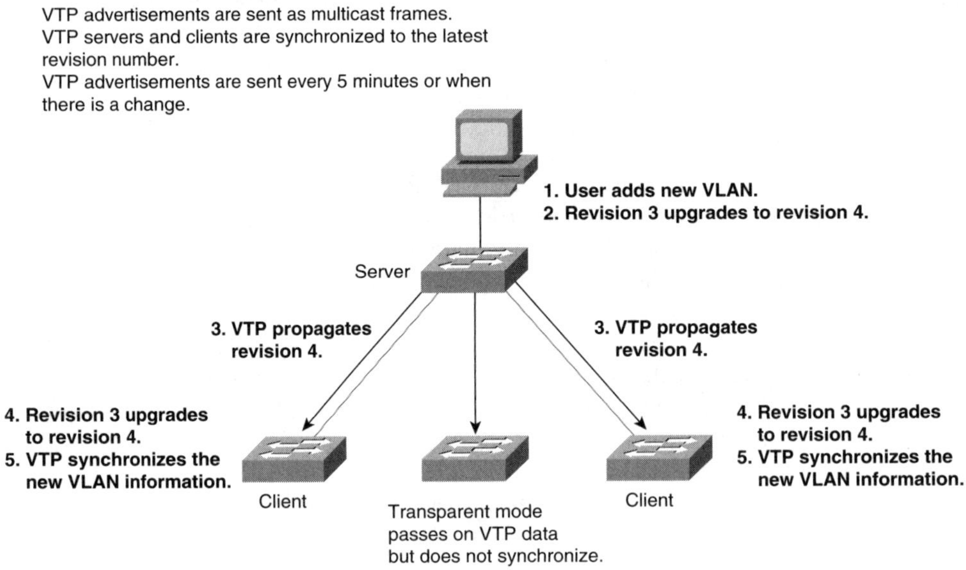

Figure 2-13 *VTP Advertisements*

Because a VTP-transparent switch does not participate in VTP, that switch does not advertise its VLAN configuration or synchronize its VLAN database upon receipt of a VTP advertisement.

Note The overwrite process means that if the VTP server deletes all VLANs and advertises with a higher revision number, the client devices in the VTP domain also delete their VLANs. Use this feature with caution.

The ensuing sections discuss the following properties of VTP:

■ VTP pruning

■ VTP versions

■ VTP message types

■ VTP authentication

- Best practices for VTP implementation

- Configuring VTP

- Verifying the VTP configuration

- Troubleshooting VTP

VTP Pruning

VTP pruning uses VLAN advertisements to determine when a trunk connection is flooding traffic needlessly. By default, a trunk connection carries traffic for all VLANs in the VTP management domain. Commonly, some switches in an enterprise network do not have local ports configured in each VLAN. In Figure 2-14, Switches 1 and 4 support ports statically configured in the red VLAN.

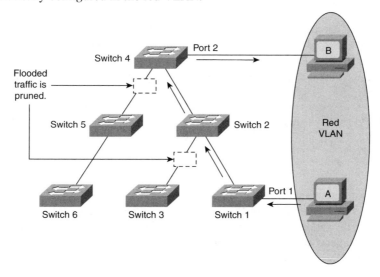

Figure 2-14   *VTP Pruning*

VTP pruning increases available bandwidth by restricting flooded traffic to those trunk links that the traffic must use to access the appropriate network devices. Figure 2-14 shows a switched network with VTP pruning enabled. The broadcast traffic from Station A is not forwarded to Switches 3, 5, and 6 because traffic for the red VLAN has been pruned on the links indicated on Switches 2 and 4.

Note   Regardless of whether you use VTP pruning support, Catalyst switches run an instance of STP for each VLAN. An instance of STP exists for each VLAN, even if no ports are active in the VLAN or if VTP pruning removes the VLANs from an interface. As a result, VTP pruning prevents flooded traffic from propagating to switches that do not have members in specific VLANs. However, VTP pruning does not eliminate the switches' knowledge of pruned VLANs.

VTP Versions

Cisco Catalyst switches support three different versions of VTP: versions 1, 2, and 3. It is important to decide which version to use because they are not interoperable. In addition, Cisco recommends running only one VTP version for network stability. This chapter emphasizes VTP versions 1 and 2 because VTP version 3 is not the most frequently used version of the VTP.

VTP Versions 1 and 2

VTP version 2 supports these features that are not implemented in VTP version 1:

■ **Token Ring support:** VTP version 2 supports Token Ring LAN switching and Token Ring VLANs.

■ **Unrecognized Type-Length-Value (TLV) support:** A VTP version 2 server or client propagates configuration changes to its other trunks even for TLVs that it cannot parse. VTP version 2 servers can still save unrecognized TLVs in NVRAM. This could be useful if not all devices are at the same version or release level.

Note   TLV optional information may be encoded as a type-length-value or TLV element inside the protocol. One of the advantages of using a TLV representation is that TLV sequences are easily searched using generalized parsing functions.

■ **Version-independent transparent mode:** In VTP version 1, a VTP-transparent switch inspects VTP messages for the domain name and version and forwards a message only if the version and domain name match. Because only one domain is supported in the Supervisor Engine software, VTP version 2 forwards VTP messages in transparent mode—without checking the version.

■ **Consistency checks:** VTP version 2 performs VLAN consistency checks (such as VLAN names and values) only when you enter new information through the CLI or via the Simple Network Management Protocol (SNMP). VTP version 2 does not perform checks when new information is obtained from a VTP message or when information is read from NVRAM. If the message digest algorithm 5 (MD5) on a received VTP message is correct, VTP version 2 accepts the information. Use VTP version 2 in a Token Ring environment, because VTP version 1 does not support Token Ring VLANs.

If all switches in a domain are capable of running VTP version 2, enable VTP version 2 on one VTP server. The VTP server propagates the version number to the other VTP version 2–capable switches in the VTP domain.

VTP Version 3

VTP version 3 is supported in Cisco CatOS Software versions 8.1 and above and all the latest Cisco IOS images. VTP version 3 differs from earlier VTP versions in that it does not directly handle VLANs. Instead, it is responsible for distributing a list of databases over an administrative domain. The following items are enhancements in VTP version 3:

- Support for extended VLANs (1025 to 4094)

- Support for the creation and advertising of Private VLANs

- Improved server authentication

- Enhancements to a mechanism for protection from the "wrong" database accidentally being inserted into a VTP domain

- Interaction with VTP versions 1 and 2

- Configurable on a per-port basis

Note   Check the config guide of a platform to find the VTP version supported.

VTP version 3 has the same features as VTP versions 1 and 2 except for the addition of the modes of primary and secondary server and the concept of database consistency.

Note   This book focuses only on VTP version 1 and 2 because VTP version 3 is still not common in the field and is not the focus of the exam.

VTP Messages Types

VTP uses various messages types for its communication. The following are the message types for VTP.

Summary Advertisements

By default, Catalyst switches issue summary advertisements in 5-minute increments. Summary advertisements inform adjacent Catalysts of the current VTP domain name and the configuration revision number.

When the switch receives a summary advertisement packet, the switch compares the VTP domain name to its own VTP domain name. If the name is different, the switch simply ignores the packet. If the name is the same, the switch then compares the configuration revision to its own revision. If its own configuration revision is higher or equal, the packet is ignored. If it is lower, an advertisement request is sent.

Subset Advertisements

When you add, delete, or change a VLAN in a Catalyst, the server Catalyst where the changes are made increments the configuration revision and issues a summary advertisement. One or several subset advertisements follow the summary advertisement. A subset advertisement contains a list of VLAN information. If there are several VLANs, more than one subset advertisement can be required to advertise all the VLANs.

Advertisement Requests

A switch needs a VTP advertisement request in these situations:

■   The switch has been reset.

■   The VTP domain name has been changed.

■   The switch has received a VTP summary advertisement with a higher configuration revision than its own.

Upon receipt of an advertisement request, a VTP device sends a summary advertisement. One or more subset advertisements follow the summary advertisement.

VTP Authentication

VTP domains can be secured by using the VTP password feature. It is important to make sure that all the switches in the VTP domain have the same password and domain name; otherwise, a switch will not become a member of the VTP domain. Cisco switches use MD5 to encode passwords in 16-byte words. These passwords propagate inside VTP summary advertisements. In VTP, passwords are case-sensitive and can be 8 to 64 characters in length. The use of VTP authentication is a recommended practice.

Best Practices for VTP implementation

VTP is often used in a new network to facilitate the implementation of VLANs. However, as the network grows larger, this benefit can turn into a liability. If a VLAN is deleted by accident on one server, it is deleted throughout the network. If a switch that already has a VLAN database defined is inserted into the network, it can hijack the VLAN database by deleting added VLANs. Because of this, it is the recommended practice to configure all switches to transparent VTP mode and manually add VLANs as needed, especially in a larger campus network. Usually VTP configuration is good for small environments.

Configuring VTP

To configure a VTP server in Cisco IOS in configuration mode for VTP versions 1 and 2, follow these steps from privileged EXEC mode:

Step 1.   Enter global configuration mode:

```
Switch# configure terminal
```

Step 2.   Configure the VTP mode as server:

```
Switch(config)# vtp mode server
```

Step 3.   Configure the domain name:

```
Switch(config)# vtp domain domain_name
```

Step 4.   (Optional.) Enable VTP version 2:

```
Switch(config)# vtp version 2
```

Step 5.   (Optional.) Specify a VTP password:

```
Switch(config)# vtp password password_string
```

Step 6.   (Optional.) Enable VTP pruning in the management domain:

```
Switch(config)# vtp pruning
```

Note   Make sure the VTP password and VTP version are the same on all the switches that are part of the VTP domain.

Example 2-13 shows configuration of a Catalyst switch as a VTP server in Cisco IOS in global configuration mode.

Example 2-13   *Cisco IOS VTP CLI Configuration*

```
Switch# configure terminal
Switch(config)# vtp mode server
Setting device to VTP SERVER mode.
Switch(config)# vtp domain Lab_Network
Switch(config)# end
```

Verifying the VTP Configuration

Use the **show vtp status** command to display information about the VTP configuration and current state in Cisco IOS.

Example 2-14 shows how to verify the VTP configuration by using the **show vtp status** command. The output describes the VTP version, number of VLANs supported locally, VTP operating mode, VTP domain name, and VTP pruning mode.

Example 2-14   *Displaying VTP Status*

```
Switch# show vtp status

VTP Version                    : 2
Configuration Revision         : 247
Maximum VLANs supported locally : 1005
Number of existing VLANs       : 33
VTP Operating Mode             : Server
VTP Domain Name                : Lab_Network
VTP Pruning Mode               : Enabled
VTP V2 Mode                    : Disabled
VTP Traps Generation           : Disabled
MD5 digest                     : 0x45 0x52 0xB6 0xFD 0x63 0xC8 0x49 0x80
Configuration last modified by 0.0.0.0 at 8-12-99 15:04:4
```

Use the **show vtp counters** command to display statistics about VTP operation. Example 2-15 displays VTP statistics in Cisco IOS. If there are any problems regarding the VTP operation, the **show** command in Example 2-15 helps look for VTP message type updates.

Example 2-15   *Displaying VTP Statistics in Cisco IOS*

```
Switch# show vtp counters

VTP statistics:
Summary advertisements received  : 7
Subset advertisements received   : 5
Request advertisements received  : 0
Summary advertisements transmitted : 997
Subset advertisements transmitted : 13
Request advertisements transmitted : 3
Number of config revision errors : 0
Number of config digest errors   : 0
Number of V1 summary errors      : 0


VTP pruning statistics:

Trunk            Join Transmitted Join Received    Summary advts received from
                                                   non-pruning-capable device
---------------- ---------------- ---------------- ------------------
Fa5/8            43071            42766            5
```

Troubleshooting VTP

Problems with VTP configuration are usually a result of improperly configured trunk links, domain names, VTP modes, or passwords.

Perform the following steps to troubleshoot VTP issues in which VTP is not updating the configuration on other switches when VLAN configuration changes occur:

Step 1.   Make sure the switches are connected through trunk links. VTP updates are exchanged only over trunk links. Check to make sure all switch-to-switch connections are using the same trunking protocol. In addition, verify that the operation of each link partner's operation speed and duplex is the same by using the **show interface** command in Cisco IOS.

Step 2.   Make sure the VTP domain name, which is case-sensitive, is configured exactly the same way on the appropriate switches. Switches exchange VTP updates only between switches in the same VTP domain. Use the **show vtp status** command to verify these configurations.

Step 3.   Check whether the switch is in VTP transparent mode. Only switches in VTP server or VTP client mode update their VLAN configuration based on VTP updates from other switches. Use the **show vtp status** command to verify the configured VTP modes.

Step 4.   If you are using VTP passwords, make sure to use the same password and authentication on all switches in the VTP domain.

Private VLANs

In some situations, you need to prevent Layer 2 connectivity between end devices on a switch in the same VLAN without placing the devices in different IP subnets. This setup prevents IP address wasting. Private VLANs enable the isolation at Layer 2 of devices in the same IP subnet. You can restrict some ports on the switch to reach only specific ports that have a default gateway or backup server attached. With this setting, devices can belong to the same VLAN but still be prevented from communicating with one another. Private VLANs are heavily deployed in the ISP environment—especially the web hosting environment. The following topics related to Private VLANs are discussed in the next section:

■   Private VLANs overview.

■   Private VLANs and port types.

■   Given an enterprise VLAN network design that contains Private VLANs, create an implementation and verification plan; then successfully execute that plan.

■   Private VLAN configuration.

■   Port protected feature.

Private VLANs Overview

Service providers often have devices from multiple clients, in addition to their own servers, on a single Demilitarized Zone (DMZ) segment or VLAN. As security issues proliferate, it becomes necessary to provide traffic isolation between devices, even though they might exist on the same Layer 3 segment and VLAN. Most Cisco IOS-based switches implement Private VLANs to keep some switch ports shared and some switch ports isolated, although all ports exist on the same VLAN.

The traditional solution to address these Internet service provider (ISP) requirements is to provide one VLAN per customer, with each VLAN having its own IP subnet. A Layer 3 device then provides interconnectivity between VLANs and Internet destinations.

The following are the challenges with this traditional solution:

■ Supporting a separate VLAN per customer can require a high number of Layer 3 interfaces on service provider network devices.

■ Spanning tree becomes more complicated with many VLAN iterations.

■ Network address space must be divided into many subnets, which wastes space and increases management complexity.

■ Multiple ACL applications are required to maintain security on multiple VLANs, resulting in increased management complexity.

Private VLANs and Port Types

A port in a Private VLAN can be one of the following three types:

■ **Isolated:** An isolated port has complete Layer 2 separation from other ports within the same Private VLAN, except for the promiscuous ports. Private VLANs block all traffic to isolated ports, except the traffic from promiscuous ports. Traffic received from an isolated port is forwarded to only promiscuous ports. As shown in Figure 2-15, PC 5 and PC 6 belong to same isolated Private VLAN, but they cannot communicate with each other—only with promiscuous.

■ **Promiscuous:** A promiscuous port can communicate with all ports within the Private VLAN, including the community and isolated ports. A promiscuous port is only part of one primary VLAN, but each promiscuous port can map to more than one secondary Private VLAN. Promiscuous ports are generally router ports, backup or shared servers, or VLAN interfaces. As shown in Figure 2-15, the router port and the shared server port is the one that needs to communicate to everyone.

■ **Community:** Community ports communicate among themselves and with their promiscuous ports. These interfaces are isolated at Layer 2 from all other interfaces in other communities, or in isolated ports within their Private VLAN. As shown in Figure 2-15, PC1 and PC2's ports belong to the community Private VLAN A and PC3, and PC4 belongs to the community Private VLAN B. PC 1 and PC2 can communicate with each other and the promiscuous port but not with PC 3 and PC4, which are part of a different community.

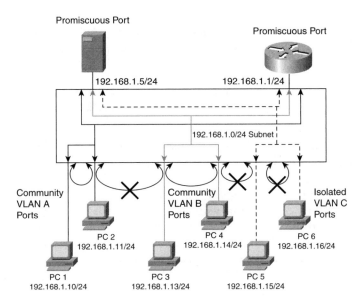

Figure 2-15   *Private VLAN Port Types and VLANs*

Private VLAN ports are associated with a set of supporting VLANs that create the Private VLAN structure. A Private VLAN uses VLANs in the following ways:

- **A primary Private VLAN:** The high-level VLAN of the Private VLAN. A primary Private VLAN can be composed of many secondary Private VLANs with the secondary Private VLANs belonging to the same subnet of the primary Private VLAN. It carries traffic from promiscuous ports to isolated, community, and other promiscuous ports in the same primary Private VLAN.

- **A secondary Private VLAN:** Every secondary Private VLAN is a child to a primary Private VLAN and is mapped to one primary Private VLAN. End devices are attached to secondary Private VLANs.

The following are the two types of secondary Private VLANs:

- **Community Private VLANs:** Ports that belong to the community Private VLAN can communicate with the other ports in the same community and promiscuous ports of the Private VLAN, as shown in Figure 2-15, where PC 1 and PC 2, which belong to community Private VLAN A, can communicate with each other but (as indicated by the X) not with PC 3 and PC 4, which belong to community Private VLAN B.

- **Isolated Private VLANs:** Ports that belong to an isolated Private VLAN can communicate only with promiscuous ports. Isolated ports cannot communicate with other ports in the same isolated Private VLAN, as shown in Figure 2-15, where PC 5 and PC 6, although in the same isolated Private VLAN, cannot communicate with each other but can communicate with the promiscuous ports. Each Private VLAN has only one isolated Private VLAN.

Note A promiscuous port can service only one primary VLAN. A promiscuous port can service one isolated VLAN or many community VLANs.

Private VLAN span across multiple switches by trunking the primary, isolated, and community VLANs to other devices that support Private VLAN.

Figure 2-16 illustrates an example of implementing Private VLANs in a service-provider environment. Here, a service provider has three customers under one primary Private VLAN. Customer A belongs to community Private VLAN 100, Customer B belongs to community Private VLAN 200, and Customer C belongs to isolated Private VLAN 300. Despite belonging to the same subnet, Customer A's, Customer B's, and Customer C's network devices cannot communicate with one another. All devices that reside in Customer A's community Private VLANs can communicate with one another even though the devices are spread across multiple switches. In addition, all devices that reside in Customer B's community Private VLANs can communicate with one another. However, devices in Customer C's isolated Private VLAN cannot communicate with one another.

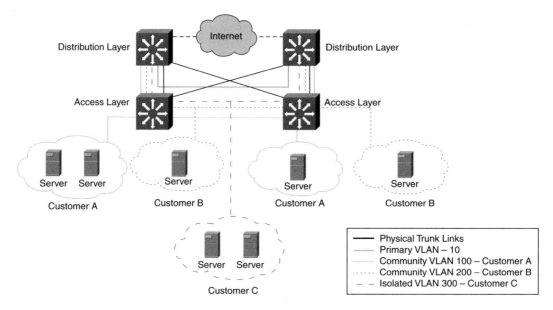

Figure 2-16 *Private VLAN Implementations*

Private VLAN Configuration

To configure a Private VLAN, follow these steps:

Step 1. Set VTP mode to transparent.

Step 2. Create the secondary Private VLANs

Step 3. Create the primary Private VLAN.

Step 4.   Associate the secondary Private VLAN with the primary Private VLAN. Only one isolated Private VLAN can be mapped to a primary Private VLAN, but more than one community Private VLAN can be mapped to a primary Private VLAN.

Step 5.   Configure an interface as an isolated or community port.

Step 6.   Associate the isolated port or community port with the primary-secondary Private VLAN pair.

Step 7.   Configure an interface as a promiscuous port.

Step 8.   Map the promiscuous port to the primary-secondary Private VLAN pair.

Configuring Private VLANs in Cisco IOS

To configure Private VLANs in Cisco IOS, perform the following steps:

Step 1.   Enter VLAN global configuration mode to configure the Private VLANs:

```
Switch(config)# vlan pvlan-id
```

Step 2.   Configure the VLANs as a type of Private VLAN:

```
Switch(config-vlan)# private-vlan {community | isolated | primary}
```

Step 3.   Exit the configuration mode:

```
Switch(config-vlan)# exit
```

Step 4.   Enter the VLAN global configuration mode to configure primary VLAN:

```
Switch(config)# vlan primary-vlan-id
```

Step 5.   If it is a primary VLAN, make sure to associate the Layer 2 secondary VLAN to the primary VLAN:

```
Switch(config-vlan)# private-vlan association {secondary-vlan-list |
  add secondary-vlan-list | remove secondary-vlan-list}
```

Step 6.   Select the interface configuration mode for the primary VLAN:

```
Switch(config)# interface vlan primary-vlan-id
```

Step 7.   Map secondary VLANs to the Layer 3 VLAN interface of a primary VLAN to allow Layer 3 switching of Private VLAN ingress traffic:

```
Switch(config-if)# private-vlan mapping {secondary-vlan-list | add
  secondary-vlan-list | remove secondary-vlan-list}
```

Step 8.   Select the LAN port interface to configure as the Private VLAN host or promiscuous port:

```
Switch(config)# interface type slot/port
```

Step 9.   Configure the LAN port for Layer 2 operation if the default behavior is a Layer 3 operation:

```
Switch(config-if)# switchport
```

Step 10.   Configure the Layer 2 port as a Private VLAN port either as host or promiscuous port:

```
Switch(config-if)# switchport mode private-vlan {host | promiscuous}
```

Step 11. To access Private VLAN ports, associate the community or isolated Private VLAN to the Private VLAN:

```
Switch(config-if)# switchport private-vlan host-association primary-
    vlan-id secondary-vlan-id
```

Step 12. For promiscuous ports, configure the interface by mapping the port to the Private VLAN:

```
Switch(config-if)# switchport private-vlan mapping primary-vlan-id
    {secondary-vlan-list | add secondary-vlan-list | remove secondary-
    vlan-list}
```

Step 13. Exit the configuration mode.

Note In Cisco IOS, you can switch between different configuration modes without exiting to the global configuration mode. For example, if you configure an interface-level command, you can also type any other level command and the mode goes into that particular mode. For example, for any global parameter, the mode switches to global configuration mode.

Verifying Private VLAN

Always verify the configuration. Following are some of the commands commonly used to verify Private VLAN configuration:

- show interface *type slot/port* switchport

- show vlan private-vlan

Example 2-16 illustrates the commands used to verify the configuration of Private VLANs in Cisco IOS. The **interface switchport** commands are usually good for verifying the interface config and mode of the port, as shown in Example 2-16.

Example 2-16 *Verifying Private VLANs*

```
Switch# show vlan private-vlan
Primary Secondary Type Interfaces
------- --------- ---------------- --------------------------------------------
100 200 community
100 300 isolated


Switch# show interfaces FastEthernet 5/2 switchport
Name: Fa5/2
Switchport: Enabled
Administrative Mode: private-vlan host
Operational Mode: down
Administrative Trunking Encapsulation: negotiate
```

```
Negotiation of Trunking: On
Access Mode VLAN: 1 (default)
Trunking Native Mode VLAN: 1 (default)
Administrative private-vlan host-association: 100 (VLAN0200) 300 (VLAN0300)
Administrative private-vlan mapping: none
Operational private-vlan: none
Trunking VLANs Enabled: ALL
Pruning VLANs Enabled: 2-1001
Capture Mode Disabled
```

Private VLAN Configuration Example

This subsection provides examples to configure Private VLANs in campus networks. It discusses how to configure on a single switch and then how to configure across two switches.

Single Switch Private Configuration

Figure 2-17 is the basis for this example. A corporate DMZ contains two DNS servers, one web server and one SMTP server. All servers and their connecting router are in the same subnet. DNS servers are redundant copies, so they need to communicate with each other to update their entries. In addition to that, they also need to communicate with the Internet. The Web Server and the SMTP server need to communicate with the Internet, but for security purposes, the SMTP server should not be reachable from the Web or the DNS servers. The web server needs to be accessible from the Internet but not from the SMTP server.

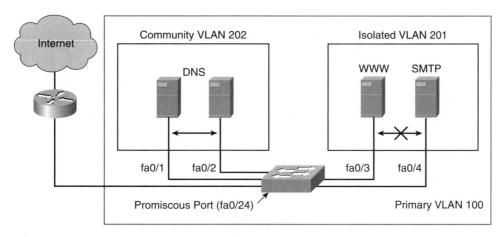

Figure 2-17 *Private VLANs Single Switch Example*

Network designers can use this configuration either using access control lists, or more simply with Private VLANs. The port to the Internet would be set to promiscuous. A

Community VLAN would be created to host both DNS servers, and an isolated VLAN would be created to host the Web and the SMTP servers.

Example 2-17 illustrates the configuration of Private VLAN in detail. When the switch is set to VTP transparent mode, the first task is to create the VLANs. Notice that in this configuration the primary VLAN 100 is associated to both the isolated 201 and the community 202.

Example 2-17   *Private VLAN Configuration for Single Switch Scenario*

```
sw(config)# vtp mode transparent
sw(config)# vlan 201
sw(config-vlan)# private-vlan isolated
sw(config)# vlan 202
sw(config-vlan)# private-vlan community
sw(config-vlan)# vlan 100
sw(config-vlan)# private-vlan primary
sw(config-vlan)# private-vlan association 201,202
sw(config-vllan)# interface fastethernet 0/24
sw(config-if)# switchport mode private-vlan promiscuous
sw(config-if)# switchport private-vlan mapping 100 201,202
sw(config-if)# interface range fastethernet 0/1 - 2
sw(config-if)# switchport mode private-vlan host
sw2(config-if)# switchport private-vlan host-association 100 202
sw(config-if)# interface range fastethernet 0/3 - 4
sw(config-if)# switchport mode private-vlan host
sw2(config-if)# switchport private-vlan host-association 100 201
```

When the Private VLANs is defined, configure each port to associate to a private VLAN mode. Interface fastethernet 0/1 and fastethernet 0/2 are DNS ports, so associate Private VLAN 100 to 202. Interface fastethernet 0/3 and fastethernet 0/4 are WWW and SMTP servers, so associate Private VLAN 100 to 201. Private VLANs 201 and 202 are mapped to the promiscuous port as a result of being associated with primary Private VLAN 100. Traffic can flow to and from Private VLAN 201 and 202 and to and from the promiscuous port that is a router port on interface 0/24. Keep in mind that all devices in Private VLAN 201, Private VLAN 202, and on the promiscuous port are in the same subnet.

Private VLAN Configuration Across Switches

As with regular VLANs, Private VLANs can span multiple switches. A trunk port carries the primary VLAN and secondary VLANs to a neighboring switch just like any other VLAN. A feature of Private VLANs across multiple switches is that traffic from an isolated port in one switch does not reach an isolated port on another switch. Configure Private VLANs on all switches on the path, which includes devices that have no Private VLAN ports to maintain the security of your Private VLAN configuration, and avoid using other VLANs configured as Private VLANs. As illustrated in Figure 2-18, the switches SWA and SWB have the same Private VLANs spread on two different switches and are connected through the trunk link.

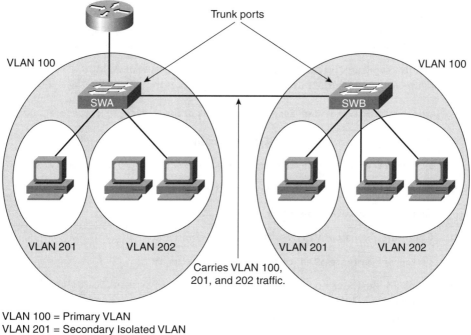

VLAN 100 = Primary VLAN
VLAN 201 = Secondary Isolated VLAN
VLAN 202 = Secondary Community VLAN

Figure 2-18   *Private VLANs Across Switches*

Because VTP does not support Private VLANs, configure the Private VLANs manually on all switches in the Layer 2 network. If the primary and secondary VLAN associations are configured in some switches but not all in the path, the Private VLAN databases and mapping will be different in each switch in the path.. This situation can result in unnecessary flooding of Private VLAN traffic on those switches.

To trunk Private VLANs on a host port or a port that is supposed to carry multiple secondary VLANs, the Private VLAN trunk feature is also available. A Private VLAN trunk port can carry multiple secondary and non-Private VLANs. Packets are received and transmitted with secondary or regular VLAN tags on the Private VLAN trunk ports.

The Private VLAN host trunk feature is supported only with 801.1Q encapsulation. Isolated trunk ports enable you to combine traffic for all secondary ports over a trunk. Promiscuous trunk ports enable you to combine the multiple promiscuous ports required in this topology in a single trunk port that carries multiple primary VLANs. The following are some guidelines for using the Private VLAN trunk feature:

■   Use isolated Private VLAN trunk ports when you anticipate the use of Private VLAN isolated host ports to carry multiple VLANs, either normal VLANs or for multiple

Private VLAN domains. This makes it useful for connecting a downstream switch that does not support Private VLANs.

■   Private VLAN promiscuous trunks are used in situations where a Private VLAN promiscuous host port is normally used but where it is necessary to carry multiple VLANs, either normal VLANs or for multiple Private VLAN domains. This makes it useful for connecting an upstream router that does not support Private VLANs.

■   The following are the commands to configure the Private VLAN trunk feature. To configure a Layer 2 interface as a Private VLAN trunk port, use the interface command:

```
switchport private-vlan association trunk primary_vlan_ID secondary_vlan_ID
```

■   If the port is set to promiscuous, use the **mapping** command:

```
switchport private-vlan mapping [trunk] primary_vlan_ID secondary_vlan_list
```

■   Once the trunk is configured, allow VLANs with the command

```
switchport private-vlan trunk allowed vlan vlan_list
```

■   Configure the native VLAN with following command

```
switchport private-vlan trunk native vlan vlan_id
```

Example 2-18 illustrates how to configure the Private VLAN trunk feature on the interface fastethernet 5/2. In Example 2-18, primary Private VLAN is 3 and port is trunking to carry secondary Private VLANs 301 and 302 traffic.

Example 2-18   *Private VLAN Trunk Configuration*

```
Switch# configure terminal
SWAwitch(config)# interface fastethernet 5/2
Switch(config-if)# switchport mode private-vlan trunk secondary
Switch(config-if)# switchport private-vlan trunk native vlan 10
Switch(config-if)# switchport private-vlan trunk allowed vlan 10, 3,301-302
Switch(config-if)# switchport private-vlan association trunk 3 301
Switch(config-if)# switchport private-vlan association trunk 3 302
Switch(config-if)# end
```

Example 2-19 shows how to verify the configuration of the port configured for a Private VLAN trunk feature. As shown in the example, port fastethernet 5/2 is configured as the secondary Private VLAN trunk and it is an operational trunk.

Example 2-19   *Private VLAN Verification Commands*

```
Switch# show interfaces fastethernet 5/2 switchport
Name: Fa5/2
Switchport: Enabled
Administrative Mode: private-vlan trunk secondary
```

```
Operational Mode: private-vlan trunk secondary
Administrative Trunking Encapsulation: negotiate
Operational Trunking Encapsulation: dot1q
Negotiation of Trunking: On
Access Mode VLAN: 1 (default)
Trunking Native Mode VLAN: 1 (default)
Administrative Native VLAN tagging: enabled
Voice VLAN: none
Administrative private-vlan host-association: none
Administrative private-vlan mapping: none
Administrative private-vlan trunk native VLAN: 10
Administrative private-vlan trunk Native VLAN tagging: enabled
Administrative private-vlan trunk encapsulation: dot1q
Administrative private-vlan trunk normal VLANs: none
Administrative private-vlan trunk associations:
    3 (VLAN0003) 301 (VLAN0301)
Administrative private-vlan trunk mappings: none
Operational private-vlan: none
Operational Normal VLANs: none
Trunking VLANs Enabled: ALL
Pruning VLANs Enabled: 2-1001
```

Port Protected Feature

Cisco lower-end switches, such as the Cisco 2960 series switches, don't support Private VLANs, but they have a more limited feature, Private VLAN edge (protected port). Protected ports are a simple version of private VLANs. Traffic can flow only between a protected and unprotected port and between an unprotected and unprotected port. Traffic between protected ports is blocked. By default, ports are unprotected, as shown in Figure 2-19. In Figure 2-19, the two protected ports cannot communicate to each other, only with the unprotected ports.

The Private VLAN edge (protected port) is a feature that has only local significance to the switch (unlike Private VLANs), and there is no isolation provided between two protected ports located on different switches. A protected port does not forward any traffic (unicast, multicast, or broadcast) to any other port that is also a protected port in the same switch. Traffic cannot be forwarded between protected ports at Layer 2. All traffic passing between protected ports must be forwarded through a Layer 3 (L3) device.

Configuring Link Aggregation with EtherChannel

In a network where resources might be located far from where users might need them, some links between switches or between switches and servers become heavily solicited. These links' speed can be increased to a certain point but not ad infinitum. EtherChannel is a technology that enables circumventing this issue by creating logical links made of several physical links.

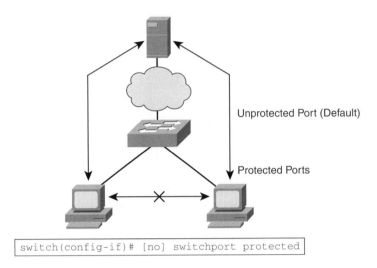

Unprotected Port (Default)

Protected Ports

```
switch(config-if)# [no] switchport protected
```

Figure 2-19 *Port Protected (Private VLAN Edge)*

This section examines the benefits of EtherChannel and the various technologies available to implement it and also the types of EtherChannel protocol. In addition to that, it explains how to configure Layer 2 EtherChannels and how to load balance traffic between physical links inside a given EtherChannel bundle. EtherChannels can also operate in a Layer 3 mode. The following topics are discussed in detail in the next section:

■ Understand the benefits of EtherChannel.

■ Compare the Port Aggregation Protocol (PAgP) and the Link Aggregation Protocol (LACP).

■ Given an enterprise VLAN network design that contains Layer 2 EtherChannel links, configure and verify EtherChannels.

■ EtherChannel load balancing options.

Describe EtherChannel

The increasing deployment of higher-speed switched Ethernet to the desktop attributes to the proliferation of bandwidth-intensive intranet applications. Any-to-any communications of new intranet applications, such as video to the desktop, interactive messaging, VoIP, and collaborative white-boarding, are increasing the need for scalable bandwidth within the core and at the edge of campus networks. At the same time, mission-critical applications call for resilient network designs. With the wide deployment of faster switched Ethernet links in the campus, users need to either aggregate their existing resources or upgrade the speed in their uplinks and core to scale performance across the network backbone.

Traffic coming from several VLANs at 100 Mbps aggregate on the access switches at the bottom and need to be sent to distribution switches in the middle. Obviously, bandwidth larger than 100 Mbps must be available on the link between two switches to accommodate the traffic load coming from all the VLANs. A first solution is to use a faster port speed, such as 1 Gbps or 10 Gbps. As the speed increases on the VLANs links, this solution finds its limitation where the fastest possible port is no longer fast enough to aggregate the traffic coming from all VLANs. A second solution is to multiply the numbers of physical links between both switches to increase the overall speed of the switch-to-switch communication. A downside of this method is that there must be a strict consistency in each physical link configuration. A second issue is that spanning tree may block one of the links, as shown in Figure 2-20. In Figure 2-20, the second links are in spanning-tree blocking mode between access and distribution.

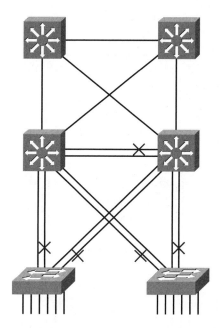

Figure 2-20   *Ethernet Without EtherChannel*

EtherChannel is a technology that was originally developed by Cisco as a LAN switch-to-switch technique of grouping several Fast or Gigabit Ethernet ports into one logical channel, as shown in Figure 2-21, where now all the links between access and distribution switches are bundled into EtherChannel and in forwarding mode. This technology has many benefits:

■   It relies on the existing switch ports: There is no need to upgrade the switch-to-switch link to a faster and more expensive connection.

■ Most of the configuration tasks can be done on the EtherChannel interface instead of each individual port, thus ensuring configuration consistency throughout the switch-to-switch links.

■ EtherChannel provides redundancy: As the overall link is seen as one logical connection, the loss of one physical link does not create a change in the topology. Spanning-tree recalculation does not need to take place. As long as at least one physical link is present, the EtherChannel is functional, even if its overall throughput decreases.

■ Load balancing is possible between the links part of the same EtherChannel. Depending on the hardware platform, you can implement one or several methods, such as source-MAC to destination-MAC or source-IP to destination-IP load balancing across the physical links.

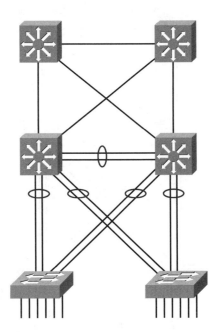

Figure 2-21   *Ethernet with EtherChannel*

Up to eight physical links can be bundled together into a single logical EtherChannel link. Keep in mind that the logic of EtherChannel is to increase the bandwidth between switches. EtherChannel cannot only be supported in switches but also is very popular in nonswitch devices such as servers. In any case, EtherChannel creates a logical point-to-point link. EtherChannel links can be between two switches or between an EtherChannel-enabled server and a switch but cannot send traffic to two different switches through the same EtherChannel link. One EtherChannel link always connects two devices only, and these devices' individual port configurations must be consistent. If the physical ports of one side are configured as trunks, the physical ports of the other side must also be configured as trunks. Each EtherChannel has a logical port channel interface. A configuration applied to the port channel interface affects all physical interfaces assigned to that interface. (Such commands can be STP commands or commands to configure a Layer 2 EtherChannel as a trunk or an access port.)

The EtherChannel technology can be used to bundle ports of the same type. On a Layer 2 switch, EtherChannel is used to aggregate access ports or trunks. Keep in mind that EtherChannel creates an aggregation that is seen as one logical link. When several EtherChannel bundles exist between two switches, spanning tree might block one of the bundles to prevent redundant links. When spanning tree blocks one of the redundant links, it blocks one EtherChannel, thus blocking all the ports belonging to this EtherChannel link. Where there is only one EtherChannel link, all physical links in the EtherChannel are active because spanning tree sees only one (logical) link.

On Layer 3 switches, convert the ports to routed ports. EtherChannel links can also be created on Layer 3 links. This functionality is highlighted in Chapter 4, "Implementing Inter-VLAN Routing."

PAgP and LACP Protocols

EtherChannel uses one of the two management protocols to create Port-Channel. These protocols ensure that when EtherChannel is created, all ports have the same type of configuration. In EtherChannel, it is mandatory that all ports have the same speed, duplex setting, and VLAN information. Any port modification after the creation of the channel also changes all the other channel ports. The following are the two known protocols to create EtherChannel:

- **The Port Aggregation Protocol (PAgP)** is a Cisco Proprietary protocol that aids in the automatic creation of Fast EtherChannel links. When an EtherChannel link is configured using PAgP, PAgP packets are sent between EtherChannel–capable ports to negotiate the forming of a channel. When PAgP identifies matched Ethernet links, it groups the links into an EtherChannel. Spanning tree adds the EtherChannel as a single bridge port.

- **LACP** is part of an IEEE specification (802.3ad) that also enables several physical ports to be bundled together to form an EtherChannel. LACP enables a switch to negotiate an automatic bundle by sending LACP packets to the peer. It performs a similar function as PAgP with Cisco EtherChannel. Because LACP is an IEEE standard, you can use it to facilitate EtherChannels in mixed-switch environments. In a Cisco environment, both protocols are supported.

The following subsections discuss each protocol in more detail.

PAgP Modes

PAgP packets are sent every 30 seconds. PAgP checks for configuration consistency and manages link additions and failures between two switches.

The PAgP helps create the EtherChannel link by detecting each side's configuration and making sure they are compatible. Table 2-7 shows the different settings for PAgP.

Table 2-7   *Different Setting Options for PAgP*

Mode	Purpose
Auto	Places an interface in a passive negotiating state in which the interface responds to the PAgP packets that it receives but does not initiate PAgP negotiation (default).
Desirable	Places an interface in an active negotiating state in which the interface initiates negotiations with other interfaces by sending PAgP packets.
On	Forces the interface to channel without PAgP. Interfaces configured in the "on" mode do not exchange PAgP packets.
Non-silent	If a switch is connected to a partner that is PAgP-capable, configure the switch interface for non-silent operation. The non-silent keyword is always used with the auto or desirable mode. If you do not specify non-silent with the auto or desirable mode, silent is assumed. The silent setting is for connections to file servers or packet analyzers; this setting enables PAgP to operate, to attach the interface to a channel group, and to use the interface for transmission.

Note   Table 2-7 depicts the mode for PagP. The names of the modes are similar to the DTP protocol, but they have different functions.

As shown in Figure 2-22, the modes need to be compatible on each side. Figure 2-22 illustrates the modes option setting on both sides and its results. If one configures a side to be in Auto mode, it will be placed in a passive state, waiting for the other side to initiate the EtherChannel negotiation. If the other side is also set to Auto, the negotiation never starts and the EtherChannel does not form. If one deconfigures all modes by using the **no** command or if no mode is configured, the interface is placed in an Off mode and EtherChannel is disabled.

Notice the "On" form. This command manually places the interface in EtherChannel without any negotiation. It works only if the other side is also set to On. If the other side is set to negotiate parameters through PAgP, no EtherChannel will form because the On side will not negotiate.

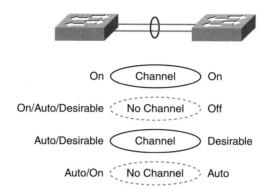

Figure 2-22 *PAgP Modes Setting*

LACP Modes

LACP provides the same negotiation benefits as PAgP. LACP helps create the EtherChannel link by detecting each side's configuration and making sure they are compatible so that the EtherChannel link can be enabled when needed. Table 2-8 shows the different settings for LACP.

Just like with PAgP, modes must be compatible on both sides for the EtherChannel link to form, as shown in Figure 2-23. Figure 2-23 displays the different options setting on both sides of the links and its results if EtherChannel is created. The On form is mentioned here again because it creates an EtherChannel configuration unconditionally, or LACP dynamic negotiation.

Table 2-8 *LACP Modes Options*

Mode	Purpose
Passive	Places a port in a passive negotiating state. In this state, the port responds to the LACP packets that it receives but does not initiate LACP packet negotiation (default).
Active	Places a port in an active negotiating state. In this state, the port initiates negotiations with other ports by sending LACP packets.
On	Forces the interface to the channel without PAgP or LACP.

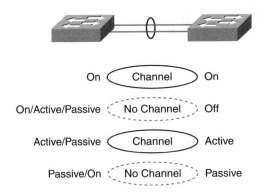

Figure 2-23   *LACP Modes*

The following are some additional parameters that you can use when configuring LACP:

- **System priority:** Each switch running LACP must have a system priority. The system priority can be specified automatically or through the command-line interface (CLI). The switch uses the MAC address and the system priority to form the system ID.

- **Port priority:** Each port in the switch must have a port priority. The port priority can be specified automatically or through the CLI. The port priority and the port number form the port identifier. The switch uses the port priority to decide which ports to put in standby mode when a hardware limitation prevents all compatible ports from aggregating.

- **Administrative key:** Each port in the switch must have an administrative key value, which can be specified automatically or through the CLI. The administrative key defines the capability of a port to aggregate with other ports, determined by these factors:

  - The port physical characteristics, such as data rate, duplex capability, and point-to-point or shared medium

  - The configuration constraints that you establish

Note   All the preceding options of LACP are optional to configure. Usually, defaults are the best to use. To configure any of these options, refer to your configuration guide.

When enabled, LACP attempts to configure the maximum number of compatible ports in a channel. In some instances, LACP cannot aggregate all the compatible ports. For example, the remote system might have more restrictive hardware limitations. When this occurs, all the ports that cannot be actively included in the channel are put in a hot standby state and used only if one of the channeled ports fails.

Configure Port Channels Using EtherChannel

Before implementing EtherChannel in a network, a network engineer should plan the steps necessary to make it successful. Prior planning can help reduce any problems during the installation by logically organizing the steps necessary and providing checkpoints and verification, as necessary. The following guideline is helpful for planning the EtherChannel:

- The first step is to identify the ports for the EtherChannel on both switches. This helps identify any issues with previous configurations on the ports and ensures that the proper connections are available.

- The network designer should already have decided whether this is going to be a Layer 3 or a Layer 2 connection. If it is a Layer 2 connection, each interface should have the appropriate protocol identified (PAgP or LACP), have a channel group number to associate all the given interfaces to a port group, and know whether negotiations should occur.

- If this is a Layer 3 connection, a new virtual interface is created. This port-channel interface is then given an IP address. Each of the physical interfaces is then made into an EtherChannel by specifying the same channel group number as the port-channel interface number.

- When the connections are established, a couple of commands can ensure that both sides of the EtherChannel have formed and are providing aggregated bandwidth.

Guidelines for Configuring EtherChannel

This subsection describes the recommendations and guidelines for configuring EtherChannel. Follow these guidelines and restrictions when configuring EtherChannel interfaces:

- **EtherChannel support:** All Ethernet interfaces on all modules support EtherChannel (maximum of eight interfaces) with no requirement that interfaces be physically contiguous or on the same module.

- **Speed and duplex:** Configure all interfaces in an EtherChannel to operate at the same speed and in the same duplex mode. Also, if one interface in the bundle is shut down, it is treated as a link failure, and traffic traverses other links in the bundle.

- **Switched port analyzer (SPAN) and EtherChannel:** An EtherChannel does not form if one of the interfaces is a SPAN destination port.

- **Layer 3 EtherChannels:** Assign Layer 3 addresses to the port-channel logical interface, not to the physical interfaces in the channel.

- **VLAN match:** All interfaces in the EtherChannel bundle must be assigned to the same VLAN or be configured as a trunk. In addition, Native VLANs should be matched across all the links on both switches.

■ **Range of VLANs:** An EtherChannel supports the same allowed range of VLANs on all the interfaces in a trunking Layer 2 EtherChannel. If the allowed range of VLANs is not the same, the interfaces do not form an EtherChannel, even when set to auto or desirable mode. For Layer 2 EtherChannels, either assign all interfaces in the EtherChannel to the same VLAN or configure them as trunks.

■ **STP path cost:** Interfaces with different STP port path costs can form an EtherChannel as long as they are otherwise compatibly configured. Setting a different STP port path costs does not, by itself, make interfaces incompatible for the formation of an EtherChannel.

■ **Port channel versus interface configuration:** After you configure an EtherChannel, any configuration that you apply to the port-channel interface affects the EtherChannel. Any configuration that you apply to the physical interfaces affects only the specific interface you configured.

Layer 2 EtherChannel Configuration Steps

Configuring a Layer2 EtherChannel requires the following three or four steps:

Step 1. Specify the interfaces that will compose the EtherChannel group. Using the range commands enables you to select several interfaces and configure them all together. A good practice is to start by shutting down these interfaces, so that incomplete configuration will not start to create activity on the link:

```
Switch(config)# interface range interface_type [interface_trange]
```

Step 2. Specify the channeling protocol to be used. This command is not applicable to all catalyst platforms. You can also specify the channeling protocol at Step 3:

```
Switch(config-if-range)# channel-protocol {pagp | lacp}
```

Step 3. Create the port-channel interface, if necessary, and assign the specified interfaces to it:

```
Switch(config-if-range)# channel-group number mode {active | on |
  {auto [non-silent]} | {desirable [non-silent]} | passive
```

Step 4. Specify the port-channel interface. When in the interface configuration mode, you can configure additional parameters. The physical interfaces will inherit these parameters. When this configuration is complete, you can reenable the physical ports in the EtherChannel bundle:

```
Switch(config)# interface port-channel number
Switch(config-if)# Interface parameters
```

Example 2-20 shows a Layer 2 EtherChannel bundle between two switches using LACP. As shown in Figure 2-24, each switch shows two ports that are left to their default configuration. The switch on the left created EtherChannel 2, and the switch on the right created EtherChannel 5. These numbers are locally significant and do not need to match the partner's configuration. The actual configuration of the link is then conducted on the EtherChannel interface. The link is configured to be unconditionally in 802.1Q trunk mode, and some VLANs are pruned.

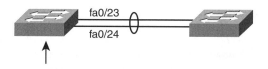

Figure 2-24 *EtherChannel Configuration*

Example 2-20 *EtherChannel Configuration*

```
Switch(config)# interface fastethernet 0/23
Switch(config-if)# channel-group 2 mode active
Switch(config)# interface fastethernet 0/24
Switch(config-if)# channel-group 2 mode active
Switch(config)# interface port-channel 2
Switch(config-if)# switchport trunk encapsulation dot1q
Switch(config-if)# switchport mode trunk
Switch(config-if)# switchport trunk native VLAN 99
Switch(config-if)# switchport trunk allowed VLAN 2,3,99
!!!Remote Switch configuration
RSwitch(config)# interface fastethernet 0/23
RSwitch(config-if)# channel-group 5 mode active
RSwitch(config)# interface fastethernet 0/24
RSwitch(config-if)# channel-group 5 mode active
RSwitch(config-if)# switchport trunk encapsulation dot1q
RSwitch(config)# interface port-channel 5
RSwitch(config-if)# switchport mode trunk
RSwitch(config-if)# switchport trunk native VLAN 99
RSwitch(config-if)# switchport trunk allowed VLAN 2,3,99
```

Example 2-20 follows these guidelines from the previous guidelines:

- **Speed and duplex:** Configure all interfaces in an EtherChannel to operate at the same speed and in the same duplex mode.

- **VLAN match:** All interfaces in the EtherChannel bundle must be assigned to the same VLAN or be configured as a trunk. Also make sure that all the interfaces are part of the same native VLANs on both switches.

- **Range of VLANs:** An EtherChannel supports the same allowed range of VLANs on all the interfaces in a trunking Layer 2 EtherChannel.

Keep in mind that the EtherChannel interface configuration must be compatible with the underlying physical ports' configuration. In the preceding example, initially there is no specific configuration on each individual port for trunking, which implies that the default dynamic auto mode is applied. In this mode, ports detect whether the other side is a trunk and dynamically changes to trunk mode if needed. This mode is compatible with the trunk mode configured on the EtherChannel interface. The physical ports inherit the EtherChannel configuration and change to trunk mode.

Verifying EtherChannel

This subsection discuss how to verify EtherChannel is correctly established and working. You can use several commands to verify an EtherChannel configuration. On any physical interface member of an EtherChannel bundle, the show interfaces type port/mod EtherChannel can provide information on the role of the interface in the EtherChannel, as shown in Example 2-21.

In Example 2-21, the interface fastethernet 0/24 is part of the EtherChannel bundle 1. The protocol for this EtherChannel is LACP.

Example 2-21   *EtherChannel Verification Command for Interface*

```
Switch# show interfaces fa0/24 etherchannel
Port state     = Up Sngl-port-Bndl Mstr Not-in-Bndl
Channel group = 1       Mode = Active         Gcchange = -
Port-channel  = null   GC   =   -            Pseudo port-channel = Po1
Port index    = 0      Load = 0x00           Protocol =    LACP
```

Also, the show etherchannel number port-channel can be used to display information about a specific port-channel.

In Example 2-22, Port-channel 1 consists of two physical ports, fa0/23 and fa0/24. It uses LACP in active mode. It is properly connected to another switch with a compatible configuration. This is why the port-channel is said to be in use.

Example 2-22   *EtherChannel Verification Port-Channel Command*

```
Switch#show etherchannel 1 port-channel
                Port-channels in the group:
                ---------------------------

Port-channel: Po7     (Primary Aggregator)
Age of the Port-channel   = 195d:03h:10m:44s
Logical slot/port    = 0/1           Number of ports = 2
Port state           = Port-channel Ag-Inuse
Protocol             =    LACP
Ports in the Port-channel:
Index   Load   Port    EC state        No of bits
------+------+------+-----------------+-----------
   0     55     fa0/23   Active    4
   1     45     fa0/24   Active    4
```

When several port-channel interfaces are configured on the same device, the **show etherchannel summary** command is useful for simply displaying one-line information per port-channel, as shown in Example 2-23.

In Example 2-23, the switch has three EtherChannels configured, group 2 and group 7 use LACP, and group 9 uses PAgP. Each EtherChannel has the member interfaces listed as well. It also indicates that all three groups are Layer 2 EtherChannels and that they are all in use. (This is shown by the letters SU next to the Port-channel number.)

Example 2-23   show etherchannel summary *Command Output*

```
Switch# show etherchannel summary
Flags:  D - down         P - bundled in port-channel
        I - stand-alone s - suspended
        H - Hot-standby (LACP only)
        R - Layer3       S - Layer2
        U - in use       f - failed to allocate aggregator
        M - not in use, minimum links not met
        u - unsuitable for bundling
        w - waiting to be aggregated
        d - default port
Number of channel-groups in use: 2
Number of aggregators:          2
Group  Port-channel  Protocol     Ports
------+------------+-----------+-----------------------------------------------
2      Po2(SU)       LACP         g0/49(P) g0/50(P) g0/51(P) g0/52(P)
7      Po7(SU)       LACP         g0/47(P) g0/48(P)
9      Po9(SU)       PAgP         g0/8(P) g0/9(P)
```

The **show-running** command also displays a section of your configuration relevant to EtherChannel groups. The argument interface is useful for displaying information about a physical interface part of an EtherChannel or to display information about the port-channel interface itself.

In Example 2-24, interface gigabitethernet 0/48 is part of EtherChannel bundle 7. It is set to trunk mode to ensure that its configuration will be compatible with the configuration of the Port-channel interface.

Example 2-24   show running-config interface *Command Output*

```
Switch# show running-config interface g0/48
Building configuration...
Current configuration : 154 bytes
interface GigabitEthernet0/48
 switchport access vlan 41
 switchport trunk encapsulation dot1q
 switchport mode trunk
 channel-group 7 mode active
end
```

In Example 2-25, the Port-channel interface is a Layer 2 EtherChannel set to trunk mode.

Example 2-25 show running-config interface port-channel *Command Output*

```
Switch# show running-config interface port-channel 7
Building configuration...
Current configuration : 92 bytes
interface Port-channel7
 switchport trunk encapsulation dot1q
 switchport mode trunk
end
```

EtherChannel Load Balancing Options

When the EtherChannel becomes one entity, the traffic is load balanced across multiple links. This subsection describes the configuration of load balancing among the ports included in an EtherChannel.

Load balancing traffic across port members of the same EtherChannel is a key element in an EtherChannel configuration. As shown in Figure 2-25, two workstations communicate with a router through a switch. The link between the router and the switch is an EtherChannel link relying on two physical ports. Suppose that the majority of the traffic is going from the PCs toward the router. How should the traffic be load balanced across the two physical links? If load balancing is based on the destination IP address, most traffic will go through the same physical link. Because the router has only one single IP address for its bundled interface, this IP address will be associated to a first physical port, and all traffic destined to it will go through a single physical link. This renders the load-balancing mechanism inefficient. On the other hand, if load balancing is based on the source MAC address, the traffic might be far better balanced across both physical links because each PC has its MAC address seen on the switch.

As a rule, use the load-balancing option that provides the greatest variety in your configuration. For example, if the traffic on a channel is going to only a single MAC address, using the destination-MAC address always chooses the same link in the channel; using source addresses might result in better load balancing.

Note EtherChannel balances traffic load across the links in a channel. The default and the load balancing methods available can vary among the Cisco switch families. The 2960, 3560, 3750 default to src-mac, whereas the 4550 and 6500 families default to src-dst-ip. This is the recommended option for Layer 3 switches.

Load balancing is applied globally for all EtherChannel bundles in the switch. To configure EtherChannel load balancing, use the **port-channel load-balance** command. Load balancing can be based on these variables. The load-balancing keywords are as follows:

- **src-mac:** Source MAC addresses
- **dst-mac:** Destination MAC addresses

- **src-dst-mac:** Source and destination MAC addresses

- **src-ip:** Source IP addresses

- **dst-ip:** Destination IP addresses

- **src-dst-ip:** Source and destination IP addresses (default)

- **src-port:** Source TCP/User Datagram Protocol (UDP) port

- **dst-port:** Destination TCP/UDP port

- **src-dst-port:** Source and destination TCP/UDP port

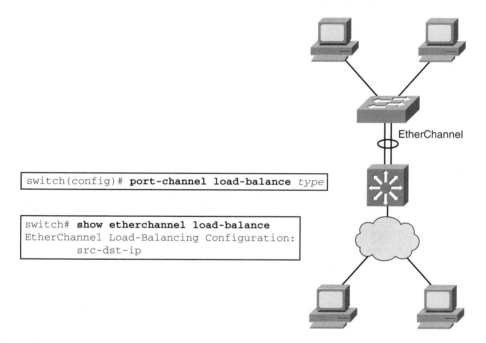

Figure 2-25 *EtherChannel Load Balancing*

Each mode is self-explanatory. For example, with source-MAC address forwarding, when packets are forwarded to an EtherChannel, they are distributed across the ports in the channel based on the source -MAC address of the incoming packet. Therefore, to provide load balancing, packets from different hosts use different ports in the channel, but packets from the same host use the same port in the channel. (And the MAC address learned by the switch does not change.)

With destination-MAC address forwarding, when packets are forwarded to an EtherChannel, they are distributed across the ports in the channel based on the destination-MAC address of the frame. Therefore, packets to the same destination are forwarded over the same port, and packets to a different destination are sent on a different port in the channel.

In Example 2-26, the EtherChannel load-balancing mechanism was configured to use source and destination IP addresses pairs. This rule is applied to IPv4 and IPv6 traffic, whereas the non-IP load-balancing mechanism uses source and destination MAC address pairs. It has been noticed that using source-destination IP load balancing, the balancing ends up more like 70-30 on the links.

Example 2-26   *EtherChannel Load Balancing*

```
Switch(config)# port-channel load-balance src-dst-ip
Switch(config)# exit
Switch# show etherchannel load-balance
EtherChannel Load-Balancing Configuration:
        src-dst-ip

EtherChannel Load-Balancing Addresses Used Per-Protocol:
Non-IP: Source XOR Destination MAC address
  IPv4: Source XOR Destination IP address
IPv6: Source XOR Destination IP address
```

Summary

In review, a VLAN is a logical grouping of switch ports that connects nodes of virtually any type, regardless of physical location. VLAN segmentation is based on traffic flow patterns. A VLAN is usually defined as end to end or local. An end-to-end VLAN spans the entire switched network, whereas a local VLAN is limited to the switches in the Building Access and Building Distribution submodules. The creation of a VLAN implementation plan depends on the business and technical requirements.

Furthermore, a trunk is a Layer 2 point-to-point link between networking devices that can carry the traffic of multiple VLANs. ISL and 802.1Q are the two trunking protocols that connect two switches. The 802.1Q protocol is an open-standard protocol also used for VLAN trunking.

VTP is used to distribute and synchronize information about VLANs configured throughout a switched network. VTP pruning helps to stop flooding of unnecessary traffic on trunk links. VTP configuration sometimes needs to be added to small network deployments, whereas VTP transparent mode is usually privileged for larger networks. When configuring VLANs over several switches, ensure that the configuration is compatible throughout switches in the same domain.

In addition, device communication within the same VLAN can be fine-tuned using Private VLANs. A Private VLAN is associated to a primary VLAN, and then mapped to one or several ports. A primary VLAN can map to one isolated and several community VLANs.

Private VLANs can span across several switches using regular 802.1Q trunks or Private VLAN trunks.

To increase bandwidth and provide redundancy, use EtherChannel by aggregating individual, similar links between switches. EtherChannel can be dynamically configured between switches using either the Cisco proprietary PAgP or the IEEE 802.3ad LACP. EtherChannel is configured by assigning interfaces to the EtherChannel bundle and configuring the resulting port-channel interface. EtherChannel load balances traffic over all the links in the bundle. The method that is chosen directly impacts the efficiency of this load-balancing mechanism.

Review Questions

Use the questions here to review what you learned in this chapter. The correct answers are found in Appendix A, "Answers to Chapter Review Questions."

1. True or False: It is important to have the same native VLAN on both switch link partners for ISL trunking.

2. True or False: The Cisco Catalyst 6500 supports up to 1024 VLANs in the most recent software releases.

3. True or False: When removing the native VLAN from a trunk port, CDP, Port Aggregation Protocol (PAgP), and DTP then use the lowest-numbered VLAN to send traffic.

4. True or False: Hosts that are members of different community VLANs can communicate to each other but not to members of isolated VLANs.

5. True or False: In VTP client mode, switches can add and delete VLANs.

6. True or False: Token Ring support is available in VTP version 1.

Questions 7 through 9 are based on the configuration in Example 2-27.

Example 2-27   *Configuration Example for Questions 7 Through 9*

```
Catalyst6500-IOS# show run interface gigabitEthernet 3/9
Building configuration...

Current configuration : 137 bytes
!
interface GigabitEthernet3/9
mtu 9216
no ip address
switchport
switchport access vlan 5
switchport trunk encapsulation dot1q
end
```

7. If the interface in Example 2-27 negotiates trunking, what would be the Native VLAN?

    a. VLAN 1.

    b. VLAN 5.

    c. VLAN 9216.

    d. There would be no Native VLAN if the port negotiated trunking.

8. Under what condition can the interface in Example 2-27 negotiate ISL trunking?

    a. If the port is a member of an EtherChannel.

    b. If the link partner defaults to ISL trunking for negotiated ports.

    c. If the link partner is configured for trunking in the On mode.

    d. The interface cannot negotiate trunking because it is configured statically for 802.1Q trunking.

9. Which statement is true for the configuration of the interface in Example 2-27?

    a. The interface is a member of VLAN 5 and may negotiate to a trunk port.

    b. The interface may negotiate to an ISL trunk with a Native VLAN of 5.

    c. The interface may negotiate to an 802.1Q trunk and operate with a Native VLAN of 1.

    d. The interface will not negotiate to a trunk port because it is configured in access VLAN 5.

    e. If a host workstation is connected to the interface, it must be configured for trunking.

Questions 10 through 12 are based on the configuration in Example 2-28.

Example 2-28   *Configuration Example for Questions 10 Through 12*

```
svs-san-6509-2# show interfaces gigabitEthernet 3/9 switchport
Name: Gi3/9
Switchport: Enabled
Administrative Mode: dynamic auto
Operational Mode: down
Administrative Trunking Encapsulation: dot1q
Negotiation of Trunking: On
Access Mode VLAN: 1 (default)
Trunking Native Mode VLAN: 2 (VLAN0002)
Voice VLAN: none
Administrative private-vlan host-association: none
Administrative private-vlan mapping: none
Operational private-vlan: none
Trunking VLANs Enabled: ALL
```

```
Pruning VLANs Enabled: 2-1001
Capture Mode Disabled
Capture VLANs Allowed: ALL
```

10. What is the trunk Native VLAN based on in Example 2-28?

    a. VLAN 1.

    b. VLAN 2.

    c. VLAN 5.

    d. There would be no Native VLAN if the port negotiated trunking.

11. Based on Example 2-28, what statement is true if the link partner (peer switch) is configured for the dynamic trunking mode?

    a. The interface cannot negotiate to a trunk port because it is configured for dot1q encapsulation.

    b. The interface cannot negotiate to a trunk port because the Native VLAN and access VLANs are mismatched.

    c. The interface can negotiate to a trunk port if the peer is configured for the dynamic desirable trunking mode.

    d. The interface can negotiate to a trunk port if access VLAN is the same on both sides.

12. What is the interface's access mode VLAN in Example 2-28?

    a. VLAN 1

    b. VLAN 2

    c. VLAN 5

    d. VLAN 1001

13. How does implementing VLANs help improve the overall performance of the network?

    a. By isolating problem employees

    b. By constraining broadcast traffic

    c. By grouping switch ports into logical communities

    d. By forcing the Layer 3 routing process to occur between VLANs

14. What are the advantages of using local VLANs over end-to-end VLANs? (Choose two.)

    a. Eases management

    b. Eliminates the need for Layer 3 devices

   c. Allows for a more deterministic network

   d. Groups users by logical commonality

   e. Keeps users and resources on the same VLAN

15. Which prompt indicates that you are in VLAN configuration mode of Cisco IOS?

   a. Switch#

   b. Switch(vlan)#

   c. Switch(config)#

   d. Switch(config-vlan)#

16. Which switch port mode unconditionally sets the switch port to access mode regardless of any other DTP configurations?

   a. Access

   b. Nonegotiate

   c. Dynamic auto

   d. Dynamic desirable

17. What information is contained in the FCS of an ISL-encapsulated frame?

   a. CRC calculation

   b. Header encapsulation

   c. ASIC implementation

   d. Protocol-independence

18. 802.1Q uses an internal tagging mechanism, where a tag is inserted after the _____ field.

   a. Type

   b. SA

   c. Data

   d. CRC

19. Which command correctly configures a port with ISL encapsulation in Cisco IOS?

   a. Switch(config-if)# **switchport mode trunk isl**

   b. Switch(config-if)# **switchport mode encapsulation isl**

   c. Switch(config-if)# **switchport trunk encapsulation isl**

   d. Switch(config-if)# **switchport mode trunk encapsulation isl**

20. Which command correctly sets the native VLAN to VLAN 5?

   a. **switchport native vlan 5**

   b. **switchport trunk native 5**

   c. switchport native trunk vlan 5

   d. switchport trunk native vlan 5

21. If the Layer 2 interface mode on one link partner is set to dynamic auto, a trunk will be established if the link partner is configured for which types of interface modes in Cisco IOS? (Choose two.)

   a. Trunk

   b. Access

   c. Nonegotiate

   d. Dynamic auto

   e. Dynamic desirable

22. What is the default VTP mode for a Catalyst switch?

   a. Client

   b. Access

   c. Server

   d. Transparent

23. When is a consistency check performed with VTP version 2?

   a. When information is read from NVRAM

   b. When the digest on a received VTP message is correct

   c. When new information is obtained from a VTP message

   d. When you enter new information through the CLI or SNMP

24. Which command correctly sets the VTP version to version 1 in Cisco IOS global configuration mode?

   a. vtp v1-mode

   b. vtp v2-mode

   c. no vtp version

   d. no vtp version 2

25. Which of the following are valid VTP version 1 and 2 modes? (Check all that apply.)

   a. Primary server mode

   b. Server mode

   c. Client mode

   d. Transparent mode

26. After you complete the VTP configuration, which command should you use to verify your configuration?

   a.   show vtp status

   b.   show vtp counters

   c.   show vtp statistics

   d.   show vtp status counters

27. What command might correct a problem with incorrect VTP passwords?

   a.   password vtp 0

   b.   clear vtp password

   c.   clear password vtp

   d.   vtp password password_string

28. What is the purpose of pruning?

29. What are the advantages of Private VLANs?

30. Suppose you have two workstations, A and B. If both Workstations A and B are members of the same community Private VLAN, can they communicate with each other? If they are members of different community Private VLANs, can they communicate? If they are members of the same isolated Private VLAN, can they communicate? Can they both communicate to the same promiscuous ports? Explain all your answers.

31. True or False: The EtherChannel would come up if one side of the EtherChannel mode is set to Auto and other On.

32. Which of the following solutions are provided by EtherChannel? (Choose two.)

   a.   Provide redundancy

   b.   Help to overcome bandwidth limitation

   c.   Because of EtherChannel, can transmit more than one VLAN over the links between switches

   d.   Can limit the broadcast to the local switches

## Chapter 3

Implementing Spanning Tree

This chapter covers the following topics:

■ Evolution of Spanning Tree Protocols

■ Spanning Tree Protocol Basics

■ Rapid Spanning Tree Protocol

■ Multiple Spanning Tree

■ Spanning Tree Enhancements

■ Recommended Spanning Tree Practices

■ Troubleshooting STP

High availability is a primary goal for enterprise networks that rely heavily on their multi-layer switched network to conduct business. One method to ensure high availability is to provide Layer 2 redundancy of devices, modules, and links throughout the network. Network redundancy at Layer 2, however, introduces the potential for bridging loops, where packets loop endlessly between devices, crippling the network. The Spanning Tree Protocol identifies and prevents such Layer 2 loops.

This chapter overviews the Spanning Tree Protocols, including PerVLAN Rapid Spanning Tree Plus (PVRST+) and Multiple Spanning Tree (MST). This chapter also covers how to configure the protocols and how to configure Spanning Tree Protocols stability mechanisms.

Evolution of Spanning Tree Protocols

Multiple redundant paths between switches can cause loops in the network topology. If a loop exists, the potential for message duplication exists. When loops occur, some switches see stations appear on both sides of the switch. This condition confuses the forwarding algorithm and enables duplicate frames to be forwarded. To prevent loops while providing path redundancy, Spanning Tree Protocol (STP) defines a tree that spans all switches in an extended network. STP will allow only one active path and block any redundant paths, as shown in Figure 3-1. In case of failure of the active path, one of the redundant paths may become the active path.

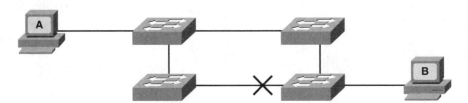

Figure 3-1   *Spanning Tree Protocol*

There are several varieties of STP:

■   The first STP, called the DEC STP, was invented in 1985 by Radia Perlman at the Digital Equipment Corporation.

■   In 1990, the IEEE published the first standard for the protocol as 802.1D based on the algorithm designed by Perlman. Subsequent versions were published in 1998 and 2004 incorporating various extensions.

■   Common Spanning Tree (CST) assumes one 802.1D spanning-tree instance for the entire bridged network, regardless of the number of VLANs. Because there is only one instance, the CPU and memory requirements for this version are lower than the others. However, because there is only one instance, there is only one root bridge and one tree. This means that traffic for all VLANs flows over the same path. This can lead to suboptimal traffic flows. Also the network is slow in converging after topology changes due to inherent 802.1D timing mechanisms.

■   Per VLAN Spanning Tree Plus (PVST+) is a Cisco enhancement of STP that provides a separate 802.1D spanning-tree instance for each VLAN configured in the network. The separate instance supports enhancement such as PortFast, BPDU guard, BPDU filter, root guard, and loop guard. Creating an instance for each VLAN increases the CPU and memory requirements but allows for per-VLAN root bridges. This allows the STP tree to be optimized for the traffic of each VLAN. Convergence of this version is similar to 802.1D; however, convergence is per-VLAN.

■   Rapid STP (RSTP), or IEEE 802.1w, is an evolution of STP that provides faster convergence of STP. This version addresses many of the convergence issues, but because it still had a single instance of STP, it did not address the suboptimal traffic flow issues. To support that faster convergence, the CPU usage and memory requirements of this version are slightly more than CST but less than PVRST+.

■   Multiple Spanning Tree (MST) is an IEEE standard inspired from the earlier Cisco proprietary Multi-Instance Spanning Tree Protocol (MISTP) implementation. To reduce the number of required STP instances, MST maps multiple VLANs that have the same traffic flow requirements into the same spanning-tree instance. The Cisco implementation provides up to 16 instances of RSTP (802.1w) and combines many VLANs with the same physical and logical topology into a common RSTP instance. Each instance supports PortFast, BPDU guard, BPDU filter, root guard, and loop guard. The CPU and memory requirements of this version are less than PVRST+ but more than RSTP.

■ PVRST+ is a Cisco enhancement of RSTP that is similar to PVST+. It provides a separate instance of 802.1w per VLAN. The separate instance supports PortFast, BPDU guard, BPDU filter, root guard, and loop guard. This version addressed both the convergence issues and the suboptimal traffic flow issues. To do this, this version has the largest CPU and memory requirements.

The RSTP algorithm is far superior to 802.1D STP and even PVST+ from a convergence perspective. It greatly improves the restoration times for any VLAN that requires a topology convergence due to link up, and it greatly improves the convergence time over BackboneFast for any indirect link failures.

Table 3-1 compares various STP protocols in terms of resources needed and convergence times. Currently MST and PVRST+ have become the predominate protocols; therefore, we focus on these protocols in this book.

Table 3-1   *Comparison of Spanning Tree Protocols*

Protocol	Standard	Resources Needed	Convergence	
CST	802.1D	Low	Slow	All VLANs
PVST+	Cisco	High	Slow	Per VLAN
RSTP	802.1w	Medium	Fast	All VLANs
PVRST+	Cisco	Very high	Fast	Per VLAN
MSTP	802.1s	Medium/high	Fast	VLAN list

Note   In Cisco switches, PVST+ is the default STP that is enabled when a VLAN is created.

Spanning Tree Protocol Basics

STP uses the concepts of root bridges, root ports, designated, and nondesignated ports to establish a loop-free path through the network. The following sections discuss the terms root bridge, root ports, designated ports, nondesignated ports in more detail. This section discusses the operation of basic STP as defined in the STP-defining IEEE 802.1D standard.

802.1D and its successor protocols provide loop resolution by managing the physical paths to given network segments. STP enables physical path redundancy while preventing the undesirable effects of active loops in the network. STP is an IEEE committee standard defined as 802.1D. Rapid Spanning Tree is defined as 802.1w.

STP and RSTP behave as follows:

- STP forces certain ports into a standby state so that they do not listen to, forward, or flood data frames. The overall effect is that there is only one path to each network segment that is active at any time.

- If there is a problem with connectivity to any of the segments within the network, STP or RSTP reestablishes connectivity by automatically activating a previously inactive path, if one exists.

STP Operation

STP initially converges on a logically loop-free network topology by performing these steps:

1. **Elects one root bridge:** The protocol uses a process to elect a root bridge. Only one bridge acts as the root bridge in a given network per VLAN. On the root bridge, all ports act as designated ports. Designated ports send and receive traffic and configuration messages, or BPDUs. In the sample scenario in Figure 3-2, switch X wins the election as the root bridge because it has the lower priority parameter.

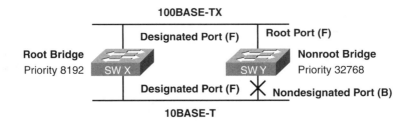

Figure 3-2   *STP Operation*

2. **Selects the root port on all nonroot bridges:** The protocol establishes one root port on each nonroot bridge. The root port is the lowest-cost path from the nonroot bridge to the root bridge. Root ports send and receive traffic. If a nonroot bridge has two or more equal-cost paths to the root; the nonroot bridge selects the port that has lowest port ID. Port ID consists of a configurable priority + Port number that defaults to the lowest port number when all eligible root ports have equal priority. In the scenario in Figure 3-2, from Switch Y, the lowest-cost path to the root bridge is through the 100BASE-TX Fast Ethernet link.

3. **Selects the designated port on each segment:** On each segment, STP establishes one designated port on the bridge that has the lowest path cost to the root bridge. In the scenario in Figure 3-2, the designated port for both segments is on the root bridge because the root bridge directly connects to both segments. The 10BASE-T Ethernet port on Switch Y is a nondesignated port because there is only one designated port per segment. The switch primarily chooses a designated port as the least-cost path to the root bridge. In the event of a tie, the bridge ID acts as the tiebreaker. Table 3-2 summarizes the port roles in a nondesignated switch.

Table 3-2 *Port Roles on a Nondesignated Switch*

Port Role	Description
Root port	This port exists on nonroot bridges and is the switch port with the best path to the root bridge. Root ports forward data traffic toward the root bridge, and the source MAC address of frames received on the root port can populate the MAC table. Only one root port is enabled per bridge.
Designated port	This port exists on root and nonroot bridges. For root bridges, all switch ports are designated ports. For nonroot bridges, a designated port is the switch port that receives and forwards data frames toward the root bridge as needed. Only one designated port is enabled per segment. If multiple switches exist on the same segment, an election process determines the designated switch, and the corresponding switch port begins forwarding frames for the segment. Designated ports can populate the MAC table.
Nondesignated port	The nondesignated port is a switch port that is not forwarding (blocking) data frames and not populating the MAC address table with the source addresses of frames seen on that segment.
Disabled port	The disabled port is a switch port that is shut down.

By examining the switch port roles on a switch, STP can determine the most desirable forwarding path for data frames.

Each Layer 2 port on a switch running STP exists in one of these five port states:

■ **Blocking:** The Layer 2 port is a nondesignated port and does not participate in frame forwarding. The port receives BPDUs to determine the location and root ID of the root switch and which port roles (root, designated, or nondesignated) each switch port should assume in the final active STP topology. By default, the port spends 20 seconds in this state (max age).

■ **Listening:** Spanning tree has determined that the port can participate in frame forwarding according to the BPDUs that the switch has received so far. At this point, the
switch port is not only receiving BPDUs, but it is also transmitting its own BPDUs
and informing adjacent switches that the switch port is preparing to participate in the
active topology. By default, the port spends 15 seconds in this state (forward delay).

■ **Learning:** The Layer 2 port prepares to participate in frame forwarding and begins
to populate the CAM table. By default, the port spends 15 seconds in this state (forward delay).

■ **Forwarding:** The Layer 2 port is considered part of the active topology; it forwards
frames and also sends and receives BPDUs.

■ **Disabled:** The Layer 2 port does not participate in spanning tree and does not forward frames.

To determine its root port (best port toward the root bridge), each switch uses a cost
value. Each port link speed is associated to a cost. The cost to the root bridge is calculat-
ed using the cumulative costs of all links between the local switch and the root bridge
that becomes the path cost.

Default individual port cost values are

■ **10 Gbps link:** Cost 1

■ **1 Gbps link:** Cost 4

■ **100 Mbps link:** Cost 19

■ **10 Mbps link:** Cost 100

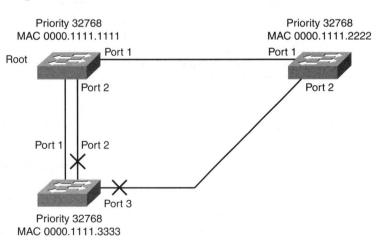

Figure 3-3 *Spanning Tree Port Cost*

In Figure 3-3, switch 0000.1111.3333 has three links that can link to the root bridge.
Suppose that all links are 100 Mbps links.

Port 1 and Port 2 would both have a cost of 19. Port 3 would have a cost of 38, which represents the overall path cost (19+19) to reach the root. Port 1 or Port 2 would be elected as root port due to both having lower path cost to the root.

When two ports have the same cost, arbitration can be done using the priority value. Priority is a combination of a default value and port number. Default value is 128. The first port will have a priority of 128.1, the second port of 128.2, and so on. With this logic, the lower port is always chosen as the root port when priority is the determining factor.

Rapid Spanning Tree Protocol

Rapid Spanning Tree Protocol (IEEE 802.1w, also referred to as RSTP) significantly speeds the recalculation of the spanning tree when the network topology changes. RSTP defines the additional port roles of Alternate and Backup and defines port states as discarding, learning, or forwarding. This section describes the differences between STP (802.1D) and RSTP (802.1w).

The 802.1D STP standard was designed with the understanding that recovering connectivity after an outage within a minute or so gives adequate performance. With the advent of Layer 3 switching in LAN environments, bridging now competes with routed solutions, in which protocols such as Open Shortest Path First (OSPF) and Enhanced Interior Gateway Routing Protocol (EIGRP) can provide an alternative path in approximately 1 second.

Cisco enhanced the original 802.1D specification with features such as UplinkFast, BackboneFast, and PortFast to speed up the convergence time of a bridged network. The drawback is that these mechanisms are proprietary and need additional configuration.

The IEEE 802.1w standard (RSTP) is an evolution, rather than a revolution, of the 802.1D standard. The 802.1D terminology remains primarily the same, and most parameters are left unchanged, so users who are familiar with 802.1D can rapidly feel at home when configuring the new protocol. In most cases, RSTP performs better than the Cisco proprietary extensions, with negligible additional configuration. In addition, 802.1w can revert to 802.1D to interoperate with legacy bridges on a per-port basis. Reverting to 802.1D negates the benefits of 802.1w for that particular segment.

RSTP selects one switch as the root of an active spanning-tree–connected topology and assigns port roles to individual ports on the switch, depending on whether the ports are part of the active topology.

RSTP provides rapid connectivity following the failure of a switch, switch port, or LAN. A new root port and the designated port of the connecting bridge transition to forwarding through an explicit handshake protocol between them. RSTP enables switch-port configuration so that the ports transition to forwarding directly when the switch reinitializes.

On Cisco Catalyst switches, a rapid version of PVST+, called PVRST+, is the per-VLAN version of the RSTP implementation. All the current generation of Catalyst switches supports PVRST+.

RSTP Port States

RSTP has only three port states, corresponding to the three possible operational statuses: discarding, learning, and forwarding. The RSTP 802.1w discarding state represents a merger of the 802.1D STP port states of disabled, blocking, and listening.

Table 3-3 describes the characteristics of RSTP port states.

Table 3-3   *RSTP Port States*

Port State	Description
Discarding	This state is seen in both a stable active topology and during topology synchronization and changes. The discarding state prevents the forwarding of data frames, thus "breaking" the continuity of a Layer 2 loop.
Learning	This state is seen in both a stable active topology and during topology synchronization and changes. The learning state accepts data frames to populate the MAC table to limit flooding of unknown unicast frames.
Forwarding	This state is seen only in stable active topologies. The forwarding switch ports determine the topology. Following a topology change, or during synchronization, the forwarding of data frames occurs only after a proposal and agreement process.

IEEE 802.1D STP mixes the state of a port, whether blocking or forwarding traffic, with the role it plays in the active topology (root port, designated port, and so on). For example, from an operational point of view, there is no difference between a port in the blocking state and a port in the listening state. Both discard frames and do not learn MAC

addresses. The real difference lies in the role the spanning tree assigns to the port. It can safely be assumed that a listening port is either designated or root and is on its way to the forwarding state. Unfortunately, when in the forwarding state, there is no way to infer from the port state whether the port is root or designated. RSTP considers there to be no difference between a port in blocking state and a port in listening state; both discard frames, and neither learns MAC addresses. RSTP decouples the role of a port from the state of a port. In all port states, a port will accept and process BPDU frames. Table 3-4 provides a comparison of 802.1D port states with RSTP port states.

Table 3-4   *Comparison of 802.1D Port States with RSTP Port States*

Operational Status	STP Port State	RSTP Port State	Port Included in Active Topology
Enabled	Blocking	Discarding	No
Enabled	Listening	Discarding	No
Enabled	Learning	Learning	Yes
Enabled	Forwarding	Forwarding	Yes
Disabled	Disabled	Discarding	No

RSTP Port Roles

The port role defines the ultimate purpose of a switch port and the way it handles data frames. One strength of RSTP is that port roles and port states can transition independently of each other. RSTP defines the port roles as follows:

- **Root:** The root port is the switch port on every nonroot bridge that is the chosen path to the root bridge. Only one root port can be on every switch. The root port assumes the forwarding state in a stable active topology. In Figure 3-4, the root port is marked as R.

- **Designated:** Each segment has at least one switch port as the designated port for that segment. In a stable, active topology, the switch with the designated port receives frames on the segment that are destined for the root bridge. There can be only one designated port per segment. The designated port assumes the forwarding state. All switches that are connected to a given segment listen to all BPDUs and determine the switch that will be the designated switch for a particular segment. In Figure 3-4, the designated port is marked as D.

- **Alternate:** The alternate port is a switch port that offers an alternative path toward the root bridge. The alternate port assumes a discarding state in a stable, active topology. An alternate port is present on nondesignated switches and makes a transition to a designated port if the current designated path fails. In Figure 3-4, the alternate port is marked as A.

- **Backup:** The backup port is an additional switch port on the designated switch with a redundant link to the segment for which the switch is designated. A backup port has a higher port ID than the designated port on the designated switch. The backup port assumes the discarding state in a stable, active topology. In Figure 3-4, the backup port is marked as B.

- **Disabled:** A port that has no role within the operation of spanning tree.

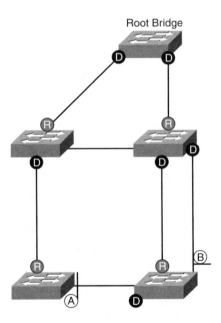

Figure 3-4 *RSTP Port Roles*

Root and designated port roles include the port in the active topology. Alternate and backup port roles exclude the port from the active topology. Table 3-5 compares the 802.1D port role and the RSTP port roles.

Establishing the additional port roles allows RSTP to define a standby switch port before a failure or topology change. The alternate port moves to the forwarding state if a failure occurs on the designated port for the segment.

Table 3-5 *802.1D and 802.1w Port Type and Port State Comparison*

802.1D Port Role	RSTP Port Role	802.1D Port State	RSTP Port State
Root port	Root port	Forwarding	Forwarding
Designated port	Designated port	Forwarding	Forwarding
Nondesignated port	Alternative or backup port	Blocking	Discarding
Disabled	Disabled	—	Discarding
Transition	Transition	Listening Learning	Learning

Rapid Transition to Forwarding

Rapid transition to forwarding is the most important feature introduced with IEEE 802.1w. Before the introduction of 802.1w, the spanning tree algorithm waited passively for the network to converge before transitioning a port to the forwarding state. The RSTP algorithm confirms that a port transition to forwarding is safe without relying on a timer configuration. To achieve fast convergence on a port, the protocol relies on two new variables:

- Link type
- Edge port

Link type provides a categorization for each port participating in RSTP. The link type is automatically derived from the duplex mode of a port. A port that operates in full-duplex is assumed to be point-to-point, whereas a half-duplex port is considered a shared port by default. This automatic link type setting can be overridden by explicit configuration. In switched networks today, most links operate in full-duplex mode and are treated as point-to-point links by RSTP. This makes them candidates for rapid transition to the forwarding state. Figure 3-5 illustrates the RSTP link type depending on the port operating mode.

Table 3-6 defines RSTP link types.

Ports that are directly connected to end stations typically cannot create bridging loops in the network; therefore, they are allowed to transition directly to forwarding, skipping the listening and learning stages. Such ports are designated as edge ports through manual configuration. An edge port does not generate a topology change when its link transitions. If an edge port receives a BPDU, it immediately loses its edge port status and becomes a normal spanning-tree port.

Edge ports, the equivalent of PortFast-enabled ports, and point-to-point links are candidates for rapid transition to a forwarding state. Before the link type parameter can be considered for the purpose of expedient port transition, RSTP must determine the port role.

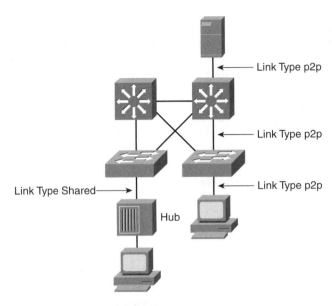

Figure 3-5   *RSTP Link Types*

Table 3-6   *RSTP Link Types*

Link Type	Description
Point-to-point	Port operating in full-duplex mode. It is assumed that the port is connected to a single switch device at the other end of the link.
Shared	Port operating in half-duplex mode. It is assumed that the port is connected to shared media where multiple switches might exist.

- **Root ports:** Do not use the link type parameter. Root ports can make a rapid transition to the forwarding state as soon as the port receives the BPDU of the root and it puts the nondesignated ports in blocking state. This operation is called sync.

- **Alternative and backup ports:** Do not use the link type parameter in most cases because these ports need to arrive at these states based on the operation of the RSTP. The only times you would configure link type parameter explicitly is when you understand the final state of these ports due to your full understanding of the topology.

- **Designated ports:** Make the most use of the link type parameter. Rapid transition to the forwarding state for the designated port occurs only if the link type parameter indicates a point-to-point link.

An RSTP edge port is a switch port that is never intended to be connected to another switch device, as shown in Figure 3-6. It immediately transitions to the forwarding state when enabled.

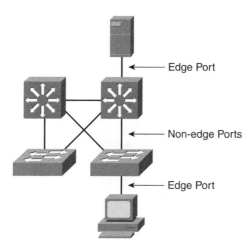

Figure 3-6 *RSTP Edge Ports*

The edge port concept is well known to Cisco spanning-tree users because it corresponds to the PortFast feature (explained in a later section titled "Portfast") . All ports that directly connect to end stations anticipate that no switch device will be connected to them, so they immediately transition to the STP forwarding state, thereby skipping the time-consuming listening and learning stages. Neither edge ports nor PortFast-enabled ports generate topology changes when the port transitions to a disabled or enabled status.

Unlike PortFast, an edge port that receives a BPDU immediately loses its edge port status and becomes a normal spanning-tree port. When an edge port receives a BPDU, it generates a topology change notification (TCN).

The Cisco RSTP implementation maintains the PortFast keyword for edge port configuration, thus making an overall network transition to RSTP more seamless. Configuring an edge port where the port will be attached to another switch can have negative implications for RSTP when it is in the "sync" state.

When a port is selected by the spanning tree algorithm to become a designated port, 802.1D still waits two times the *forward delay* seconds (2 × 15 by default) before it transitions it to the forwarding state. In RSTP, this condition corresponds to a port with a designated role but a blocking state. Figure 3-7 is a step-by-step illustration of the fast transition achieved in RSTP. Suppose a new link is created between the root and Switch A. Both ports on this link are put in a designated blocking state until they receive a BPDU from their counterpart.

When a designated port is in a discarding or learning state (and only in this case), it sets the proposal bit on the BPDUs it sends out. This is what occurs for port p0 of the root bridge, as shown in Step 1 of Figure 3-7. Because Switch A receives superior information, it immediately knows that p1 is the new root port. Switch A then starts a sync process that puts nonedge designated ports in blocking state as it needs to verify that all its ports are in-sync with the new superior BPDU received.

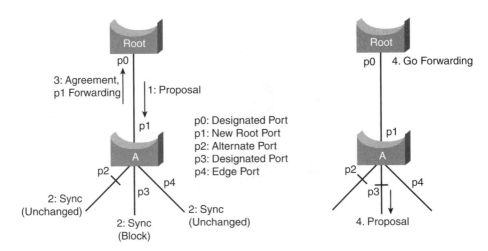

Figure 3-7 *Proposal and Agreement in RSTP*

To illustrate the effect of the sync mechanism on different kind of ports, suppose that there exists an alternative Port p2 and a designated forwarding Port p3 on Switch A. To be in sync, Switch A just needs to block Port p3 and assign it the discarding state. Now that all of its ports are in sync, Switch A can unblock its newly selected root, Port p1, and send an agreement message to reply to the root. This message is a copy of the proposal BPDU with the agreement bit set instead of the proposal bit. This ensures that Port p0 knows exactly to which proposal the agreement it receives corresponds.

When p0 receives that agreement, it can immediately transition to the forwarding state. Root then starts to propose to its neighbor and attempts to quickly transition to the forwarding state. The proposal agreement mechanism is fast because it does not rely on any timers. This wave of handshakes propagates quickly toward the edge of the network and quickly restores connectivity after a change in the topology. If a designated discarding port does not receive an agreement after it sends a proposal, it slowly transitions to the forwarding state by falling back to the traditional 802.1D listening-learning sequence. This can occur if the remote bridge does not understand RSTP BPDUs or if the port of the remote bridge is blocking.

When a bridge loses its root port, it can put its best alternate port directly into forwarding mode. The selection of an alternate port as the new root port generates a topology change. The 802.1w topology change mechanism, discussed in the next section, clears the appropriate entries in the MAC address tables of the upstream bridges.

RSTP Topology Change Mechanism

When an 802.1D bridge detects a topology change, it first notifies the root bridge by using a reliable mechanism. After the root bridge is aware of a change in the topology of the network, it sets the TC flag on the BPDUs that it sends out, which then gets relayed to all the bridges in the network through the normal mechanism. When a bridge receives a BPDU with the TC flag bit set, it reduces its bridging-table aging time to forward-delay seconds, ensuring a relatively quick flushing of stale information.

In the scenario in Figure 3-8, a link between the root bridge and Bridge A is added. Suppose there already is an indirect connection between Bridge A and the root bridge (via C to D in Figure 3-8). The spanning tree algorithm blocks a port and disables the bridging loop. First, as they come up, both ports on the link between the root and Bridge A are put in the listening state. Bridge A can now hear the root directly. It immediately propagates its BPDUs on the designated ports toward the leaves of the tree. As soon as Bridges B and C receive this new superior information from Bridge A, they immediately relay the information toward the leaves. In a few seconds, Bridge D receives a BPDU from the root and instantly blocks Port p1. Spanning tree is efficient in how it calculates the new topology of the network. The only problem now is that twice the forward delay must elapse before the link between the root and Bridge A eventually ends up in the forwarding state, as shown in Figure 3-9. This means 30 seconds of disruption of traffic (the entire A, B, and C part of the network is isolated) because the 8021.D algorithm lacks a feedback mechanism to clearly advertise that the network converges in a matter of seconds.

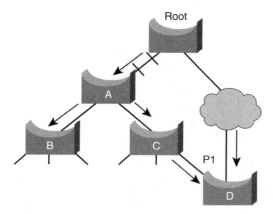

Figure 3-8   *Topology Change Initiated in 802.1D*

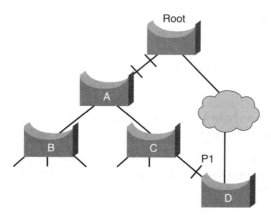

Figure 3-9   *Converged Topology in 802.1D*

In RSTP, only nonedge ports that are moving to the forwarding state cause a topology change. Unlike with 802.1D, loss of connectivity does not generate a topology change. In other words, a port that is moving to blocking does not cause the respective bridge to generate a TC BPDU.

When an RSTP bridge detects a topology change, as depicted in Figure 3-10, it performs these actions:

1. The RSTP bridge starts the TC While timer with a value equal to twice the hello time for all its nonedge designated ports and its root port, if necessary. The TC While timer is the interval during which the RSTP bridge actively informs the rest of the bridges in the network of a topology change.

2. The RSTP bridge flushes the MAC addresses associated with all nonedge ports.

3. As long as the TC While timer is running on a port, the BPDUs sent out of that port have the TC bit set. While the timer is active, the bridge sends BPDUs even on the root port.

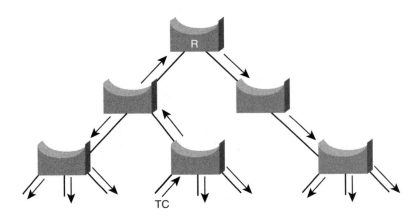

Figure 3-10 *Topology Change Mechanism in RSTP*

When a bridge receives a BPDU with the TC bit set from a neighbor, the bridge performs these actions:

1. The bridge clears the MAC addresses learned on all its ports, except the one that received the topology change.

2. The bridge starts the TC While timer and sends BPDUs with TC set on all its designated ports and root port; RSTP does not use the specific TCN BPDU anymore unless a legacy bridge needs to be notified.

The topology change propagation is now a one-step process. In fact, the initiator of the topology change is flooding this information throughout the network, as opposed to with 802.1D, where only the root sends BPDUs with the TC bit set. This mechanism is much faster than the 802.1D equivalent. In RSTP implementation, there is no need to wait for the root bridge to be notified and then maintain the topology change state for the whole network for the value of the max age timer plus the value of the forward delay timer.

Now, you can see how RSTP deals with a similar situation, as shown in Figure 3-10. Both ports on the link between A and the root are put in designated blocking as soon as they come up. Thus far, everything behaves as in a pure 802.1D environment. However, at this stage, a negotiation takes place between Switch A and the root. As soon as A receives the BPDU of the root, it blocks the nonedge designated ports. This operation is called sync. When this is done, Bridge A explicitly authorizes the root bridge to put its port in the forwarding state. Figure 3-11 illustrates the result of this process on the network. The link between Switch A and the root bridge is blocked, and both bridges exchange BPDUs.

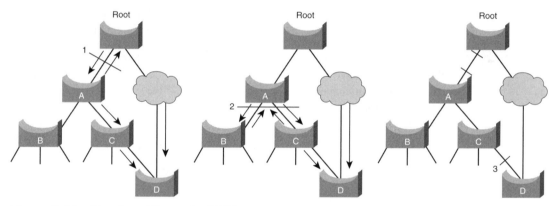

Figure 3-11   *Topology Change in RSTP*

When Switch A blocks its nonedge designated ports, the link between Switch A and the root is put in the forwarding state. There still cannot be a loop. Instead of blocking above Switch A, the network now blocks below Switch A. However, the potential bridging loop is cut at a different location. This cut travels down the tree along with the new BPDUs originated by the root through Switch A. At this stage, the newly blocked ports on Switch A also negotiate a quick transition to the forwarding state with their neighbor ports on Switch B and Switch C that both initiate a sync operation. Other than the root port toward A, Switch B only has edge-designated ports. Therefore, it has no port to block to authorize Switch A to go to the forwarding state. Similarly, Switch C only has to block its designated port to D.

Remember that the final topology is exactly the same as the 802.1D example, which means that port p1 on D ends up blocking. This means that the final network topology is reached, just in the time necessary for the new BPDUs to travel down the tree. No timer is involved in this quick convergence. The only new mechanism introduced by RSTP is the acknowledgment that a switch can send on its new root port to authorize immediate transition to the forwarding state and bypass the twice-the-forward-delay long listening and learning stages.

Bridge Identifier for PVRST+

Spanning-tree operation requires that each switch have a unique BID. In the original 802.1D standard, the BID was composed of the bridge priority and the MAC address of the switch, and all VLANs were represented by a CST. Because PVST+ or PVRST+ requires that a separate instance of spanning tree run for each VLAN, the BID field is required to carry VLAN ID (VID) information. This is accomplished by reusing a portion of the Priority field as the extended system ID to carry a VID. The extended system ID is not restricted to PVRST+ but also useful in PVST+ and in the MST configurations.

To accommodate the extended system ID, the original 802.1D 16-bit bridge priority field is split into two fields, resulting in these components in the BID, as shown in Figure 3-12:

- **Bridge priority:** A 4-bit field still used to carry bridge priority. Because of the limited bit count, the priority is conveyed in discreet values in increments of 4096 rather than discreet values in increments of 1, as they would be if the full 16-bit field was available. The default priority, in accordance with IEEE 802.1D, is 32,768, which is the midrange value.

- **Extended system ID:** A 12-bit field carrying, in this case, the VID for PVST+.

- **MAC address:** A 6-byte field with the MAC address of a single switch.

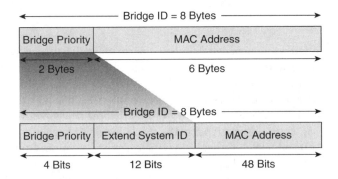

Figure 3-12 *Bridge Identifier with Extended System ID*

By virtue of the MAC address, a BID is always unique. When the priority and extended system ID are prepended to the switch MAC address, each VLAN on the switch can be represented by a unique BID.

If no priority has been configured, every switch will have the same default priority, and the election of the root for each VLAN is based on the MAC address. This method is a random means of selecting the ideal root bridge; for this reason, it is advisable to assign a lower priority to the switch that should serve as the root bridge.

Only four high-order bits of the 16-bit Bridge Priority field carry actual priority. Therefore, priority can be incremented only in steps of 4096, onto which are added the VLAN number, as shown in Table 3-7. For example, for VLAN 11: If the priority is left at default, the 16-bit Priority field will hold 32768 + 11 = 32779.

Table 3-7   *Bridge Priority with Extended System ID*

Priority Value (Hex)	Priority Value (Dec)
0	0
1	4096
2	8192
.	.
8 (default)	32768
.	.
F	61440

Compatibility with 802.1D

RSTP can operate with legacy STPs. However, it is important to note that 802.1w's inherent fast-convergence benefits are lost when interacting with legacy bridges.

Each port maintains a variable that defines the protocol to run on the corresponding segment. If the port consistently keeps receiving BPDUs that do not correspond to its current operating mode for two times the hello time, it switches to the other STP mode.

Cisco Spanning Tree Default Configuration

Cisco Catalyst switches support three types of spanning tree:

- PVST+
- PVRST+
- MST

The default spanning tree mode for Cisco Catalyst switches is PVST+. In this mode, a separate STP instance runs for each VLAN. The direct consequence is that, as the STP calculation is done the same way for each VLAN, the same switch becomes root bridge for all VLANs. Each change of topology has exactly the same impact on all VLANs.

Redundant links are blocked the same way, at the same location of the network. There is no load sharing between redundant links in this configuration.

PortFast

Spanning Tree PortFast causes an interface configured as a Layer 2 access port to enter the forwarding state immediately, bypassing the listening and learning states. Enable PortFast on Layer 2 access ports connected to a single workstation or server to allow those devices to connect to the network immediately, rather than waiting for spanning tree to converge. In Figure 3-13, a server and workstation are attached to an access switch through ports that have the PortFast feature enabled.

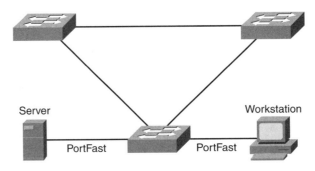

Figure 3-13   *Sample PortFast Scenario*

Figure 3-13 illustrates the modification in the STP state machine for interfaces configured for the PortFast feature. As illustrated in the figure, the STP state jumps directly from blocking to forwarding without going through the listening and learning state. In addition, PortFast suppresses topology change notifications.

Note   The purpose of PortFast is to minimize the time that access ports wait for STP to converge. The advantage of enabling PortFast is to prevent DHCP timeouts. Use this feature solely on access ports except in specific network designs. When enabling PortFast on a port connecting to another switch, there is a risk of creating a bridging loop.

Configuring the PortFast Feature

On Cisco IOS–based Catalyst switches, use the following interface command to enable or disable the PortFast feature:

```
[no] spanning-tree portfast
```

Example 3-1 illustrates a user configuring the PortFast feature and verifying the configuration.

Example 3-1 *Configuration and Verification of PortFast on Cisco IOS–Based Catalyst Switches*

```
Switch# configure terminal
Enter configuration commands, one per line. End with CNTL/Z.
Switch(config)# interface FastEthernet 3/27
Switch(config-if)# spanning-tree portfast
%Warning: portfast should only be enabled on ports connected to a single
host. Connecting hubs, concentrators, switches, bridges, etc... to this
interface  when portfast is enabled, can cause temporary bridging loops.
Use with CAUTION

%Portfast has been configured on FastEthernet3/27 but will only
have effect when the interface is in a non-trunking mode.
Switch(config-if)# end
Switch#
Switch# show spanning-tree interface FastEthernet 3/27 portfast
VLAN0001            enabled
```

On building access switches, enable PortFast globally so that there is no need to explicitly enable PortFast on each port individually. Remember to explicitly disable PortFast on uplink ports that connect to distribution layer switches. Enabling Portfast globally affects only the access ports and does not affect trunk ports. Use the interface level command **spanning-tree portfast trunk** to enable portfast on trunk port.

Use the following command to enable PortFast globally in global configuration mode:

spanning-tree portfast default

PortFast is a highly recommended configuration on end-user ports and server ports along with disabling negotiation of channeling and trunking. The end result of these configurations is to enable immediate forwarding frames on link up. On Cisco IOS-based Catalyst switches, use the following command to place an interface into this desired configuration:

switchport mode host

Example 3-2 shows a user configuring an interface for connecting to a host.

Example 3-2 *Configuration of Host Interface on Cisco IOS–Based Catalyst Switch*

```
SwitchB# configure terminal
Enter configuration commands, one per line.  End with CNTL/Z.
SwitchB(config)# interface fastEthernet 3/9
SwitchB(config-if)# switchport host
switchport mode will be set to access
spanning-tree portfast will be enabled
channel group will be disabled
SwitchB(config-if)# end
SwitchB#
```

Configuring the Basic Parameters of PVRST+

To implement PVRST+, perform these steps:

1. Enable PVRST+ globally. PVRST+ should be configured on all switches in the broadcast domain, as shown in Figure 3-14.

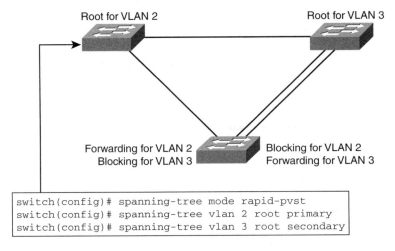

Figure 3-14 *Sample Topology for PVRST+*

2. Designate and configure a switch to be the root bridge.

3. Designate and configure a switch to be the secondary (backup) root bridge.

4. Enable load sharing on uplinks using priority and cost parameters.

5. Verify the configuration.

Example 3-3 illustrates how to display the RSTP information for VLAN2 on a nonroot switch in topology, as shown in Figure 3-14.

Example 3-3 *Verifying PVRST+ Using the* **show spanning-tree** *Command*

```
Cat6503E# show spanning-tree vlan 2

VLAN0002
  Spanning tree enabled protocol rstp
  Root ID     Priority     32768
```

```
           Address      000b.fcb5.dac0
           Cost         38
           Port         7 (FastEthernet0/7)
           Hello Time   2 sec  Max Age 20 sec  Forward Delay 15 sec

  Bridge ID  Priority   32770  (priority 32768 sys-id-ext 2)
             Address    0013.5f1c.e1c0
             Hello Time  2 sec  Max Age 20 sec  Forward Delay 15 sec
             Aging Time 300

Interface             Role Sts Cost      Prio.Nbr Type
------------------    ---- --- --------- -------- ------------------------------
Fa0/7                 Root FWD 19        128.7    P2p
Fa0/8                 Root FWD 19        128.8    P2p
```

Multiple Spanning Tree

Multiple Spanning Tree (MST) extends the IEEE 802.1w RST algorithm to multiple spanning trees. The main purpose of MST is to reduce the total number of spanning-tree instances to match the physical topology of the network and thus reduce the CPU cycles of a switch. PVRST+ runs STP instances for each VLAN and does not take into consideration the physical topology that might not require many different STP topologies. MST, on the other hand, uses a minimum number of STP instances to match the number of physical topologies present.

Figure 3-15 shows a common network design, featuring an access Switch A, connected to two Building Distribution submodule Switches D1 and D2. In this setup, there are 1000 VLANs, and the network administrator typically seeks to achieve load balancing on the access switch uplinks based on even or odd VLANs—or any other scheme deemed appropriate.

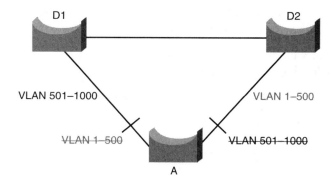

Figure 3-15 *VLAN Load Balancing*

Figure 3-15 illustrates two links and 1000 VLANs. The 1000 VLANs map to two MST instances. Rather than maintaining 1000 spanning trees, each switch needs to maintain only two spanning trees, reducing the need for switch resources. This concept of two MST instances for the topology, as shown in Figure 3-15, extends to 4096 VLANs. MST converges faster than PVRST+ and is backward compatible with 802.1D STP, 802.1w (RSTP), and the Cisco PVSTP+ architecture.

MST allows for the building of multiple spanning trees over trunks by grouping and associating VLANs to spanning-tree instances. Each instance may have a topology that is independent of other spanning-tree instances. This architecture provides multiple forwarding paths for data traffic and enables load balancing. A failure in one forwarding path does not affect other instances with different forwarding paths; hence, this architecture improves network fault tolerance.

In large networks, using different VLANs and a different spanning-tree topology enables better administration of the network and use of the redundant paths available. An MST spanning-tree instance might exist only on bridges that have compatible VLAN instance assignments. Configuring a set of bridges with the same MST configuration information allows them to participate in a specific set of spanning-tree instances. The term MST region refers to the set of interconnected bridges that have the same MST configuration.

Implementation of MST is not required if the Enterprise Campus Model is being employed because the number of active VLAN instances, and hence the STP instances, would be small and stable due to the design.

In the scenario described in Figure 3-15, only two different final logical topologies exist and therefore require only two spanning-tree instances. There is no need to run 1000 instances if, as shown in Figure 3-15, half of the 1000 VLANs map to a different spanning-tree instance.

In a network running MST, as depicted in Figure 3-16, the following is true:

■   The desired load-balancing scheme is still possible because half the VLANs follow one separate instance.

■   The switch utilization is low because it has to handle only two instances.

From a technical standpoint, MST is the best solution for the scenario presented in Figure 3-16. Because MST is a newer protocol, however, the following issues could arise:

■   The protocol is more complex than the usual spanning tree and thus requires additional training of the operation staff.

■   Interaction with legacy bridges is sometimes challenging.

MST enables you to build multiple spanning trees over trunks by grouping VLANs and associating them with spanning-tree instances. Each instance can have a topology independent of other spanning-tree instances. This architecture provides multiple active forwarding paths for data traffic and enables load balancing.

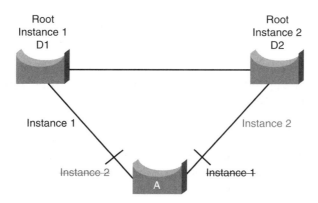

Figure 3-16   *MST*

Network fault tolerance is improved over Common Spanning Tree (CST) because a failure in one instance (forwarding path) does not necessarily affect other instances. This VLAN-to-MST grouping must be consistent across all bridges within an MST region.

In large networks, you can more easily administer the network and use redundant paths by locating different VLAN and spanning-tree assignments in different parts of the network. A spanning-tree instance can exist only on bridges that have compatible VLAN instance assignments.

You must configure a set of bridges with the same MST configuration information, which allows them to participate in a specific set of spanning-tree instances. Interconnected bridges that have the same MST configuration are referred to as an MST region. Bridges with different MST configurations or legacy bridges running 802.1D are considered separate MST regions.

MST Regions

The main enhancement introduced by MST is the ability to map several VLANs to a single spanning-tree instance. This raises the problem, however, of determining what VLAN is to be associated with what instance. More precisely, based on received BPDUs, devices need to identify these instances and the VLANs that are mapped to the instances.

In the case of the 802.1Q standard, all instances map to a unique and common instance and are therefore less complex. In the case of PVST+, each VLAN carries the BPDUs for its respective instance (one BPDU per VLAN).

Each switch that runs MST in the network has a single MST configuration that consists of three attributes:

- An alphanumeric configuration name (32 bytes)
- A configuration revision number (2 bytes)

■ A 4096-element table that associates each of the potential 4096 VLANs supported on the chassis to a given instance

To be part of a common MST region, a group of switches must share the same configuration attributes. It is up to the network administrator to properly propagate the configuration throughout the region.

To ensure a consistent VLANs-to-instance mapping, the protocol must exactly identify the boundaries of the regions. For that purpose, the characteristics of the region are included in BPDUs. Switches do not propagate the exact VLANs-to-instance mapping in the BPDU because the switches need to know only whether they are in the same region as a neighbor. Therefore, switches only send a digest of the VLANs-to-instance mapping table, along with the revision number and the name. When a switch receives a BPDU, it extracts the message digest, a numerical value derived from the VLANs-to-instance mapping table through a mathematical function, and compares it with its own computed digest. If the digests differ, the port receiving the BPDU is at the boundary of a region.

In generic terms, a port is at the boundary of a region if the designated bridge on its segment is in a different region or if it receives legacy 802.1D BPDUs. In Figure 3-17, the port on B1 is at the boundary of Region A, whereas the ports on B2 and B3 are internal to Region B.

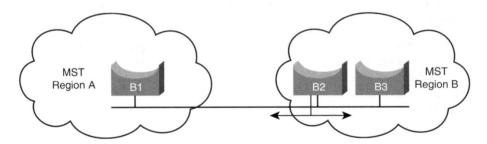

Figure 3-17   *Switches in Different MST Regions*

Extended System ID for MST

As with PVRST+, the 12-bit Extended System ID field is used in MST, as shown in Figure 3-18. In MST, this field carries the MST instance number.

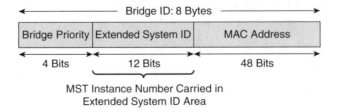

Figure 3-18   *MST Bridge ID*

Configuring MST

Enabling MST is a multistep process that involves mapping ranges of VLANs to a single MSTI.

Because MST is applicable to multiple VLANs, it requires some additional configuration beyond that needed for PVRST+. After you enable MST with the command **spanning-tree mode mst**, you must configure regions and instances with additional configuration commands.

Consider Figure 3-19 with three switches with six VLANs that need to be implemented. Spanning tree must be configured across these three switches. The Switches A and B are distribution switches. Either of them would be a possible candidate to perform the root bridge role.

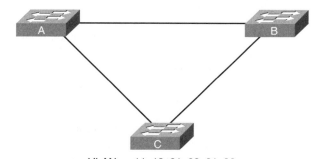

VLANs – 11, 12, 21, 22, 31, 32

Figure 3-19 *MST Sample Scenario*

A possible solution is to use MST with two instances, each instance grouping half the needed VLANs. Switch A would be the root for the first instance with odd VLANs assigned to it, Switch B would be the root for the second instance with even VLANs assigned to it.

Table 3-8 shows the various steps involved in configuring MST in a network, and Example 3-4 shows a user configuring Switches A and B to reflect the final configuration, as shown in Figure 3-20. Switch A is configured root for instance 1 and Switch B is configured root for instance 2, but the rest of the configuration, including name and VLAN grouping to instances, are identical.

Table 3-8 *Steps to Configure MST in IOS-Based Cisco Catalyst Switches*

Step	Description	Notes and Comments
1.	Enters MST configuration submode. Switch(config)# **spanning-tree mst configuration**	You can use the no keyword to clear the MST configuration.
2.	Displays the current MST configuration. Switch(config-mst)# **show current**	This command can be used in configuration mode to display the current configuration before making changes.

continues

Table 3-8   *Steps to Configure MST in IOS-Based Cisco Catalyst Switches (continued)*

Step	Description	Notes and Comments
3.	`Switch(config-mst)# `**`name`**` name`	
4.	Sets the MST configuration revision number. `Switch(config-mst)# `**`revision`** `revision_number`	The revision number can be any unassigned 16-bit integer. It is not incremented automatically when you commit a new MST configuration.
5.	Maps the VLANs to an MST instance. `Switch(config-mst)# `**`instance`** `instance_number `**`vlan`**` vlan_range`	If you do not specify the vlan keyword, you can use the no keyword to unmap all the VLANs that were mapped to an MST instance. If you specify the vlan keyword, you can use the no keyword to unmap a specified VLAN from an MST instance.
6.	`Switch(config-mst)# `**`show pending`**	Displays the new MST configuration to be applied.
7.	`Switch(config-mst)# `**`end`**	Applies the configuration and exit MST configuration submode.
8.	`Switch(config-mst)# `**`spanning-tree`** **`mst`**` instance_number `**`root primary|`** **`secondary`**	Assigns root bridge for MST instance. This syntax makes the switch root primary or secondary (only active if primary fails). It sets primary priority to 24576 and secondary to 28672.
9.	`Switch(config)# `**`spanning-tree extend`** **`system-id`**	This enables MAC address reduction, also known as extended system ID in Cisco IOS Software.
10.	`Switch(config-if)# `**`spanning-tree mst`** **`pre-standard`**	This command is required if the neighboring switch is using a prestandard version of MST.

Example 3-4   *Configuring MST for Topology Shown in Figure 3-20*

```
SwitchA(config)# spanning-tree mode mst
SwitchA(config)# spanning-tree mst configuration
SwitchA(config-mst)# name XYZ
SwitchA(config-mst)# revision 1
SwitchA(config-mst)# instance 1 vlan 11, 21, 31
SwitchA(config-mst)# instance 2 vlan 12, 22,32
```

```
SwitchA(config)# spanning-tree mst 1 root primary
SwitchB(config)# spanning-tree mode mst
SwitchB(config)# spanning-tree mst configuration
SwitchB(config-mst)# name XYZ
SwitchB(config-mst)# revision 1
SwitchB(config-mst)# instance 1 vlan 11, 21, 31
SwitchB(config-mst)# instance 2 vlan 12, 22,32
SwitchB(config)# spanning-tree mst 2 root primary
```

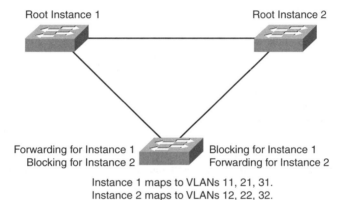

Root Instance 1   Root Instance 2

Forwarding for Instance 1   Blocking for Instance 1
Blocking for Instance 2   Forwarding for Instance 2

Instance 1 maps to VLANs 11, 21, 31.
Instance 2 maps to VLANs 12, 22, 32.

Figure 3-20 *Topology with MST Configured*

Example 3-5 illustrates a user changing the spanning-tree mode to MST and configuring the MST region by mapping the range of VLANs to Instance 1.

Example 3-5 *Sample Output of Configuring MST and Mapping VLANs to Instances on Cisco IOS–Based Catalyst Switches*

```
Switch# configure terminal
Enter configuration commands, one per line.  End with CNTL/Z.
Switch(config)# spanning-tree mode mst
Switch(config)# spanning-tree mst configuration
Switch(config-mst)# show current
Current MST configuration
```

```
Name          []
Revision  0
Instance  Vlans mapped
--------  ------------------------------------------------------------
0         1-4094

          ------------------------------------------------------------
Switch(config-mst)# name cisco
Switch(config-mst)# revision 1
Switch(config-mst)# instance 1 vlan 1-10
Switch(config-mst)# show pending
Pending MST configuration
Name          [cisco]
Revision  1
Instance  Vlans mapped
--------  ------------------------------------------------------------
0         11-4094
1         1-10
Switch(config-mst)# end
```

The **show current** command in Example 3-5 displays the current MST configuration on the switch. The **show pending** command details the uncommitted MST configuration. Catalyst switches discard the pending configuration if the administrator aborts the configuration changes by using the **abort** command. In addition, Catalyst switches save the MST configuration when issuing the **end** command, as shown in Example 3-5.

Example 3-6 illustrates a user displaying MST protocol information for MSTIs configured on the switch.

Example 3-6 *Displaying MST Protocol Information on Cisco IOS–Based Catalyst Switches*

```
Switch# show spanning-tree mst
###### MST00          vlans mapped:   5-4094
Bridge       address 0009.e845.6480  priority  32768 (32768 sysid 0)
Root         this switch for CST and IST
Configured   hello time 2, forward delay 15, max age 20, max hops 20

Interface        Role Sts Cost      Prio.Nbr Type
---------------- ---- --- --------- -------- -------------------------------
Fa3/24           Desg FWD 2000000   128.152  Shr
Fa3/32           Desg FWD 200000    128.160  P2p
Fa3/42           Back BLK 200000    128.170  P2p


###### MST01          vlans mapped:   1-2
Bridge       address 0009.e845.6480  priority  32769 (32768 sysid 1)
```

```
Root        this switch for MST01
Interface         Role Sts Cost       Prio.Nbr Type
---------------- ---- --- --------- -------- ------------------------------
Fa3/24            Desg FWD 2000000    128.152  Shr
Fa3/32            Desg FWD 200000     128.160  P2p
Fa3/42            Back BLK 200000     128.170  P2p
###### MST02         vlans mapped:    3-4
Bridge        address 0009.e845.6480  priority  32770 (32768 sysid 2)
Root        this switch for MST02
Interface         Role Sts Cost       Prio.Nbr Type
---------------- ---- --- --------- -------- ------------------------------
Fa3/24            Desg FWD 2000000    128.152  Shr
```

Example 3-7 illustrates a user displaying MST protocol information for a specific MSTI.

Example 3-7 *Displaying MST Protocol Instance Information*

```
Switch# show spanning-tree mst 1

###### MST01           vlans mapped:    1-2
Bridge        address 0009.e845.6480  priority  32769 (32768 sysid 1)
Root        this switch for MST01


Interface         Role Sts Cost       Prio.Nbr Type
---------------- ---- --- --------- -------- ------------------------------
Fa3/24            Desg FWD 2000000    128.152  Shr
Fa3/32            Desg FWD 200000     128.160  P2p
Fa3/42            Back BLK 200000     128.170  P2p
```

Example 3-8 illustrates a user displaying MST protocol information for a specific interface.

Example 3-8 *Displaying MST Protocol Information for a Specific Interface*

```
Switch# show spanning-tree mst interface FastEthernet 3/24

FastEthernet3/24 of MST00 is designated forwarding
Edge port: no            (default)       port guard : none      (default)
Link type: shared        (auto)          bpdu filter: disable   (default)
Boundary : internal                      bpdu guard : disable   (default)
Bpdus sent 81, received 81


Instance Role Sts Cost       Prio.Nbr Vlans mapped
-------- ---- --- --------- -------- ------------------------------
0        Desg FWD 2000000    128.152  5-4094
```

```
1             Desg FWD 2000000   128.152  1-2
2             Desg FWD 2000000   128.152  3-4
```

Example 3-9 illustrates a user displaying detailed information for a specific instance.

Example 3-9   *Displaying MST Protocol Details*

```
Switch# show spanning-tree mst 1 detail

###### MST01         vlans mapped:    1-2
Bridge      address 0009.e845.6480  priority  32769 (32768 sysid 1)
Root        this switch for MST01
FastEthernet3/24 of MST01 is designated forwarding
Port info            port id        128.152  priority    128  cost      2000000
Designated root      address 0009.e845.6480  priority  32769  cost            0
Designated bridge    address 0009.e845.6480  priority  32769  port id  128.152
Timers: message expires in 0 sec, forward delay 0, forward transitions 1
Bpdus (MRecords) sent755, received 0

FastEthernet3/32 of MST01 is designated forwarding
Port info            port id        128.160  priority    128  cost       200000
Designated root      address 0009.e845.6480  priority  32769  cost            0
Designated bridge    address 0009.e845.6480  priority  32769  port id  128.160
Timers: message expires in 0 sec, forward delay 0, forward transitions 1
Bpdus (MRecords) sent 769, received 1

FastEthernet3/42 of MST01 is backup blocking
Port info            port id        128.170  priority    128  cost       200000
Designated root      address 0009.e845.6480  priority  32769  cost            0
Designated bridge    address 0009.e845.6480  priority  32769  port id  128.160
Timers: message expires in 5 sec, forward delay 0, forward transitions 0
Bpdus (MRecords) sent 1, received 769
```

Spanning Tree Enhancements

STP is a mature protocol, benefiting from years of development and production deployment; however, STP makes assumptions about the quality of the network and it can fail. Those failures are generally high profile failures because of the extent to which they impact the network. STP is designed to never open, even temporarily, a loop during its operation. However, like any protocol, it is based on some assumptions that might not be valid in the network. To help STP converge faster and for the protocol behavior to match your network infrastructure, several features are available to filter the way Bridge Protocol Data Units (BPDU) are sent or received, and to alter the way the network should react if an unexpected network topology change occurs.

Note Unless otherwise explicitly stated, STP in this section refers to all versions of STP such as 802.1D, PVST+, PVRST+ and MST.

For example, 802.1D does not prevent unwanted devices from becoming the root bridge of the spanning tree, and no mechanism exists to selectively discard BPDUs from certain ports. The Cisco STP toolkit provides tools to better manage STP. Features such as Root Guard and BPDU Guard solve the problem of unauthorized or inappropriate devices causing network topology changes.

In addition, network device failures can cause bridging loops or black holes in the network. The Cisco Unidirectional Link Detection (UDLD) and Loop Guard features prevent network device failures that are due to faulty hardware or software errors.

Problems such as link duplex mismatch, unidirectional link failure, frame corruption, resource errors, and misconfigurations can disrupt the spanning tree, which in turn disrupts network traffic. As a result, understanding how to troubleshoot spanning-tree problems is critical in maintaining high network availability. The following best practices for spanning tree prevent problems and aid in quick network recovery if unforeseen anomalous events occur.

This remaining section of this chapter introduces the STP enhancements with sample configurations. This section also discusses how to tune STP for higher availability and resiliency.

STP does not provide for checks and balances to ensure high availability in multilayer switched networks. As a result, Cisco introduced features such as the following to help fine-tune and increase resiliency of STP:

■   **BPDU Guard:** Prevents accidental connection of switching devices to PortFast-enabled ports, as shown in Figure 3-21. Connecting switches to PortFast-enabled ports can cause Layer 2 loops or topology changes.

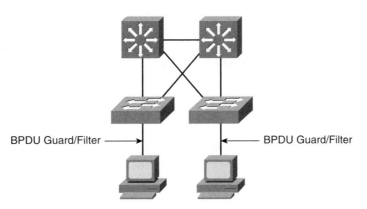

Figure 3-21 *Enabling BPDU Guard/Filter at Access Ports*

■ **BPDU filtering:** Restricts the switch from sending unnecessary BPDUs out access ports.

■ **Root Guard:** Prevents switches connected on ports configured as access ports from becoming the root switch.

BPDU Guard

BPDU Guard puts an interface configured for STP PortFast in the err-disable state upon receipt of a BPDU, as shown in Example 3-10. The BPDU Guard disables interfaces as a preventive step to avoid a potential bridging loop.

Example 3-10 *BPDU Guard Log Messages on a Catalyst Switch*

```
2009 May 12 15:13:32 %SPANTREE-2-RX_PORTFAST:Received BPDU on PortFast enable port.
Disabling 2/1
2009 May 12 15:13:32 %PAGP-5-PORTFROMSTP:Port 2/1 left bridge port 2/1
```

The STP BPDU Guard shuts down PortFast-configured interfaces that receive BPDUs, rather than putting them into the STP blocking state (the default behavior). In a valid configuration, PortFast-configured interfaces should not receive BPDUs. Reception of a BPDU by a PortFast-configured interface signals an invalid configuration, such as connection of an unauthorized device. BPDU Guard provides a secure response to invalid configurations, because the administrator must manually reenable the err-disabled interface after fixing the invalid configuration. It is also possible to set up a time-out interval after which the switch automatically tries to reenable the interface. However, if the invalid configuration still exists, the switch err-disables the interface again.

To enable BPDU Guard or to disable BPDU Guard on a Cisco IOS–based Catalyst switch, use the following global configuration command:

`[no] ` **`spanning-tree portfast edge bpduguard default`**

Example 3-11 illustrates a user configuring and verifying the spanning-tree PortFast BPDU Guard feature.

At the interface level, you can enable BPDU guard on any port by using the **spanning-tree bpduguard enable** interface configuration command without also enabling the PortFast feature. When the port receives a BPDU, it is put in the error-disabled state.

Example 3-11 *Configuring and Verifying BPDU Guard on Cisco IOS–Based Catalyst Switches*

```
Switch# configure terminal
Enter configuration commands, one per line. End with CNTL/Z.
Switch(config)# spanning-tree portfast edge bpduguard default
Switch(config)# end
Switch# show spanning-tree summary totals
```

```
Root bridge for: none.
PortFast BPDU Guard is enabled
Etherchannel misconfiguration guard is enabled
UplinkFast is disabled
BackboneFast is disabled
Default pathcost method used is short


Name                   Blocking Listening Learning Forwarding STP Active
-------------------- --------- --------- -------- ---------- ---------
             34 VLANs 0         0         0         36         36
```

BPDU Filtering

BPDU filtering supports the ability to prevent Catalyst switches from sending BPDUs on PortFast-enabled interfaces. Ports configured for the PortFast feature typically connect to host devices. Hosts do not participate in STP and hence drop the received BPDUs. As a result, BPDU filtering prevents unnecessary BPDUs from being transmitted to host devices.

When enabled globally, BPDU filtering has these attributes:

■ It affects all operational PortFast ports on switches that do not have BPDU filtering configured on the individual ports.

■ If BPDUs are seen, the port loses its PortFast status, BPDU filtering is disabled, and the STP sends and receives BPDUs on the port as it would with any other STP port on the switch.

■ Upon startup, the port transmits ten BPDUs. If this port receives any BPDUs during that time, PortFast and PortFast BPDU filtering are disabled.

When enabled on an individual port, BPDU filtering has these attributes:

■ It ignores all BPDUs received.

■ It sends no BPDUs.

Table 3-9 lists all the possible PortFast BPDU filtering combinations.

If you enable BPDU Guard on the same interface as BPDU filtering, BPDU Guard has no effect because BPDU filtering takes precedence over BPDU Guard.

To enable PortFast BPDU filtering globally on the switch, use the following command on Cisco IOS–based Catalyst switches:

```
spanning-tree portfast bpdufilter default
```

Table 3-9 *PortFast BPDU Filtering Port Configurations*

Per-Port Configuration	Global Configuration PortFast State		PortFast BPDU Filtering State
Default	Enable	Enable	Enable
Default	Enable	Disable	Disable
Default	Disable	Not applicable	Disable
Disable	Not applicable	Not applicable	Disable
Enable	Not applicable	Not applicable	Enable

To enable PortFast BPDU filtering on a specific switch port, enter this command:

```
Switch(config-if)# spanning-tree bpdufilter enable
```

To verify the configuration, use the following command on Cisco IOS–based Catalyst switches:

```
show spanning-tree summary
```

Example 3-12 illustrates verification of spanning-tree configuration on the switch.

Example 3-12 *Verifying Portfast BPDU Filter Status on a Cisco Catalyst Switch*

```
PxD1# show spanning-tree summary
Switch is in pvst mode
Root bridge for: none
Extended system ID          is enabled
Portfast Default            is disabled
PortFast BPDU Guard Default is disabled
Portfast BPDU Filter Default is disabled
Loopguard Default           is disabled
EtherChannel misconfig guard is enabled
UplinkFast                  is disabled
BackboneFast                is disabled
Configured Pathcost method used is short
Name            Blocking Listening Learning Forwarding STP Active
-------------- ---- -------- ------- -------- ---------- --------
VLAN0001            2        0        0          6          8
---------------- -- -------- ------- -------- ---------- --------
1 vlan              2        0        0          6          8
```

Example 3-13 illustrates how to verify the PortFast BPDU filtering status on a specific switch port.

Example 3-13 *Verifying PortFast BPDU Filtering on a Specific Switch Port*

```
Switch# show spanning-tree interface fastEthernet 4/4 detail

Port 196 (FastEthernet4/4) of VLAN0010 is forwarding
   Port path cost 1000, Port priority 160, Port Identifier 160.196.
   Designated root has priority 32768, address 00d0.00b8.140a
   Designated bridge has priority 32768, address 00d0.00b8.140a
   Designated port id is 160.196, designated path cost 0
   Timers:message age 0, forward delay 0, hold 0
   Number of transitions to forwarding state:1
   The port is in the portfast mode by portfast trunk configuration
   Link type is point-to-point by default
   Bpdu filter is enabled
   BPDU:sent 0, received 0
```

Root Guard

Root Guard is useful in avoiding Layer 2 loops during network anomalies. The Root Guard feature forces an interface to become a designated port to prevent surrounding switches from becoming a root switch. In other words, Root Guard provides a way to enforce the root bridge placement in the network. Catalyst switches force Root Guard–enabled ports to be designated ports. If the bridge receives superior STP BPDUs on a Root Guard–enabled port, the port moves to a root-inconsistent STP state (effectively equal to a listening state), and the switch does not forward traffic out of that port. As a result, this feature effectively enforces the position of the root bridge.

Figure 3-22 shows a sample topology to illustrate the Root Guard feature. Switches A and B comprise the core of the network, and Switch A is the root bridge for a VLAN. Switch C is an access layer switch. The link between Switch B and Switch C is blocking on the Switch C side. Figure 3-22 shows the flow of STP BPDUs with arrows.

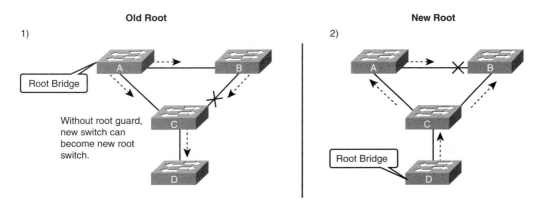

Figure 3-22 *Network Topology with Root Guard Disabled*

In Figure 3-22, when Switch D is connected to Switch C, it begins to participate in STP. If the priority of Switch D is 0 or any value lower than that of the current root bridge, Switch D becomes the root bridge for that VLAN based on normal STP guidelines. In this specific scenario, however, having Switch D as the root causes the Gigabit Ethernet link that is connecting the two core switches to block, thus causing all the data in that particular VLAN to flow via a 100-Mbps link across the access layer. If there is more data flowing between the core switches in that VLAN than this link may accommodate, packet loss can occur, causing performance issues or network connectivity problems. An even worse scenario might occur if Switch D is unstable and causes frequent reconvergence of the root bridge.

The Root Guard feature can protect against such issues. After the Root Guard feature is enabled on a port, the switch does not enable that port to become an STP root port. The port remains as an STP-designated port. In addition, if a better BPDU is received on the port, Root Guard disables (err-disables) the port rather than processing the BPDU. If an unauthorized device starts sending BPDUs with a better bridge ID, the normal STP process would elect the new switch as the root switch. By disabling the port, the network topology is protected.

The current design recommendation is to enable Root Guard on all access ports so that a root bridge is not established through these ports. In Figure 3-22, enable Root Guard on Switches A, B, and C on the following ports:

- **Switch A (Distribution/Core):** Any access port

- **Switch B (Distribution/Core):** Any access port

- **Switch C (Access):** Any access port including the port connecting to Switch D

In this configuration, Switch C blocks the port connecting to Switch D when it receives a better (superior) BPDU. The port transitions to a special STP state (root-inconsistent), which is effectively the same as the listening state. No traffic passes through the port in root-inconsistent state.

When Switch D stops sending superior BPDUs, the port unblocks again and goes through regular STP transition of listening and learning, and eventually to the forwarding state. Recovery is automatic; no intervention is required.

In addition, Catalyst switches log the following message when a Root Guard–enabled port receives a superior BPDU:

```
%SPANTREE-2-ROOTGUARDBLOCK: Port 1/1 tried to become non-designated in VLAN 77.
    Moved to root-inconsistent state
```

To enable Root Guard on a Layer 2 access port to force it to become a designated port, or to disable Root Guard, use the following interface-level command on Cisco IOS–based Catalyst switches:

```
[no] spanning-tree guard root
```

Example 3-14 illustrates a user enabling the Root Guard feature on FastEthernet interface 5/8 and verifying the configuration.

Example 3-14   *Configuring and Verifying Root Guard on Cisco IOS–Based Catalyst Switches*

```
Switch# configure terminal
Enter configuration commands, one per line. End with CNTL/Z.
Switch(config)# interface FastEthernet 5/8
Switch(config-if)# spanning-tree guard root
Switch(config-if)# end
Switch# show running-config interface FastEthernet 5/8
Building configuration...
Current configuration: 67 bytes
!
interface FastEthernet5/8
switchport mode access
spanning-tree guard root
end
!
```

Example 3-15 shows how to determine whether any interfaces are in root-inconsistent state.

Example 3-15   *Displaying Root-Inconsistent Interfaces on Cisco IOS–Based Catalyst Switches*

```
Switch# show spanning-tree inconsistentports
Name                    Interface                Inconsistency
------------------      ---------------------    -----------------
VLAN0001                FastEthernet3/1          Port Type Inconsistent
VLAN0001                FastEthernet3/2          Port Type Inconsistent
VLAN1002                FastEthernet3/1          Port Type Inconsistent
VLAN1002                FastEthernet3/2          Port Type Inconsistent
Number of inconsistent ports (segments) in the system :4
```

Note   Ports in root inconsistent recover automatically with no human intervention after the port stop receiving superior BPDUs. The port goes through the listening state to the learning state, and eventually transitions to the forwarding state.

Preventing Forwarding Loops and Black Holes

Prevention of forwarding loops and black holes in a network is a required aspect of network design. Black holes in the network are created when a device that receives frames has no forwarding information for that packet and thus essentially drops all such packets. Cisco Catalyst switches support two important features to address such conditions:

- **Loop Guard:** The Loop Guard STP feature improves the stability of Layer 2 networks by preventing bridging loops.

- **UDLD:** UDLD detects and disables unidirectional links.

Loop Guard

Loop Guard provides additional protection against Layer 2 forwarding loops (STP loops). A bridging loop happens when an STP blocking port in a redundant topology erroneously transitions to the forwarding state. This usually occurs because one of the ports of a physically redundant topology (not necessarily the STP blocking port) has stopped receiving STP BPDUs. In STP, switches rely on continuous reception or transmission of BPDUs, depending on the port role. (A designated port transmits BPDUs, whereas a nondesignated port receives BPDUs.)

When one of the ports in a physically redundant topology stops receiving BPDUs, STP considers the topology loop-free. Eventually, the blocking port from the alternative or backup port transitions to a designated port and then moves to the STP forwarding state, creating a bridging loop.

With the Loop Guard feature, switches do an additional check before transitioning to the STP forwarding state. If switches stop receiving BPDUs on a nondesignated port with the Loop Guard feature enabled, the switch places the port into the STP loop-inconsistent blocking state instead of moving through the listening, learning, and forwarding states.

When the Loop Guard feature places a port into the loop-inconsistent blocking state, the switch logs the following message:

```
SPANTREE-2-LOOPGUARDBLOCK: No BPDUs were received on port 3/2 in vlan 3.
    Moved to loop-inconsistent state.
```

If a switch receives a BPDU on a port in the loop-inconsistent STP state, the port transitions through STP states according to the received BPDU. As a result, recovery is automatic, and no manual intervention is necessary. After the recovery, the switch logs the following message:

```
SPANTREE-2-LOOPGUARDUNBLOCK: port 3/2 restored in vlan 3.
```

To illustrate Loop Guard behavior, consider the example in Figure 3-23. Switch A is the root switch. Due to unidirectional link failure on the link between Switch B and Switch C, Switch C is not receiving BPDUs from Switch B.

Without Loop Guard, the STP blocking port on Switch C transitions to the STP listening state after the max age timer expires, and ultimately to the forwarding state after two times the forward delay time. When the port moves into the forwarding state, a bridging loop occurs, as shown in Figure 3-24.

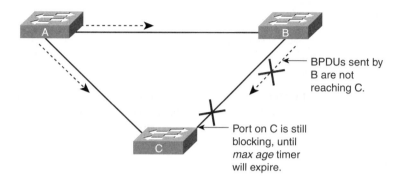

Figure 3-23   *Unidirectional Link Without Loop Guard*

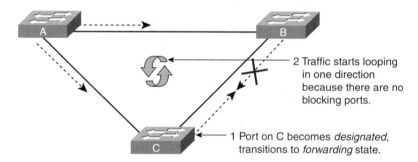

Figure 3-24   *Bridging Loop Without Loop Guard*

With the Loop Guard feature enabled, the blocking port on Switch C transitions into the STP loop-inconsistent state when the max age timer expires, as shown in Figure 3-25. A port in the STP loop-inconsistent state does not pass data traffic; hence, a bridging loop does not occur. The loop-inconsistent state is effectively equal to the blocking state.

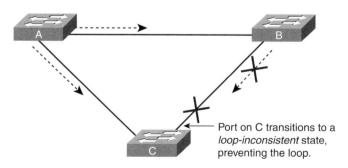

Figure 3-25   *Unidirectional Link with Loop Guard*

You configure the Loop Guard feature on a per-port basis, although the feature blocks inconsistent ports on a per-VLAN basis. For example, on a trunk port, if BPDUs are not received for only one particular VLAN, the switch blocks only that VLAN (that is, moves the port for that VLAN to the loop-inconsistent STP state). In the case of an Ether

Channel interface, the channel status goes into the inconsistent state for all the ports belonging to the channel group for the particular VLAN not receiving BPDUs. (Recall that Catalyst switches consider EtherChannel as one logical port from the STP point of view.)

Enable the Loop Guard feature on all nondesignated ports, and not just for blocking ports. More precisely, Loop Guard should be enabled on root and alternative ports for all possible combinations of active topologies. Before enabling Loop Guard, however, consider all possible failover scenarios. Figure 3-26 shows a sample scenario and indicates the ports configured for Loop Guard.

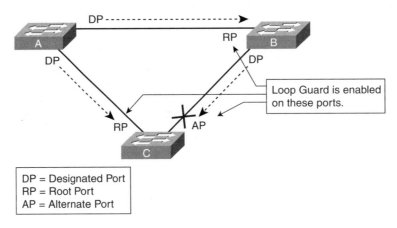

Figure 3-26 *Loop Guard–Enabled Ports*

Loop Guard is disabled by default on Catalyst switches. Use the following interface-level configuration command to enable Loop Guard on Cisco IOS–based Catalyst switches:

```
Switch(config-if)# spanning-tree guard loop
```

When you enable Loop Guard globally for application to all ports, the switch enables Loop Guard only on ports considered to be point-to-point links. Catalyst switches consider full-duplex ports as point-to-point links. It is still possible to configure, or override, the global configuration of Loop Guard on a per-port basis.

To enable Loop Guard globally on Cisco IOS–based Catalyst switches, use the following global configuration command:

```
spanning-tree loopguard default
```

To disable Loop Guard on any specific interface on Cisco IOS–based Catalyst switches, issue the following interface configuration command:

```
no spanning-tree loopguard
```

Disabling loop guard moves all loop-inconsistent ports to the listening state.

To verify the Loop Guard status on an interface, issue the following EXEC command on Cisco IOS–based Catalyst switches:

```
show spanning-tree interface interface-id detail
```

Example 3-16 illustrates a user verifying the status of Loop Guard on interface FastEthernet 3/42.

Example 3-16 *Verifying the Status of Loop Guard on an Interface on Cisco IOS–Based Catalyst Switches*

```
Switch# show spanning-tree interface FastEthernet 3/42 detail
Port 170 (FastEthernet3/42) of VLAN0001 is blocking
   Port path cost 19, Port priority 128, Port Identifier 128.170.
   Designated root has priority 8193, address 0009.e845.6480
   Designated bridge has priority 8193, address 0009.e845.6480
   Designated port id is 128.160, designated path cost 0
   Timers: message age 1, forward delay 0, hold 0
   Number of transitions to forwarding state: 0
   Link type is point-to-point by default
   Loop guard is enabled on the port
   BPDU: sent 1, received 4501
```

UDLD

A unidirectional link occurs when traffic is transmitted between neighbors in one direction only. Unidirectional links can cause spanning-tree topology loops. Uni-Directional Link Detection (UDLD) enables devices to detect when a unidirectional link exists and also to shut down the affected interface. UDLD is useful on a fiber ports to prevent network issues resulting in miswiring at the patch panel causing the link to be in up/up status but the BPDUs are lost.

UDLD is a Layer 2 protocol that works with Layer 1 mechanisms to determine the physical status of a link. At Layer 1, auto-negotiation takes care of the physical signaling and fault detection. UDLD performs tasks that auto-negotiation cannot, such as detecting the identities of neighbors and shutting down misconnected ports. When enabling both auto-negotiation and UDLD, Layer 1 and Layer 2 detections work together to prevent physical and logical unidirectional connections and the malfunctioning of other protocols.

With UDLD enabled, the switch periodically sends UDLD protocol packets to its neighbor and expects the packets to be echoed back before a predetermined timer expires. If the timer expires, the switch determines the link to be unidirectional and shuts down the port. The default interval for UDLD message is 15 seconds, which is configurable for faster detection.

UDLD is a Layer 2 protocol enabled between adjacent switches. It uses MAC 01-00-0c-cc-cc-cc with Subnetwork Access Protocol (SNAP) High-Level Data Link Control (HDLC) protocol type 0x0111. UDLD packets contain information about sending the port's device ID and port ID and the neighbor's device ID and port ID. Neighbor devices with UDLD enabled send the same hello message. The link is bidirectional if devices on both sides receive each other's UDLD packets.

In Normal mode, UDLD simply changes the UDLD-enabled port to an undetermined state if it stops receiving UDLD messages from its directly connected neighbor. Aggressive mode UDLD is a variation of UDLD, and when a port stops receiving UDLD packets, UDLD tries to reestablish the connection with the neighbor. After eight failed retries, the port state changes to the err-disable state, which effectively disables the port.

Aggressive mode is the preferred method of configuring UDLD. By preventing this one-way communication, UDLD can be useful in spanning-tree networks. UDLD is used when a link should be shut down because of a hardware failure that is causing unidirectional communication. In an EtherChannel bundle, UDLD shuts down only the physical link that has failed.

To reenable the port after correcting the problem, use the following interface-level commands in Cisco Catalyst switches:

```
Switch(config-if)# shutdown
Switch(config-if)# no shutdown
```

STP prevents loops in the network by detecting loops and blocking the redundant ports. This loop detection is based on BPDUs received on switch ports. If a switch receives the same root BPDU from more than one port, it chooses the best port to the root bridge and blocks the other, redundant ports. Because receiving BPDUs is a critical part of the loop-prevention process, it is important to detect unidirectional links by another method to ensure that BPDUs are sent in the appropriate direction on all links at all times. Otherwise, a unidirectional link ultimately leads to spanning-tree loops or black holes for routed traffic. For instance, if a Layer 3 or routed interface is experiencing a unidirectional link condition but the interface stays up, the switch continues to forward traffic to that interface, but the packet never reaches the far-end device. In this situation, a routing black hole exists. The solution to preventing these issues is to use aggressive mode UDLD.

To illustrate this concept, consider the three switches shown in Figure 3-27. Switch A is the root bridge, and the link between Switch B, and Switch C is in the blocking state because a physical loop is present in the network.

Now consider a situation where the link between Switches B and C becomes unidirectional, as shown in Figure 3-28. Switch B can receive traffic from Switch C, but Switch C cannot receive traffic from Switch B. On the segment between Switches B and C, Switch B is the designated bridge sending the root BPDUs, and Switch C expects to receive the BPDUs. Switch C waits until the max-age timer (20 seconds) expires before it takes action. When this timer expires, Switch C moves through the listening and learning states of STP and then eventually to the STP forwarding state on the port toward Switch B. At this moment, both Switch B and Switch C are forwarding to each other, and essentially, there is no blocking port in the network. This situation is a network loop where severe connectivity issues exist.

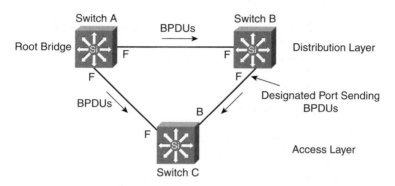

Figure 3-27 *Steady State STP Behavior in the Topology*

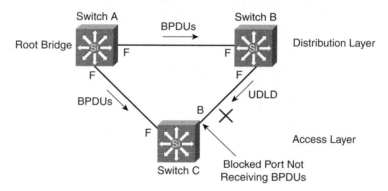

Figure 3-28 *Unidirectional Condition in the Topology*

Aggressive mode UDLD running on Switches B and C in this scenario would detect the condition and would take corrective action before STP moves into the forwarding state.

UDLD works by exchanging UDLD protocol packets between connected switches. For UDLD to function correctly, it must be enabled on switches on both sides of the link. A UDLD-enabled switch sends UDLD protocol packets with its own device ID and port ID to the neighboring device. The UDLD is in determined status if the switch sees its own information in the packet sent by the neighbor. If the device does not see itself in the neighboring device's UDLD protocol packets, the link is determined as unidirectional.

Table 3-10 describes the default status for the UDLD on a global and an interface basis.

UDLD can be enabled globally for all fiber interfaces or on a per-interface basis.

Table 3-10   *UDLD Default Configuration Status*

Feature	Default Status
UDLD global enable state	Globally disabled
UDLD per-interface enable state for fiber-optic media	Enabled on all Ethernet fiber-optic interfaces
UDLD per-interface enable state for twisted-pair (copper) media	Disabled on all Ethernet 10/100 and 1000BASE-TX interfaces

To enable UDLD on an interface, use this command:

```
Switch(config-if)# udld enable [aggressive]
```

To enable UDLD globally on all fiber-optic interfaces, use this command:

```
Switch(config)# udld { enable | aggressive }
```

To disable UDLD on an individual nonfiber-optic interface, use this command:

```
switch(config-if)# no udld enable
```

To disable UDLD on an individual fiber-optic interface, use this command:

```
switch(config-if)# no udld port
```

Example 3-17 shows a user configuring and verifying aggressive mode UDLD on interface GigabitEthernet 5/1 on a Cisco IOS-based Catalyst switch.

Example 3-17   *Configuration and Verification of UDLD on Cisco Switches*

```
SwitchA# configure terminal
Enter configuration commands, one per line.  End with CNTL/Z.
SwitchA(config)# interface gigabitEthernet 5/1
SwitchA(config-if)# udld port aggressive
SwitchA(config-if)# end
SwitchA#
SwitchA#show udld gigabitEthernet 5/1


Interface Gi5/1
---
Port enable administrative configuration setting: Enabled / in aggressive mode
Port enable operational state: Enabled / in aggressive mode
Current bidirectional state: Bidirectional
Current operational state: Advertisement - Single neighbor detected
Message interval: 15
Time out interval: 5

    Entry 1
    ---
```

```
Expiration time: 38
Device ID: 1
Current neighbor state: Bidirectional
Device name: FOX06310RW1
Port ID: Gi1/1
Neighbor echo 1 device: FOX0627A001
Neighbor echo 1 port: Gi5/1

Message interval: 15
Time out interval: 5
CDP Device name: SwitchB
```

To summarize, UDLD and aggressive mode UDLD are critical features recommended on all ports to prevent various issues that can potentially cause network outages.

Comparison Between Aggressive Mode UDLD and Loop Guard

Loop Guard and aggressive mode UDLD functionality overlap insofar as both protect against STP failures caused by unidirectional links. These two features are different, however, in their approach to the problem and in functionality. Table 3-11 compares and contrasts the Loop Guard and aggressive mode UDLD features.

Table 3-11 *Comparison Between Loop Guard and Aggressive Mode UDLD*

	Loop Guard	**Aggressive Mode UDLD**
Configuration	Per port	Per port
Action granularity	Per VLAN	Per port
Auto-recovery	Yes	Yes, with err-disable timeout feature
Protection against STP failures caused by unidirectional links	Yes, when enabled on all root ports and alternative ports in redundant topology	Yes, when enabled on all links in redundant topology
Protection against STP failures caused by problem in software resulting in designated switch not sending BPDUs	Yes	No
Protection against miswiring	No	Yes

The most noticeable difference between aggressive mode UDLD and Loop Guard is with regard to STP. Aggressive mode UDLD cannot detect failures caused by problems in software in the designated switch not sending the BPDU. Problems resulting from software failures are less common than failures caused by unidirectional links that result from hardware failures. Nevertheless, aggressive mode UDLD is more robust in its capability to detect unidirectional links on EtherChannel. Loop Guard blocks all interfaces of the EtherChannel in such a failure by putting the EtherChannel into the loop-inconsistent state for a VLAN or for all VLANs, whereas aggressive mode UDLD disables the single port exhibiting problems. In addition, aggressive mode UDLD is not dependent on STP, so it supports Layer 3 links as well.

In addition, Loop Guard does not support shared links or interfaces that are unidirectional on switch Bootup. If a port is unidirectional on switch Bootup, the port never receives BPDUs and becomes a designated port. Loop Guard does not support this scenario, because the behavior is not distinguishable from normal STP operation. Aggressive mode UDLD does provide protection against such a failure scenario.

Enabling both aggressive mode UDLD and Loop Guard provides the highest level of protection against bridging loops and black holes in multilayer switched networks.

Flex Links

Flex Links is a Layer 2 availability feature that provides an alternative solution to STP and allows users to turn off STP and still provide basic link redundancy. Flex Links can coexist with spanning tree turned in the distribution layer switches; however, the distribution layer is unaware of Flex Links feature. This enhancement enables a convergence time of less than 50 milliseconds. In addition, this convergence time remains consistent regardless of the number of VLANs or MAC addresses configured on switch uplink ports.

Flex Links is based on defining an active/standby link pair on a common access switch. Flex Links are a pair of Layer 2 interfaces, either switchports or port channels, that are configured to act as a backup to another Layer 2 interface, as shown in Figure 3-29.

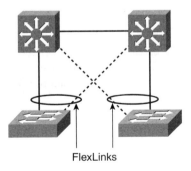

FlexLinks

Figure 3-29 *Configuring Flex Links in the Network*

Flex Links are configured on one Layer 2 interface (the active link) by assigning another Layer 2 interface as the Flex Links or backup link. The Flex Links can be on the same switch or on another switch in the stack. When one of the links is up and forwarding traffic, the other link is in standby mode, ready to begin forwarding traffic if the other link shuts down. At any given time, only one of the interfaces is in the linkup state and forwarding traffic. If the primary link shuts down, the standby link starts forwarding traffic. When the active link comes back up, it goes into standby mode and does not forward traffic. Flex Links are supported only on Layer 2 ports and port channels, not on VLANs or on Layer 3 ports.

Follow these guidelines to configure Flex Links:

- You can configure only one Flex Links backup link for any active link, and it must be a different interface from the active interface.

- An interface can belong to only one Flex Links pair. An interface can be a backup link for only one active link. An active link cannot belong to another Flex Links pair.

- Neither of the links can be a port that belongs to an EtherChannel. However, you can configure two port channels (EtherChannel logical interfaces) as Flex Links, and you can configure a port channel and a physical interface as Flex Links, with either the port channel or the physical interface as the active link.

- A backup link does not have to be the same type (Fast Ethernet, Gigabit Ethernet, or port channel) as the active link. However, you should configure both Flex Links with similar characteristics so that there are no loops or changes in behavior if the standby link begins to forward traffic.

- STP is disabled on Flex Links ports. A Flex Links port does not participate in STP, even if the VLANs present on the port are configured for STP. When STP is not enabled, be sure that there are no loops in the configured topology.

Flex Links are configured at the interface level with the command:

`switchport backup interface`

Example 3-18 shows how to configure an interface with a backup interface and to verify the configuration.

Example 3-18 *Configuration and Verification of Flex Links*

```
Switch# configure terminal
Switch(conf)# interface fastethernet1/0/1
Switch(conf-if)# switchport backup interface fastethernet1/0/2
Switch(conf-if)# end
Switch# show interface switchport backup
Switch Backup Interface Pairs:
Active Interface        Backup Interface        State
--------------------------------------------------------------------
FastEthernet1/0/1       FastEthernet1/0/2       Active Up/Backup Standby
```

Recommended Spanning Tree Practices

There are many arguments in favor of using large Layer 2 domains in a corporate network. There are also good reasons why you should avoid Layer 2 in the network. The traditional way of doing transparent bridging requires the computation of a spanning tree for the data plane. Spanning means that there will be connectivity between any two devices that have at least one path physically available between them in the network. Tree means that the active topology will use a subset of the links physically available so that there is a single path between any two devices. (For example, there is no loop in the network.) Note that this requirement is related to the way frames are forwarded by bridges, not to the STP that is just a control protocol in charge of building such a tree. This behavior can result in a single copy being delivered to all the nodes in the network without any duplicate frames. This approach has the following two main drawbacks:

- **Networkwide failure domain:** A single source can send traffic that is propagated to all the links in the network. If an error condition occurs and the active topology includes a loop, because Ethernet frames do not include a Time-To-Live (TTL) field, traffic might circle around endlessly, resulting in networkwide flooding and link saturation.

- **No multipathing:** Because the forwarding paradigm requires the active topology to be a tree, only one path between any two nodes is used. That means that if there are N redundant paths between two devices, all but one will be simply ignored. Note that the introduction of a per-VLAN tree allows working around this constraint to a certain extent.

To limit the impact of such limitations, the general recommendation is to use Layer 3 connectivity at the distribution or core layer of the network, keeping Layer 2 for the access layer. as shown in Figure 3-30. Using Layer 3 between the distribution and core layer allows multipathing (up to 16 paths) using Equal-Cost Multipathing (ECMP) without dependency of STP and is strongly preferred unless there is a need to extend Layer 2 across a data center pod (distribution block). ECMP refers to the situation in which a router has multiple equal-cost paths to a prefix, and thus load-balances traffic over each path. Newer technologies, such as Catalyst 6500 Virtual Switching System or Nexus 7000 virtual Port Channel (vPC), enable multipathing at Layer 2.

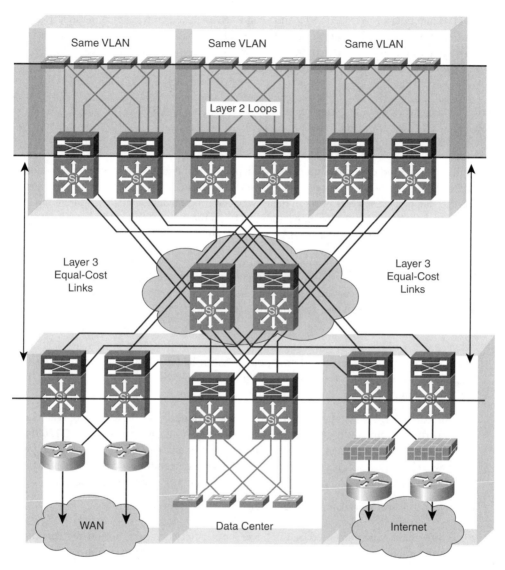

Figure 3-30 *Avoiding Spanning Layer 2 Domain in an Enterprise Network*

In modern networks, a 50-second convergence time is usually not acceptable. For this reason, Rapid Spanning Tree is widely preferred over legacy 802.1D implementations. In networks where a large number of VLANs are configured over many switches, it might be necessary to group STP instances with MST Protocol. Most of the time, the same VLAN would not be configured over many switches. VLANs would be local to a floor, thus spanning across a limited number of switches. In this configuration, RSTP provides the best efficiency.

RSTP is far superior to 802.1D STP and even PVST+ from a convergence perspective. It greatly improves the restoration times for any VLAN that requires a topology convergence due to link up, and it also greatly improves the convergence time over BackboneFast for any indirect link failures.

Note   If a network includes other vendor switches, you should isolate the different STP domains with Layer 3 routing to avoid STP compatibility issues.

Even if the recommended design does not depend on STP to resolve link or node failure events, STP is required to protect against user-side loops. A loop can be introduced on the user-facing access layer ports in many ways. Wiring mistakes, misconfigured end stations, or malicious users can create a loop. STP is required to ensure a loop-free topology and to protect the rest of the network from problems created in the access layer.

Note   Some security personnel have recommended disabling STP at the network edge. This practice is not recommended because the risk of lost connectivity without STP is far greater than any STP information that might be revealed.

Spanning tree should be used and its topology controlled by root bridge manual designation. When the tree is created, use the STP toolkit to enhance the overall mechanism performances and reduce the time lost during topology changes.

To configure a VLAN instance to become the root bridge, enter the **spanning-tree vlan** *vlan_ID* **root** command to modify the bridge priority from the default value (32768) to a significantly lower value. Manually placing the primary and secondary bridges along with enabling STP toolkit options enables you to support a deterministic configuration where you know which ports should be forwarding and which ports should be blocking.

Figure 3-31 illustrates recommended placements for STP toolkit features:

- Loop guard is implemented on the Layer 2 ports between distribution switches and on the uplink ports from the access switches to the distribution switches.

- Root guard is configured on the distribution switch ports facing the access switches.

- UplinkFast is implemented on the uplink ports from the access switches to the distribution switches.

- BPDU guard or root guard is configured on ports from the access switches to the end devices, as is PortFast.

- The UDLD protocol enables devices to monitor the physical configuration of the cables and detect when a unidirectional link exists. When a unidirectional link is detected, UDLD shuts down the affected LAN port. UDLD is often configured on ports linking switches.

■ Depending on the security requirements of an organization, the port security feature can be used to restrict a port's ingress traffic by limiting the MAC addresses that are allowed to send traffic into the port.

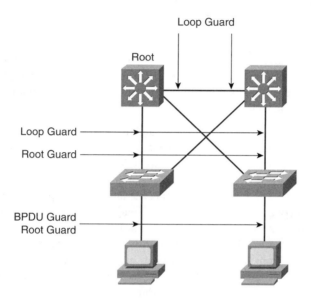

Figure 3-31 *STP Toolkit Recommendation*

Troubleshooting STP

Bridging loops generally characterize STP problems. Troubleshooting STP involves identifying and preventing such loops.

The primary function of STP is to prevent loops created by redundant links in bridged networks. STP operates at Layer 2 of the OSI model. STP fails in specific cases, such as hardware or software anomalies. Troubleshooting these situations is typically difficult depending on the design of the network.

Potential STP Problems

The following subsections highlight common network conditions that lead to STP problems:

■ Duplex mismatch

■ Unidirectional link failure

- Frame corruption

- Resource errors

- PortFast configuration error

- Inappropriate STP diameter parameter tuning

Duplex Mismatch

Duplex mismatch on point-to-point links is a common configuration error. Duplex mismatch occurs specifically when one side of the link is manually configured as full duplex and the other side is using the default configuration for auto-negotiation. Such a configuration leads to duplex mismatch.

The worst-case scenario for a duplex mismatch is when a bridge that is sending BPDUs is configured for half duplex on a link while its peer is configured for full duplex. In Figure 3-32, the duplex mismatch on the link between Switch A and Switch B could potentially lead to a bridging loop. Because Switch B is configured for full duplex, it starts forwarding frames even if Switch A is already using the link. This is a problem for Switch A, which detects a collision and runs the back-off algorithm before attempting another transmission of its frame. If there is enough traffic from Switch B to Switch A, every packet (including the BPDUs) sent by Switch A is deferred or has a collision and is subsequently dropped. From an STP point of view, because Switch B no longer receives BPDUs from Switch A, it assumes the root bridge is no longer present. Consequently, Switch B moves its port to Switch C into the forwarding state, creating a Layer 2 loop.

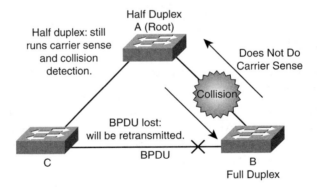

Figure 3-32   *Duplex Mismatch*

Unidirectional Link Failure

A unidirectional link is a frequent cause for a bridging loop. An undetected failure on a fiber link or a problem with a transceiver usually causes unidirectional links. With STP enabled to provide redundancy, any condition that results in a link maintaining a physical link connected status on both link partners but operating in a one-way communication state is detrimental to network stability because it could lead to bridging loops and routing black holes. Figure 3-33 shows such an example of a unidirectional link failure affecting STP.

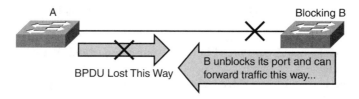

Figure 3-33   *Unidirectional Link Failure*

The link between Switch A and Switch B is unidirectional and drops traffic from Switch A to Switch B while transmitting traffic from Switch B to Switch A. Suppose, however, that the interface on Switch B should be blocking. An interface blocks only if it receives BPDUs from a bridge that has a better priority. In this case, all the BPDUs coming from Switch A are lost, and Switch B eventually moves to the forwarding state, creating a loop. Note that in this case, if the failure exists at startup, STP does not converge correctly. In addition, rebooting of the bridges has absolutely no effect on this scenario.

To resolve this problem, configure aggressive mode UDLD to detect incorrect cabling or unidirectional links and automatically put the affected port in err-disable state. The general recommended practice is to use aggressive mode UDLD on all point-to-point interfaces in any multilayer switched network.

Frame Corruption

Frame corruption is another cause for STP failure. If an interface is experiencing a high rate of physical errors, the result may be lost BPDUs, which may lead to an interface in the blocking state moving to the forwarding state. However, this case is rare because STP default parameters are conservative. The blocking port needs to miss consecutive BPDUs for 50 seconds before transitioning to the forwarding state. In addition, any single BPDU that is successfully received by the switch breaks the loop. This case is more common for nondefault STP parameters and aggressive STP timer values. Frame corruption is generally a result of a duplex mismatch, bad cable, or incorrect cable length.

Resource Errors

Even on high-end switches that perform most of their switching functions in hardware with specialized application-specific integrated circuits (ASIC), STP is performed by the CPU (software-based). This means that if the CPU of the bridge is over-utilized for any reason, it might lack the resources to send out BPDUs. STP is generally not a processor-intensive application and has priority over other processes; therefore, a resource problem is unlikely to arise. However, you need to exercise caution when multiple VLANs in PVST+ mode exist. Consult the product documentation for the recommended number of VLANs and STP instances on any specific Catalyst switch to avoid exhausting resources.

PortFast Configuration Error

As discussed in the previous "PortFast" section, the PortFast feature, when enabled on a port, bypasses the listening and learning states of STP, and the port transitions to the forwarding mode on linkup. The fast transition can lead to bridging loops if configured on incorrect ports.

In Figure 3-34, Switch A has Port p1 in the forwarding state and Port p2 configured for PortFast. Device B is a hub. Port p2 goes to forwarding and creates a loop between p1 and p2 as soon as the second cable plugs in to Switch A. The loop ceases as soon as p1 or p2 receives a BPDU that transitions one of these two ports into blocking mode. The problem with this type of transient loop condition is that if the looping traffic is intensive, the bridge might have trouble successfully sending the BPDU that stops the loop. The BPDU Guard prevents this type of event from occurring.

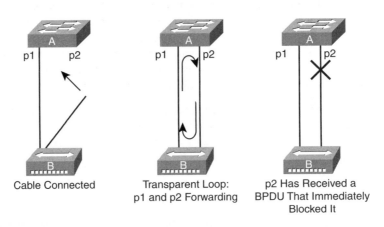

Cable Connected   Transparent Loop: p2 Has Received a
                         p1 and p2 Forwarding   BPDU That Immediately
                                                    Blocked It

Figure 3-34 *PortFast Configuration Error*

Troubleshooting Methodology

Troubleshooting STP issues can be difficult if logical troubleshooting procedures are not deployed in advance. Occasionally, rebooting of the switches might resolve the problem temporarily, but without determining the underlying cause of the problem, the problem is likely to return.

The following steps provide a general overview of a methodology for troubleshooting STP:

Step 1.   Develop a plan.

Step 2.   Isolate the cause and correct an STP problem.

Step 3.   Document findings.

The following subsections explain the approach to troubleshooting Layer 2 bridging loops in more detail.

Develop a Plan

It is critical to develop a plan of action for potential STP issues. To create a plan, you must understand the following basic characteristics of your network:

- Topology of the bridged network

- Location of the root bridge

- Location of the blocked ports and, therefore, the redundant links

Knowing the basic characteristics is essential in troubleshooting any Layer 2 issue. In addition, knowledge of the network helps to focus attention on the critical ports on key devices, because most of the STP troubleshooting steps simply involve using **show** commands to identify error conditions. Knowing which links on each device is redundant helps to quickly stop a bridging loop by disabling those links.

Isolate the Cause and Correct an STP Problem

If there is a STP loop in your network, follow these steps:

Step 1.   Identify a bridging loop.

Step 2.   Restore connectivity.

Step 3.   Check the port status.

Step 4.   Check for resource errors.

Step 5.   Disable unneeded features.

Identify a Bridging Loop

The best way to identify a bridging loop is to capture the traffic on a saturated link and to determine whether duplicate packets are propagating. If all users in a specific bridging domain have connectivity issues at the same time, a bridging loop is a possible cause. Check the port utilization on devices and look for abnormal values. In addition, you might see other protocols break down due to the bridging loops. For example, HSRP might complain of duplicate IP addresses if a loop causes it to see its own packets. Another common message during a loop is constant flapping of MAC addresses between interfaces. In a stable network, MAC addresses do not flap. In addition, be careful not to associate a bridging loop with a packet storm caused by another anomalous event such as an Internet worm or virus.

Restore Connectivity

Bridging loops have severe consequences on a bridged network. Administrators generally do not have time to look for the cause of a loop, however, preferring to restore connectivity as soon as possible and identify potential issues later. Restoring connectivity consists of the following two actions:

- **Breaking the loop:** A simple solution is to manually disable every port that is providing redundancy in the network. Identify the part of the network that is more affected and start disabling ports in that area. If possible, start by disabling ports that should be in the blocking state. Check to see whether network connectivity is restored while disabling one port at a time.

■   **Logging events:** If it is not possible to identify the source of the problem or if the problem is transient, enable logging and increase the logging level of STP events on the switches experiencing the failure. At a minimum, enable logging on switches with blocked ports because the transition of a blocked port to forwarding state creates the loop.

To log detailed events or to identify STP problems, use debug commands on Cisco IOS–based Catalyst switches. Debugging commands, if used with care, can help identify the source of the problem.

Use the following command to enable STP debugging:

`debug spanning-tree events`

Example 3-19 shows sample debug output for spanning-tree events.

Use the following command from global configuration mode to capture debug information into the logging buffer of a Catalyst switch.

`logging buffered`

Example 3-19   *Spanning-Tree Events Debug on Cisco IOS–Based Catalyst Switches*

```
Switch# debug spanning-tree events
Spanning Tree event debugging is on
Switch#
*Mar  5 21:23:14.994: STP: VLAN0013 sent Topology Change Notice on Gi0/3
*Mar  5 21:23:14.994: STP: VLAN0014 sent Topology Change Notice on Gi0/4
*Mar  5 21:23:14.994: STP: VLAN0051 sent Topology Change Notice on Po3
*Mar  5 21:23:14.994: STP: VLAN0052 sent Topology Change Notice on Po4
*Mar  5 21:23:15.982: %LINEPROTO-5-UPDOWN: Line protocol on Interface Giga-
bitEthernet0/1, changed state to down
*Mar  5 21:23:16.958: STP: VLAN0001 Topology Change rcvd on Po1
```

Note   When troubleshooting an IP subnet that spans multiple switches, it might be efficient to check the syslog server to collectively look at all the switches' logged messages. However, if loss of network connectivity to the syslog server occurs, not all messages might be available.

Check Port Status

Investigate the blocking ports first and then the other ports. The following are several guidelines for troubleshooting port status:

- **Blocked ports:** Check to make sure the switch reports receiving BPDUs periodically on root and blocked ports. Issue the following command on Cisco IOS–based Catalyst switches to display the number of BPDUs received on each interface:

```
show spanning-tree vlan vlan-id detail
```

  Issue the command multiple times to determine whether the device is receiving BPDUs.

- **Duplex mismatch:** To look for a duplex mismatch, check on each side of a point-to-point link. Simply use the **show interface** command to check the speed and duplex status of the specified ports.

- **Port utilization:** An overloaded interface may fail to transmit vital BPDUs and is also an indication of a possible bridging loop. Use the **show interface** command to determine interface utilization using the load of the interface and packet input and output rates.

- **Frame corruption:** Look for increases in the input error fields of the **show interface** command.

Look for Resource Errors

High CPU utilization can lead to network instability for switches running STP. Use the **show processes cpu** command to check whether the CPU utilization is approaching 100 percent. Cisco Catalyst switches prioritize control packets such as BPDU over any lower-priority traffic; hence, the switch would be stable with higher CPU if it were just processing low-priority traffic. As a general rule of thumb, if the CPU exceeds 70 percent, action should be taken to rectify any problem or to consider re-architecting the network to prevent any potential future problems.

Disable Unneeded Features

Disabling as many features as possible reduces troubleshooting complexity. EtherChannel, for example, is a feature that bundles several different links into a single logical port. It might be helpful to disable this feature while troubleshooting. In general, simplifying the network configuration reduces the troubleshooting effort. If configuration changes are made during the troubleshooting effort, note the changes. An alternative way is to save the configuration by maintaining a copy of the configuring in bootflash or on a TFTP server. After the root cause is found and fixed, the removed configurations can be easily reapplied.

Document Findings

When the STP issue is isolated and resolved, it is important to document any learnings from the incident as part of improving the plan for future issues. Not documenting any configuration or network design changes to the previous plan might result in difficulty troubleshooting during the next STP issue. Documentation of the network is critical for eventual up time of the business. Significant amounts of outages can be prevented by planning ahead. In some cases, some links can be disabled to break the loop without impacting the business during business hours, and troubleshooting can be performed after-hours. Without clear documentation, the network will begin to affect all critical functions, and as network administrators, it is critical to have the proper documentation to reduce the time to stabilize the network. Documentation includes the IP addresses of all the devices, passwords, root and the secondary root, and the proper configuration of all switch to switch or switch to router links. Also, knowing the network topology diagram with port number information can help determine quickly how the problem is manifested in the network. Having known good configuration is also essential to recover the network quickly.

Summary

The Spanning Tree Protocol is a fundamental protocol to prevent Layer 2 loops and at the same time provide redundancy in the network. This chapter covered the basic operation and configuration of RSTP and MST. Enhancements now enable STP to converge more quickly and run more efficiently.

- RSTP provides faster convergence than 802.1D when topology changes occur.

- RSTP enables several additional port roles to increase the overall mechanism's efficiency.

- **show spanning-tree** is the main family of commands used to verify RSTP operations.

- MST reduces the encumbrance of PVRST+ by allowing a single instance of spanning tree to run for multiple VLANs.

The Cisco STP enhancements provide robustness and resiliency to the protocol. These enhancements add availability to the multilayer switched network. These enhancements not only isolate bridging loops but also prevent bridging loops from occurring.

To protect STP operations, several features are available that control the way BPDUs are sent and received:

- BPDU guard protects the operation of STP on PortFast-configured ports.

- BPDU filter is a variant that prevents BPDUs from being sent and received while leaving the port in forwarding state.

- Root guard prevents root switch being elected via BPDUs received on a root-guard-configured port.

- Loop guard detects and disables an interface with Layer 2 unidirectional connectivity, protecting the network from anomalous STP conditions.

- UDLD detects and disables an interface with unidirectional connectivity, protecting the network from anomalous STP conditions.

- In most implementations, the STP toolkit should be used in combination with additional features, such as Flex Links.

Spanning Tree Protocol troubleshooting is achieved with careful planning and documentation before the problem and following a set of logical troubleshooting steps to identify and correct the problem. The troubleshooting exercise needs to be completed with documenting findings and making appropriate changes to the planning document.

References

Cisco Spanning Tree Protocol Configuration Guide:
http://www.cisco.com/en/US/docs/switches/lan/catalyst6500/ios/12.2SX/configuration/guide/spantree.html.

Cisco Optional STP Features Configuration Guide:
http://www.cisco.com/en/US/docs/switches/lan/catalyst6500/ios/12.2SX/configuration/guide/stp_enha.html.

Review Questions

Use the questions here to review what you learned in this chapter. The correct answers are found in Appendix A, "Answers to Chapter Review Questions."

1. True or False: MST is always preferred if you have more than a single VLAN.

2. True or False: Secondary root bridges have a lower bridge priority than primary root bridges.

3. Which one of the following is the best bridge priority configuration for a spanning-tree root switch?

   a. 0

   b. 1

   c. 4096

   d. 8192

   e. 65536

4. What command is used to configure a distribution switch as the primary root of a spanning tree?

   a. **spanning-tree vlan** *vlan-id* **primary**

   b. **spanning-tree vlan** *vlan-id* **root primary**

   c. **spanning-tree root primary**

   d. **spanning-tree bridge root**

   e. None of the above

5. How many operational states does RSTP have?

   a. 1

   b. 2

   c. 3

   d. 4

   e. None of the above

6. What is a typical convergence time in network topology of just two directly connected RSTP-enabled switches?

   a. 15 seconds

   b. 50 seconds

   c. 20 seconds

   d. 2 seconds

   e. <1 second

7. What is the default message interval for BPDUs in RSTP mode?

   a. 1 second

   b. 15 seconds

   c. 20 seconds

   d. 2 seconds

   e. <1 second

8. True or False: Enabling PortFast is recommended on all ports to improve STP convergence.

9. Upon which one of the following features does the BPDU Guard depend?

   a. PortFast

   b. BPDU filtering

   c. UplinkFast

   d. Root Guard

10. How does the Root Guard feature recover from the root-inconsistent state?

    a. Automatically when the port stops receiving superior BPDUs

    b. Automatically when the port stops receiving inferior BPDUs

    c. Using an err-disable timeout mechanism

    d. Manual shutdown/no shutdown of the port

    e. Reload of the switch

11. BPDU filtering should be enabled only on ports connected to which of the following devices?

    a. Hosts

    b. Routers

    c. Switches

    d. Hubs

12. Select an activity that is not a recommended step in troubleshooting STP issues and Layer 2 loops.

    a. Identifying the loop

    b. Restoring connectivity

    c. Rebooting the root switch or secondary root switch

    d. Checking for bad hardware

    e. Checking for port errors

13. Which command is used to collect debugging data regarding STP events on Catalyst switches?

    a. **logging spanning-tree events**

    b. **logging events spanning-tree**

    c. **debug stp events**

    d. **debug spanning-tree events**

    e. None of the above

Chapter 4

Implementing Inter-VLAN Routing

This chapter covers the following topics:

- Describing Inter-VLAN Routing

- Configuring Inter-VLAN Routing

- Implementing Dynamic Host Configuration Protocol in a Multilayer Switched Environment

- Deploying CEF-Based Multilayer Switching

Network topologies generally associate VLANs with individual networks or subnetworks. However, network devices in different VLANs cannot communicate with each other without a Layer 3 switch or a router to forward traffic between the VLANs. The initial VLAN design recommends that each VLAN is associated with a different subnet as a best practice, therefore inter-VLAN routing is required to route traffic between VLANs. Cisco provides several solutions to enable inter-VLAN routing. Many Catalyst switches have integrated Layer 3 routing capabilities using hardware switching to achieve line-rate performance. In addition, several families of switches use Layer 3 modules to provide inter-VLAN routing.

This chapter discusses the advantages and disadvantages of different methods of inter-VLAN routing. In addition, it discusses how to plan, implement, and verify inter-VLAN routing using a variety of methods. This chapter also discusses how to configure and implement Dynamic Host Configuration Host (DHCP). Finally, it mentions how a multilayer switch forwards Layer 3 traffic using CEF. CEF is one of the Cisco methods of switches. This chapter goes into detail on how CEF builds and utilizes hardware tables to perform multilayer switching.

Upon completing this chapter, you will be able to implement inter-VLAN routing in a campus network. This ability includes being able to meet these objectives:

■   Given an enterprise network, design, plan, implement, and verify inter-VLAN routing using an external router or a multilayer switch, using either switch virtual interfaces or routed interfaces.

■   Understand DHCP operation and its implementation and verification in given enterprise network.

■   Implement and verify Cisco Express Forwarding (CEF) on a Cisco Catalyst multilayer switch.

Describing Inter-VLAN Routing

Following the recommendation from Campus design, the distribution and Collapsed Core switches always have many VLANs terminating to these switches. Switches at the distribution layer, or in a collapsed core, will almost certainly have multiple VLANs connected to them. A switch with multiple VLANs requires a means of passing Layer 3 traffic to communicate between those VLANs.

This section describes the process and the various methods of routing traffic from VLAN to VLAN. A router that is external to the Layer 2 switch hosting the VLANs can perform inter-VLAN routing. In addition, Cisco Catalyst multilayer switch can be used to perform both intra-VLAN frame forwarding and inter-VLAN routing.

This section focuses on how to perform inter-VLAN packet transfer using an external router and a multilayer switch. These sections focus on the following objectives:

■   Introduction to inter-VLAN routing

■   Inter-VLAN routing with an external router

■   Inter-VLAN routing with switch virtual interfaces

■   Routing with routed ports

Introduction to Inter-VLAN Routing

Because VLANs isolate traffic to a defined broadcast domain and subnet, network devices in different VLANs cannot communicate with each other natively. As shown in Figure 4-1, the devices in different VLANs cannot communicate without any Layer 3 device. The devices in each VLAN can communicate to the network devices in another VLAN only through a Layer 3 routing device, referred to as an inter-VLAN router (see Figure 4-2). Cisco recommends the implementation of routing in the distribution or core switches of the multilayer switched network to terminate local VLANs. This helps to isolate network problems and to prevent them from affecting the campus backbone. In addition, packet manipulation and control of the traffic across VLANs is simplified by routing in the distribution layer instead of the core layer.

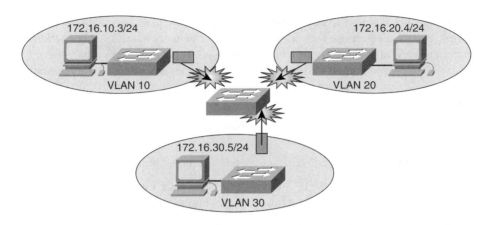

Figure 4-1 *VLAN Isolation*

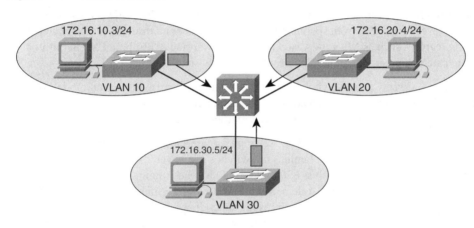

Figure 4-2 *Inter-VLAN Routing*

The following devices can provide inter-VLAN routing:

■   Any Layer 3 multilayer Catalyst switch

■   Any external router with an interface that supports trunking (router-on-a-stick)

■   Any external router or group of routers with a separate interface in each VLAN

Note   Adding an external router with an individual interface in each VLAN is a nonscal-able solution, especially when between 20 and 50 VLANs exist in the network. In addition, adding an external router for inter-VLAN routing on trunk interfaces does not scale beyond 50 VLANs. This chapter discusses only using Layer 3 switches and external routers with trunk interfaces (router-on-a-stick) to route VLANs. Furthermore, Cisco IOS routers support trunking in specific Cisco IOS Software feature sets, such as the IP Plus Feature set. Refer to the documentation on Cisco.com for software requirements before deploying inter-VLAN routing on Cisco IOS routers.

Router-on-a-stick is simple to implement because routers are usually available in every network, but most enterprise networks use multilayer switches to achieve high packet-processing rates using hardware switching. In addition, Layer 3 switches usually have packet-switching throughputs in the millions of packets per second (pps), whereas traditional general-purpose routers provide packet switching in the range of 100,000 pps to more than 1 million pps.

All the Catalyst multilayer switches support three different types of Layer 3 interfaces:

- **Routed port:** A pure Layer 3 interface similar to a routed port on a Cisco IOS router.

- **Switch virtual interface (SVI):** A virtual VLAN interface for inter-VLAN routing. In other words, SVIs are the virtual routed VLAN interfaces.

- **Bridge virtual interface (BVI):** A Layer 3 virtual bridging interface.

Because of high-performance switches such as the Catalyst 6500 and Catalyst 4500, almost every function, from spanning tree to routing, is done through hardware switching using features such as MLS and Cisco Express Forwarding (CEF)-based MLS, both of which are discussed in detail in later sections of this chapter.

All Layer 3 Cisco Catalyst switches support routing protocols, but several models of Catalyst switches require enhanced software for specific routing protocol features. Table 4-1 lists the Catalyst switches and their capabilities to support Layer 3.

Catalyst switches use different default settings for interfaces. For example, all members of the Catalyst 3550 and 4500 families of switches use Layer 2 interfaces by default, whereas members of the Catalyst 6500 family of switches running Cisco IOS use Layer 3 interfaces by default. Recall that default interface configurations do not appear in the running or startup configuration. As a result, depending on which Catalyst family of switches is used, the **switchport** or **no switchport** command might be present in the running-config or startup-config files.

Note   As mentioned in previous chapters, the default configurations do not appear in the running or start-up config. For some Cisco switches, the **switchport** command is the default config and for others the **no switchport** command is the default config.

Inter-VLAN Routing Using an External Router (Router-on-a-Stick)

If a switch supports multiple VLANs but has no Layer 3 capability to route packets between those VLANs, the switch must be connected to a device external to the switch that possesses this capability. That device is normally a router, although it could be a multilayer switch (discussed in later subsections). This setup is not a high performance solution but it is quite simple. It just needs a single trunk link between the switch and the router. This single physical link should be Fast Ethernet or greater, although 802.1Q is supported on some new router 10-Mb Ethernet interfaces.

Table 4-1   *Cisco Catalyst Switches with Inter-VLAN Routing Support*

Type of Switch	Inter-VLAN Routing Capability	Inter-VLAN Routing Solution
Catalyst 2940/2950/2955/2960/2970	No	Not applicable
Catalyst 3560/3750/3760	Yes	Integrated
Catalyst 4000/4500/4948	Yes	Catalyst 4000 running Cisco CatOS with Supervisor I or II, using the Layer 3 module, WS-X4232-L3 Catalyst 4000 with a Supervisor II+, III, IV, or V running Cisco IOS using integrated routing
Catalyst 6500	Yes	Catalyst 6500 with an MSFC, MSFC II, or MSFC III daughter card running Cisco CatOS on the supervisors and Cisco IOS on the MSFC Catalyst 6500 with MSFC, MSFC II, or MSFC III running Cisco Native IOS Catalyst 6500 using a legacy MSM module

Figure 4-3 shows a configuration where the router is connected to a core switch using a single 802.1Q trunk link. This configuration is commonly referred to as router-on-a-stick. The router can receive packets on one VLAN, for example on VLAN 10, and forward them to another VLAN, for example on VLAN 20. To support 802.1Q trunking, subdivide the physical router interface into multiple, logical, addressable interfaces, one per VLAN. The resulting logical interfaces are called subinterfaces.

Assume that client PC-1 needs to send traffic to server PC-2, as shown in Figure 4-4. Because the hosts are on different VLANs, transferring this traffic requires a Layer 3 device. In this example, an external router connects to the switch via an 802.1Q trunk—a router-on-a-stick.

Table 4-2 describes the actions necessary for traffic to be routed between VLANs using an external router, as illustrated in Figure 4-4.

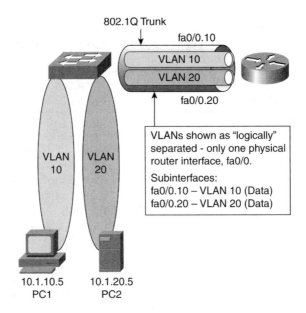

Figure 4-3   *Inter-VLAN Routing Using External Router*

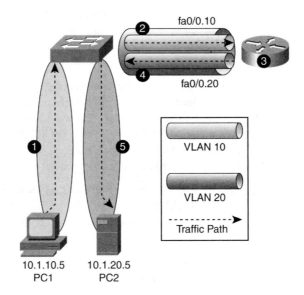

Figure 4-4   *Router-on-a-Stick Forwarding Path*

Table 4-2   *Router-on-a-Stick Forwarding Path Steps*

Step	Action
1	The frame is transmitted by the source device and enters the switch where it is associated with a specific VLAN.
2	The switch determines (from the destination MAC address) that the frame must be forwarded across a trunk link. It adds an 802.1Q tag to the frame header and forwards to the router.
3	Based on the 802.1Q tag received, the router accepts the packets from VLAN10 on its subinterface in that VLAN. The router performs Layer 3 processing based on the destination network address. Because the destination network is associated with a VLAN accessed over the trunk link, the router adds the appropriate 802.1Q tag to the frame header.
4	The router then routes the packet out the appropriate subinterface on VLAN20.
5	The switch removes the 802.1Q tag from the frame. The switch determines from the destination MAC address that the frame will be transmitted through an access mode port in VLAN 20, so the frame is transmitted as an untagged Ethernet frame.

External Router: Advantages and Disadvantages

Every method of inter-VLAN routing has it advantages and disadvantages. The following are the advantage of the router-on-a-stick method:

■ It works with any switch that supports VLANs and trunking because Layer 3 services are not required on the switch. Many switches do not contain Layer 3 forwarding capability, especially switches used at the access layer of a hierarchical network, as listed in Table 4-1. If using Local VLANs, mostly none of the switches at the access layer have Layer 3 forwarding capability. Depending on the network design, it might be possible to have no Layer 3-capable switches at all.

■ The implementation is simple. Only one switch port and one router interface require configuration. If the switch enables all VLANs to cross the trunk (the default), it literally takes only a few commands to configure the switch.

■ The router provides communication between VLANs. If the network design includes only Layer 2 switches, this makes the design and troubleshooting traffic flow simply because only one place in the network exists where VLANs inter-connect.

The following are some of the disadvantages of using the external router for inter-VLAN routing:

- The router is a single point of failure.

- A single traffic path may become congested. With a router-on-a-stick model, the trunk link is limited by the speed of the router interface shared across all trunked VLANs. Depending on the size of the network, the amount of inter-VLAN traffic, and the speed of the router interface, congestion could result with this design.

- Latency might be higher as frames leave and re-enter the switch chassis multiple times and the router makes software-based routing decisions. Latency increases any time traffic must flow between devices. Additionally, routers make routing decisions in software, which always incurs a greater latency penalty than switching with hardware.

Inter-VLAN Routing Using Switch Virtual Interfaces

In the early days of switched networks, switching was fast (often at hardware speed) and routing was slow (routing had to be processed in software). This prompted network designers to extend the switched part of the network as much as possible. Access, distribution, and core layers were often partly configured to communicate at Layer 2. This architecture is referred as switched, as shown in Figure 4-5. This topology created loop issues. To solve these issues, spanning-tree technologies were used to prevent loops while still enabling flexibility and redundancy in inter-switch connections.

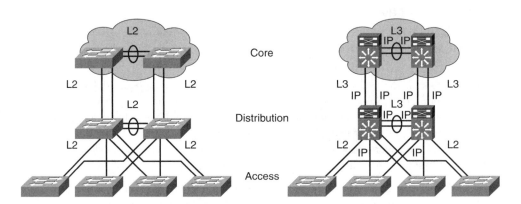

Figure 4-5 *Routed Versus Switched Campus Architecture*

As network technologies evolved, routing became faster and cheaper. Today, routing can be performed at hardware speed. One consequence of this evolution is that routing can be brought down to the core and the distribution layers without impacting network performance. As many users are in separate VLANs, and as each VLAN is usually a separate subnet, it is logical to configure the distribution switches as Layer 3 gateways for the users of each access switch VLAN. This implies that each distribution switch must have IP addresses matching each access switch VLAN. This architecture is referred to as routed, as shown in Figure 4-5.

As reflected in Figure 4-5, between the distribution and the core layer, implement Layer 3 ports instead of L2. Because dynamic routing protocols can dynamically adapt to any change in the network topology, this new topology also eliminates Layer 2 loops. Between access and distribution switches, where Layer 2 connections remain, FlexLink technology can be used to activate only one link at a time or Layer 2 EtherChannel can be used, thus removing the risk of loops and the need for spanning tree.

An SVI is a virtual interface configured within a multilayer switch compared to external router configuration where the trunk is needed, as shown in Figure 4-6. An SVI can be created for any VLAN that exists on the switch, as illustrated in Figure 4-6. Only one VLAN associates with one SVI. An SVI is "virtual" in that there is no physical port dedicated to the interface, yet it can perform the same functions for the VLAN as a router interface would and can be configured in much the same way as a router interface (IP address, inbound/outbound ACLs, and so on). The SVI for the VLAN provides Layer 3 processing for packets to or from all switch ports associated with that VLAN.

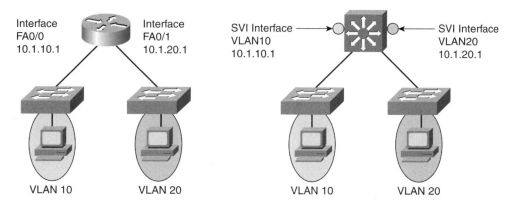

Figure 4-6   *SVI Versus External Router*

By default, an SVI is created for the default VLAN (VLAN1) to permit remote switch administration. Additional SVIs must be explicitly created. SVIs are created the first time the VLAN interface configuration mode is entered for a particular VLAN SVI (for instance, when the command interface vlan ## is entered). The VLAN number used corresponds to the VLAN tag associated with data frames on an 802.1Q encapsulated trunk or to the VLAN ID (VID) configured for an access port. For instance, if creating an SVI as a gateway for VLAN 10, name the SVI interface VLAN 10. Configure and assign an IP address to each VLAN SVI that is to route traffic off of and onto a VLAN.

Whenever the SVI is created, make sure that particular VLAN is present in the VLAN database manually or learned via VTP. As shown in Figure 4-6, the switch should have VLAN 10 and VLAN 20 present in the VLAN database; otherwise, the SVI interface will stay down.

The following are some of the reasons to configure SVI:

■   To provide a gateway for a VLAN so that traffic can be routed into or out of that VLAN

■   To provide fallback bridging if it is required for nonroutable protocols

Note   Using fallback bridging, non-IP packets can be forwarded across the routed interfaces. This book focuses only on inter-VLAN routing, so only IP connectivity is discussed.

■   To provide Layer 3 IP connectivity to the switch

■   To support routing protocol and bridging configurations

SVI: Advantages and Disadvantages

The following are some of the advantage of SVI:

■   It is much faster than router-on-a-stick because everything is hardware switched and routed.

■   No need for external links from the switch to the router for routing.

■   Not limited to one link., Layer 2 EtherChannels can be used between the switches to get more bandwidth.

■   Latency is much lower because it doesn't need to leave the switch.

The following are some of the disadvantages:

■   It needs a Layer 3 switch to perform Inter-VLAN routing, which is more expensive.

Routing with Routed Ports

A routed port is a physical port that acts similarly to a port on a traditional router with Layer 3 addresses configured. Unlike an access port, a routed port is not associated with a particular VLAN. A routed port behaves like a regular router interface. Also, because Layer 2 functionality has been removed, Layer 2 protocols, such as STP and VTP, do not function on a routed interface. However, protocols such as LACP, which can be used to build either Layer 2 or Layer 3 EtherChannel bundles, would still function at Layer 3.

Note   Routed interfaces don't support subinterfaces as with Cisco IOS routers.

Routed ports are used for point-to-point links; connecting WAN routers and security devices are examples of the use of routed ports. In the campus switched network, routed ports are mostly configured between the switches in the campus backbone and between switches in the campus backbone and building distribution switches if Layer 3 routing is applied in the distribution layer. Figure 4-7 illustrates an example of routed ports for point-to-point links in a campus switched network.

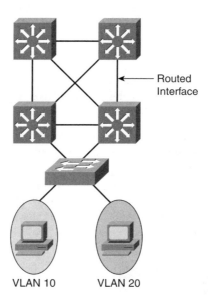

Figure 4-7   *Inter-VLAN Routing with Routed Ports*

To configure routed ports, make sure to configure the respective interface as a Layer 3 interface using the **no switchport** interface command, if the default configurations of the interfaces are Layer 2 interfaces as with the Catalyst 3560 family of switches. In addition, assign an IP address and other Layer 3 parameters as necessary. After assigning the IP address, make certain that IP routing is globally enabled and that applicable routing protocols are configured.

The number of routed ports and SVIs that can be configured on a switch is not limited by software. However, the interrelationship between these interfaces and other features configured on the switch may overload the CPU due to hardware limitations, so a network engineer should fully consider these limits before configuring these features on numerous interfaces.

Routed Port: Advantage and Disadvantages

Following are some of the advantages of routed ports:

■   A multilayer switch can have SVI and routed ports in a single switch.

■   Multilayer switches forward either Layer 2 or Layer 3 traffic in hardware, so it helps to do routing faster.

L2 EtherChannel Versus L3 EtherChannel

The EtherChannel technology is available to bundle ports of the same type. On a Layer 2 switch, EtherChannel can aggregate access ports such as servers that support EtherChannel or trunk links to connect switches. As each EtherChannel link is seen as one logical connection, ports that are member of an EtherChannel can load balance traffic on all the links that are up.

On Layer 3 switches, switched ports can be converted to routed ports. These ports do not perform switching at Layer 2 anymore, but become Layer 3 ports similar to those found on router platforms. Routed Layer 3 ports can also form EtherChannel just like Layer 2.

On a multilayer switch, it is easy to configure Layer 2 EtherChannels or Layer 3 EtherChannels, depending on what type of devices connect and depending on their position in the network. The configuration requires that ports on both sides are configured the same way: switch ports (access or trunk) or routed ports. As shown in Figure 4-8, the bottom switch is Layer 2-only because it is an access switch, so Layer 2 EtherChannel is configured. At the distribution or the core layer, where Layer 3 links are recommended, Layer 3 EtherChannels are configured.

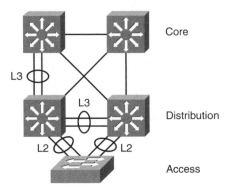

Figure 4-8   *Layer 2 Versus Layer 3 EtherChannel*

Configuring Inter-VLAN Routing

This section focuses on the configuration of Inter-VLAN routing using various methods. The following are some of the configurations discussed in this section:

■   Inter-VLAN configuration with external router

■   Inter-VLAN configuration with SVI

■   Routing configuration with routed ports

■   Verifying and troubleshooting inter-VLAN routing

■   Layer 3 EtherChannel configuration

■   Routing protocol configuration

Inter-VLAN Configuration with External Router

Before implementing inter-VLAN routing, a network engineer should plan the steps necessary to make it successful.

Implementation Planning

Prior planning can help reduce any problems during the installation by logically organizing the steps necessary and providing checkpoints and verification, as necessary. Following are the key points to plan the implementation for the external router configuration method:

■ You need to know how many VLANs need routing and their VLAN_Ids. In addition, know what ports connect to the router.

■ A router interface providing inter-VLAN routing on a trunk link must be configured with a subinterface for each VLAN for which it will perform routing. Each subinterface on the physical link must then be configured with the same trunk encapsulation protocol. That protocol, usually 802.1Q (many Cisco switches also support the ISL protocol, but it is considered legacy technology), must match the encapsulation type configured on the switch side of the link, so you need to know the type of encapsulation.

■ Make sure to have the same native VLAN on both devices. Because traffic on the native VLAN is not tagged, all native VLAN frames will be received as untagged Ethernet frames. Beginning with Cisco IOS version 12.1(3)T, the creation of a subinterface for the native VLAN is allowed. If the native VLAN is configured as a subinterface, the command **encapsulation dot1q** *<vlan>* **native** is used. With older IOS versions, the physical interface is configured as the gateway for the native VLAN, with no encapsulation command—just an IP address. All other, non-native VLANs have an 802.1Q tag inserted into their frames. These non-native VLANs are configured as subinterfaces on the router, and the VLANs must be defined as using 802.1Q encapsulation, with the VLAN associated with them being identified. The subinterface command **encapsulation dot1q** *vlan* accomplishes this task.

Note   The subinterface number of the slot/port number configuration is arbitrary and does not need to match the encapsulation configuration. However, to make configuration easily readable, configure the subinterface ID number as the VLAN ID number.

Because a switch port defined as a trunk forwards all Ethernet VLANs by default, no configuration is required on the switch for the non-native VLANs. Additional configuration might exist if the trunk is configured to enable only some VLANs to use the trunk, but the figure assumes the default behavior.

To configure inter-VLAN routing using router-on-a-stick, perform the following steps:

Step 1.   Enable trunking on the switch port connecting to the router. (Refer to Chapter 2, "Implementing VLANs in Campus Networks" for details on configuring trunking on multilayer switches.)

Step 2.   Enable the router interface by issuing the **no shutdown** interface command on the router.

```
router(config)# interface interface_id
router(config-if)# no shutdown
```

Step 3.   On the router, create the subinterfaces for each VLAN that requires inter-VLAN routing.

```
router(config)# interface interface_id slot/port.subinterface
```

Step 4.   On the router, configure the trunking encapsulation and IP address on the subinterfaces corresponding to the VLANs.

```
router(config-subif)# encapsulation [dot1Q | isl] vlan-id {native}
router(config-subif)# ip address ip_address subnet_mask
```

Note   The **encapsulation dot1Q 1 native** command was introduced in Cisco IOS version 12.1(3)T. The **native** keyword indicates the native VLAN. Recall from Chapter 2 that Cisco switches and routers do not tag the native VLAN. The alternative method of configuring the native VLAN is to configure the Layer 3 properties, such as the IP address, on the main interface rather than on the subinterface.

Example 4-1 shows an example of configuring inter-VLAN routing between VLAN 1 and VLAN 2 on an external router on the interface FastEthernet0/0 and a Catalyst switch running Cisco IOS on interface FastEthernet 4/2. Configuration of a router is followed by the switch configuration to configure an interface as a trunk port.

Note   In Example 4-1, VLAN 100 is used as native VLAN because this security best practice for switching is to use a dummy/unused VLAN for native VLAN.

Example 4-1   *Inter-VLAN Routing Using External Router*

```
Router(config)# interface FastEthernet0/0
Router(config-if)#no shutdown
Router(config)# interface FastEthernet 0/0.1
Router(config-subif) description VLAN 1
Router(config-subif)# encapsulation dot1Q 1 native
Router(config-subif)# ip address 10.1.1.1 255.255.255.0
Router(config-subif)# exit
Router(config)# interface FastEthernet 0/0.2
```

```
Router(config-subif)# description VLAN 2
Router(config-subif)# encapsulation dot1Q 2
Router(config-subif)# ip address 10.2.2.1 255.255.255.0
Router(config-subif)# exit
Router(config)# end
#####Cisco IOS switch Trunking Configuration Connected to Interface
FastEthernet0/0
switch(config)# interface FastEthernet 4/2
switch(config-if)# switchport trunk encapsulation dot1q
switch(config-if)# switchport mode trunk
switch(config-if)# end
```

Inter-VLAN Configuration with SVI

Implementation Plan

As previously discussed, before implementing inter-VLAN routing on a multilayer switch, a network engineer should plan the steps necessary to make it successful. Prior planning can help prevent any problems during the installation by logically organizing the necessary steps and providing checkpoints and verification, as necessary:

- The first step is to identify the VLANs that require a Layer 3 gateway within the multilayer switch. It is possible that not all VLANs will require the capability to reach other VLANs within the enterprise. For example, a company might have a VLAN in use in an R&D laboratory. The network designer determines that this VLAN should not have connectivity with other VLANs in the enterprise or to the Internet. However, the R&D VLAN is not a local VLAN but spans the switch fabric due to the presence of an R&D server in the data center, so it cannot simply be pruned from the trunk between the multilayer switch and the R&D lab switch. Such a VLAN might be configured without a Layer 3 gateway as one way of ensuring the desired segregation.

- If a VLAN that is to be routed by an SVI interface does not already exist on the multilayer switch, it must be created. Then create the SVI interface for each VLAN that needs to be routed within the multilayer switch.

- Find out what protocols needs to be configured on the SVI; for example, IP and such. Assuming the enterprise uses only IP as a routed protocol, a network engineer would then configure each SVI interface with an appropriate IP address and mask. Following this, the SVI interface needs to be enabled using the **no shutdown** interface command.

- If SVIs are used to provide Layer 3 forwarding services to their assigned VLAN (as opposed to only giving those VLANs the capability to reach the switch), all routed protocols in use in the enterprise must have their routing function enabled within the multilayer switch. (Layer 3 routing is not enabled by default in a multilayer switch.)

- Depending on the size of the network and the design provided by the network architect, the multilayer switch might need to exchange dynamic routing protocol updates with one or more other routing devices in the network. A network engineer must determine whether this need exists, and if so, configure an appropriate dynamic routing protocol on the multilayer switch. The choice of protocol may be specified by the network designer, or the choice may be left to the network engineer.

■   Finally, after carefully considering the network structure, a network engineer can decide to exclude certain switchports from contributing to the SVI line-state up-and-down calculation. Any such switchports would be configured with the autostate exclude feature. Autostate is discussed more in the "SVI Autostate" section.

Note   In addition, the number of VLANs and SVIs supported per Catalyst family is not always the same. For example, a switch can support 256 VLANs but only 64 SVIs (routed VLAN interfaces). Refer to Chapter 2 for details about the number of VLANs supported per Catalyst switch, and always refer to product release notes for the latest details about the number of VLANs and SVIs supported per Catalyst family of switch.

Switch Virtual Interface Configuration

To configure an SVI for inter-VLAN routing on a Catalyst switch, such as the Catalyst 6000 Series, perform these steps:

Step 1.   Specify an SVI by using a VLAN interface command:

```
Switch(config)# interface vlan vlan-id
```

Step 2.   Assign an IP address to the VLAN:

```
Switch(config-if)#ip address ip_address subnetmask
```

Step 3.   Enable the interface:

```
Switch(config-if) #no shutdown
```

Step 4.   (Optional.) Enable IP routing on the router:

```
Switch(config) #ip routing
```

Step 5.   (Optional.) Specify an IP routing protocol or use static routes:

```
Switch(config)# router ip_routing_protocol options
```

Note   A routing protocol is only needed to communicate the VLANs subnets to other routers and is not essential to route between the SVIs on the same device, because SVIs are seen as connected interfaces.

Figure 4-9 shows a multilayer switch providing inter-VLAN routing for VLAN 10 and VLAN 20.

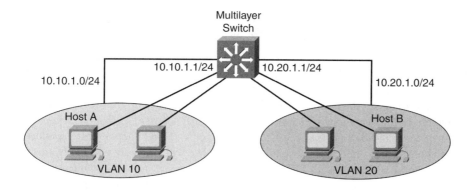

Figure 4-9 *Inter-VLAN Routing with SVI Configuration*

Example 4-2 shows the configuration of IP routing on a Catalyst 3560 by creating VLAN interfaces and assigning IP addresses and subnet masks to the interfaces. In addition, RIP is enabled as the routing protocol.

Example 4-2 *Inter-VLAN Routing Using SVIs*

```
Switch# configure terminal
Enter configuration commands, one per line.  End with CNTL/Z.
Switch(config)# ip routing
Switch(config)# router rip
Switch(config-router)# network 10.0.0.0
Switch(config)# interface vlan 10
Switch(config-if)# ip address 10.10.1.1 255.0.0.0
Switch(config-if)# no shutdown
Switch(config-if)# interface vlan 20
Switch(config-if)# ip address 10.20.1.1 255.255.255.0
Switch(config-if)# no shutdown
```

SVI Autostate

By default, when SVI is created and enabled, the line state of an SVI with multiple ports on a VLAN is in the up state when it meets these conditions:

- The VLAN exists and is active in the VLAN database on the switch.

- The VLAN interface exists and is not administratively down.

- At least one Layer 2 (access or trunk) port exists on the switch, has a link in the up state on this VLAN, and is in the spanning-tree forwarding state on the VLAN.

The SVI interface is up when one Layer 2 port in that VLAN is in spanning-tree forwarding mode. When a VLAN has multiple ports, the default action is to take the SVI down as soon as all the ports belonging in the VLAN go down. This feature helps minimize problems such as routing black holes, which happens when a routing protocol uses VLAN interfaces and misinterprets a VLAN interface as fully operational if there is no interface up in that VLAN.

In some cases, when a port connects to some monitoring equipment and intrusion prevention sensors, the port stays up because it is only connected to the monitoring equipment. and because of that the VLAN interface stays up. The monitoring ports are not used for activating any data transfers like host ports, and it stays up most of the time. The switchport **autostate exclude** commands help in that scenario so that the VLAN goes down when all other ports in the VLAN (those connected to active hosts) go down except the ones configured with **autostate exclude**. The SVI autostate exclude feature configures a port so that it is not included in the SVI line-state up-and-down calculation and the SVI interface goes down if all others ports in that VLAN goes down, even if the ports configured with this feature stayed up. A network engineer would therefore need to carefully consider the implications of activating this feature on a trunk link.

To configure a Layer 2 switchport for **autostate exclude**, follow these two steps:

Step 1.   Select an interface for configuration:

```
Switch(config)# interface interface_id
```

Step 2.   Exclude the access port/trunk in defining the status of an SVI (up or down). This command would commonly be used for ports used for monitoring, for instance, so that a monitoring port did not cause the SVI to remain up when no other ports are active in the VLAN:

```
Switch(config-if)# switchport autostate exclude
```

Configuring Routed Port on a Multilayer Switch

To configure routed ports, make sure to configure the respective interface as a Layer 3 interface using the **no switchport** interface command, if the default configurations of the interfaces are Layer 2 interfaces as with the Catalyst 3560 family of switches. In addition, assign an IP address and other Layer 3 parameters as necessary. The rest of the steps are similar, as mentioned in the configuration of Inter-VLAN routing using SVI.

Note   Entering the **no switchport** interface configuration command shuts down the interface and then reenables it, which might generate messages on the device to which the interface is connected. When you use this command to put the interface into Layer 3 mode, you delete any Layer 2 characteristics configured on the interface.

To configure the routed ports, follow the following steps:

Step 1.   Select the interface for configuration:

```
Switch(config)# interface interface_id
```

Step 2.   Convert this port from a physical Layer 2 port to a physical Layer 3 interface:

```
Switch(config)# no switchport
```

Step 3.   Configure the IP address and IP subnet mask. This address will be used by hosts on the segment connected to this interface for communication to the switch on this interface, or as the default gateway to other networks:

```
Switch(config-if)# ip address ip_address subnet_mask
```

Step 4.   Enable the switch interface:

```
Switch(config-if)# no shutdown
```

Step 4.   (Optional.) Enable IP routing on the router:

```
Switch(config)# ip routing
```

Step 5.   (Optional.) Specify an IP routing protocol or use static routes:

```
Switch(config)# router ip_routing_protocol options
```

Example 4-3 illustrates the configuration of routed ports for a Catalyst 3560 switch running Cisco IOS. In this example, if the port is a Layer 2 port, the switch returns an error message upon attempted configuration.

Example 4-3   *Configuration of Routed Ports in Cisco IOS*

```
Core(config)# interface GigabitEthernet 1/1
Core(Coreonfig-if)# no switchport
Core(config-if)# ip address 10.10.1.1 255.255.255.252
Core(config-if)# exit
Core(config)# interface GigabitEthernet 1/2
Core(config-if)# ip address 10.20.1.254 255.255.255.252
% IP addresses may not be configured on L2 links.
Core(config-if)# no switchport
Core(config-if)# ip address 10.20.1.254 255.255.255.252
```

Verifying Inter-VLAN Routing

This subsection focuses on commands used to verify configuration of InterVLAN routing. The verification commands are similar across any inter-VLAN routing methods. The following commands are useful to inter-VLAN routing verifications:

- **show ip interface** *interface_type_port | svi_number*

- **show interface** *interface_type_port | svi_number*

- **show running interface** *type_port | svi_number*

- **ping**

- **show vlan**

- **show interface trunk**

Note   The **show vlan** and **show interface trunk** commands are covered in Chapter 2.

The **show interfaces** command can be used to display the interface IP address configuration and status of a port. The interface can be used for SVI interface status, EtherChannel interface status, or a port status and its configuration. Example 4-4 shows the output of the **show interfaces vlan** command.

Example 4-4   show interface *Command for Inter-VLAN Verification*

```
Switch# show interfaces vlan 20
Vlan20 is up, line protocol is up
Hardware is Ethernet SVI, address is 00D.588F.B604 (bia 00D.588F.B604)
Internet address is 10.1.20.1/24
MTU 1500 bytes, BW 1000000 Kbit, DLY 10 usec,
reliability 255/255, txload 1/255, rxload 1/255
Encapsulation ARPA, loopback not set
ARP type: ARPA, ARP Timeout 04:00:00
Last input never, output never, output hang never
Last clearing of "show interface" counters never
Input queue: 0/75/0/0 (size/max/drops/flushes); Total output drops: 0
Queueing strategy: fifo
Output queue: 0/40 (size/max)
5 minute input rate 0 bits/sec, 0 packets/sec
5 minute output rate 0 bits/sec, 0 packets/sec
0 packets input, 0 bytes, 0 no buffer
Received 0 broadcasts, 0 runts, 0 giants, 0 throttles
0 input errors, 0 CRC, 0 frame, 0 overrun, 0 ignored
0 packets output, 0 bytes, 0 underruns
0 output errors, 0 interface resets
0 output buffer failures, 0 output buffers swapped out
```

In Example 4-4, the SVI interface for VLAN 20 shows a status of up/up because at least one port is active in VLAN 20. Note that the hardware is reported as Ethernet SVI indicating the virtual nature of the interface. The remainder of the output is similar to what would be seen on any router interface.

The **show running-config** command can be used to display the interface configuration of a Layer 3 routed interface. In Example 4-5, the interface is configured as a Layer 3 routed interface, as evident by the disabling of Layer 2 functionality through use of the **no switchport** command. Recall that the 30-bit mask means two IP addresses exist in that subnet, which means the switch interfaces might be connecting to only a single external device on this subnet, such as a router or firewall.

Example 4-5   show running-config *Command*

```
Switch# show running-config interface FastEthernet 2/8
Building configuration...
!
interface FastEthernet2/8
   no switchport
   ip address 172.16.22.2 255.255.255.252<output omitted>
```

In addition to this, the network administrator can use the **show ip interface** command to check and verify the IP properties configured on the ports.

As shown in Example 4-6, interface fasthethernet0/24 is a routed port with the IP address 10.1.10.1.

Example 4-6   show ip interface *Command*

```
switch# show ip interface fastethernet0/24
FastEthernet0/24 is up, line protocol is up
   Internet address is 10.1.10.1/24
   Broadcast address is 255.255.255.255
   Address determined by setup command
   MTU is 1500 bytes
   Helper address is not set
   Directed broadcast forwarding is disabled
   Multicast reserved groups joined: 224.0.0.10
   Outgoing access list is not set
   Inbound  access list is not set
   Proxy ARP is enabled
   Local Proxy ARP is disabled
   Security level is default
   Split horizon is enabled
   ICMP redirects are always sent
   ICMP unreachables are always sent
   ICMP mask replies are never sent
   IP fast switching is enabled
   IP CEF switching is enabled
```

After the router is properly configured and is connected to the network, it can communicate with other nodes on the network. To test IP connectivity to hosts, use the **ping** command.

Troubleshooting Inter-VLAN Problems

To troubleshoot inter-VLAN routing issues, the following are some checkpoint implementations:

■ Correct VLANs on switches and trunks.

■ Correct routes.

■ Correct primary and secondary root bridges.

■ Correct IP address and subnet masks.

Table 4-3 lists the common problems that can be seen during Inter-VLAN routing configuration.

Table 4-3 *Common Inter-VLAN Routing Problems*

Problem	Possible Cause
Missing VLAN	VLAN might not be defined across all the switches. VLAN might not be enabled on the trunk ports. Ports might not be in the right VLANs.
Layer 3 interface misconfiguration	Virtual interface might have the wrong IP address or subnet mask. Virtual interface might not be up. Virtual interface number might not be match with the VLAN number. Routing has to be enabled to route frames between VLAN. Routing might not be enabled.
Routing protocol misconfiguration	Every interface or network needs to be added in the routing protocol. The new interface might not be added to the routing protocol. Routing protocol configuration is needed only if VLAN subnets needs to communicate to the other routers, as previously mentioned in this chapter.
Host misconfiguration	Host might not have the right ip or subnetmask. Each host has to have the default gateway that is the SVI or Layer 3 interface to communicate the other networks and VLAN. Host might not be configured with the default gateway.

Note   You need to know on a particular VLAN that the IP addresses should be taken from the range used for the subnet/VLAN and that the mask should match; otherwise, the host and SVI—even though in the same VLAN—might not able to communicate because they are in the different networks.

To plan how to troubleshoot the inter-VLAN problems, you need to first understand the implementation and design layout of the topology before starting the troubleshooting. The following subsection discusses the example of a troubleshooting plan.

Example of a Troubleshooting Plan

A company XYZ adding a new floor to the current network and based on this the current requirements are to make sure the users on the new floor 5 can communicate with users on other floors. The current issue is that users on floor 5 cannot communicate with user on the other floor. Following is the example of the implementation plan to install a new VLAN for their use and make sure it is routing to other VLANs.

Your implementation plan lists the following steps:

Step 1.   Create a new VLAN 500 on the fifth floor switch and on the distribution switches. Name it Accounting_dept.

Step 2.   Identify the ports needed for the users and switches. Set the **switchport access VLAN** command to 500 and make sure the trunk is configured using the configuration mentioned in Chapter 2 between the switches and VLAN 500 is allowed on the trunk.

Step 3.   Create an SVI interface on the distribution switches and make sure the IP address are assigned.

Step 4.   Verify connectivity.

The troubleshooting plan might look like this:

1.   If a new VLAN has been created:

   ■ Was the VLAN created on all the switches?

   ■ If VTP is configured, make sure VLANs are defined on the VTP server and are getting propagated across all the domains.

   ■ Verify with a **show vlan** command.

2.   Make sure ports are in the right VLAN and trunking is working as expected:

   ■ Did all access ports get the command **switchport access VLAN 510** added?

   ■ Were there any other ports that should have been added? If so, make those changes.

   ■ Were these ports previously used? If so, make sure there are no extra commands enabled on these ports that can cause conflicts. If not, is the port enabled?

   ■ Are the access ports set to switchport access and not trunks? If not, issue the command **switchport mode access.**

   ■ Are the trunk ports set to trunk mode and manually prune all the VLAN.

   ■ Is manual pruning of VLANs a possibility? If so, make sure that the trunks necessary to carry this VLAN traffic have the VLAN in the allowed statements.

3.   If SVI interfaces are created

   ■ Is the VLAN virtual interface already created with the correct IP address and subnet mask?

- Is it enabled?

- Is the routing enabled?

- Is this SVI added in the routing protocol

4. Verify connectivity.

    - Are all the links between the different switches on the path enabling this VLAN to be transported?

    - Are all the links between switches in trunk mode?

    - Is this VLANs allowed on all trunks?

    - Is spanning-tree blocking one of those links?

    - Are the ports enabled?

    - Does the host have the right default gateway assigned.

    - Also make sure the default route or some routing protocol is enabled if it needs to talk to other routers.

Configuration of Layer 3 EtherChannel

To configure Layer 3 EtherChannel, follow these steps for configuring and verifying a Layer 3 EtherChannel interface:

Step 1.   Create a virtual Layer 2 interface:

```
Switch(config)# interface port-channel 1
```

Step 2.   Change the interface to Layer 3 to enable the use of the IP address command:

```
Switch(config-if)# no switchport
```

Step 3.   Assign an IP address to the port-channel interface because this will be a Layer 3 interface:

```
Switch(config-if)# ip address ip_address subnet_mask
```

Step 4.   Navigate to the interface that is to be associated with the EtherChannel bundle:

```
Switch(config)# interface range interface_id portnumber_range
```

Step 5.   The independent Layer 2 and Layer 3 functionality of the port must be removed so that the port can function as part of a group. This step is important. On a Layer 3 switch, interfaces are by default in Layer 2 mode. If you set the port-channel interface to a layer and if the physical ports are in another mode (Layer 3), the EtherChannel will not form:

```
Switch(config-if-range)# no switchport
```

Step 6.   Assign all the physical interfaces in the range to the EtherChannel group. Make sure the channel mode is set up right on both sides. Depending on the mode, the EtherChannel can use lacp or pagp (as discussed in Chapter 2):

```
Switch(config-if-range) # channel-group channel-group-number mode
{auto [non-silent] | desirable [non-silent] | on} | {active | passive}
```

Note   It is important to match the EtherChannel configuration on both sides on the switches, and the IP addresses on the Portchannel Interfaces should be on the same subnets/VLAN to communicate.

Figure 4-10 shows a sample configuration for two switches using a Layer 3 EtherChannel bundle. The left switch has created a virtual interface with an IP address, and the physical interfaces are assigned to the matching channel-group number. The same is true with the right switch. Again, the virtual portchannel interfaces do not need to have the same number as any of the partner switches.

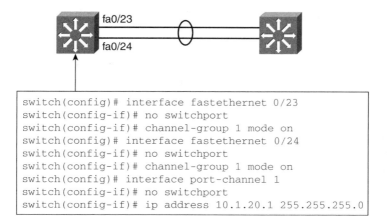

```
switch(config)# interface fastethernet 0/23
switch(config-if)# no switchport
switch(config-if)# channel-group 1 mode on
switch(config)# interface fastethernet 0/24
switch(config-if)# no switchport
switch(config-if)# channel-group 1 mode on
switch(config)# interface port-channel 1
switch(config-if)# no switchport
switch(config-if)# ip address 10.1.20.1 255.255.255.0
```

Figure 4-10   *Layer 3 EtherChannel Configuration*

As illustrated in Figure 4-10, the following guidelines are followed to create the Layer 3 EtherChannel:

■ **Speed and duplex:** Configure all interfaces in an EtherChannel to operate at the same speed and in the same duplex mode.

■ **Interface mode:** As the port-channel interface is a routed port, the **no switchport** command was applied to it. The physical interfaces are by default switched, which is a mode incompatible with a router port. This is why the **no switchport** command was also applied to the physical ports, to make their mode compatible with the EtherChannel interface mode.

- **Layer 3 configuration:** Ensure the two switches connected using Layer 3 EtherChannel are configured with the IP addresses belonging to the same VLAN subnet with the correct subnet mask.

- **Verifying the EtherChannel configuration:** After EtherChannel is configured, use the following commands to verify and troubleshoot EtherChannel:

- **show interface port-channel** *channel-group-number*

- **show etherChannel** *channel-group-number* **summary**

- **show spanning-tree vlan** *vlan-number* **detail**

Note   This chapter discusses only the configuration for Layer 3 port-channel. The concepts of EtherChannel and Layer 2 EtherChannel configuration is discussed in detail in Chapter 2.

Routing Protocol Configuration

As soon as a multilayer switch is configured with Layer 3 IP addresses, it starts behaving like a router in the sense that it has connections to different subnets. Communication between these subnets can no longer be achieved using Layer 2 protocols. A major difference between a multilayer switch and a router is that a multilayer switch does not route until some Layer 3 or SVI interfaces are created.

When routing is enabled, the network administrator configures static routes and dynamic routing, just like on a router, as shown in Figure 4-11. In Figure 4-11, EIGRP is configured. Notice the passive interface commands. On a Layer 3 switch, a common recommendation is to enable dynamic routing only on those interfaces that need to exchange routing information with neighbors.

Wherever needed, summarization should also be configured to limit the size of the routing tables.

Verifying Routing Protocol

To verify whether the routing protocol is working as expected, use the **show ip route** and **show ip protocol** commands.

On a Layer 3 switch, just like on a router, use the **show ip route** command to display which Layer 3 routes are known to the local multilayer switch, as shown in Example 4-7. Each route type is identified by a code D, for example, which means routes are learned via EIGRP. In Example 4-7, the 10.1.10.0/24 subnet is directly connected (which can be identified with the letter C at the left of the route); the other routes are known via EIGRP (which can be identified with the letter D at the left of the route).

Both 10.1.2.0/24 and 10.1.3.0/24 subnets are learned via 10.1.10.10. Their administrative distance is 90, and the cost to each of these networks is 28416. The link to 10.1.10.10

goes through the VLAN 10 interface. Notice that VLAN 10 here is the name of the SVI, the Layer 3 interface, through which the networks are reachable.

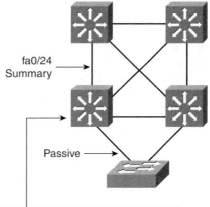

fa0/24
Summary

Passive

```
sw(config)# ip routing
sw(config)# router eigrp 100
sw(config-router)# no auto-summary
sw(config-router)# network 10.0.0.0
sw(config-router)# passive-interface default
sw(config-router)# no passive-interface fa0/24
sw(config)# interface f0/24
sw(config-if)# description Uplink
sw(config-if)# ip summary-address eigrp 100 10.1.0.0 255.255.240.0
```

Figure 4-11   *Routing Protocol Configuration*

Example 4-7   show ip route *Command*

```
switch# show ip route
Codes: C - connected, S - static, R - RIP, M - mobile, B - BGP
       D - EIGRP, EX - EIGRP external, O - OSPF,
       IA - OSPF inter area
       N1 - OSPF NSSA external type 1,
       N2 - OSPF NSSA external type 2
       E1 - OSPF external type 1, E2 - OSPF external type 2
       i - IS-IS, su - IS-IS summary, L1 - IS-IS level-1,
       L2 - IS-IS level-2
       ia - IS-IS inter area, * - candidate default,
       U - per-user static route
       o - ODR, P - periodic downloaded static route
Gateway of last resort is not set
     10.0.0.0/8 is variably subnetted, 13 subnets, 2 masks
D       10.1.3.0/24 [90/28416] via 10.1.10.10, 08:09:49, Vlan10
D       10.1.2.0/24 [90/28416] via 10.1.10.10, 08:09:49, Vlan10
C       10.1.10.0/24 is directly connected, Vlan10
```

The **show ip protocol** command shows information about the routing protocols that are enabled on the switch or router, as shown in Example 4-8.

Example 4-8   show ip protocol *Command*

```
Switch# show ip protocol
Routing Protocol is "eigrp 1"
  Outgoing update filter list for all interfaces is not set
  Incoming update filter list for all interfaces is not set
  Default networks flagged in outgoing updates
  Default networks accepted from incoming updates
  EIGRP metric weight K1=1, K2=0, K3=1, K4=0, K5=0
  EIGRP maximum hopcount 100
  EIGRP maximum metric variance 1
  Redistributing: eigrp 1
  Automatic network summarization is in effect
  Maximum path: 4
  Routing for Networks:
    10.0.0.0
  Passive Interface(s):
    Vlan1
    Vlan11
  Routing Information Sources:
    Gateway         Distance      Last Update
    10.100.117.202       90       20:25:10
    10.100.113.201       90       20:25:10
  Distance: internal 90 external 170
```

Implementing Dynamic Host Configuration Protocol in a Multilayer Switched Environment

As defined in RFC 2131, Dynamic Host Configuration Protocol (DHCP) provides configuration parameters to Internet hosts. DHCP consists of two components: a protocol for delivering host-specific configuration parameters from a DHCP server to a host, and a mechanism for allocating network addresses to hosts. DHCP is built on a client/server model in which designated DHCP server hosts allocate network addresses and deliver configuration parameters to dynamically configured hosts. By default, Cisco multilayer switches running Cisco IOS Software include DHCP server and relay agent software.

Distribution multilayer switches often act as Layer 3 gateways for clients connecting to the access switches on various VLANs. Therefore, the DHCP service can be provided directly by the distribution switches, as shown in Figure 4-12. Alternatively, DHCP services can be concentrated in an external, dedicated DHCP server, as also reflected in Figure 4-12. In that case, distribution switches need to redirect the incoming clients DHCP requests to the external DHCP server.

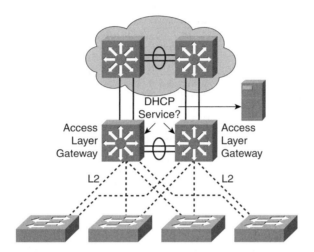

Figure 4-12   *DHCP in Campus Environment*

This section focuses on the following objectives:

■   DHCP operation

■   DHCP configuration and verification

DHCP Operation

Following are the steps that define the DHCP operation. Figure 4-13 illustrates the layout of the DHCP processs.

Step 1.   As illustrated in Figure 4-13, in the DHCP process, the client sends a DHCPDISCOVER broadcast message to locate a Cisco IOS DHCP server.

Step 2.   A DHCP server offers configuration parameters (such as an IP address, a MAC address, a domain name, and a lease for the IP address) to the client in a DHCPOFFER unicast message. A DHCP client might receive offers from multiple DHCP servers and can accept any one of the offers; however, the client usually accepts the first offer it receives. Additionally, the offer from the DHCP server is not a guarantee that the IP address will be allocated to the client; however, the server usually reserves the address until the client has had a chance to formally request the address.

Step 3.   The client returns a formal request for the offered IP address to the DHCP server in a DHCPREQUEST broadcast message.

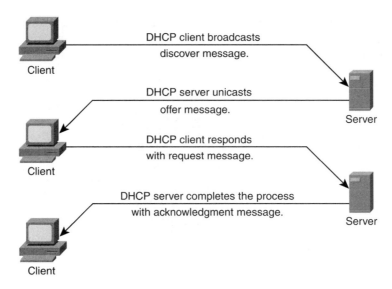

Figure 4-13   *DHCP Process*

Step 4.   The DHCP server confirms that the IP address has been allocated to the client by returning a DHCPACK unicast message to the client.

Configuring DHCP and Verifying DHCP

This subsection discusses the configuration and verification of DHCP. As previously discussed, the DHCP server can be configured on the router/multilayer switches or reside on the external server, and the multilayer switch or router can act as a DHCP relay agent.

Configure DHCP on the Multilayer Switch

To configure the DHCP service on a multilayer switch, follow these steps:

Step 1.   For DHCP configuration use the **ip dhcp pool** command, as shown in Figure 4-14.

Step 2.   Within the dhcp pool configuration submode, configure the network value, which indicates in which subnet should be the offered addresses. Additionally, also configure items such as default-gateway, lease duration, subnetmask, and DNS server IP addresses, and many others.

Step 3.   By default, the switch offers addresses taken from the whole range. To exclude some addresses, in global configuration mode, use the **ip dhcp excluded-address** command followed by the range of addresses to exclude from the DHCP offers. For a discontinuous address range, configure several ip dhcp excluded-addresses for each DHCP scope if needed.

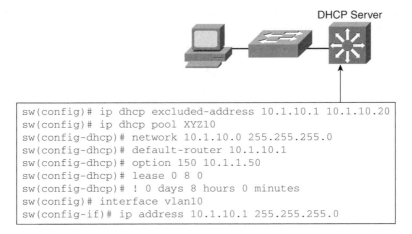

```
sw(config)# ip dhcp excluded-address 10.1.10.1 10.1.10.20
sw(config)# ip dhcp pool XYZ10
sw(config-dhcp)# network 10.1.10.0 255.255.255.0
sw(config-dhcp)# default-router 10.1.10.1
sw(config-dhcp)# option 150 10.1.1.50
sw(config-dhcp)# lease 0 8 0
sw(config-dhcp)# ! 0 days 8 hours 0 minutes
sw(config)# interface vlan10
sw(config-if)# ip address 10.1.10.1 255.255.255.0
```

Figure 4-14   *DHCP Configuration on the Router/Switch*

A last important point to notice is that a multilayer switch can only offer IP addresses for a subnet in which it has an IP address. In other words, the switch in Figure 4-14 could not offer IP addresses in a 10.1.10.0/24 subnet if the switch itself did not have a Layer 3 IP address in this subnet. After this Layer 3 address is configured, all devices connecting to the switch through this interface can request an IP address. If the Layer 3 interface is a router port, all devices connecting to this routed port can request a DHCP IP address. If the Layer 3 interface in an SVI, all devices in the SVI VLAN in this scenario VLAN 10 can request a DHCP IP address. Figure 4-14 shows the configuration of DHCP on the switch for VLAN 10 with subnet 10.1.10.0. With the DHCP request, it mentions the default gateway and lease information.

Configure DHCP Relay

DHCP is a client-server application, in which the DHCP client, usually a desktop computer, contacts a DHCP server for configuration parameters using a broadcast request. Today's enterprise networks consist of multiple VLANs, where inter-VLAN routing routes between the subnetworks. Because Layer 3 devices do not pass broadcasts by default, each subnet requires a DHCP server unless the routers are configured to forward the DHCP broadcast using the DHCP relay agent feature using **ip helper-address** command. The **ip helper-address** command not only forwards DHCP UDP packets but also forwards TFTP, DNS, Time, NetBIOS, name server, and BOOTP packets by default.

As illustrated in Figure 4-15, an **ip helper-address** command must be configured under the multilayer switch Layer 3 interface. This **ip helper-address** command points to the corporate DHCP server IP address. As shown in Figure 4-15, under VLAN 10, using **ip helper-address** command points to the DHCP server address 10.1.100.1.

When the switch receives a DHCP request broadcast message from a client, the switch forwards this request, as a unicast message, to the IP address specified under the **ip**

helper command. With this feature, the switch relays the dialog between the DHCP client and the DHCP server. When the switch receive the packets, it makes sure it assign an IP address only from the range of the subnet in which the client resides.

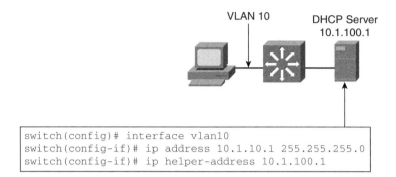

Figure 4-15   *Configuration of the IP Helper Address*

Verifying DHCP Operation

To verify the DHCP operation, use the following two commands:

■ **show ip dhcp binding**

■ **debug ip dhcp server packet**

Example 4-9 shows the output of the command **show ip dhcp** binding to find out the IP address assigned by the DHCP service on the switch and information regarding the IP addresses such as lease, MAC address, and so on.

Example 4-9   show ip dhcp binding *Command Output*

```
switch# show ip dhcp binding
Bindings from all pools not associated with VRF:
IP address    Client-ID/          Lease expiration      Type
              Hardware address/
              User name
10.1.10.21    0100.1bd5.132a.d2   Jun 25 2009 06:09 AM   Automatic
10.1.10.22    0100.4096.a46a.90   Jun 25 2009 09:40 AM   Automatic
10.1.10.23    0100.4096.aa98.95   Jun 25 2009 11:28 AM   Automatic
```

Example 4-10 shows the output of the debug command to verify the DHCP services on the switch. As illustrated, a client with mac-address 0100.1bd5.132a.d2 sends the request on VLAN 6. The DHCP server responds with the IP address 10.1.10.21, and then clients send the acceptance and DHCP services reply with the acknowledgment.

Example 4-10   debug dhcp *Command Output*

```
switch# debug ip dhcp server packet
DHCPD: DHCPDISCOVER received from client 0100.1bd5.132a.d2 on interface Vlan6.
DHCPD: Sending DHCPOFFER to client 0100.1bd5.132a.d2 (10.1.10.21).
DHCPD: broadcasting BOOTREPLY to client 001b.d513.2ad2.
DHCPD: DHCPREQUEST received from client 0100.1bd5.132a.d2.
DHCPD: Sending DHCPACK to client 0100.1bd5.132a.d2 (10.1.10.21).
DHCPD: broadcasting BOOTREPLY to client 001b.d513.2ad2.
```

Deploying CEF-Based Multilayer Switching

Layer 3 switching provides a wire-speed mechanism by which to route packets between VLANs using tables that store Layer 2 and Layer 3 forwarding information in the hardware.

CEF-based MLS is an efficient forwarding model of Layer 3 switching implemented on the latest generation of Cisco multilayer switches. CEF-based MLS is topology-based, where the control plane and data plane are separate. The control plane downloads the routing table information to the data plane for hardware switching. CEF uses a specific process to build forwarding tables in the hardware and then uses that table's information to forward packets at line speed. This section explains the mechanisms involved in Layer 2 and Layer 3 switching.

This section focuses on the following objectives:

■   Understand multilayer switching concepts and processing.

■   Describe the different switching methods that are available on a Cisco switch.

■   In a given enterprise environment describe, configure, and verify CEF on a Cisco switch.

Multilayer Switching Concepts

Traditionally, a switch makes forwarding decisions by looking at the Layer 2 header, whereas a router makes forwarding decisions by looking at the Layer 3 header.

A multilayer switch combines the functionality of a switch and a router into one device, thereby enabling the device to switch traffic when the source and destination are in the same VLAN and to route traffic when the source and destination are in different VLANs (that is, different subnets). A switch offloads a significant portion of the normal software-based routing process (packet rewrite) to hardware, so its Layer 3 forwarding process has also been termed switching, hence the term multilayer switching.

Layer 2 forwarding in hardware is based on the destination MAC address. The Layer 2 switch learns MAC address locations based on the source MAC address contained in incoming frames. The MAC address table lists MAC address and VLAN pairs with associated interfaces.

Layer 3 forwarding is based on the destination IP address. Layer 3 forwarding occurs when a packet is routed from a source in one subnet to a destination in another subnet. When a multilayer switch sees its own MAC address in the Layer 2 header, it recognizes that the packet is either destined for itself or has been sent to the switch so that it can act as a gateway toward the destination. If the packet is not destined for the multilayer switch, the destination IP address is compared against the Layer 3 forwarding table for the longest match. In addition, any router ACL checks are performed.

Traditionally, switches were handling Layer 2 frames at hardware speed, whereas routers were handling Layer 3 packets at software speed. Today, technology enables multilayer switches to route packets at hardware speed.

This subsection discusses the following topics:

- Explaining Layer 3 switch processing

- Distributed hardware forwarding

Explaining Layer 3 Switch Processing

Recall that a multilayer switch combines the functionality of a switch and a router into one device. Because a switch offloads a significant portion of the normal software-based routing process (packet rewrite) to the hardware, a multilayer switch processes more packets, faster than a traditional router by using specialized ASIC hardware instead of microprocessor-based engines.

Because Layer 3 switches provide both wire-speed Ethernet routing and switching services, they are optimized for the campus LAN or intranet and are generally preferred over traditional routers for routing within such an environment.

A Layer 3 switch performs three major functions:

- Packet switching

- Route processing

- Intelligent network services

The latter subsections discuss how the packets traverse through the multilayer switch.

Frame Rewrite

When packets transit through a router or multilayer switch, the following verifications must occur, as shown in Figure 4-16:

- The incoming frame checksum is verified to ensure that no frame corruption or alteration occurs during transit.

- The incoming IP header checksum is verified to ensure that no packet corruption or alteration occurs during transit.

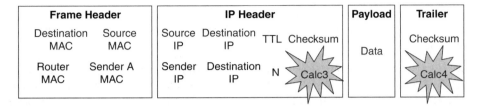

Figure 4-16 *Incoming Packet*

IP unicast packets are rewritten on the output interface, as illustrated in Figure 4-17 and described as follows:

- The destination MAC address changes from the router MAC address to the next-hop MAC address.

- The source MAC address changes from the sender MAC address to the outgoing router MAC address.

- The destination MAC address changes from the router MAC address to the next-hop MAC address.

- The TTL is decremented by one, and as a result, the IP header checksum is recalculated.

- The frame checksum must be recalculated.

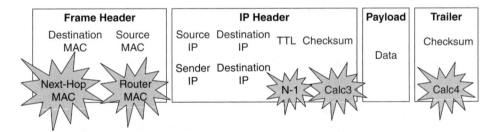

Figure 4-17 *Rewritten Packets*

The switch obtains the information needed for the frame rewriting process from internal tables such as CAM and TCAM tables. Some of these tables are cached in ASICs or RAM. These tables are covered in the following subsections.

CAM and TCAM Tables

This subsection describes the multilayer switching table architectures and how the CAM and TCAM tables are used.

Multilayer switches build routing, bridging, QoS, and ACL tables for centralized or distributed switching in hardware using high-speed memory tables. Switches perform lookups in these tables for result information, such as to determine whether a packet with a specific destination IP address is supposed to be dropped according to an ACL. These tables support high-performance lookups and search algorithms such that multilayer switches maintain line-rate performance.

Multilayer switches deploy these memory tables using specialized memory architectures, referred to as content addressable memory (CAM), and ternary content addressable memory (TCAM). CAM tables provide only two results: 0 (true) or 1 (false). CAM is most useful for building tables that search on exact matches such as MAC address tables. TCAM provides three results: 0, 1, and "don't care." TCAM is most useful for building tables for searching on the longest matches, such as IP routing tables organized by IP prefixes.

In addition, Catalyst switch architecture supports the capability to perform multiple lookups into multiple distinct CAM and TCAM regions in parallel. As a result of this capability to perform multiple lookups simultaneously, Catalyst switches do not suffer any performance degradation by enabling additional hardware-switching features such as QoS and IP ACL processing.

The following summarizes the tables:

- **CAM table:** The primary table used to make Layer 2 forwarding decisions. The table is built by recording the source MAC address and inbound port of all incoming frames. When a frame arrives at the switch with a destination MAC address of an entry in the CAM table, the frame is forwarded out through only the port that is associated with that specific MAC address.

- **TCAM table:** Stores ACL, QoS, and other information generally associated with Layer 3 and up layer processing.

Table lookups are performed with efficient search algorithms. A key is created to compare the frame to the table content. For example, the destination MAC address and VLAN ID (VID) of a frame would constitute the key for Layer 2 table lookup. This key is input into a hashing algorithm, which produces, as the output, a pointer into the table. The system uses the pointer to access a specific entry in the table, thus eliminating the need to search the entire table.

In specific high-end switch platforms, the TCAM is a portion of memory designed for rapid, hardware-based table lookups of Layer 3 and Layer 4 information. In the TCAM, a single lookup provides all Layer 2 and Layer 3 forwarding information for frames, including CAM and ACL information.

TCAM matching is based on three values: 0, 1, or x (where x is either number), hence the term *ternary*. The memory structure is broken into a series of patterns and associated masks.

In a Layer 2 table, all bits of all information are significant for frame forwarding (for example, VLANs destination MAC addresses and destination protocol types). However, in more complicated tables associated with upper-layer forwarding criteria, a full analysis might not be required; some bits of information might be too inconsequential to analyze.

For example, an ACL might require a match on the first 24 bits of an IP address but not concerned with the last 8 bits. This capability to "care" about only certain bits is a key factor to the lookup process for the TCAM table.

Figure 4-18 displays an example of the TCAM table that would be used by a CEF prefix lookup to make a routing decision. Because the entry searched for, 10.1.10.10, does not appear as a pattern in the TCAM table when all bits are compared, the search continues with the patterns and fall back where only the first 24 bits are compared that happen to be the next match in this case, resulting in a hit.

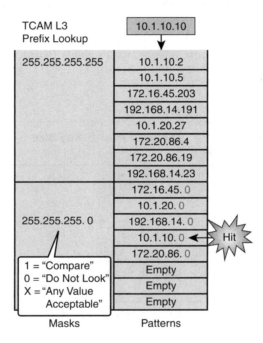

Figure 4-18 *TCAM Layout*

Although the figure uses an example of TCAM for routing lookups, the TCAM is also used to match patterns for QoS and ACLs (including VACLs), where multiple factors might be part of the input key, for example destination IP address and port number for an ACL entry.

Moreover, TCAM is divided into multiple protocol regions such as one region for ACL, one region for multicast, and one for IP-PREFIX, as shown in Table 4-4. TCAM also defines three different match options that correlate to specific match regions. These match regions are as follows:

■   **Exact-match region:** Consists of Layer 3 entries for regions such as IP adjacencies. IP adjacencies are the next-hop information (MAC address) for an IP address. Other examples of exact-match regions are Layer 2 switching tables and UDP flooding tables.

- **Longest-match region:** Consists of multiple "buckets" or groups of Layer 3 address entries organized in decreasing order by mask length. All entries within a bucket share the same mask value and key size. The buckets change their size dynamically by borrowing address entries from neighboring buckets. Although the size of the whole protocol region is fixed, as mentioned in Table 4-4, several platforms support configuration of the region size. For most platforms, the reconfigured size of the protocol region is effective only after the next system reboot.

- **First-match region:** Consists of regions that stop lookups after the first match of the entry. An example of when a first-match region is used is for ACL entries.

Table 4-4 illustrates the common protocol regions, lookup type, and key size found on Catalyst switches. The size of the regions and the ability to configure the region varies on each Catalyst switch family.

Table 4-4   *Common TCAM Protocol Regions*

Region Name	Cisco IOS Region Name	Lookup Type	Key Size	Sample Result
IP adjacency	ip-adjacency	Exact-match	32 bits	MAC address rewrite information
IP prefix	ip-prefix	Longest-match	32 bits	Next-hop routing information
IP multicast	ip-mcast	Longest-match	64 bits	Next-hop routing information
Layer 2 switching	l2-switching	Exact-match	64 bits	Destination interface and VLAN
UDP flooding	udp-flooding	Exact-match	64 bits	Next-hop routing or MAC address rewrite information
Access lists	access-list	First-match	128 bits	Permit, deny, or wildcard

Distributed Hardware Forwarding

In this subsection, the focus is on the concept of control and data planes.

Layer 3 switching software employs a distributed architecture in which the control path and data path are relatively independent. The control path code, such as routing protocols, runs on the route processor, whereas the Ethernet interface module and the switching fabric forward most of the data packets.

Figure 4-19 shows a distributed hardware forwarding overview.

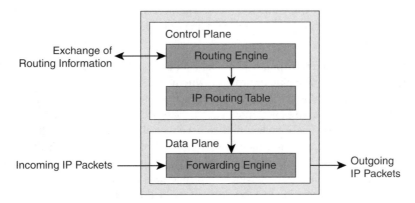

Figure 4-19   *Distributed Hardware Forwarding Overviews*

Each interface module includes a microcoded processor that handles all packet forwarding. Following are the main functions of the control layer between the routing protocol and the firmware datapath microcode:

■ Managing the internal data and control circuits for the packet-forwarding and control functions

■ Extracting the other routing and packet-forwarding-related control information from the Layer 2 and Layer 3 bridging and routing protocols and the configuration data, and then conveying the information to the interface module for control of the data path

■ Collecting the data path information, such as traffic statistics, from the interface module to the route processor

■ Handling certain data packets sent from the Ethernet interface modules to the route processor

Cisco Switching Methods

A Cisco router can use one of following three methods to forward packets:

■ **Process Switching:** In process switching, the router strips off the Layer 2 header for each incoming frame, looks up the Layer 3 destination network address in the routing table for each packet, and then sends the frame with rewritten Layer 2 header, including computed cyclical redundancy check (CRC), to the outgoing interface. All these operations are done by software running on the CPU for each individual frame. Process switching is the most CPU-intensive method available in Cisco routers. It can greatly degrade performance and is generally used only as a last resort or during troubleshooting.

- **Fast Switching:** After the lookup of the first packet destined for a particular IP network, the router initializes the fast-switching cache used by the Fast switching mode. When subsequent frames arrive, the destination is found in this fast-switching cache. The frame is rewritten with corresponding link addresses and is sent over the outgoing interface.

- **Cisco Express Forwarding (CEF):** The default-switching mode. CEF is less CPU-intensive than fast switching or process switching. A router with CEF enabled uses information from tables built by the CPU, such as the routing table and ARP table, to build hardware-based tables known as the Forwarding Information Base (FIB) and adjacency tables. These tables are then used to make hardware-based forwarding decisions for all frames in a data flow, even the first. Although CEF is the fastest switching mode, there are limitations, such as other features that are not compatible with CEF or rare instances in which CEF functions can actually degrade performance, such as CEF polarization in a topology using load-balanced Layer 3 paths.

This section discusses the multilayer switching forwarding methods.

A Layer 3 switch makes forwarding decisions using one of following two methods, which are platform-dependent:

- **Route caching:** Also known as flow-based or demand-based switching, a Layer 3 route cache is built within hardware functions as the switch sees traffic flow into the switch. This is functionally equivalent to Fast Switching in Router IOS.

- **Topology-based switching:** Information from the routing table is used to populate the route cache, regardless of traffic flow. The populated route cache is called the FIB. CEF is the facility that builds the FIB. CEF is discussed in more detailed in later sections. This is functionally equivalent to CEF in Router IOS.

Route Caching

For route caching to function, the destination MAC address of an incoming frame must be that of a switch interface with Layer 3 capability, either an SVI or routed interface. The first packet in a stream is switched in software by the route processor because no cache entry exists yet for the new flow. The forwarding decision that is made by the route processor is then programmed into a cache table (the hardware forwarding table), and all subsequent packets in the flow are switched in the hardware. Entries are only created in the hardware-forwarding table as the switch sees new traffic flows and will time out after they have been unused for a period of time. As shown in Figure 4-20, when the host sends its first packet the traffic goes through the router processor and then the route processor fills up the cache.

Because entries are created only in the hardware cache as flows are seen by the switch, route caching always forwards at least one packet in a flow using software, which is "slow" by comparison to CEF-based forwarding in which the routing table are already loaded in hardware.

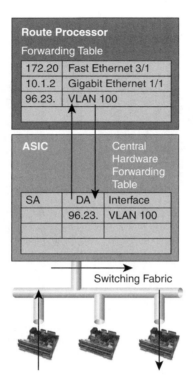

Figure 4-20   *Route Caching*

Topology-Based Switching

Layer 3 switching using topology-based switching is even faster than route caching. CEF uses information in the routing table to populate a route cache (known as a Forwarding Information Base [FIB]) without traffic flows being necessary to initiate the caching process.

Because this hardware FIB exists regardless of traffic flow, assuming a destination address has a route in the routing table, all packets that are part of a flow, even the first, will be forwarded by the hardware, as shown in Figure 4-21. Because of this increased performance, topology-based switching is currently the predominate method of switching versus route caching.

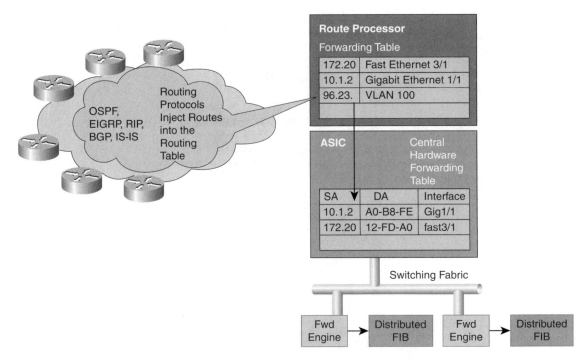

Figure 4-21   *Logical Topology-Based Switching*

CEF can occur at following two different locations on the switch:

- **Centralized switching:** Carries out forwarding decisions on a specialized ASIC that is central to all interfaces of a Layer 3 switch. With centralized switching, routing, ACL, QoS, and forwarding decisions are made on the supervisor engine in a modular chassis or by Layer 3 engines in fixed-port density Layer 3 switches. As a result, all frames to be routed or switched must pass through the centralized engine via a fabric or bus. Furthermore, with centralized switching, the hardware-switching performance of the Catalyst switch is based on the central forwarding engine and the fabric or bus architecture.

  Examples of Catalyst switches that are engineered for centralized switching are the Catalyst 4500 family of switches and the Catalyst 6500 family of switches without the use of Distributed Forwarding Cards (DFC).

- **Distributed switching:** Interfaces or line modules on Layer 3 switches handle forwarding decisions independently. With distributed switching, a centralized switching engine synchronizes Layer 3 forwarding, routing, and rewrite tables to local tables on distributed switching–capable modules. As a result, individual line cards or ports make forwarding decisions without the aid of the centralized switching engine; frames pass between ports directly across the fabric. In other words, switches using distributed switching place additional copies of the CEF FIB and adjacency table on line modules or interfaces for routing and switching of frames. System performance with distributed switching is equal to the aggregate of all forwarding engines. Distributed forwarding enables Catalyst switches to achieve rates of more than 100 million pps. The Catalyst 6500 supports distributed switching through the use of the Switch Fabric module or with a Supervisor 720 that has an integrated fabric and DFC line modules. The Catalyst 6500 maintains use of a centralized distributing switching engine even when using distributed switching–capable line modules for backward compatibility. Figure 4-21 presents the primary features that differentiate centralized switching from distributed switching.

CEF Processing

CEF uses special strategies to switch data packets to their destinations expediently. It caches the information generated by the Layer 3 routing engine even before the switch encounters any data flows. CEF caches routing information in one table (the FIB) and caches Layer 2 next-hop addresses and frame header rewrite information for all FIB entries in another table, called the adjacency table (AT), as shown in Figure 4-22.

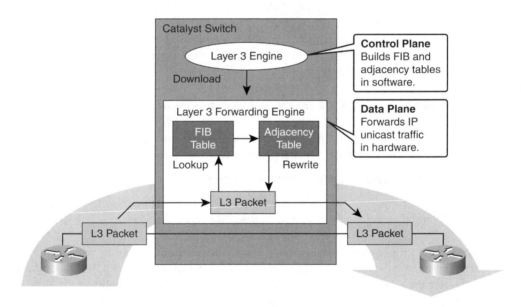

Figure 4-22 *CEF Operation*

As illustrated in Figure 4-22, CEF separates the control plane hardware from the data plane hardware and switching. ASICs in switches are used to separate the control plane and data plane, thereby achieving higher data throughput. The control plane is responsible for building the FIB table and adjacency tables in software. The data plane is responsible for forwarding IP unicast traffic using hardware.

The following is a summary of these tables:

■   **FIB:** Derived from the IP routing table and arranged for maximum lookup through-
    put. CEF IP destination prefixes are stored in the TCAM table, from the most-specific
    to the least-specific entry. The FIB lookup is based on the Layer 3 destination address
    prefix (longest match), so it matches the structure of CEF entries within the TCAM.
    When the CEF TCAM table is full, a wildcard entry redirects frames to the Layer 3
    engine. The FIB table is updated after each network change but only once and con-
    tains all known routes—there is no need to build a route-cache by central processing
    initial packets from each data flow. Each change in the IP routing table triggers a simi-
    lar change in the FIB table because it contains all next-hop addresses associated with
    all destination networks.

■   **AT:** The adjacency table is derived from the ARP table and contains Layer 2 header
    rewrite (MAC) information for each next hop contained in the FIB. Nodes in the net-
    work are said to be adjacent if they are within a single hop from each other. The adja-
    cency table maintains Layer 2 next-hop addresses and link-layer header information
    for all FIB entries. The adjacency table is populated as adjacencies are discovered.
    Each time an adjacency entry is created (such as through the ARP protocol), a link-
    layer header for that adjacent node is precomputed and stored in the adjacency table.
    When the adjacency table is full, a CEF TCAM table entry points to the Layer 3 en-
    gine to redirect the adjacency.

The following types of adjacencies exist for special processing:

■   **Punt adjacency:** Used for packets that require special handling by the Layer 3 engine
    or for features that are not yet supported by hardware switching.

■   **Drop or discard adjacency:** Used to drop ingress packets.

■   **Null adjacency:** Used to drop packets destined for a Null0 interface. The use of a
    Null0 interface is for access filtering of specific source IP packets.

Not all packets can be processed in the hardware. When traffic cannot be processed in
the hardware, it must receive software processing by the Layer 3 engine. This traffic does
not receive the benefit of expedited hardware-based forwarding. A number of different
packet types might force the Layer 3 engine to process them. Some examples of IP
exception packets follow:

■   Use IP header options (Packets that use TCP header options are switched in hardware
    because they do not affect the forwarding decision.)

■   Have an expiring IP Time-To-Live (TTL) counter

■   Are forwarded to a tunnel interface

■   Arrive with nonsupported encapsulation types

■   Are routed to an interface with nonsupported encapsulation types

- Exceed the maximum transmission unit (MTU) of an output interface and must be fragmented

- NAT

Some Cisco switches actually use different hardware to control the different planes. For example, the Cisco Catalyst 6500 is a modular switch that uses the Multilayer Switch Feature Card (MSFC) for control-plane operations, and the supervisor Policy Feature Card (PFC) for the data-plane operations.

CEF Operation and Use of TCAM

The following list details the characteristics of CEF operation and its use of the TCAM:

- Longest-match lookups in the FIB table are done for the Layer 3 destination address prefixes.

- CEF uses the IP routing table on the Layer 3 forwarding engine to build the FIB. Arrangement of the FIB is for maximum lookup throughput.

- CEF builds the adjacency table from the ARP table. The adjacency table contains Layer 2 rewrite (MAC) information for the next hop.

- FIB entries in the TCAM table are populated from the most specific to the least specific entry.

- Adjacency (rewrite) information and statistics are maintained by specialized components.

- CEF maintains one-to-one CEF-to-adjacency mappings for accurate statistics tracking.

- When the FIB table in TCAM is full, a wildcard entry redirects unmatched entries to the software switching Layer 3 forwarding engine.

- When the adjacency table in TCAM is full, an entry in the FIB table points to the Layer 3 forwarding engine to redirect the adjacency lookup.

- FIB and adjacency tables are dynamically updated when an ARP entry for a destination next hop changes, ages out, or is removed; the routing table changes; or next-hop rewrite information changes.

CEF Modes of Operation

As previously discussed in detail in the "Topology-Based Routing" section, CEF operates in one of two modes.

- **Central CEF mode:** The CEF FIB and adjacency tables reside on the route processor, and the route processor performs the express forwarding. Use this CEF mode when line cards are not available for CEF switching, or when features are not compatible with distributed CEF.

■   **Distributed Cisco Express Forwarding (dCEF) mode:** When dCEF is enabled, line cards maintain identical copies of the FIB and adjacency tables. The line cards can perform the express forwarding by themselves, relieving the main processor of involvement in the switching operation. dCEF uses an interprocess communications (IPC) mechanism to ensure synchronization of FIBs and adjacency tables on the route processor and line cards.

Address Resolution Protocol Throttling

An important feature of CEF-based Catalyst switches is Address Resolution Protocol (ARP) throttling; this feature requires explanation before CEF-based MLS is explored further. Make note that the ARP table builds the CEF adjacency table. This concept is explored in more detail throughout this chapter; however, it is important to consider when reading this section.

When a router is directly connected to a segment shared by multiple hosts such as Ethernet interfaces, the router maintains an additional prefix for the subnet. This subnet prefix points to a glean adjacency. When a router receives packets that need to be forwarded to a specific host, the adjacency database is gleaned for the specific prefix. If the prefix does not exist, the subnet prefix is consulted, and the glean adjacency indicates that any addresses within this range should be forwarded to the Layer 3 engine ARP processing.

One example where glean adjacencies are used is where a Catalyst switch receives a packet for which no rewrite information exists. To obtain rewrite information, the Layer 3 engine sends ARP requests to next hop to obtain the rewrite information. Catalyst switches using CEF-based MLS forward only the first several packets to the Layer 3 engine for new destinations without rewrite information. The switch installs a throttling adjacency such that the switch drops subsequent packets to the specific destination address in hardware until an ARP response is received. The switch removes the throttling adjacency when an ARP reply is received from the Layer 3 engine (and a complete rewrite adjacency is installed for the host). The switch removes the throttling adjacency if no ARP reply is seen within 2 seconds (to enable more packets through to the Layer 3 engine to reinitiate ARP). This relieves the Layer 3 engine from excessive ARP processing (or ARP-based denial-of-service [DoS] attacks).

Figure 4-23 shows an example of ARP throttling; an explanation of its stepwise behavior follows. Figure 4-23 depicts the Layer 3 forwarding engine and hardware switching forwarding engine as two separate hardware components for illustrative purposes.

ARP throttling consists of the following steps:

Step 1.   Host A sends a packet to Host B.

Step 2.   The switch forwards the packet to the Layer 3 engine based on the "glean" entry in the FIB.

Step 3.   The Layer 3 engine sends an ARP request for Host B and installs the drop adjacency for Host B in the hardware.

Step 4.   Host B responds to the ARP request.

Step 5.   The Layer 3 engine installs adjacency for Host B and removes the drop adjacency.

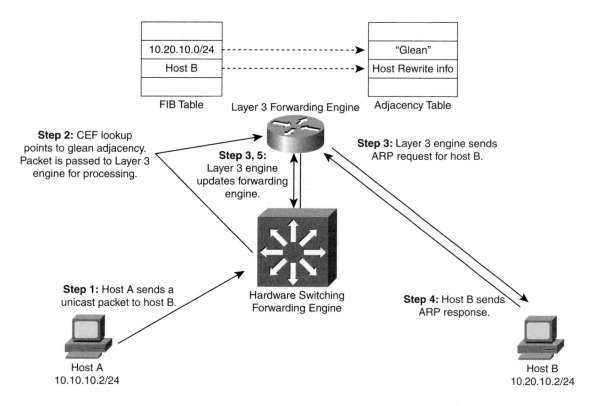

Figure 4-23   *ARP Throttling*

Figure 4-24, later in this chapter using the same example as in Figure 4-23, shows step-wise how the packet is routed in a multilayer switch using CEF in a larger context.

Sample CEF-Based MLS Operation

Before a multilayer switch can route frames in the hardware, it sets up the necessary routing information in the hardware. After the switch has set up the necessary routing information in the hardware, frame routing in the hardware can start. Figure 4-24 illustrates the steps for how a frame is routed in a multilayer switch using CEF.

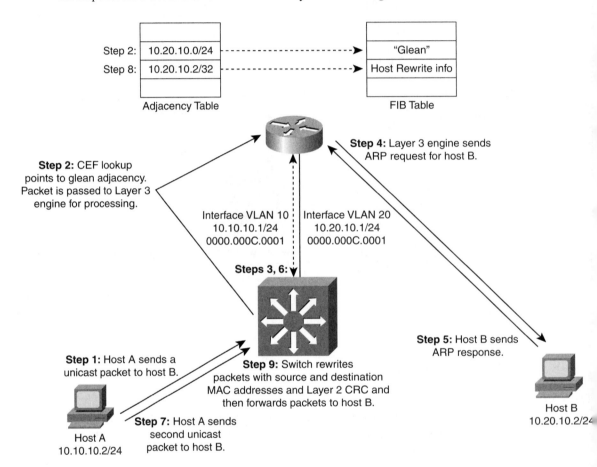

Figure 4-24   *Stepwise CEF Operation*

These steps assume the switch does not initially have rewrite information for the destination:

Step 1.   Host A sends a packet to Host B. The switch recognizes the frame as a Layer 3 packet because the destination MAC (0000.000c.0001) matches the Layer 3 engine MAC.

Step 2.   The switch performs a CEF lookup based on the destination IP address (10.20.10.2) in the hardware. The packet hits the CEF FIB entry for the connected (VLAN 20) network and is redirected to the Layer 3 engine using a "glean" adjacency. The hardware-switching CEF table cannot forward this packet because it does not have rewrite information.

Step 3.   The Layer 3 engine installs an ARP throttling adjacency in the switch for Host B's IP address, because an ARP entry does not exist for Host B because Hosts A and B have not previously communicated.

Step 4.   The Layer 3 engine sends an ARP request for Host B on VLAN 20.

Step 5.   Host B sends an ARP response to the Layer 3 engine.

Step 6.   The Layer 3 engine installs the resolved adjacency in its local adjacency table, and the hardware-switching components install the adjacency as well (removing the ARP throttling adjacency).

Step 7.   The switch receives another packet for Host B (10.20.10.2).

Step 8.   The switch performs a Layer 3 lookup and finds a CEF entry for Host B. The entry points to the adjacency with rewrite information for Host B.

Step 9.   The switch rewrites packets per the adjacency information (source and destination MAC address) and forwards the packet to Host B on VLAN 20.

Note   The ARP throttling adjacency drops the first packet in any communication between Hosts A and B due to ARP processing when no ARP entries exist for Hosts A and B.

CEF-Based MLS Load Sharing

CEF does support load sharing (equal-cost or nonequal-cost). However, CEF does not support all the load-sharing features found in software-based CEF. With the current version of software on a Catalyst 6500 switch, a single FIB entry may have up to six adjacencies for load sharing per destination.

To achieve evenly distributed load balancing across multiple interfaces, CEF selects a particular adjacency based on the hash (mathematical equivalent) of the following packet characteristics:

■   Source IP address

■   Destination IP address

■   Source and destination IP Layer 4 ports

In addition, parallel paths can exist and enable CEF to perform load balancing. Per-destination load balancing enables the Layer 3 switch to use multiple paths to achieve load sharing for packets going to different destinations. Packets for a given source-destination host pair are guaranteed to take the same path, even if multiple paths are available. This ensures that packets for a given host pair arrive in order. Per-destination load balancing is enabled by default when you allow CEF, and it is the load balancing method of choice for most situations.

However, this is also a potential limitation of CEF. Because CEF by default would always select the same path for a given host pair, in a topology with multiple Layer 3 paths between a given host pair, where packet-based load balancing would normally occur across the multiple paths, CEF "polarizes" the traffic by using only one path for a given host pair, thus effectively negating the load balancing benefit of the multiple paths for that particular host pair.

Because per-destination load balancing depends on the statistical distribution of traffic, load sharing becomes more effective as the number of source-destination pairs increases. Thus, in an environment where there is a broad distribution of traffic among host pairs, CEF polarization is of minimal concern. However, in an environment where data flow between a small number of host pairs creates a disproportionate percentage of the packets traversing the network, CEF polarization can become a serious problem. CEF load balancing can be "tuned," so a network engineer who anticipates a problem with CEF polarization would want to ensure that such tuning was performed within the enterprise network.

The default load-sharing method and hashing algorithms vary slightly per Catalyst switch family. Consult the product documentation for specifics about load-sharing support on each Catalyst switch.

Configuring CEF and Verifying CEF Configuration

This section discusses how to configure and verify CEF.

CEF-Based MLS Configuration

Cisco Catalyst switches that use the CEF-based MLS architecture use CEF by default. For Catalyst switches that support CEF-based MLS, CEF and per-destination load balancing with CEF are enabled by default. As a result, no configuration is required for CEF-based MLS.

Network administrators should not disable CEF on Catalyst switches for any reason except under the supervision of a Cisco TAC engineer for the specific purpose of troubleshooting. Disabling CEF on Cisco Catalyst switches yields low switching performance and can result in undesirable behavior.

CEF-Based MLS Verification

To verify the CEF information, use the following commands to help verify any issues with CEF:

- **show interface** *type number*: Provides stats for hardware switching Layer 3 packets

- **show ip cef:** Verifies the FIB

- **show ip cef** [*type mod/port* | *vlan_interface*] [**detail**]: Verifies the detailed information about a particular vlan or interface

- **show adjacency** *type mod/port* | *port-channel number*} | **detail** | **internal** | **summary:** Verifies adjacency table

Example 4-11 shows the output of show interface commands. In Example 4-11, the lines beginning L2 Switched, L3 in Switched, and L3 out Switched indicate the Layer 3 hardware-switching statistics. Catalyst switches do not instantaneously update hardware-switching statistics for CLI show commands. For example, on the Catalyst 4500 family of switches running Cisco IOS, interface statistics might take up to 30 seconds to be updated in **show** commands. Furthermore, each Catalyst family of switches has its own troubleshooting methodology and commands for viewing hardware switching statistics. Consult Cisco.com for more details.

Example 4-11 *Displaying Layer 3 Switching Statistics on the Cisco IOS–Based Catalyst 6500 Family of Switches*

```
Router# show interface port-channel 9
Port-channel9 is up, line protocol is up (connected)
 Hardware is EtherChannel, address is 00d0.039b.e80a (bia 00d0.039b.e800)
 Description: POINT-TO-POINT TO CORE-4
! Output omitted for brevity
 Output queue: 0/40 (size/max)
 5 minute input rate 0 bits/sec, 0 packets/sec
5 minute output rate 0 bits/sec, 0 packets/sec
  L2 Switched: ucast: 205744 pkt, 34282823 bytes - mcast: 216245 pkt, 66357101
    bytes
  L3 in Switched: ucast: 367825 pkt, 361204150 bytes - mcast: 0 pkt, 0 bytes mcast
  L3 out Switched: ucast: 248325 pkt, 243855150 bytes
     682964 packets input, 431530341 bytes, 0 no buffer
Received 311465 broadcasts (50899 IP multicast)
     0 runts, 0 giants, 0 throttles
     0 input errors, 0 CRC, 0 frame, 0 overrun, 0 ignored
     0 watchdog, 0 multicast, 0 pause input
     0 input packets with dribble condition detected
     554167 packets output, 309721969 bytes, 0 underruns
     0 output errors, 0 collisions, 8 interface resets
     0 babbles, 0 late collision, 0 deferred
     0 lost carrier, 0 no carrier, 0 PAUSE output
     0 output buffer failures, 0 output buffers swapped out
```

The Layer 3 Engine CEF table determines the hardware-switching CEF table. As such, when troubleshooting any CEF issues, the first step is to view the software CEF table. You can use the **show ip cef** command to display information about entries in the FIB. Example 4-12 output shows only general information about entries in the FIB, such as the destination network address, associated interface, and next hop (or local action, such as drop).

Example 4-12　show ip cef *Command*

```
Switch# show ip cef
Prefix              Next Hop              Interface
0.0.0.0/32          receive
1.0.0.0/24          attached             GigabitEthernet0/2
1.0.0.0/32          receive
1.0.0.1/32          receive
1.0.0.55/32         1.0.0.55             GigabitEthernet0/2
```

In addition, the **show ip cef** command with a detail option for a particular port or interface provides additional information. The output shows that CEF is enabled and various statistics about the number of routes and how many have been added or removed from the FIB. Example 4-13 shows that SVI VLAN 10 connects directly to the 10.1.10.0 network because it has a glean adjacency associated with that network. Recall that a glean adjacency is in the CEF adjacency table when multiple hosts are directly connected to the multilayer switch through a single port or interface.

Example 4-13　show ip cef detail *Command*

```
Switch# show ip cef vlan 10 detail
IP CEF with switching (Table Version 11), flags=0x0
  10 routes, 0 reresolve, 0 unresolved (0 old, 0 new), peak 0
  13 leaves, 12 nodes, 14248 bytes, 14 inserts, 1 invalidations
  0 load sharing elements, 0 bytes, 0 references
  universal per-destination load sharing algorithm, id 4B936A24
  2(0) CEF resets, 0 revisions of existing leaves
  Resolution Timer: Exponential (currently 1s, peak 1s)
  0 in-place/0 aborted modifications
  refcounts:  1061 leaf, 1052 node


  Table epoch: 0 (13 entries at this epoch)


10.1.10.0/24, version 6, epoch 0, attached, connected
0 packets, 0 bytes
  via Vlan10, 0 dependencies
    valid glean adjacency
```

CEF populates the adjacency tables when MAC addresses are learned via the ARP process. As a result, the adjacency table includes the MAC address rewrite information and destination interface for the adjacent node. All IP routing entries in the CEF table correspond to a next-hop address (adjacency).

When a switch hardware-switches an ingress packet with the destination MAC address as itself, it looks up the destination IP address in the CEF table. The first match in the CEF table points to an adjacency entry that contains the MAC rewrite information and destination interface. The switch rewrites the packet accordingly and sends it out the destination interface.

A single CEF entry might point to multiple adjacency entries when multiple paths to a destination exist. In addition, when a router is connected directly to several hosts, the FIB table on the router maintains a prefix for the subnet rather than for the individual host prefixes. The subnet prefix points to a glean adjacency. When packets need to be forwarded to a specific host, the adjacency database is gleaned for the specific prefix.

Certain IP prefixes or addresses require exception processing. Switches require exception processing of packets when hardware switching does not support routing of the frame or when the Layer 3 engine requires processing of the packet. Examples of packets that require exception processing include interfaces configured for NAT and received packets with IP options.

To display adjacency table information, use the **show adjacency** command. Example 4-14 shows the adjacency summary.

Example 4-14   show adjacency *Command*

```
Switch# show adjacency
Protocol Interface              Address
IP       GigabitEthernet0/3     2.0.0.55(5)
IP       GigabitEthernet0/2     1.0.0.55(5)
```

Example 4-15 displays the adjacency table in more detailed.

Example 4-15   show adjacency detail *Command*

```
Switch# show adjacency gigabitethernet 1/5 detail
Protocol Interface              Address
IP       GigabitEthernet1/5     172.20.53.206(11)
                                504 packets, 6110 bytes
                                00605C865B82
                                000164F83FA50800
                                ARP         03:49:31
```

Note   Information is displayed about the number of packets and bytes forwarded using this adjacency entry. Also, both the next-hop MAC address (used by the switch as the destination MAC for outgoing frame headers) and the local MAC address (used by the switch as the source MAC for outgoing frame headers), are displayed. The local MAC address is also followed by the well-known Ethertype value to be used for encapsulating the protocol displayed; in this instance, 0800 denotes the Ethertype value for IP, which would be inserted into the frame header.

In addition, the **show cef drops** command displays an indication of packets that are being dropped due to adjacencies that are either incomplete or nonexistent. The symptoms of an incomplete adjacency include random packet drops during a ping test. Following are two known reasons for incomplete or nonexistent adjacencies:

■   The router cannot use ARP successfully for the next-hop interface.

■   After a **clear ip arp** or a **clear adjacency** command, the router marks the adjacency as incomplete, and then it fails to clear the entry.

Troubleshooting CEF

In terms of troubleshooting, understanding the basic operation of multilayer switches is paramount; multilayer switching requires a hierarchical approach to troubleshooting because several switching components determine the packet flow, not a single processing engine. CEF-based MLS configuration, verification, and troubleshooting vary slightly per Catalyst switch family but do have some commonalities.

Previous subsections discussed several CEF troubleshooting techniques on the Layer 3 engine. Recall that the Layer 3 engine does not actually contain the hardware FIB and adjacency table. Instead, these tables are located in specialized hardware components in supervisor engines and line cards. The following highlights a stepwise approach to troubleshooting a unicast route on a CEF-based Catalyst switch. The troubleshooting steps are not inclusive but do review the hierarchical approach to troubleshooting CEF-based MLS:

Step 1.   Verify that the IP routing information on the Layer 3 engine is correct. Use the **show ip route** or **show ip route destination-network** command to verify that the destination network routing entry exists and is associated with a valid next-hop address. If the route does not exist or the next-hop address is incorrect, troubleshooting of routing protocol, next-hop interfaces, or route configuration is required.

Step 2.   Verify that the next-hop address has a valid next-hop MAC address by using the **show ip arp** *IP-address* command. If the entry is incomplete, troubleshooting of the ARP process is required.

Step 3.   Verify that the IP route entry in the FIB on the Layer 3 engine contains the same next-hop address as in Step 1 by using the **show ip cef destination-network** command.

Step 4.   Verify that the CEF adjacency table contains the same rewrite information as the ARP table from Step 2 by using the **show adjacency detail | begin** *next_hop_IP_address* command.

Step 5.   When all other troubleshooting steps have been exhausted and the CEF-based MLS switch is still experiencing unicast routing issues, verify the population of the FIB and adjacency table in TCAM under the supervision of a TAC engineer.

Summary

This chapter discussed in detail Layer 3 routing and its implementation, including coverage of inter-VLAN routing and router-on-a-stick, DHCP services, and the forwarding path of multilayer switching using CEF. This chapter can be summarized as follows:

- Inter-VLAN routing provides communication between the devices in different VLANs. Recall that a VLAN is a single broadcast domain, and the devices within a VLAN cannot communicate beyond VLAN boundaries unless through a Layer 3 device. Multilayer switches support two types of Layer 3 interfaces: routed ports and SVIs (VLAN interfaces).

- Routed ports are point-to-point connections such as those that interconnect the building distribution submodules and the campus backbone submodules when using Layer 3 in the distribution layer.

- SVIs are VLAN interfaces that route traffic between VLANs and VLAN group ports. In multilayer switched networks with Layer 3 in the distribution layer and Layer 2 in the access layer, SVIs can route traffic from VLANs on the access-layer switches.

- Using router-on-a -stick is an alternative and legacy method of implementing inter-VLAN routing for low-throughput and latency-tolerant applications.

- On multilayer switches, Layer 3 links can be aggregated using Layer 3 EtherChannels. When a Layer 3 interface is configured, routing can be enabled.

- DHCP functions can be configured on the switches.

- Multilayer switches can forward traffic based on either Layer 2 or Layer 3 header information. Multilayer switches rewrite frame and packet headers using information from tables cached in hardware. Layer 3 (multilayer) switching is high-performance packet switching in hardware. Multilayer switching can use centralized or distributed switching, and route caching or topology-based switching. Multilayer switching functionality can be implemented using Cisco Express Forwarding (CEF), which utilizes two tables in hardware to forward packets: a Forwarding Information Base (FIB) and an Adjacency Table (AT).

Review Questions

Use the questions here to review what you learned in this chapter. The correct answers are found in Appendix A, "Answers to Chapter Review Questions."

1. True or False: An SVI is a physical Layer 3 interface, whereas a routed port is a virtual Layer 3 interface.

2. True or False: Multilayer switches generally outperform routers of multiple Ethernet interfaces.

3. True or False: A router can forward DHCP requests across VLAN or IP subnet boundaries by using the DHCP relay agent feature.

Questions 4 and 5 are based on the configuration in Example 4-16.

Example 4-16   Configuration for Questions 4 and 5

```
switch# show run interface vlan 10
Building configuration...


Current configuration : 60 bytes
!
interface Vlan10
 ip address 10.1.1.1 255.255.255.0
 no ip proxy-arp
end
switch# show run int vlan 20
Building configuration...


Current configuration : 60 bytes
!
interface Vlan20
 ip address 10.2.1.1 255.255.255.0
 no ip proxy-arp
end
```

4. Based on Example 4-16, can the hosts that reside in VLAN 20 communicate with hosts on VLAN 10 if their default gateway is set to 10.2.1.1?

   a. Yes, if the hosts on VLAN 10 have their default gateway set to 10.1.1.1.

   b. No, the default gateway of the hosts that reside in VLAN 20 should be set to 10.1.1.1.

   c. Yes, but there is no need to define default gateways.

   d. No, because the routing protocol or static routes are not defined.

5. Based on Example 4-16, if the hosts that reside on VLAN 10 have their default gateway defined as 10.1.1.1 and ICMP can ping 10.2.1.1 but not a host that resides in VLAN 20, what could be a possible reason?

   a. Hosts on VLAN 10 are not configured with the correct default gateway.

   b. Hosts on VLAN 20 are not configured with the correct default gateway.

   c. The routing protocol or static routes are not defined on the Layer 3 switch.

   d. VLAN 20 is not defined in the switch database.

6. When performing router-on-a-stick inter-VLAN routing, a router interface is subdi-vided into what?

    a. VLAN subinterfaces

    b. 802.1q subinterfaces

    c. Layer 3 subinterfaces

    d. EtherChannel subinterfaces

7. Which two commands should be used to configure a router and switch to identify VLAN 10 as the native VLAN on an 802.1Q trunk link? (Choose two.)

    a. encapsulation dot1q vlan 10 native

    b. encapsulation dot1q 10 native

    c. encapsulation dot1q native vlan 10

    d. switchport trunk dot1q native vlan 10

    e. switchport mode trunk dot1q vlan 10 native

    f. switchport trunk native vlan 10

8. Place the following five items in the proper order of processing (Note: Not all steps are included.)

    a. If necessary, an input router ACL check is performed.

    b. The Layer 2 and Layer 3 header are rewritten.

    c. The Layer 2 forwarding engine forwards the frame.

    d. The Layer 2 engine performs the input VLAN ACL lookup.

    e. The destination IP address is compared against the Layer 3 forwarding table for the longest match.

9. Which of the following are NOT reasons for configuring an SVI? (Choose two.)

    a. To provide fallback bridging if it is required for nonroutable protocols

    b. To provide Layer 3 IP connectivity to the switch

    c. To provide failover if the primary SVI for a VLAN fails

    d. To provide a gateway for a VLAN so that traffic can be routed into or out of that VLAN

    e. To provide connectivity to an external router for inter-VLAN routing

10. On which of the following ports would a network engineer be most likely to use the **autostate exclude** command?

   a. An 802.1Q trunk port connected to an external router

   b. A monitoring port connected to an intrusion prevention sensor

   c. The secondary SVI for a VLAN

   d. A routed interface on a multilayer switch

   e. All of the above

11. When must the command **ip routing** be used when configuring SVIs on a multilayer switch?

   a. When an SVI is being used to provide IP connectivity to the switch itself for a given VLAN.

   b. When the SVI is being configured as part of a Layer 2 EtherChannel bundle.

   c. When EIGRP is not being used as a routing protocol.

   d. When an SVI is being used to provide Layer 3 IP forwarding services to its assigned VLAN.

   e. Never; IP routing is enabled by default on a multilayer switch.

12. How is a port on a multilayer switch configured as a routed port?

   a. By configuring an IP address and subnet mask on the port

   b. By using the command **switchport mode routed**

   c. By removing the Layer 2 switching capability of the switch port

   d. By using the command **no switchport mode**

13. Which two of the following are Layer 3 switching modes on a Cisco Catalyst multilayer switch? (Choose two.)

   a. Fast switching

   b. Topology-based switching

   c. CEF switching

   d. Rapid switching

   e. Route caching

   f. Distributed fast switching

14. What are the names of the two hardware tables created by CEF? (Choose two.)

    a. Cisco Express Forwarding Table

    b. Forwarding Information Table

    c. Adjacency Table

    d. Forwarding Information Base

    e. Link-State Table

15. When a multilayer switch connects directly to several hosts, the FIB table on the switch maintains a prefix for the subnet rather than for the individual host prefixes. This adjacency is known as which of the following?

    a. Punt adjacency

    b. Subnet adjacency

    c. Connected adjacency

    d. Glean adjacency

    e. Host-route adjacency

16. Which of the following is the solution if part of an adjacency is an "incomplete" or a "drop" adjacency?

    a. Troubleshoot routing protocols to ensure that the routing table is properly populated.

    b. Verify that the IP host exists on a media that is accessible to the host that is trying to ARP resolve.

    c. Debug CEF to observe all messages for CEF operations.

    d. Disable and then reenable CEF on the multilayer switch.

    e. Check that unsupported software features have not been enabled.

17. What command is used on Cisco IOS switches to change the interface from a Layer 3 interface to a Layer 2 interface?

    a. **switchport mode access**

    b. **ip routing**

    c. **switchport**

    d. **switchport mode trunk**

18. Which Cisco IOS command enables IP routing on a Catalyst switch?

  a.   **ip routing**

  b.   **interface** *vlan-id*

  c.   **ip address** *n.n.n.n mask*

  d.   **router** *ip_routing_protocol*

19. What is the function of a DHCP relay agent?

20. Which of the following UDP protocols are forwarded in addition to DHCP when a Layer 3 interface is configured with the **ip helper-address** command? (Select all that apply.)

  a.   Mobile IP

  b.   DNS

  c.   Time

  d.   FTP

Chapter 5

Implementing High Availability and Redundancy in a Campus Network

This chapter covers the following topics:

- Understanding High Availability

- Implementing High Availability

- Implementing Network Monitoring

- Implementing Redundant Supervisor Engines in Catalyst Switches

- Understanding First Hop Redundancy Protocols

- Cisco IOS Server Load Balancing

A network with high availability provides an alternative means that enables constant access to all infrastructure paths and key servers. High availability is not just about adding redundant devices. It implies planning to understand where the points of failure occur and designing the network so that an alternative solution exists to compensate for the loss of these points of failure.

This chapters provides an overview on how to implement a high-availability solution according to a given network design and requirements. This includes building a resilient network with optimal redundancy for high availability. Monitoring the network using SNMP, Syslog, and IP SLA are key elements to ensure the high availability of the network.

This chapter also covers supervisor redundancy options such as RPR, RPR+, SSO, and NSF. For ensuring first hop gateway redundancy, the Hot Standby Router Protocol (HSRP), Virtual Router Redundancy Protocol (VRRP) and Gateway Load Balancing Protocol (GLBP) are needed. First hop redundancy protocols (FHRP) allow for nondisruptive failover between available redundant gateways. HSRP/VRRP allow for one primary router per subnet with other routers acting as standby/backup. GLBP allows load balancing across multiple gateways for the same subnet. The first hop redundancy protocols are explained in detail in this chapter.

Understanding High Availability

High availability is technology that enables networkwide resilience to increase IP network availability. Network applications must cross different network segments—from the Enterprise Backbone, Enterprise Edge, and Service Provider Edge, through the Service Provider Core. All segments must be resilient to recover quickly enough for faults to be transparent to users and network applications. This chapter describes the high availability concept, how resiliency is built, and how the network is designed to always offer a path between any pair of end points.

Components of High Availability

High availability is an organizational objective with the goal of preventing outages or at least minimizing downtime. Achieving high availability is hard work. It takes ongoing effort and iterated improvement.

To start making progress on providing high availability requires integrating multiple components, as shown in Figure 5-1.

- Redundancy

- Technology (including hardware and software features)

- People

- Processes

- Tools

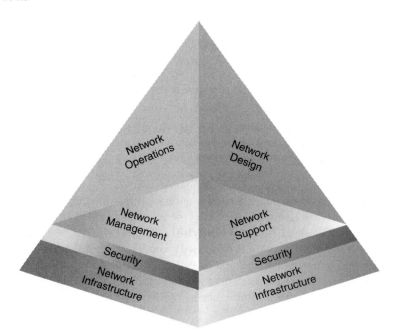

Figure 5-1 *Components of High Availability*

The network redundancy and technology components are relatively easy to accomplish because these elements can be purchased and deployed. A traditional network designer will expect to be involved with these two aspects of high availability.

No matter how much and how well redundancy and technology are designed and deployed, high availability is not achieved unless the people component (sufficient labor pool with the right skills, training, and mindset), the process component (company expectations, change control process, and so on), and the tools component (network management, good documentation) are present. If any one of the three high-availability components is insufficiently addressed, incidents will happen and outages will occur. Initially, the network designer might not be able to fix the people, processes, and tools in an organization. Often, it takes a consultant doing a post outage design review to talk about these components and suggest changes.

Redundancy

Redundancy designs attempt to eliminate single points of failure, where one failed device or design element brings down service.

A redundant design can use several mechanisms to prevent single points of failure:

- Geographic diversity and path diversity are often included.

- Dual devices and links are common, as shown in Figure 5-2.

- Dual WAN providers are common.

- Dual data centers are sometimes used, especially for large companies and large e-commerce sites.

- Dual collocation facilities, dual phone central office facilities, and dual power substations can be implemented.

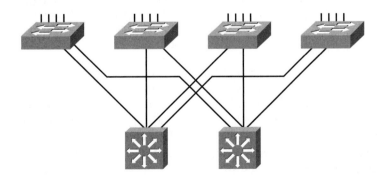

Figure 5-2   *Redundant Campus Network*

Redundant design must trade off cost versus benefit. It takes time to plan redundancy and verify geographic diversity of service providers. Additional links and equipment cost money to purchase and maintain. These options must be balanced against risks, costs of downtime, and so on. The time and money invested in redundancy designs needs to be spent where they will have the most impact. Consequently, redundancy is most frequently found in network, data center, or e-commerce module cores, and then in critical WAN links or Internet service provider (ISP) connections. Additional e-commerce module redundancy can double up elements in the path between users and applications, and the applications and back-end databases and mainframes.

Technology

Several Cisco routing continuity options, such as Cisco Nonstop Forwarding (NSF) and Stateful Switchover (SSO) exist, and graceful restart capabilities improve availability. These technologies allow processor failover without a link flap, continued forwarding of packets, and maintenance of Border Gateway Protocol (BGP) adjacencies.

Techniques exist to detect failure and trigger failover to a redundant device. These techniques include service monitoring for Cisco IOS IP Service Level Agreements (SLA) and Object Tracking. Object Tracking enables you to track specific objects on the network, such as the interface line protocol state, IP routing, and route reachability, and to take action when the tracked object's state changes.

Other technologies also contribute to high availability. For example, fast routing convergence and server load balancers help maintain high availability. Firewall stateful failover can maintain user or application sessions across a firewall device failover.

People

Redundant equipment and links and advanced technology are just the beginning of high availability. In the Prepare, Plan, Design, Implement, Operate, and Optimize (PPDIOO) methodology, the people component is vitally important, too. Staff work habits and skills can impact high availability. For example, attention to detail enhances high availability, whereas carelessness hurts availability. Reliable and consistent wiring and configurations are easier to manage and troubleshoot.

The level of staff skills and technical training are important elements when it comes to taking full advantage of redundancy. Devices must be configured correctly. Lab testing is important to understand the circumstances that activate failover, and what failover will and will not accomplish. Thoroughness in lab testing often translates into less downtime in production. For example, nonstateful firewall failover might be adequate in terms of passing traffic. However, a practical understanding of the application can show that with nonstateful failover, application sessions will lock up for an extended period of time until an application timeout causes session reestablishment. Designs that include failover must be tested for the entire system, not just for individual components.

Good communication and documentation are also important. The network administrators need to communicate with other network, security, application, and server teams. The network documentation should cover why things are designed the way they are and how the network is supposed to work. Failover behavior is complex enough that it is unwise to have to recapture failover logic and boundary conditions every time some part of the design changes.

Field experience leads to the observation that if people are not given time to do the job right, they will cut corners. Testing and documentation are often the first items to be eliminated. Lack of thorough testing and documentation can have long-term consequences on the ability to maintain, expand, and troubleshoot the network.

If the design target is just "adequate" coverage, falling short of that target can lead to a poor design. Designs should be better than adequate to ensure that no part of the implementation or operation of the high-availability network is inadequate.

One other organizational recommendation is to align staff teams with services. If the corporate web page depends on staff who report to other managers, the manager of the e-commerce site might compete for staff time with the network engineering or operations manager. In most cases, the person who does the staff evaluation and provides the pay bonus generally gets most of the attention. This organizational structure can make it difficult to get routine testing or maintenance done for the e-commerce site if the staff does not report to the e-commerce manager. The owner or expert on key service applications and other components should be identified and included in design and redesign efforts.

Processes

Sound, repeatable processes can lead to high availability. Continual process improvement as part of the PPDIOO methodology plays a role in achieving high availability. Organizations need to build repeatable processes and gradually improve them. Tasks that are always implemented as a special one-time occurrence represent a lost opportunity to learn as an organization.

Organizations should build repeatable processes in the following ways:

- By documenting change procedures for repeated changes (for example, Cisco IOS Software upgrades)

- By documenting failover planning and lab testing procedures

- By documenting the network implementation procedure so that the process can be revised and improved the next time components are deployed

Organizations should use labs appropriately, as follows:

- Lab equipment should accurately reflect the production network.

- Failover mechanisms are tested and understood.

- New code is systematically validated before deployment.

Because staff members tend to ignore processes that consume a lot of time or appear to be a waste of time, organizations also need meaningful change controls in the following ways:

- Test failover and all changes before deployment.

- Plan well, including planning rollbacks in detail.

- Conduct a realistic and thorough risk analysis.

The following management of operational changes is also important:

- Perform regular capacity management audits.

- Track and manage Cisco IOS versions.

- Track design compliance as recommended practices change.

- Develop plans for disaster recovery and continuity of operations.

Tools

Organizations are starting to monitor service and component availability. With proper failover, services should continue operating when single components fail. Without component monitoring, a failure to detect and replace a failed redundant component can lead to an outage when the second component subsequently fails.

Performance thresholds and reporting the top N devices with specific characteristics (Top N reporting) are useful, both for noticing when capacity is running out, and also for correlating service slowness with stressed network or server resources. Monitoring packet loss, latency, jitter, and drops for WAN links or ISPs is also important. Those metrics can be the first indication of an outage or of a potential deterioration of an SLA that could affect delivery of services.

Good documentation, such as the following, provides an extremely powerful set of tools:

- Network diagrams help in planning and in fixing outages more quickly. Out-of-date documentation can lead to design errors, lack of redundancy, and other undesirable consequences.

- Documentation explaining how and why the network design evolved helps capture knowledge that can be critical when a different person needs to make design changes, reexamine how failover works, or make other changes.

- Key addresses, VLANs, and servers should be documented.

- Documentation tying services to applications and virtual and physical servers can be incredibly useful when troubleshooting.

Resiliency for High Availability

Network level, system-level resiliency, and network monitoring are required components to provide high availability. High availability should be considered at every level of the network. In the context of this course, however, the focus is on network-level resiliency. You should still organize high availability at the system level. In a switched network, this means making sure that heavily solicited or key switches have redundant power supplies, or that duplicate devices are available to replace failed components of the network.

Another part of high availability ensures that you are informed when an element of your network fails. This is configured through monitoring and management features—the status or the failure of any element in your network should be immediate reported to a location with an immediate notification of the issue.

Network-Level Resiliency

Network-level resiliency is built with device and link redundancy. Device redundancy refers to having backup or redundant devices in the network to provide switching or routing or services functionality. Link redundancy refers to having multiple or duplicate links between any two devices. When possible and needed, duplicate links are installed between devices. If one physical link fails, the redundant one can hold the load while you replace the first one. These redundant links can be set in a standby mode, where one link is active and the other one is blocked by the spanning tree, or in a load-balancing mode, with EtherChannel. Also, if the links are Layer 3 instead, load balancing is possible.

Another element of high availability at network level is fast convergence. When a link fails, the redundant link or path should take precedence immediately to avoid situations in which frames or packets are dropped due to slow convergence time. In this perspective, Rapid Spanning Tree Protocol (RSTP) is preferred over 802.1D STP. With the same logic in mind, fast convergence should apply to Layer 3 connections. Wherever possible, efficient routing protocols, such as OSPF or EIGRP, would be preferred to slower routing protocols such as RIP to increase convergence speed.

Monitoring the various network elements involves several components. The first one is to synchronize time between interconnecting devices and the monitoring station. Knowing precisely when an event occurs is fundamental to managing failures and recoveries. The second element is to track events related to devices status. This can be done using Syslog and SNMP. SNMP cannot monitor some elements. For example, your link to the next hop may be up, but a failure in the network renders your gateway unreachable. This event might be undetected by the local device-monitoring configuration. To circumvent this kind of issue, IP SLA is a protocol dedicated to testing connectivity between devices. It is an important addition to monitor the network with increased accuracy.

High Availability and Failover Times

The overall failover time in the data center is the combination of convergence at Layer 2, Layer 3, and Layer 4 components. Figure 5-3 shows failover times of high-availability protocols.

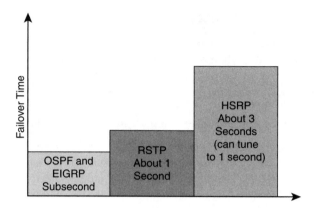

Figure 5-3 *Failover Time of High-Availability Protocols in Network*

The network components have different recovery times:

- Tuned routing protocols can failover in less than 1 second. Open Shortest Path First (OSPF) and Enhanced Interior Gateway Routing Protocol (EIGRP) can both achieve subsecond convergence time with recommended timer configurations.

- RSTP converges in about 1 second. RSTP permits subsecond convergence time for minor failures when logical ports are under watermarks and can take 1 second to 2 seconds for major failure conditions.

- EtherChannel can failover in approximately 1 second. When a link fails, Cisco EtherChannel technology redirects traffic from the failed link to the remaining links in less than 1 second.

- Default HSRP timers are 3 seconds for the hello time and 10 seconds for the hold time. A recommended practice is to configure the timers with a hello time of 1 second and a hold time of 3 seconds so that convergence occurs in less than 3 seconds. You can adjust the convergence time down to subsecond values, but you must consider the CPU load.

- Stateful service modules typically failover within 3 to 5 seconds. The convergence time for Cisco Catalyst 6500 Series Firewall Services Module (FWSM) is approximately 5 seconds with recommended timers, and the Caching Services Module (CSM) is approximately 5 seconds with recommended timers. Cisco Application Control Engine (ACE) can achieve failovers in approximately 1 second with its active/active configuration.

- The least tolerant TCP/IP stacks are the Windows Server and Windows XP client stacks, which have approximately a 9-second tolerance. Each of the TCP/IP stacks built into the various operating systems have a different level of tolerance for determining when a TCP session will drop. Other TCP/IP stacks such as those found in Linux, Hewlett-Packard (HP), and IBM systems are more tolerant and have a longer window before tearing down a TCP session.

Optimal Redundancy

Providing optimal redundancy is important to ensure high availability. The key is not to provide too much redundancy resulting in an overly complicated or expensive to build and maintain network nor too little to compromise the required high availability.

As a recommended practice, the core and distribution layers are built with redundant switches and fully meshed links that provide maximum redundancy and optimal convergence, as shown in Figure 5-4. Access switches should have redundant connections to redundant distribution switches. The network bandwidth and capacity is engineered to withstand a switch or link failure, usually recovering within 120 ms to 200 ms. OSPF and EIGRP timer manipulation quickly attempts to redirect the flow of traffic away from a router that has experienced a failure toward an alternate path.

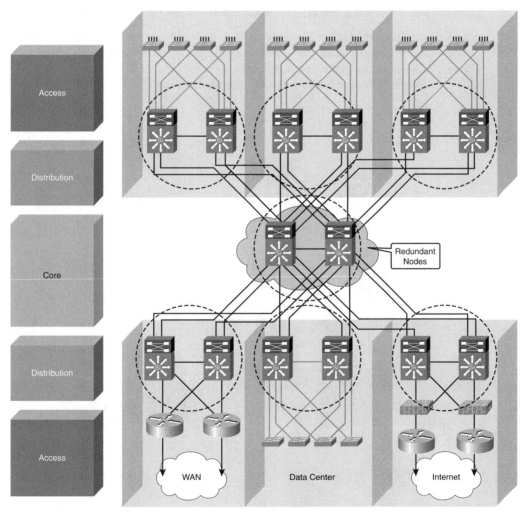

Figure 5-4 *Optimal Redundancy in Multilayer Network*

In a fully redundant topology with tuned IGP timers, adding redundant supervisors with Cisco NSF and SSO might cause longer convergence times than single supervisors with tuned IGP timers. NSF attempts to maintain the flow of traffic through a router that has experienced a failure. NSF with SSO is designed to maintain the link up with neighbors while preserving the routing capabilities during a routing convergence event.

In nonredundant topologies, using Cisco NSF with SSO and redundant supervisors can provide significant resiliency improvements.

Provide Alternate Paths

Although dual distribution switches connected individually to separate core switches will reduce peer relationships and port counts in the core layer, this design does not provide sufficient redundancy. If a link or core switch failure occurs, traffic is dropped.

An additional link providing an alternative path to a second core switch from each distribution switch offers redundancy to support a single link or node failure, as shown in Figure 5-5. A link between the two distribution switches is needed to support summarization of routing information from the distribution layer to the core.

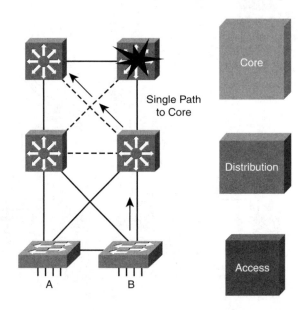

Figure 5-5 *Redundancy Through Alternate Paths*

Avoid Too Much Redundancy

In Figure 5-6, a third switch is added to the distribution switches in the center. This extra switch adds unneeded complexity to the design and leads to these design questions:

- Where should the root switch be placed? With this design, it is not easy to determine where the root switch is located.

- What links should be in a blocking state? It is hard to determine how many ports will be in a blocking state.

- What are the implications of STP and RSTP convergence? The network convergence is definitely not deterministic.

- When something goes wrong, how do you find the source of the problem? The design is much harder to troubleshoot.

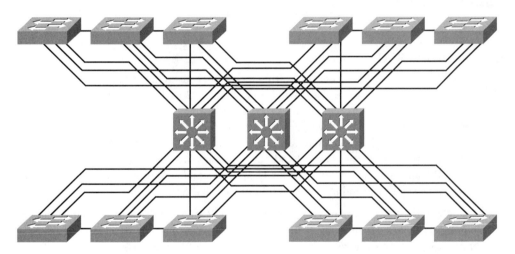

Figure 5-6 *Network with Too Much Redundancy*

Avoid Single Point of Failure

Avoiding single points of failure is another key element to high availability. If there is only one path to a device or a network, the loss of the path is unrecoverable. Redundancy is relatively easy to implement at the distribution or the core layers, where duplicate links and duplicate devices can exist to interconnect the other elements of the network. Redundancy is more difficult to achieve at the access layer. An access switch failure is a single point of failure that causes an outage for the end devices connected to it. You can reduce the outage to 1 to 3 seconds in this access layer by utilizing SSO in a Layer 2 environment or Cisco NSF with SSO in a Layer 3 environment, as shown in Figure 5-7.

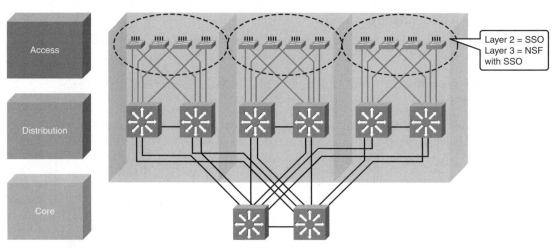

Figure 5-7 *Avoiding Single Point of Failure*

Cisco NSF with SSO

Cisco NSF with SSO is a supervisor redundancy mechanism in Cisco IOS Software that enables extremely fast supervisor switchover at Layers 2 to 4. SSO enables the standby route processor (RP) to take control of the device after a hardware or software fault on the active RP. SSO synchronizes startup configuration, startup variables, and running configuration, as well as dynamic runtime data including Layer 2 protocol states for trunks and ports, hardware Layer 2 and Layer 3 tables (MAC, Forwarding Information Base [FIB], and adjacency tables) and ACLs and QoS tables. NSF with SSO is explained more in the supervisor redundancy section of this chapter.

Cisco NSF is a Layer 3 function that works with SSO to minimize the amount of time a network is unavailable to its users following a switchover. The main objective of Cisco NSF is to continue forwarding IP packets following an RP switchover, as shown in Figure 5-8. Cisco NSF is supported by the EIGRP, OSPF, Intermediate System-to-Intermediate System (IS-IS), and Border Gateway Protocol (BGP) for routing. A router running these protocols can detect an internal switchover and take the necessary actions to continue forwarding network traffic using CEF while recovering route information from the peer devices. With Cisco NSF, peer-networking devices continue to forward packets while route convergence completes and do not experience routing flaps.

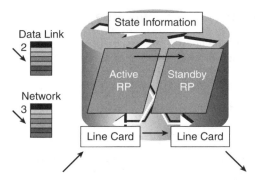

Figure 5-8 *Cisco Nonstop Forwarding with Stateful Switchover*

Routing Protocols and NSF

Cisco NSF enables for the continued forwarding of data packets along known routes while the routing protocol information is being restored following a switchover. With Cisco NSF, peer-Cisco NSF devices do not experience routing flaps because the interfaces remain up during a switchover and adjacencies do not reset. Data traffic is forwarded while the standby RP assumes control from the failed active RP during a switchover. User sessions established prior to the switchover are maintained.

The capability of the intelligent line cards to remain up through a switchover and kept current with the FIB on the active RP is crucial to Cisco NSF operation. While the control plane builds a new routing protocol database and restarts peering agreements, the data plane relies on pre-switchover forwarding-table synchronization to continue forwarding traffic.

Note   Transient routing loops or black holes might be introduced if the network topology changes before the FIB is updated.

After the routing protocols have converged, CEF updates the FIB table and removes stale route entries, and then it updates the line cards with the refreshed FIB information.

The switchover must be completed before the Cisco NSF dead and hold timers expire, or else the peers will reset the adjacency and reroute the traffic.

Implementing High Availability

When designing a campus network, the network engineer needs to plan the optimal use of the highly redundant devices. Carefully consider when and where to invest in redundancy to create a resilient and highly available network.

Note   This section assumes that the reader has knowledge about STP and HSRP protocol operation. If you are not familiar with these topics, refer to Chapter 3, "Implementing Spanning Tree," for information about Spanning Tree Protocol and the "Understanding First Hop Redundancy Protocols" section later in this chapter for information about HSRP.

Distributed VLANs on Access Switches

If the enterprise campus requirements must support VLANs spanning multiple access layer switches, the design model uses a Layer 2 link for interconnecting the distribution switches, as shown in Figure 5-9. This design is more complex than the Layer 3 interconnection of the distribution switches. The Spanning Tree Protocol (STP) convergence process initiates for uplink failures and recoveries.

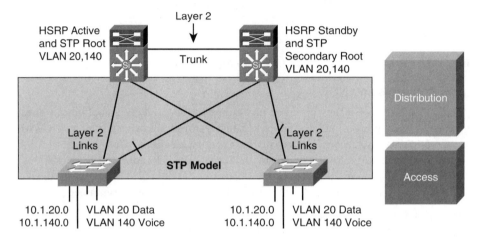

Figure 5-9   *Distributed VLANs on Access Layer Switches*

You should take the following steps to improve this suboptimal design:

- Use Rapid STP (RSTP) as the version of STP.

- Provide a Layer 2 trunk between the two distribution switches to avoid unexpected traffic paths and multiple convergence events.

- Place the Hot Standby Router Protocol (HSRP) primary and the STP primary root on the same distribution layer switch if you choose to load balance VLANs across up-links. The HSRP and RSTP root should be colocated on the same distribution switches to avoid using the interdistribution link for transit.

Local VLANs on Access Switches

In this time-proven topology, no VLANs span between access layer switches across the distribution switches, as shown in Figure 5-10. A subnet equals a VLAN that, in turn, equals an access switch because VLAN is restricted to one access switch only. The root for each VLAN is aligned with the active HSRP instance. From a STP perspective, both access layer uplinks are forwarding, so the only convergence dependencies are the default gateway and return-path route selection across the distribution-to-distribution Layer 3 link.

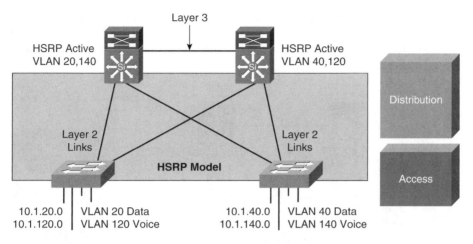

Figure 5-10 *VLANs Restricted to Access Layer Switches*

> **Note**   This recommended design provides the highest availability.

With this design, a distribution-to-distribution Layer 3 link is required for route summarization. A recommended practice is to map the Layer 2 VLAN number to the Layer 3 subnet for ease of use and management.

Layer 3 Access to the Distribution Interconnection

In this time-proven topology, no VLANs span between access layer switches across the distribution switches, as shown in Figure 5-11. A subnet equals a VLAN that, in turn, equals an access switch. The root for each VLAN is aligned with the active HSRP instance. From a STP perspective, both access layer uplinks are forwarding, so the only convergence dependencies are the default gateway and return-path route selection across the distribution-to-distribution link.

With this design as well, a distribution-to-distribution Layer 3 link is required for route summarization. A recommended practice is to map the Layer 2 VLAN number to the Layer 3 subnet for ease of use and management.

Daisy Chaining Access Layer Switches

In the topology shown in Figure 5-12 before failures, no links block from a STP or RSTP perspective. Both uplinks are available to actively forward and receive traffic. Both distribution nodes can forward return-path traffic from the rest of the network toward the access layer for devices attached to all members of the stack or chain.

Two scenarios can occur if a link or node in the middle of the chain or stack fails. In the first case, the standby HSRP peer (Dist-B) can go active as it loses connectivity to its primary peer (Dist-A), forwarding traffic outbound for the devices that still have connectivity to it. The primary HSRP peer remains active and also forwards outbound traffic for its half of the stack. Although this is not optimum, it is not detrimental from the perspective of outbound traffic.

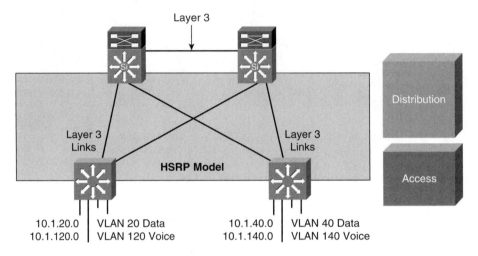

Figure 5-11 *Layer 3 to Access Layer Switches*

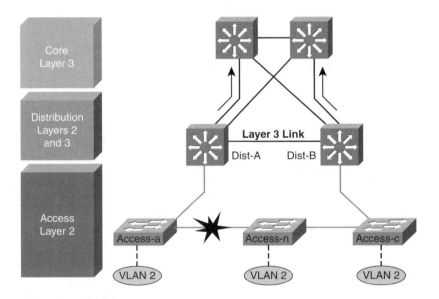

Figure 5-12 *Daisy Chaining Access Layer Switches*

Another scenario, as shown in Figure 5-13, illustrates the issue with this design for the return traffic. The core switch sees both the distribution layer switches advertise the VLAN 2 subnet and does equal cost load balancing for the traffic destined to VLAN 2 to both the Dist-A and Dist-B. Therefore, return-path traffic has a 50 percent chance of arriving on a distribution switch that does not have physical connectivity to the half of the stack where the traffic is destined. The traffic that arrives on the wrong distribution switch is dropped.

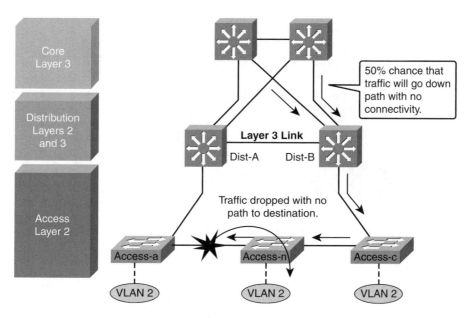

Figure 5-13   *Challenges with Daisy Chaining Access Layer Switches*

The solution to this issue with this design is to provide alternative connectivity across the stack in the form of a direct connection between the Access-a and Access-c switches in the stack. This link needs to be carefully deployed so that the appropriate STP behavior occurs in the access layer if the stack is greater than three switches. It is preferred to implement StackWise access switches, which is explained in the next section.

An alternative design uses a Layer 2 link between the distribution switches.

StackWise Access Switches

StackWise technology in the access layer supports the recommended practice of using a Layer 3 connection between the distribution switches without having to use a loopback cable or perform extra configuration, as shown in Figure 5-14.

The true stack creation provided by the Cisco Catalyst 3750 Series switches makes using stacks in the access layer much less complex than chains or stacks of other models. A stack of 3750 switches appears as one node from the network topology perspective.

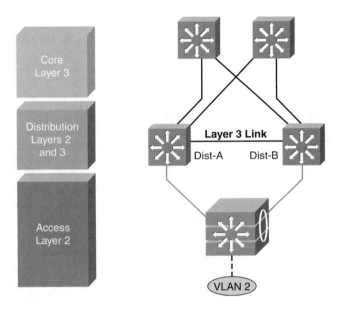

Figure 5-14 *StackWise in Access Layer Switches*

Too Little Redundancy

Figure 5-15 shows a less than optimal design where VLANs span multiple access layer switches. Without a Layer 2 link between the distribution switches, the design is a looped Figure-8 topology. One access layer uplink will be blocking. HSRP hellos are exchanged by transiting the access switches.

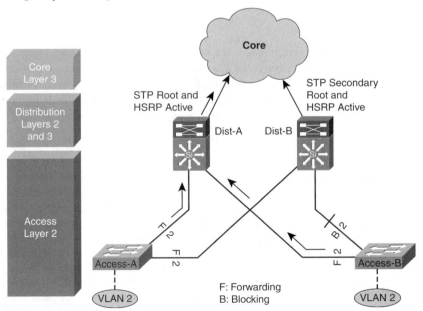

Figure 5-15 *Network with Too Little Redundancy*

Initially, traffic is forwarded from both access switches to the Distribution A switch that supports the STP root and the primary or active HSRP peer for VLAN 2. However, this design will black-hole traffic and be affected by multiple convergence events with a single network failure.

As shown in Figure 5-16, when the uplink from Access A switch to the Distribution A switch fails, there are three convergence events:

■   Access A switch sends traffic across its active uplink to Distribution B switch to get to its default gateway. The traffic is black-holed at Distribution B switch because Distribution B switch does not initially have a path to the primary or active HSRP peer on Distribution A switch due to the STP blocking. The traffic is dropped until the standby HSRP peer takes over as the default gateway after not receiving HSRP hellos from Distribution A switch.

Note   With aggressive HSRP timers, you can minimize this period of traffic loss to approximately 900 ms.

■   The indirect link failure is eventually detected by Access B switch after the maximum-age (max_age) timer expires, and Access B switch removes blocking on the uplink to Distribution B switch. With standard STP, transitioning to forwarding can take as long as 50 seconds. If BackboneFast is enabled with Per VLAN Spanning Tree Plus (PVST+), this time can be reduced to 30 seconds, and RSTP can reduce this interval to as little as 1 second.

■   After STP and RSTP converge, the distribution nodes reestablish their HSRP relationships, and Distribution A switch (the primary HSRP peer) preempts. This causes yet another convergence event when Access A switch end points start forwarding traffic to the primary HSRP peer. The unexpected side effect is that Access A switch traffic goes through Access B switch to reach its default gateway. The Access B switch uplink to Distribution B switch is now a transit link for Access A switch traffic, and the Access B switch uplink to Distribution A switch must now carry traffic for both the originally intended Access B switch and for Access A switch.

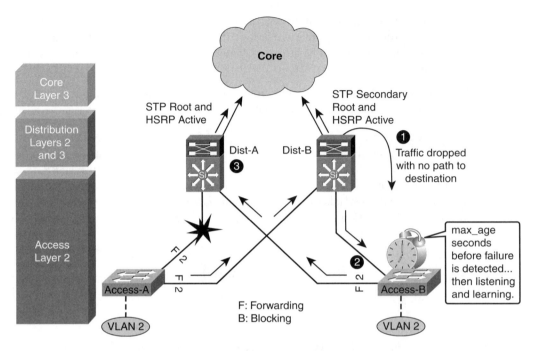

Figure 5-16 *Challenges with Too Little Redundancy Network Design*

Implementing Network Monitoring

When designing a campus network, when redundancy is created, managing redundancy can be achieved by monitoring the network, through SNMP and Syslog (System Logging), and testing connectivity with an IP SLA. This section describes these various elements and explains how to implement them.

Network Management Overview

Network management is a set of tools and processes to help manage the network, as shown in Figure 5-17. Network administrators use network management so they can be confident in the performance of the network. The following are some of the capabilities of well-configured network management:

- Ability to verify the network is working well and behaving in the planned manner

- Ability to characterize the performance of the network

- Ability to understand how much traffic is flowing and where it is flowing in the network

- Ability to troubleshoot the network

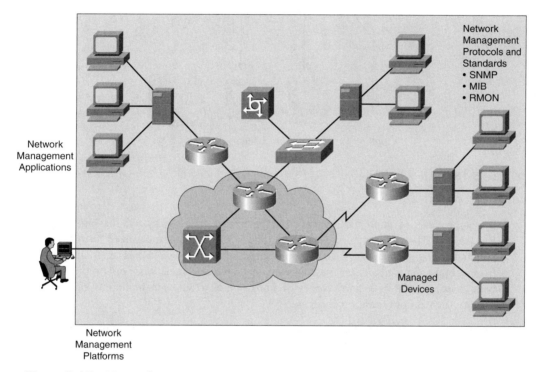

Figure 5-17 *Network Management*

The following tools are used extensively for typical enterprise network management:

- Syslog

- SNMP

- IP SLA

Syslog

The Cisco IOS system message logging (syslog) process enables a device to report and save important error and notification messages, either locally or to a remote logging server. Syslog messages can be sent to local console connections, the system buffer, or remote syslog servers, as shown in Figure 5-18. Syslog enables text messages to be sent to a syslog server using UDP port 514.

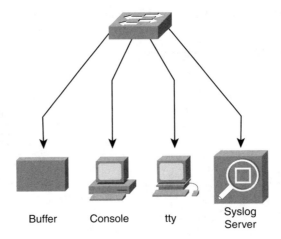

Buffer   Console   tty   Syslog Server

Figure 5-18 *Reporting Options for a Cisco Device*

Syslog provides a comprehensive reporting mechanism that logs system messages in plain English text. The syslog messages include both messages in a standardized format (called system logging messages, system error messages, or simply system messages) and output from debug commands. These messages are generated during network operation to assist with identifying the type and severity of a problem or to aid users in monitoring router activity such as configuration changes.

The system message and error reporting service (syslog) is an essential component of any network operating system. The system message service reports system state information to a network manager.

Cisco devices produce syslog messages as a result of network events. Every syslog message contains a severity level and a facility. Many networking devices support syslog, including routers, switches, application servers, firewalls, and other network appliances.

The smaller numerical levels are the more critical syslog alarms. The complete list of syslog levels are shown in Table 5-1.

Syslog facilities are service identifiers that identify and categorize system state data for error and event message reporting. Cisco IOS Software has more than 500 facilities. The most common syslog facilities are

- IP

- OSPF protocol

- SYS operating system

- IP Security (IPsec)

- Route Switch Processor (RSP)
- Interface (IF)

Table 5-1   *Syslog Severity Level*

Syslog Severity	Severity Level
Emergency	Level 0, highest level
Alert	Level 1
Critical	Level 2
Error	Level 3
Warning	Level 4
Notice	Level 5
Informational	Level 6
Debugging	Level 7

Other facilities include Cisco Discovery Protocol, STP, multicast, IPsec, TCP, BGP, RADIUS, Telnet, and those facilities related to QoS services.

More syslog information is located at www.cisco.com/univercd/cc/td/doc/product/software/ios123/123sup/123sems/index.htm.

Syslog Message format

The system messages begin with a percent sign (%) and are structured as shown in Figure 5-19.

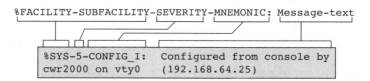

Figure 5-19   *Syslog Message Format*

- **Facility:** A code consisting of two or more uppercase letters that indicates the hardware device, protocol, or a module of the system software.
- **Severity:** A single-digit code from 0 to 7 that reflects the severity of the condition. The lower the number, the more serious the situation.
- **Mnemonic:** A code that uniquely identifies the error message.

■ **Message-text:** A text string describing the condition. This portion of the message sometimes contains detailed information about the event, including terminal port numbers, network addresses, or addresses that correspond to locations in the system memory address space.

Figure 5-19 shows a typical message that indicates the operating system (facility = SYS) is providing a notification (SEVERITY = 5) has been configured (MNEUMONIC = CON-FIG). The message text indicates that a user on VTY0 from IP address 192.168.64.25 made this change.

Note The documentation for each Cisco IOS Software release explains the meaning of these messages. For example, Catalyst 6500 system error message explanations are available at this location: www.cisco.com/en/US/products/hw/switches/ps708/products_system_message_guides_list.html.

Example 5-1 shows samples of syslog messages that Cisco IOS Software produces. The most common messages are link up and down messages and messages that a device produces when it exits from configuration mode. If ACL logging is configured, the device generates syslog messages when packets match a parameter condition. ACL logging can be useful for detecting packets that are denied access based on the security policy set by an ACL.

Example 5-1 *Sample Syslog Messages*

```
08:01:13: %LINEPROTO-5-UPDOWN: Line protocol on Interface FastEthernet0/5, changed
  state to up
08:01:23: %DUAL-5-NBRCHANGE: EIGRP-IPv4:(1) 1: Neighbor 10.1.1.1 (Vlan1) is up:
  new adjacency
08:02:31: %LINK-3-UPDOWN: Interface FastEthernet0/8, changed state to up
08:18:20: %LINEPROTO-5-UPDOWN: Line protocol on Interface FastEthernet0/5, changed
  state to down
08:18:22: %LINEPROTO-5-UPDOWN: Line protocol on Interface FastEthernet0/5, changed
  state to up
08:18:24: %LINEPROTO-5-UPDOWN: Line protocol on Interface FastEthernet0/2, changed
  state to down
08:18:24: %ILPOWER-5-IEEE_DISCONNECT: Interface Fa0/2: PD removed
08:18:26: %LINK-3-UPDOWN: Interface FastEthernet0/2, changed state to down
08:19:49: %ILPOWER-7-DETECT: Interface Fa0/2: Power Device detected: Cisco PD
08:19:53: %LINK-3-UPDOWN: Interface FastEthernet0/2, changed state to up
08:19:53: %LINEPROTO-5-UPDOWN: Line protocol on Interface FastEthernet0/2, changed
  state to up
```

System log messages can contain up to 80 characters and a percent sign (%), which follows the optional sequence number or timestamp information, if configured. Messages are displayed in this format:

seq no:timestamp: %facility-severity-MNEMONIC:description

A sequence number appears on the syslog message if the **service sequence-numbers** global configuration command is configured.

The timestamp shows the date and time of the message or event if the **service time-stamps [debug | log] [datetime uptime] [localtime |msec|show-timezone|year]** global configuration command is configured. The timestamp can be have one of three formats:

- *mm/dd hh:mm:ss*

- *hh:mm:ss* (short uptime)

- *d h* (long uptime)

Configuring Syslog

To configure a syslog server, use the command **logging** *<ip address of the Syslog server>*.

To configure from which severity level messages have to be sent to the Syslog server, use the global configuration command **logging trap** level, as shown in Example 5-2.

Example 5-2   *Configuring Syslog Trap Command*

```
sw(config)# logging trap ?
  <0-7>          Logging severity level
  alerts         Immediate action needed         (severity=1)
  critical       Critical conditions             (severity=2)
  debugging      Debugging messages              (severity=7)
  emergencies    System is unusable              (severity=0)
  errors         Error conditions                (severity=3)
  informational  Informational messages          (severity=6)
  notifications  Normal but significant conditions (severity=5)
  warnings       Warning conditions              (severity=4)
```

Messages can be sent to a syslog server. They also can be kept on the local switch. To configure the local logs, use the command **logging buffered**, as shown in Example 5-3. Valid parameters are the maximum local log size and the severity level that has to be logged: Enabling higher logging with small buffer size might mean that your logging displays only a short duration of time before newer messages overwrite the older ones. Ensure the local log size is an appropriate size for your level of logging and time frame that you would like to see in the local logs.

Example 5-3   *Configuring Syslog Buffered Command*

```
sw(config)# logging buffered ?
  <0-7>               Logging severity level
  <4096-2147483647>   Logging buffer size
  alerts              Immediate action needed        (severity=1)
  critical            Critical conditions            (severity=2)
  debugging           Debugging messages             (severity=7)
  discriminator       Establish MD-Buffer association
  emergencies         System is unusable             (severity=0)
  errors              Error conditions               (severity=3)
  informational       Informational messages         (severity=6)
  notifications       Normal but significant conditions  (severity=5)
  warnings            Warning conditions             (severity=4)
  xml                 Enable logging in XML to XML logging buffer
```

Use the **show logging** command to display the content of the local log files. When too many events are present in the log files, use the pipe argument (|) in combination with keywords such as **include** or **begin** to filter the output. Example 5-4 shows how to display all events present in the local logs that involve an error report (severity level 3) about interface link status.

Example 5-4   *Displaying Filtered System Log Messages*

```
sw# show logging | inc LINK-3
2d20h: %LINK-3-UPDOWN: Interface FastEthernet0/1, changed state to up
2d20h: %LINK-3-UPDOWN: Interface FastEthernet0/2, changed state to up
2d20h: %LINK-3-UPDOWN: Interface FastEthernet0/1, changed state to up
```

Example 5-5 shows another sample of how to display all events that start with %DUAL (therefore reporting events related to the EIGRP DUAL algorithm).

Example 5-5   *Displaying Filtered System Log Messages*

```
sw# show logg | beg %DUAL
2d22h: %DUAL-5-NBRCHANGE: EIGRP-IPv4:(10) 10: Neighbor 10.1.253.13
(FastEthernet0/11) is down: interface down
2d22h: %LINK-3-UPDOWN: Interface FastEthernet0/11, changed state to down
2d22h: %LINEPROTO-5-UPDOWN: Line protocol on Interface FastEthernet0/11, changed
state to down
```

SNMP

SNMP has become the standard for network management. SNMP is a simple solution that requires little code to implement and thus enables vendors to easily build SNMP agents for their products. Therefore, SNMP is often the foundation of network management architecture.

SNMP contains three elements, as shown in Figure 5-20:

■ Network Management Application (SNMP Manager)

■ SNMP Agents (running inside a managed device)

■ MIB Database object that describes the information in a predetermined format that the agent can use to populate the data.

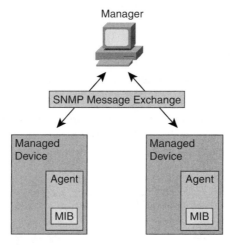

Figure 5-20 *SNMP Overview*

SNMP defines how management information is exchanged between network management applications and management agents. A network management application periodically polls the SNMP agents that reside on managed devices by querying the device for data. The periodic SNMP polling has the disadvantage that there is delay between the time that an event occurs and the time that it is noticed by the NMS. There is a trade-off between polling frequency and bandwidth usage. A network management application can display the information in a GUI on the network manager. SNMP uses the User Datagram Protocol (UDP) transport mechanism of IP to retrieve and send management information, such as MIB variables.

SNMP management agents that reside on managed devices collect and store information about the device and its operation, respond to managerial requests, and generate traps to inform the manager of certain events. SNMP traps are sent by management agents to the network management system when certain events occur. Trap-directed notification can result in substantial savings of network and agent resources by eliminating the need for some SNMP polling requests.

The management agent collects data and stores it locally in the MIB. Community strings control access to the MIB. To view or set MIB variables, the user must specify the appropriate community string for read or write access.

SNMP Versions

The initial version of the SNMP standard (SNMP version 1, or SNMPv1) is defined in RFC 1157. Following are five basic SNMP messages the network manager uses to transfer data from agents that reside on managed devices, as shown in Figure 5-21:

- **Get Request:** Used to request the value of a specific MIB variable from the agent.

- **Get Next Request:** Used after the initial Get Request to retrieve the next object instance from a table or a list.

- **Set Request:** Used to set a MIB variable on an agent.

- **Get Response:** Used by an agent to respond to a Get Request or Get Next Request from a manager.

- **Trap:** Used by an agent to transmit an unsolicited alarm to the manager. An agent sends a Trap message when a certain condition occurs, such as a change in the state of a device, a device or component failure, or an agent initialization or restart.

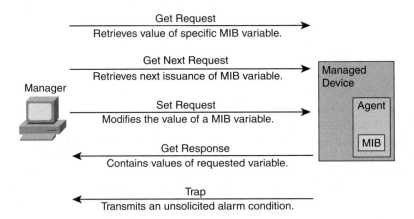

Figure 5-21   *SNMP Messages*

SNMPv2 was introduced with RFC 1441, but members of the Internet Engineering Task Force (IETF) subcommittee could not agree on the security and administrative sections of the SNMPv2 specification. There were several attempts to achieve acceptance of SNMPv2 through the release of experimental modified versions.

Community-based SNMPv2 (SNMPv2C), defined in RFC 1901, is the most common implementation. SNMPv2C deploys the administrative framework defined in SNMPv1, which uses read/write community strings for administrative access.

SNMPv2 introduces two new message types:

- **Get Bulk Request:** Reduces repetitive requests and replies and improves performance when you are retrieving large amounts of data (for example, tables).

- **Inform Request:** Alert an SNMP manager of specific conditions. Unlike SNMP Trap messages, which are unconfirmed, the NMS acknowledges an Inform Request by sending an Inform Response message back to the requesting device.

SNMPv2 adds new data types with 64-bit counters, because 32-bit counters were quickly outmoded by fast network interfaces. On Cisco routers, SNMPv2 is implemented in Cisco IOS Software Release 11.3 and later.

Note   Neither SNMPv1 nor SNMPv2 offers security features. Specifically, SNMPv1 and v2 can neither authenticate the source of a management message nor provide encryption. Because of the lack of security features, many SNMPv1 and v2 implementations are limited to a read-only capability, reducing their utility to that of a network monitor.

SNMPv3 is described in RFCs 3410 through 3415. It adds methods to ensure the secure transmission of critical data between managed devices.

SNMPv3 introduces three levels of security:

- **noAuthNoPriv:** No authentication is required, and no privacy (encryption) is provided.

- **authNoPriv:** Authentication is based on Hash-based Message Authentication Code with Message Digest 5 (HMAC-MD5) or Hash-based Message Authentication Code with Secure Hash Algorithm (HMAC-SHA). No encryption is provided.

- **authPriv:** In addition to authentication, Cipher Block Chaining-Data Encryption Standard (CBC-DES) encryption is used as the privacy protocol.

Security levels that are implemented for each security model determine which SNMP objects a user can access for reading, writing, or creating and the list of notifications that its users can receive.

On Cisco routers, SNMPv3 is implemented in Cisco IOS Software Release 12.0 and later.

SNMP Recommendations

SNMPv1 and SNMPv2 use community strings in clear text. These community strings, as with all passwords, should be carefully chosen to ensure they are not trivial. Community strings should be changed at regular intervals and in accordance with network security policies. For example, the strings should be changed when a network administrator changes roles or leaves the company. If SNMP is used only to monitor devices, use read-only communities. Ensure that SNMP messages do not spread beyond the management consoles. You can use access-lists to prevent SNMP messages from going beyond the required devices, and on the monitored devices to limit access for management systems only.

SNMPv3 is recommended because it provides authentication and encryption.

Configuring SNMP

To configure SNMP, follow these steps:

Step 1.   Configure SNMP access lists.

Step 2.   Configure SNMP community strings.

Step 3.   Configure SNMP trap receiver.

Step 4.   Configure SNMPv3 user.

The first step needed for SNMP configuration is to enable SNMP access. This is done by configuring community strings, which act somewhat like passwords. The difference is that there can be several community strings, and that each one might grant different forms of access. In Example 5-6, community *cisco* grants read-only access to the local switch, while *xyz123* grants read and write access to the local switch. The *100* at the end of the **snmp-server community** lines restricts access to sources permitted via standard access-list 100. In this case, all stations in subnet 10.1.1.0/24 can access the local switch with both communities *cisco* and *xyz123*.

Example 5-6 *Configuring SNMP*

```
sw(config)# access-list 100 permit ip 10.1.1.0 0.0.0.255 any
sw(config)# snmp-server community cisco RO 100
sw(config)# snmp-server community xyz123 RW 100
sw(config)# snmp-server trap 10.1.1.50
```

It is critical to choose community strings that are stronger to ensure higher security. Choose strings that are at least eight charters in length and contain lower/upper CAPS mixed in with special characters and numerals.

The **snmp-server trap** command has two purposes: It configures the SNMP server and instructs the switch to send its traps to this server.

There are many other SNMP options. Refer to this page for more information: www.cisco.com/en/US/docs/ios/netmgmt/configuration/guide/nm_cfg_snmp_sup_ps6350_ TSD_Products_Configuration_Guide_Chapter.html.

IP Service Level Agreement

The network has become increasingly critical for customers, and any downtime or degradation can adversely impact revenue. Companies need some form of predictability with IP services. An SLA is a contract between the network provider and its customers, or between a network department and internal corporate customers. It provides a form of guarantee to customers about the level of user experience.

An SLA specifies connectivity and performance agreements for an end-user service from a service provider. The SLA typically outlines the minimum level of service and the expected level of service. The networking department can use the SLAs to verify that the service provider is meeting its own SLAs or to define service levels for critical business applications. An SLA can also be used as the basis for planning budgets and justifying network expenditures.

Administrators can ultimately reduce the mean time to repair (MTTR) by proactively isolating network issues. They can change the network configuration based on optimized performance metrics.

Typically, the technical components of an SLA contain a guarantee level for network availability, network performance in terms of round-trip time (RTT), and network response in terms of latency, jitter, and packet loss. The specifics of an SLA vary depending on the applications an organization is supporting in the network.

IP SLA Measurements

The IP SLA measurement functionality in Cisco IOS Software enables configuration of a router to send synthetic traffic to a host computer or a router that has been configured to respond, as shown in Figure 5-22. One-way travel times and packet loss data are gathered. Certain measurements also enable jitter data to be collected.

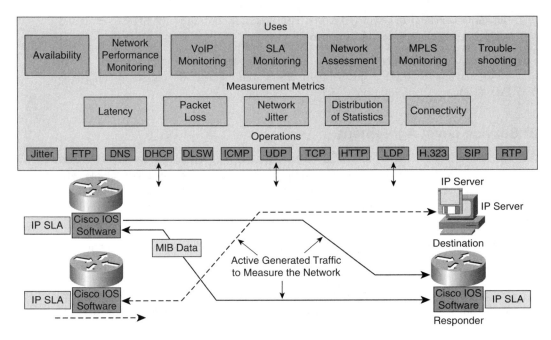

Figure 5-22 *IP SLA in Cisco IOS*

Following are several common functions for IP SLA measurements:

■   Edge-to-edge network availability monitoring

■   Network performance monitoring and network performance visibility

■   VoIP, video, and virtual private network (VPN) monitoring

■   IP service network health readiness or assessment

■   Multiprotocol Label Switching (MPLS) network monitoring

■   Troubleshooting of network operation

IP SLA measurement uses a variety of operations and actively generated traffic probes to gather many types of measurement statistics:

■   Network latency and response time

■   Packet loss statistics

■   Network jitter and voice quality scoring

■   End-to-end network connectivity

Multiple IP SLA operations (measurements) can run in a network at one time. Reporting tools use SNMP to extract the data into a database and then report on it.

IP SLA measurements enable the network manager to verify service guarantees, which increases network reliability by validating network performance, proactively identifying network issues, and easing the deployment of new IP services.

IP SLA Operations

The network manager configures a target device, protocol, and User Datagram Protocol (UDP) or TCP port number on the IP SLA source for each operation. The source uses the IP SLA control protocol to communicate with the responder before sending test packets. To increase security on IP SLA measurements control messages, the responder can utilize Message Digest 5 (MD5) authentication for securing the control protocol exchange. When the operation is finished and the response is received, the results are stored in the IP SLA MIB on the source and are retrieved using SNMP.

IP SLA operations are defined to target devices. If the operation is something such as Domain Name System (DNS) or HTTP, the target device might be any suitable computer. For operations such as testing the port used by a database, an organization might not want to risk unexpected effects and would use the IP SLA responder functionality to have a router respond in place of the actual database server. Responder functionality can be enabled in a router with one command and requires no complex or per-operation configuration.

IP SLA Source and Responder

The IP SLA source is where all IP SLA measurement probe operations are configured either by the command-line interface (CLI) or through an SNMP tool that supports IP SLA operation. The source is also the Cisco IOS device that sends probe packets. The destination of the probe might be another Cisco router or another network target, such as a web server or IP host.

Although the destination of the probe can be any IP device, the measurement accuracy is improved with an IP SLA responder. An IP SLA responder is a device that runs Cisco IOS Software and is configured as an IP SLA measurement responder with the **ip sla monitor responder** configuration command.

IP SLA Operation with Responder

The network manager configures an IP SLA operation by defining a target device, protocol, and port number on the IP SLA source. The network manager can also configure reaction conditions. The operation is scheduled to be run for a period of time to gather statistics. Figure 5-23 shows the sequence of events that occurs for each IP SLA operation that requires a responder on the target:

1. At the start of the control phase, the IP SLA source sends a control message with the configured IP SLA operation information to IP SLA control port UDP 1967 on the target router. The control message carries information such as protocol, port number, and duration:

- If MD5 authentication is enabled, MD5 checksum is sent with the control message.

- If the authentication of the message is enabled, the responder verifies it; if the authentication fails, the responder returns an authentication failure message.

- If the IP SLA measurement operation does not receive a response from a responder, it tries to retransmit the control message and eventually times out.

2. If the responder processes the control message, it sends an OK message to the source router and listens on the port specified in the control message for a specified duration. If the responder cannot process the control message, it returns an error. In Figure 5-23, UDP port 2020 will be used for the IP SLA test packets.

3. If the return code of control message is OK, the IP SLA operation moves to the probing phase, where it sends one or more test packets to the responder for response time computations. The return code is available in the **show ip sla statistics** command. In Figure 5-23, these test messages are sent on control port 2020.

4. The responder accepts the test packets and responds. Based on the type of operation, the responder might add an "in" timestamp and an "out" timestamp in the response packet payload to account for CPU time spent in measuring unidirectional packet loss, latency, and jitter to a Cisco device. These timestamps help the IP SLA source to make accurate assessments on one-way delay and the processing time in the target routers. The responder disables the user-specified port when it responds to the IP SLA measurements packet or when a specified time expires.

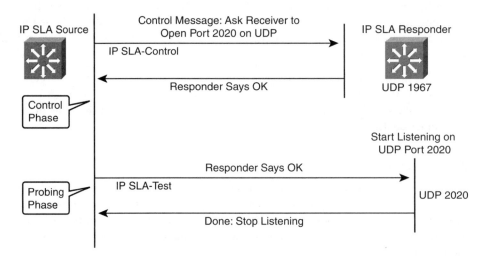

Figure 5-23 *IP SLA Operation*

IP SLA Responder Timestamps

Figure 5-24 illustrates the use of IP SLA responder timestamps in round-trip calculations. The IP SLA source uses four timestamps for the round-trip time (RTT) calculation. The IP SLA source sends a test packet at time T1.

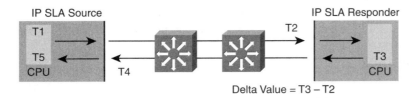

Figure 5-24   *IP SLA Responder Timestamps*

The IP SLA responder includes both the receipt time (T2) and the transmitted time (T3). Because of other high-priority processes, routers can take tens of milliseconds to process incoming packets. The delay affects the response times because the reply to test packets might be sitting in a queue while waiting to be processed. This timestamping is made with a granularity of submilliseconds. At times of high network activity, an ICMP ping test often shows a long and inaccurate response time, whereas an IP SLA–based responder shows an accurate response time. The IP SLA source subtracts T2 from T3 to produce the time spent processing the test packet in the IP SLA responder. This time is represented by a delta value.

The delta value is then subtracted from the overall RTT. The same principle is applied by the IP SLA source where the incoming T4 is also taken at the interrupt level to allow for greater accuracy as compared to T5 when the packet is processed.

An additional benefit of two timestamps at the IP SLA responder is the ability to track one-way delay, jitter, and directional packet loss. These statistics are critical because a great deal of network behavior is asynchronous. To capture one-way delay measurements, the configuration of both the IP SLA source and IP SLA responder with Network Time Protocol (NTP) is required.

Both the source and target need to be synchronized to the same clock source. The IP SLA responder provides enhanced accuracy for measurements, without the need for dedicated third-party external probe devices. It also provides additional statistics, which are not otherwise available via standard ICMP-based measurements.

Configuring IP SLA

There are many ways of implementing IP SLA. Different hardware platforms and different IOS versions might have a slightly different approach to IP SLA configuration.

Steps to configure IP SLA follow:

Step 1.   Configure IP SLA probe.

Step 2.   Activate probe.

Step 3.   Configure tracking object.

Step 4.   Configure action on tracking object.

The first step is to use the command **ip sla monitor** followed by a number to enter in IP SLA configuration mode. The number identifies the SLA test.

In Figure 5-25, the IP SLA test is done by sending an ipIcmpEcho message to the IP address 10.1.1.1, from the local interface f0/1. This message is sent every 10 seconds, as shown in the Example 5-7.

Figure 5-25   *Configuring IP SLA*

Example 5-7   *Cisco IP SLA Configuration*

```
SwitchB(config)# ip sla monitor 11
SwitchB(config-sla)# type echo prot ipIcmpEcho 10.1.1.1 source-int fa0/1
SwitchB(config-sla)# frequncy 10
SwitchB(config0sla)# exit
SwitchB(config)# ip sla monitor schedule 11 life forever start-time now
SwitchB(config)# track 1 ip sla 11 reachability
```

The 10.1.1.1 device should be configured to answer this message with **the** ip sla responder command.

At this point, the type of message is configured, along with its frequency and target address. The next step is to decide when this test should start. This is configured with the **ip sla monitor schedule** command. In Example 5-7, the test is to start immediately and to last forever.

When the IP SLA test has been defined, additional configuration is needed to determine what action should be taken when the test result is received. In Example 5-7, the track command follows the IP SLA test result. Further commands can then be configured to use the track result to decrement interfaces' priority or activate backup links.

Example 5-8   *Verifying IP SLA*

```
sw# show ip sla statistics
Round Trip Time (RTT) for Index 1
Latest RTT: NoConnection/Busy/Timeout
Latest operation start time: 11:11:22.533 eastern Thu Jul 9 2010
Latest operation return code: Timeout
```

```
Over thresholds occurred: FALSE
Number of successes: 177
Number of failures: 6
Operation time to live: Forever
Operational state of entry: Active
Last time this entry was reset: Never
```

When IP SLA is configured, the test is conducted as per the scheduled configuration. The test might succeed or fail. If you do not monitor the test results, it might fail silently. To display information about the test, use the **show ip sla statistics** command. It displays, among other parameters, the number of successes and number of failures. It also shows if the test is still being run. In Example 5-8, the sample output shows that the test is still in active state, succeeded 177 times but also failed 6 times when the command was issued. Monitoring these statistics over time can tell you if there is a connection issue discovered through the IP SLA test.

To get more information about a given IP SLA test configuration, use the **show ip sla configuration** command. Example 5-9 shows a user displaying IP SLA configuration. With **show ip sla configuration**, you can also verify which IP address is used as a source, what is the size of each packet, and what are the default timeout and frequency for the test.

Example 5-9 *Verifying IP SLA Configuration*

```
sW# sh ip sla configuration
IP SLAs, Infrastructure Engine-II

Entry number: 1
Owner:
Tag:
Type of operation to perform: echo
Target address/Source address: 10.1.3.10/10.1.253.1
Type Of Service parameter: 0x0
Request size (ARR data portion): 28
Operation timeout (milliseconds): 5000
Verify data: No
Vrf Name:
Schedule:
    Operation frequency (seconds): 5
    Next Scheduled Start Time: Start Time already passed
    Group Scheduled : FALSE
    Randomly Scheduled : FALSE
    Life (seconds): Forever
    Entry Ageout (seconds): never
    Recurring (Starting Everyday): FALSE
    Status of entry (SNMP RowStatus): Active
```

```
Threshold (milliseconds): 5000
Distribution Statistics:
    Number of statistic hours kept: 2
    Number of statistic distribution buckets kept: 1
    Statistic distribution interval (milliseconds): 20
History Statistics:
    Number of history Lives kept: 0
    Number of history Buckets kept: 15
    History Filter Type: None
```

Implementing Redundant Supervisor Engines in Catalyst Switches

The Supervisor Engine is the most important component in Catalyst modular switches, which are typically found in the campus backbone and building distribution submodules. If the Supervisor Engine fails, the switch fails to forward traffic. As a result, providing redundancy for the Supervisor Engine is the most critical form of high availability. Not all Catalyst switches are modular, and not all Catalyst switches provide redundant Supervisor Engine capability. The Catalyst 4500 and 6500 families of switches, however, do provide options for redundant Supervisor Engines.

Provisioning dual Supervisor Engines within a Catalyst family of switches, as shown in Figure 5-26, ensures high availability by providing redundancy without requiring the deployment of an entire separate switch. This solution is a cost-effective alternative to deploying multiple switches for redundancy. Even in networks that deploy multiple redundant switches, configuring redundant Supervisor Engines adds an extra level of availability assurance.

The Catalyst 4500 and Catalyst 6500 families of switches support redundant Supervisor Engines. The Catalyst 6500 family supports redundant Supervisor Engines on all chassis models, whereas the Catalyst 4500 supports redundant Supervisor Engines only in 4057R-E and 4510R-E chassis.

The Catalyst 4500 and Catalyst 6500 families of switches supports the following redundancy features:

- RPR (Route Processor Redundancy) and RPR+ (only on Catalyst 6500)

- SSO (Stateful SwitchOver)

- NSF (Non-Stop Forwarding) with SSO

NSF with SSO provides the highest level of high availability in the Catalyst 6500 and Catalyst 4500 families of switches.

Figure 5-26   *Redundant Supervisor Engines in Catalyst 6500 Switches*

Route Processor Redundancy

Route Processor Redundancy (RPR) was the first form of high availability feature in Cisco IOS Software starting with Cisco IOS Software Release 12.1(13)E. Although RPR is still available in Cisco IOS, it is no longer the preferred option. NSF with SSO provides better convergence time than RPR or RPR+.

This section briefly reviews the RPR and RPR+ features. The Catalyst 4500 and Catalyst 6500 families of switches support high availability by enabling a redundant Supervisor Engine to take over if the primary Supervisor Engine fails for both Layer 2 and Layer 3 functions. Table 5-2 shows the failover times of RPR and RPR+ on the Catalyst 6500 and 4500 families of switches.

Table 5-2   *RPR and RPR+ Failover Time Intervals*

Redundancy	Catalyst 6500 Failover Time	Catalyst 4500 Failover Time
RPR	2–4 minutes	Less than 60 seconds
RPR+	30–60 seconds	—

The Supervisor Engine involved in forwarding of traffic at both the Layer 2 and Layer 3 levels is called the active Supervisor Engine. The other Supervisor Engine, which is not forwarding traffic but is instead in a standby mode monitoring the active Supervisor Engine, is called the standby Supervisor Engine. The active and standby Supervisor Engines monitor each other through periodic communication for failure.

With RPR, any of the following events triggers a switchover from the active to the standby Supervisor Engine:

■ Route Processor (RP) or Switch Processor (SP) crash on the active Supervisor Engine.

■ A manual switchover from the CLI.

■ Removal of the active Supervisor Engine.

■ Clock synchronization failure between Supervisor Engines.

In a switchover, the redundant Supervisor Engine becomes fully operational, and the following events occur on the remaining modules during an RPR failover:

■ All switching modules are power-cycled.

■ Remaining subsystems on the MSFC (including Layer 2 and Layer 3 protocols) are initialized on the prior standby, now active, Supervisor Engine.

■ ACLs based on the new active Supervisor Engine are reprogrammed into the Supervisor Engine hardware.

Route Processor Redundancy Plus

With RPR+, the redundant Supervisor Engine remains fully initialized and configured, which shortens the switchover time if the active Supervisor Engine fails or if the network administrator performs a manual switchover.

> **Note** The active Supervisor Engine checks the image version of the standby Supervisor Engine when the standby Supervisor Engine comes online. If the image on the standby Supervisor Engine does not match the image on the active Supervisor Engine, RPR redundancy mode is used.

RPR+ enhances Supervisor redundancy compared to RPR by providing the following additional benefits:

■ **Reduced switchover time:** Depending on the configuration, the switchover time is in the range of 30 seconds to 60 seconds.

■ **No reloading of installed modules:** Because both the startup configuration and the running configuration stay continually synchronized from the active to the redundant Supervisor Engine during a switchover, no reloading of line modules occurs.

■   **Synchronization of Online Insertion and Removal (OIR) events between the active and standby:** This occurs such that modules in the online state remain online and modules in the down state remain in the down state after a switchover.

Configuring and Verifying RPR+ Redundancy

RPR+ redundancy configurations are straightforward, as illustrated in the following steps:

Step 1.   Enter the following command to start configuring redundancy modes:

   `redundancy`

Step 2.   Use the following command under redundancy configuration submode to configure RPR+:

   `mode rpr-plus`

Example 5-10 illustrates a user configuring RPR+ redundancy on a Catalyst 6500 and verifying the configuration. In Example 5-10, the standby supervisor is currently not present; therefore, the peer state is disabled in the display.

Example 5-10   *Configuring and Verifying RPR+ Redundancy*

```
Switch# configure terminal
Enter configuration commands, one per line. End with CNTL/Z.
Switch(config)# redundancy
Switch(config-red)# mode rpr-plus
Switch(config-red)# end
Switch# show redundancy states
       my state = 13 -ACTIVE
     peer state = 1 -DISABLED
           Mode = Simplex
           Unit = Primary
        Unit ID = 1

Redundancy Mode (Operational) = Route Processor Redundancy Plus
Redundancy Mode (Configured) = Route Processor Redundancy Plus
     Split Mode = Disabled
   Manual Swact = Disabled Reason: Simplex mode
 Communications = Down      Reason: Simplex mode

  client count   = 11
 client_notification_TMR = 30000 milliseconds
          keep_alive TMR = 4000 milliseconds
        keep_alive count = 0
    keep_alive threshold = 7
           RF debug mask = 0x0
```

Stateful Switchover (SSO)

RPR and RPR+ recover traffic forwarding of the switch in about a minute after a switchover of the Supervisor Engine; however, RPR and RPR+ disruptions are not transparent to the end user. For example, if the user were using an IP Phone, the call would be dropped. Even though a minute-long outage might not be significant to a typical Internet user, it is critical for IP Phone users or database applications; therefore, this poses the need for a better redundancy protocol to minimize the disruption of traffic. The Catalyst 4500 and Catalyst 6500 families of switches support SSO to provide minimal Layer 2 traffic disruption during a Supervisor switchover.

In SSO mode, the redundant Supervisor Engine starts up in a fully initialized state and synchronizes with the startup configuration and the running configuration of the active Supervisor Engine. The standby Supervisor in SSO mode also keeps in sync with the active Supervisor Engine for all changes in hardware and software states for features that are supported via SSO. Any supported feature interrupted by failure of the active Supervisor Engine is continued seamlessly on the redundant Supervisor Engine.

The following list details the current protocols and features that SSO modes support for Layer 2 redundancy. For a complete and up-to-date list, refer to Cisco.com.

- 802.3x (Flow Control)

- 802.3ad (LACP) and PAgP

- 802.1X (Authentication) and Port security

- 802.3af (Inline power)

- VTP

- Dynamic ARP Inspection/DHCP snooping/IP source guard

- IGMP snooping (versions 1 and 2)

- DTP (802.1Q and ISL)

- MST/PVST+/Rapid-PVST

- PortFast/UplinkFast/BackboneFast /BPDU Guard and filtering

- Voice VLAN

- Unicast MAC filtering

- ACL (VLAN ACLs, Port ACLs, Router ACLs)

- QOS (DBL)

- Multicast storm control/broadcast storm control

In SSO mode, ports that were active before the switchover remain active because the redundant Supervisor Engine recognizes the hardware link status of every link. The neighboring devices do not see the link-down event during the switchover except the link to the previous active Supervisor. On the Catalyst 4500 switches, the uplink on the previous active Supervisor Engine is also retained even though that Supervisor Engine might be rebooting. In such a case, no spanning-tree topology changes occur because no link states change.

On the Catalyst 6500 family of switches, the time it takes for the Layer 2 traffic to be fully operational following a Supervisor failure is between 0 and 3 seconds.

On the Catalyst 4500, subsecond switchover can be achieved for Layer 2 traffic. Layer 3 information, however, needs to be relearned after a Supervisor Engine failover with just the SSO mode of redundancy, but the newly active Supervisor Engine continues to use existing Layer 2 switching information to continue forwarding traffic until Layer 3 information is relearned. This relearning involves rebuilding ARP tables and Layer 3 CEF and adjacency tables. Until the routing converges and CEF and adjacency tables are rebuilt, packets that need to be routed are dropped.

Configuring and Verifying SSO

SSO redundancy configurations are straightforward, as illustrated in the following steps:

Step 1.   Enter the following command to start configuring redundancy modes:

```
redundancy
```

Step 2.   Use the following command under redundancy configuration submode to configure SSO:

```
mode sso
```

Example 5-11 illustrates a user configuring SSO redundancy on a Catalyst 4500 and verifying the configuration.

Example 5-11   *Configuring and Verifying SSO Redundancy*

```
Switch# configure terminal
Enter configuration commands, one per line. End with CNTL/Z.
Switch(config)# redundancy
Switch(config-red)# mode sso
Changing to sso mode will reset the standby. Do you want to continue? [confirm]
Switch(config-red)# end
Switch# show redundancy states
       my state = 13 -ACTIVE
     peer state = 8   -STANDBY HOT
           Mode = Duplex
           Unit = Primary
        Unit ID = 2
```

```
Redundancy Mode (Operational) = Stateful Switchover
Redundancy Mode (Configured) = Stateful Switchover
       Split Mode = Disabled
   Manual Swact = Enabled
 Communications = Up

   client count = 21
 client_notification_TMR = 240000 milliseconds
          keep_alive TMR = 9000 milliseconds
        keep_alive count = 0
    keep_alive threshold = 18
            RF debug mask = 0x0
```

NSF with SSO

The Catalyst 4500 and 6500 family of switches supports another form of redundancy called NSF with SSO.

NSF with SSO redundancy includes the standard SSO for Layer 2 switching; however, it also minimizes the amount of time that a Layer 3 network is unavailable following a Supervisor Engine switchover by continuing to forward IP packets using CEF entries built from the old active Supervisor. Zero packet loss or near-zero packet loss is achieved with NSF with SSO redundancy mode.

When using the NSF with SSO feature, reconvergence of supported Layer 3 routing protocols (BGP, EIGRP, OSPF, and IS-IS) happens automatically in the background while packet forwarding continues. The standby Supervisor Engine maintains the copy of the CEF entries from the active Supervisor Engine, and upon switchover, the new active Supervisor Engine uses the CEF entries while the routing protocol converges without interruption to user traffic. When the routing protocol has converged and the Routing Information Base (RIB) has been built afresh on the route processor, any stale CEF entries are removed, and packet forwarding is fully restored.

Changes have been made to the routing protocols so that upon switchover, an NSF-enabled router sends special packets that trigger routing updates from the NSF-aware neighbors without resetting the peer relationship. This feature prevents route flapping and routing changes during a Supervisor failover. NSF-aware routers understand that a neighboring NSF router can still forward packets when an RP switchover happens. NSF-aware routers are not required to be NSF routers themselves.

For information about the NSF operations for each of the routing protocols, refer to the "Configuring NSF with SSO Supervisor Engine Redundancy" configuration section of the Catalyst 6500 configuration guide at Cisco.com.

In summary, Cisco NSF provides the following benefits:

- **Improved network availability:** NSF continues forwarding network traffic and application state information so that user traffic is not interrupted after a Supervisor switchover.

- **Overall network stability:** Network stability is improved by maintaining routing protocol neighbor relationships during Supervisor failover.

Configuring and Verifying NSF with SSO

NSF is an additional configuration option for configuring SSO. For an example of how to configure SSO, refer to Example 5-11. To configure NSF for OSPF, EIGRP, and IS-IS, use the **nsf** *router-level* command. To configure BGP for NSF support, use the **bgp graceful-restart** *router-level* command.

Example 5-12 illustrates a user configuring NSF support for BGP and OSPF and verifying the configuration output.

Example 5-12   *Configuring and Verifying NSF Support for BGP and OSPF Routing Protocols*

```
Switch# configure terminal
Enter configuration commands, one per line. End with CNTL/Z.
Switch(config)# router bgp 100
Switch(config-router)# bgp graceful-restart
Switch(config-router)# exit
Switch(config)#router ospf 200
Switch(config-router)# nsf
Switch(config-router)# end
Switch# show ip bgp neighbors 192.168.200.1

BGP neighbor is 192.168.200.1, remote AS 200, external link
  BGP version 4, remote router ID 192.168.200.1
  BGP state = Established, up for 00:01:23
  Last read 00:00:17, hold time is 180, keepalive interval is 60 seconds
  Neighbor capabilities:
    Route refresh:advertised and received(new)
    Address family IPv4 Unicast:advertised and received
    Address family IPv4 Multicast:advertised and received
    Graceful Restart Capability:advertised and received
      Remote Restart timer is 120 seconds
      Address families preserved by peer:
        IPv4 Unicast, IPv4 Multicast
```

```
    Received 1539 messages, 0 notifications, 0 in queue
    Sent 100 messages, 0 notifications, 0 in queue
    Default minimum time between advertisement runs is 30 seconds

Switch# show ip ospf
Routing Process "ospf 200" with ID 192.168.20.1 and Domain ID 0.0.0.1
Supports only single TOS(TOS0) routes
Supports opaque LSA
SPF schedule delay 5 secs, Hold time between two SPFs 10 secs
Minimum LSA interval 5 secs. Minimum LSA arrival 1 secs
Number of external LSA 0. Checksum Sum 0x0
Number of opaque AS LSA 0. Checksum Sum 0x0
Number of DCbitless external and opaque AS LSA 0
Number of DoNotAge external and opaque AS LSA 0
Number of areas in this router is 1. 1 normal 0 stub 0 nssa
External flood list length 0
Non-Stop Forwarding enabled, last NSF restart 00:02:36 ago (took 34 secs)
Area BACKBONE(0)
Number of interfaces in this area is 1 (0 loopback)
 Area has no authentication
SPF algorithm executed 3 times
```

Understanding First Hop Redundancy Protocols

Hosts and servers in a subnet need a gateway to reach devices that are not in the same subnet. Because gateways perform a key role in operations of all devices, their availability is paramount. Providing redundant gateways is one solution but to ensure that they operate in a way that provides redundancy and load balancing, they need be configured for first hop redundancy protocol such as HSRP, VRRP, and GLBP. This section covers the alternatives to gateway protocols and then explains each of the first hop redundancy protocols in detail.

Introduction to First Hop Redundancy Protocol

First hop redundancy protocols such as HSRP and VRRP provide default gateway redundancy with one router acting as the active gateway router with one or more other routers held in standby mode. GLBP enables all available gateway routers to load share and be active at the same time. But before first hop redundancy protocols were available, networks relied on Proxy ARP and static gateway configuration.

Proxy ARP

Before default gateway was supported on most IP clients, networks were relying on the proxy ARP feature to reach IP devices outside the IP client subnet. Cisco IOS Software ran proxy ARP to enable hosts that had no knowledge of routing options to obtain the MAC address of a gateway that can forward packets off the local subnet.

In Figure 5-27, if the proxy ARP router receives an ARP request for an IP address that it knows is not on the same interface as the request sender, it generates an ARP reply packet giving its own local MAC address as the destination MAC address of the IP address being resolved. The host that sent the ARP request sends all packets destined for the resolved IP address to the MAC address of the router. The router then forwards the packets toward the intended host. Proxy ARP is enabled by default.

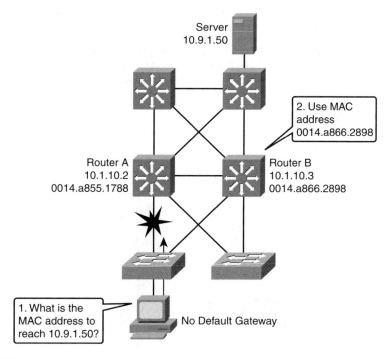

Figure 5-27   *Proxy ARP*

With proxy ARP, the end-user station behaves as if the destination device were connected to its own network segment. If the responsible router fails, the source end station continues to send packets for that IP destination to the MAC address of the failed router, and the packets are discarded.

Eventually, the proxy ARP MAC address will age out of the workstation's ARP cache. The workstation might eventually acquire the address of another proxy ARP failover router, but the workstation cannot send packets off the local segment during this failover time.

For further information on proxy ARP, refer to RFC 1027, "Using ARP to Implement Transparent Subnet Gateways."

Static Default Gateway

Now that a default gateway is configured on most devices, the Proxy ARP feature is not used anymore. Nevertheless, each client receives only one default gateway; there is no means by which to configure a secondary gateway, even if a second route exists to carry packets off the local segment.

For example, primary and secondary paths between the building access submodule and the building distribution submodule provide continuous access if a link failure occurs at the building access layer. Primary and secondary paths between the building distribution layer and the building core layer provide continuous operations should a link fail at the building distribution layer.

In Figure 5-28, Router A is responsible for routing packets to server (10.9.1.50). If Router A becomes unavailable, routing protocols can quickly and dynamically converge and determine that Router B will now transfer packets that would otherwise have gone through Router A. Most workstations, servers, and printers, however, do not receive this dynamic routing information.

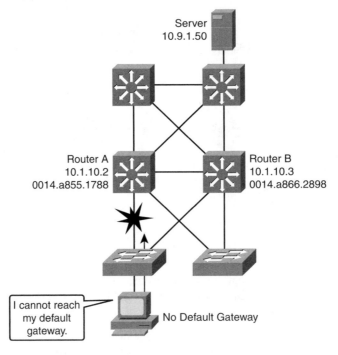

Figure 5-28   *Static Default Gateway*

End devices are typically configured with a single default gateway IP address that does not change when network topology changes occur. If the router whose IP address is configured as the default gateway fails, the local device cannot send packets off the local network segment, effectively disconnecting it from the rest of the network. Even if a redundant router exists that could serve as a default gateway for that segment, there is no dynamic method by which these devices can determine the address of a new default gateway.

Hot Standby Router Protocol (HSRP)

HSRP is a redundancy protocol developed by Cisco to provide gateway redundancy without any additional configuration on the end devices in the subnet. With HSRP configured between a set of routers, they work in concert to present the appearance of a single virtual router to the hosts on the LAN, as shown in Figure 5-29. By sharing an IP address and a MAC (Layer 2) address, two or more routers can act as a single virtual router.

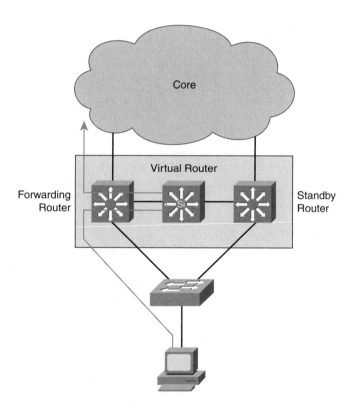

Figure 5-29   *Hot Standby Router Protocol*

The IP address of the virtual router will be configured as the default gateway for the workstations on a specific IP segment. When frames are to be sent from the workstation to the default gateway, the workstation uses ARP to resolve the MAC address associated with the IP address of the default gateway. The ARP resolution returns the MAC address of the virtual router. Frames sent to the MAC address of the virtual router can then be physically processed by the active router that is part of that virtual router group. The physical router that forwards this traffic is transparent to the end stations.

HSRP provides the mechanism for determining which router should take the active role in forwarding traffic. HSRP also has a mechanism to determine when that active role must be taken over by a standby router. The transition from one forwarding router to another is transparent to the end devices.

For example, when the active router or the links between the routers fail, the standby router stops seeing hello messages from the active router. The standby router then assumes the role of the forwarding router, as shown in Figure 5-30. Because the new forwarding router assumes both the IP and MAC address of the virtual router, the end stations see no disruption in service.

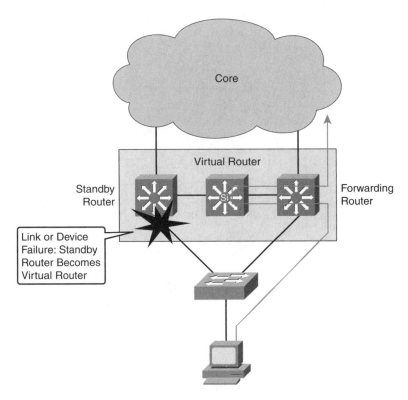

Figure 5-30   *Failover Between Active and Standby Routers*

HSRP active and standby routers send hello messages to multicast address 224.0.0.2 User Datagram Protocol (UDP) port 1985. Hello messages are used to communicate between routers in the HSRP group. All the routers in the HSRP group need to be L2 adjacent so that hello packets can be exchanged.

All the routers in an HSRP group have specific roles and interact in specific manners:

- **Virtual router:** An IP and MAC address pair that end devices have configured as their default gateway. The active router processes all packets and frames sent to the virtual router address. The virtual router processes no physical frames. There is one virtual router in an HSRP group.

- **Active router:** Within an HSRP group, one router is elected to be the active router. The active router physically forwards packets sent to the MAC address of the virtual router. There is one active router in an HSRP group.

The active router responds to traffic for the virtual router. If an end station sends a packet to the virtual router MAC address, the active router receives and processes that packet. If an end station sends an ARP request with the virtual router IP address, the active router replies with the virtual router MAC address.

In Figure 5-31, Router A assumes the active role and forwards all frames addressed to the assigned HSRP MAC address of 0000.0c07.acxx, where xx is the HSRP group identifier.

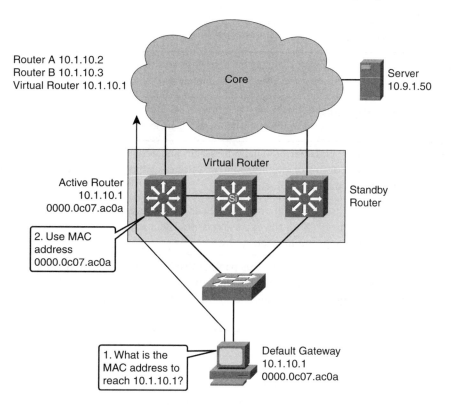

Figure 5-31 *HSRP Active Router Operation*

- **Standby Router:** Listens for periodic hello messages. When the active router fails, the other HSRP routers stop seeing hello messages from the active router. The standby router then assumes the role of the active router. There is one standby router in a HSRP group.

- **Other Routers:** There can be more than two routers in a HSRP group but only one active and one standby router is possible. The other routers remain in the initial state and if both the active and standby routers fail, all routers in the group contend for the active and standby router roles.

HSRP States

A router in an HSRP group can be in one of these states: initial, listen, speak, standby, or active. When a router exists in one of these states, it performs the actions required for that state. Not all HSRP routers in the group will transition through all states. For example, if there were three routers in the HSRP group, the router that is not the standby or active router will remain in the listen state.

Table 5-3 describes the different HSRP states.

Table 5-3 *HSRP States*

State	Definition
Initial	The beginning state. The initial state indicates that HSRP does not run. This state is entered via a configuration change or when an interface first comes up.
Listen	The router knows the virtual IP address, but the router is neither the active router nor the standby router. It listens for hello messages from those routers.
Speak	The router sends periodic hello messages and actively participates in the election of the active or standby router. A router cannot enter speak state unless the router has the virtual IP address.
Standby	The router is a candidate to become the next active router and sends periodic hello messages. With the exclusion of transient conditions, there is, at most, one router in the group in standby state.
Active	The router currently forwards packets that are sent to the group virtual MAC address. The router sends periodic hello messages. With the exclusion of transient conditions, there must be, at the most, one router in the active state in the group.

HSRP State Transition

All routers begin in the initial state, which is the starting state and indicates that HSRP is not running. This state is entered via a configuration change, such as when HSRP is enabled on an interface, or when an HSRP-enabled interface is first brought up, such as when the **no shutdown** command is issued.

The purpose of the listen state is to determine if there are already active or standby routers for the group. In the speak state, the routers are actively participating in the election of the active router or standby router or both. HSRP uses the hello and hold time to determine when it moves to different states. The timers are explained later in this chapter.

In Figure 5-32, Router A starts. As it is the first router for standby Group 1 in the subnet, it transits through the listen and speak states and then becomes the active router. Router B starts after A. While router B is in listen state, Router A is already assuming the standby and then the active role. As there is already an existing active router, B assumes the standby role.

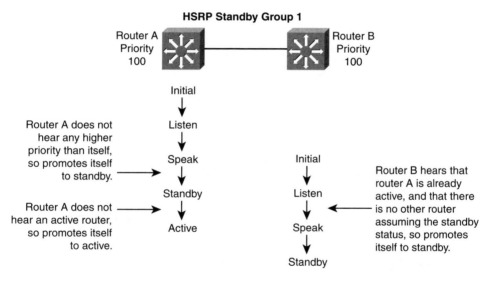

Figure 5-32 *HSRP State Transition Example*

When two routers participate in an election process, a priority can be configured to determine which router should be active. Without specific priority configuration, each router has a default priority of 100, and the router with the highest IP address is elected as the active router.

Regardless of other routers priorities or IP addresses, an active router will stay active by default. A new election occurs only if the active router is removed. When the standby router is removed, a new election is made to replace the standby. This default behavior can be changed with the option preempt, examined in later section of this chapter.

HSRP Active Router and Spanning Tree Topology

In a redundant spanning-tree topology, some links are blocked. The spanning-tree topology has no awareness about the HSRP configuration. There is no automatic relationship between the HSRP active router election process and the Spanning Tree Root Bridge election process.

When configuring both spanning tree and HSRP (or any other first hop redundancy protocol), you should make sure that the active router is the same as the root bridge for the corresponding VLAN. When the root bridge is different from the HSRP active router, a suboptimal path could result, as shown in Figure 5-33.

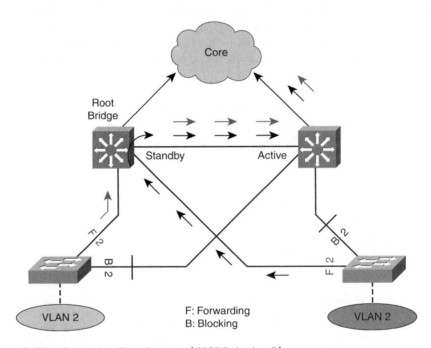

Figure 5-33 *Spanning Tree Root and HSRP Active Placement*

Configuring HSRP

Table 5-4 shows the commands needed to enable or disable HSRP on an interface.

While running HSRP, the end-user stations must not discover the actual MAC addresses of the routers in the standby group. Any protocol that informs a host of a router's actual address must be disabled. To ensure that the actual addresses of the participating HSRP routers are not discovered, enabling HSRP on a Cisco router interface automatically disables Internet Control Message Protocol (ICMP) redirects on that interface.

After the **standby ip** command is issued, the interface changes to the appropriate state. When the router successfully executes the command, the router issues an HSRP message.

Table 5-4   *HSRP Configuration Commands*

Command	Description
Switch(config-if)# **standby** *group-number* **ip** *ip-address*	Configures HSRP on this interface. Group number is optional and indicates the HSRP group to which this interface belongs. Specifying a unique group number in the **standby** commands enables the creation of multiple HSRP groups. The default group is 0. IP address is that of the virtual router IP address.
Switch(config-if)# **no standby** *group-number* **ip** *ip-address*	Disables HSRP on the interface.

HSRP Priority and Preempt

Each standby group has its own active and standby routers. The network administrator can assign a priority value to each router in a standby group, allowing the administrator to control the order in which active routers for that group are selected.

To set the priority value of a router, enter this command in interface configuration mode:

```
Switch(config-if)# standby group-number priority priority-value
```

Priority value can be from 0 to 255. The default value is 100.

During the election process, the router with the highest priority in an HSRP group becomes the active router. If a tie occurs, the router with the highest configured IP address becomes active.

To reinstate the default standby priority value, enter the **no standby priority** command.

If the routers do not have preempt configured, a router that boots up significantly faster than the others in the standby group becomes the active router, regardless of the configured priority. The former active router can be configured to resume the forwarding router role by preempting a router with a lower priority. To enable a router to resume the forwarding router role, enter this command in interface configuration mode:

```
Switch(config-if)#standby [group-number] preempt {delay} [minimum delay]
```

Figure 5-34 shows two Routers A and B configured with priorities of 110 and 90 respectively and Example 5-13 shows the configuration on Router A with preempt additional configured.

HSRP Standby Group 10

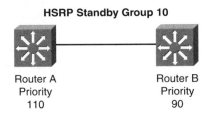

Router A
Priority
110

Router B
Priority
90

Figure 5-34   *HSRP Priority Configuration*

Example 5-13   *HSRP Priority and Preempt Configuration*

```
RouterA(config)# interface vlan 10
RouterA(config-if)# ip address 10.1.1.2 255.255.255.0
RouterA(config-if)# standby 10 ip 10.1.1.1
RouterA(config-if)# standby 10 priority 110
RouterA(config-if)# standby 10 preempt
```

To remove the interface from preemptive status, enter the **no standby group preempt** command.

HSRP Authentication

HSRP authentication prevents rogue routers on the network from joining the HSRP group.

HSRP authentication is enabled by configuration of an authentication string on all member devices of the HSRP group. The authentication string is a maximum of eight characters and the default keyword is *cisco*.

Example 5-14 shows the configuration of HSRP authentication with string value of *xyz123*.

Example 5-14   *HSRP Authentication Configuration*

```
RouterA(config)# interface vlan 10
RouterA(config-if)# ip address 10.1.1.2 255.255.255.0
RouterA(config-if)# standby 10 ip 10.1.1.1
RouterA(config-if)# standby 10 priority 110
RouterA(config-if)# standby 10 preempt
RouterA(config-if)# standby 10 authentication xyz123
```

HSRP Timer Considerations and Configuration

When an HSRP active router fails, the standby router detects the failure and assumes the active role. This mechanism relies on hello messages and holdtime intervals. The hello timer determines how often routers in the same Standby group exchange messages.

The holdtime timer determines the time before the active or standby router is declared to be down.

Ideally, to achieve fast convergence, these timers should be configured to be as low as possible. Within milliseconds after the active router fails, the standby router can detect the failure, expire the holdtime interval, and assume the active role.

Nevertheless, timers configuration should also take into account other parameters relevant to the network convergence. For example, both HSRP routers might be running a dynamic routing protocol. The routing protocol probably has no awareness of the HSRP configuration and sees both routers as individual hops toward other subnets. If HSRP failover occurs before the dynamic routing protocol converges, suboptimal routing information might still exist. In a worst-case scenario, the dynamic routing protocol continues seeing the failed router as the best next hop to other networks, and packets are lost, as shown in Figure 5-35. When configuring HSRP timers, make sure that they harmoniously match the other timers that can influence which path is chosen to carry packets in your network.

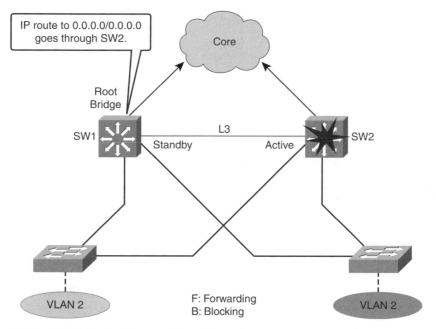

Figure 5-35 *HSRP Active Router Failure Detection*

The hello message contains the priority of the router and hellotime and holdtime parameter values. The standby timer includes an **msec** parameter to allow for subsecond failovers. Lowering the hello timer results in increased traffic for hello messages and should be used cautiously.

If an active router sends a hello message, receiving routers consider that hello message to be valid for one holdtime. The holdtime value should be at least three times the value of the hellotime. The holdtime value must be greater than the value of the hellotime.

HSRP timers can be adjusted to tune the performance of HSRP on distribution devices, thereby increasing their resilience and reliability in routing packets off the local VLAN.

By default, HSRP hellotime is 3 seconds and holdtime is 10 seconds, which means that failover time could be as much as 10 seconds for clients to start communicating with the new default gateway. In some cases, this interval might be excessive for application support. The *hellotime* and the *holdtime* parameters are both configurable. To configure the time between hello messages and the time before other group routers declare the active or standby router to be nonfunctioning, enter this command in interface configuration mode:

Switch(config-if)#**standby** *group-number* **timers** [*msec*] *hellotime holdtime*

Hello and dead timer intervals must be identical for all devices within the HSRP group.

Table 5-5 describes the options for standby message timer configuration.

To reinstate the default standby-timer values, enter the **no standby group timers** command.

The HSRP *hellotime* and *holdtime* can be set to millisecond values so that HSRP failover occurs in less than 1 second.

Preempt is an important feature of HSRP that enables the primary router to resume the active role when it comes back online after a failure or maintenance event. Preemption is a desired behavior because it forces a predictable routing path for the VLAN during normal operations and ensures that the Layer 3 forwarding path for a VLAN parallels the Layer 2 STP forwarding path whenever possible.

Table 5-5   *Standby Message Timer Configuration Options*

Variable	Description
group-number	(Optional) Group number on the interface to which the timers apply. The default is 0.
msec	(Optional) Interval in milliseconds. Millisecond timers allow for faster failover.
hellotime	Hello interval in seconds. This is an integer from 1 through 255. The default is 3 seconds.
holdtime	Time, in seconds, before the active or standby router is declared to be down. This is an integer from 1 through 255. The default is 10 seconds.

When a preempting device is rebooted, HSRP preempt communication should not begin until the distribution switch has established full connectivity to the rest of the network. This enables the routing protocol convergence to occur more quickly, after the preferred router is in an active state.

To accomplish this, measure the system boot time and set the HSRP preempt delay to a value of 50 percent greater than the boot time. This ensures that the primary distribution switch establishes full connectivity to the network before HSRP communication occurs.

For example, if the boot time for the distribution device is 150 seconds, the preempt delay should be set to 225 seconds.

Example 5-15 shows the configuration of timers and the *preempt delay* configuration commands.

Example 5-15   *Configuring HSRP Timers*

```
switch(config)# interface vlan 10
switch(config-if)# ip address 10.1.1.2 255.255.255.0
switch(config-if)# standby 10 ip 10.1.1.1
switch(config-if)# standby 10 priority 110
switch(config-if)# standby 10 preempt
switch(config-if)# standby 10 timers msec 200 msec 750
switch(config-if)# standby 10 preempt delay minimum 225
```

HSRP Versions

HSRP version 1 is the default in IOS and it enables group numbers up to 255. Because one can have up to 4095 VLANs, one has to reuse the same HSRP group number on multiple interface if needed. This is allowed even though it might cause some confusion to the administrator. HSRPv1 uses the Virtual MAC address of the form 0000.0C07.ACXX (XX = HSRP group), and the HSRPv1 hello packets are sent to multicast address 224.0.0.2.

HSRP version 2 has been added to IOS (since 12.2 46SE or later) and it enables group numbers up to 4095. This enables you to use the VLAN number as the group number.

With HSRP v2, the MAC address of the virtual router and the multicast address for the hello messages has been changed. The virtual MAC address is 0000.0C9F.FXXX (XXX=HSRP group), and hello packets are sent to multicast address 224.0.0.102.

Also, the HSRPv2 has a different packet format than HSRPv1. Ensure that the same version is configured on all routers in a HSRP group. Otherwise hello messages are not understood. Version 1 is the default. Use the following command to change the version:

```
Switch(config-if)# standby <hsrp group number> version 2
```

HSRP Interface Tracking

Interface tracking enables the priority of a standby group router to be automatically adjusted, based on the availability of the router interfaces. When a tracked interface becomes unavailable, the HSRP priority of the router is decreased. When properly configured, the HSRP tracking feature ensures that a router with an unavailable key interface will relinquish the active router role.

In Figure 5-36, the distribution switches monitor the uplink to the core switches. The uplink between the active forwarding device for the standby group and the core experiences a failure. Without HSRP enabled, the active device would detect the failed link and send an Internet Control Message Protocol (ICMP) redirect to the other device. However, when HSRP is enabled, ICMP redirects are disabled. The left switch now has the better path to the server.

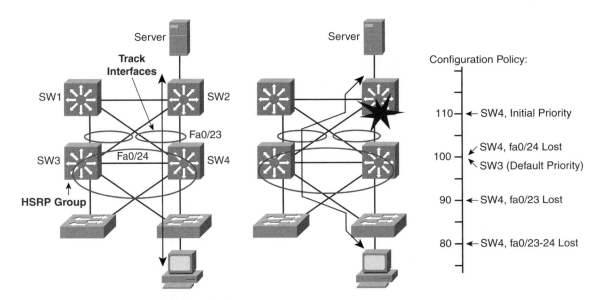

Figure 5-36 *HSRP Interface Tracking*

The HSRP group tracks the uplink interfaces. If the uplink to the core on the right switch fails, the router automatically decrements the priority on that interface and sends hello messages with the decremented priority. The switch on the left now has a higher priority and with preempt enabled becomes the active router.

To configure HSRP with interface tracking, follow these steps:

Step 1. Configure the standby group.

Step 2. Configure priority (default 100).

Step 3. Configure preempt on all devices within the HSRP group.

Step 4.   Configure the tracked interfaces and decrement (default decrement 10).

Table 5-6 describes the variables in the HSRP tracking configuration command:

```
Switch(config-if) standby [group-number] track interface-type interface-number
  [interface-priority]
```

Table 5-6   *HSRP Tracking Configuration Arguments*

Variable	Description
group-number	(Optional) Indicates the group number on the interface to which the tracking applies. The default number is 0.
interface-type	Indicates the interface type (combined with the interface number) that will be tracked.
interface-number	Indicates the interface number (combined with the interface type) that will be tracked.
interface-priority	(Optional) Indicates the amount by which the hot standby priority for the router is decremented when the interface becomes disabled. The priority of the router is incremented by this amount when the interface becomes available. The default value is 10.

A router can track several interfaces. In Figure 5-36, SW4 tracks both fa0/23 and fa0/24. The configuration policy shown in Example 5-16 states that SW4 initial priority should be 110. SW3 initial priority should be left to its default value, 100. If SW4 loses its link fa0/24 to SW1, SW4 priority should become the same as SW3 priority. If a new election needs to occur, both multilayer switches have the same chances of becoming the active router. This decrement is made because fa0/24 is not the active link but just a backup. If fa0/23 (the active uplink) is lost, SW4 priority becomes lower than SW3 priority. If both fa0/23 and fa0/24 are lost, both decrements are applied and SW4 priority becomes 80.

Example 5-16   *Configuration Example for HSRP Interface Tracking*

```
switch(config)# interface vlan 10
switch(config-if)# ip address 10.1.1.2 255.255.255.0
switch(config-if)# standby 10 ip 10.1.1.1
switch(config-if)# standby 10 priority 110
switch(config-if)# standby 10 preempt
switch(config-if)# standby 10 track fastethernet0/23 20
switch(config-if)# standby 10 track fastethernet0/24
```

To disable interface tracking, enter the **no standby group** track command.

The command to configure HSRP tracking on a multilayer switch is the same as on the external router, except that the interface type can be identified as a switch virtual interface (vlan followed by the vlan number assigned to that interface) or by a physical interface.

The internal routing device uses the same command as the external routing device to disable interface tracking.

Multiple tracking statements might be applied to an interface. For example, this might be useful if the currently active HSRP interface relinquishes its status only upon the failure of two (or more) tracked interfaces.

HSRP Object Tracking

The HSRP tracking feature can be used to track an object. When the conditions defined by this object are fulfilled, the router priority remains the same. As soon as the verification defined by the object fails, the router priority is decremented.

Tracked objects are defined in global configuration with the track keyword, as shown in Example 5-17, followed by an object number. You can track up to 500 objects.

Example 5-17   *HSRP Tracking Object Configuration*

```
switch(config)# track 1 ?
  interface   Select an interface to track
  ip          IP protocol
  list        Group objects in a list
  rtr         Response Time Reporter (RTR) entry
```

Tracked objects offer a vast group of possibilities. You can track the following:

■ **An interface:** Just like the **standby track** interface command, a tracking object can verify the interface status (line-protocol). You can also track ip routing on the interface. This option tracks whether IP routing is enabled, whether an IP address is configured on the interface, and whether the interface state is up before reporting to the tracking client that the interface is up.

■ **IP route:** A tracked IP-route object is considered up and reachable when a routing-table entry exists for the route and the route is not inaccessible. To provide a common interface to tracking clients, route metric values are normalized to the range of 0 to 255, where 0 is connected and 255 is inaccessible. You can track route reachability, or even metric values to determine best paths values to the target network. The tracking process uses a per-protocol configurable resolution value to convert the real metric to the scaled metric. The metric value communicated to clients is always such that a lower metric value is better than a higher metric value.

■ **A list of objects:** Several objects can be tracked and their result compared to determine if one or several of them should trigger the "success" of "fail" condition.

- **IP SLA:** This special case enables you to track advanced parameters, such as IP reachability, delay, or jitter.

HSRP and IP SLA Tracking

IP SLA tracking extends the HSRP interface tracking to enable it to track paths through the network.

In Figure 5-37, a Cisco IOS IP SLA measurement is being run between two switches across a network cloud.

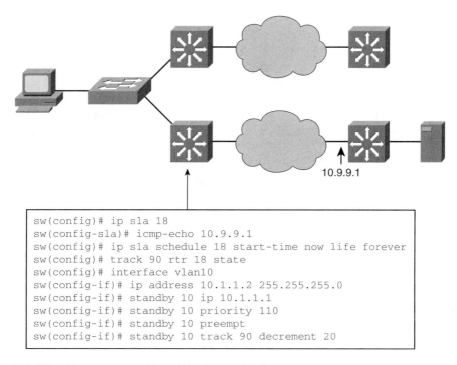

```
sw(config)# ip sla 18
sw(config-sla)# icmp-echo 10.9.9.1
sw(config)# ip sla schedule 18 start-time now life forever
sw(config)# track 90 rtr 18 state
sw(config)# interface vlan10
sw(config-if)# ip address 10.1.1.2 255.255.255.0
sw(config-if)# standby 10 ip 10.1.1.1
sw(config-if)# standby 10 priority 110
sw(config-if)# standby 10 preempt
sw(config-if)# standby 10 track 90 decrement 20
```

Figure 5-37   *Configuring HSRP and IP SLA Tracking*

If the link fails, the priority of the active switch in the HSRP group is reduced, and the other switch connection via the upper network becomes the active router to reach the server.

Figure 5-37 also shows the configuration of IP SLA with HSRP, and it includes the following steps:

Step 1.   Create an IP SLA process (18).

Step 2.   Schedule this IP SLA Process.

Step 3.   Create an object (90) to track the state of this process.

Step 4.   Track the state of this object and decrement the HSRP device priority if the object fails.

Multiple HSRP Groups

HSRP allows for only one active router in the same subnet. In a typical network, administrators would want to use all available routers to load share the traffic going across the network. Multigroup HSRP enables routers to simultaneously provide redundant backup and perform load sharing across different IP subnets.

In Figure 5-38, two HSRP-enabled routers participate in two separate VLANs, using 802.1Q. Running HSRP over trunking enables users to configure redundancy among multiple routers that are configured as front ends for VLAN IP subnets.

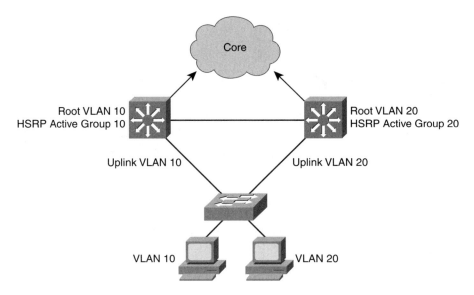

Figure 5-38   *Multiple HSRP Groups*

By configuring HSRP over trunks, users can eliminate situations in which a single point of failure causes traffic interruptions. This feature inherently provides some improvement in overall networking resilience by providing load balancing and redundancy capabilities between subnets and VLANs.

For a VLAN, configure the same device to be both the spanning-tree root and the HSRP active router. This approach ensures that the Layer 2 forwarding path leads directly to the Layer 3 active router and so achieves maximum efficiency of load balancing on the routers and the trunks.

For each VLAN, a standby group, an IP addresses, and a single well-known MAC address with a unique group identifier is allocated to the group. Although up to 255 standby groups can be configured (4095 with version 2), it is advised that the actual number of group identifiers used be kept to a minimum. When you are configuring two distribution layer switches, typically you will require only two standby group identifiers, regardless of how many standby groups are created.

Figure 5-39 shows the configuration for two HSRP groups for two VLANs and the corresponding STP root configuration.

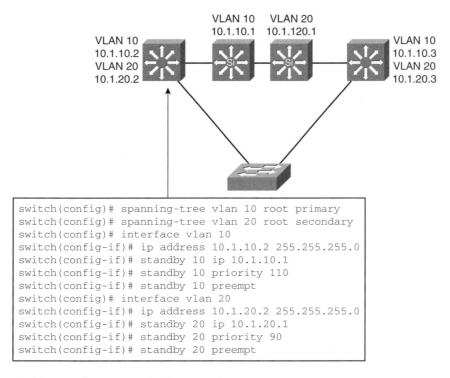

Figure 5-39   *Configuring Multiple HSRP Groups*

The left switch is root and active HSRP router for VLAN 10.

The corresponding configuration of the right switch has the switch as root and active HSRP router for VLAN 20.

HSRP Monitoring

Use the **show standby** family of commands to verify HSRP state. Several arguments can be used. **Show standby brief** simply displays a summary of the HSRP configurations, as shown in Example 5-18. For each standby group, you can verify the local router neighbors.

Example 5-18   *Monitoring HSRP with the show standby Command*

```
switch# show standby brief
                     P indicates configured to preempt.
                   |
Interface   Grp  Pri P State   Active     Standby    Virtual IP
Vl10         10   120 P Active  local      10.1.10.3  10.1.10.1
```

```
V120        20   90  P Standby 10.1.20.3 local        10.1.20.1
switch#show standby neighbor vlan10
HSRP neighbors on Vlan10
  10.1.10.3
    Active groups: 10
    No standby groups
```

When simply typing **show standby**, a complete display is provided, as shown in Example 5-19.

Example 5-19   *Displaying Detailed HSRP Standby Status*

```
switch# sh standby
Vlan10 - Group 10
  State is Active
  Virtual IP address is 10.1.10.1
  Active virtual MAC address is 0000.0c07.ac0a
    Local virtual MAC address is 0000.0c07.ac0a (v1 default)
  Hello time 3 sec, hold time 10 sec
    Next hello sent in 1.248 secs
  Preemption enabled
  Active router is local
  Standby router is 10.1.10.3, priority 90 (expires in 10.096 sec)
  Priority 120 (configured 120)
    Track interface Port-channel31 state Up decrement 30
    Track interface Port-channel32 state Up decrement 30
  Group name is "hsrp-Vl10-10" (default)
Vlan20 - Group 20
  State is Standby
  Virtual IP address is 10.1.20.1 Active virtual MAC address is 0000.0c07.ac14
    Local virtual MAC address is 0000.0c07.ac14 (v1 default)
  Hello time 3 sec, hold time 10 sec
    Next hello sent in 2.064 secs
  Preemption enabled
  Active router is 10.1.10.3, priority 120 (expires in 10.032 sec)
  Standby router is local
  Priority 90 (configured 90)
  Group name is "hsrp-Vl20-20" (default)
```

The IP address and corresponding MAC address of the virtual router are maintained in the ARP table of each router in an HSRP group. As shown in Figure 5-40, the command **show ip arp** displays the ARP cache on a multilayer switch.

HSRP offers more detailed monitoring capabilities through the IOS debugging facility. Table 5-7 describes commands used to debug HSRP.

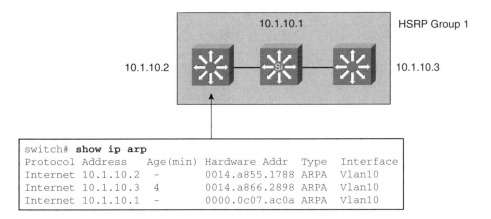

```
switch# show ip arp
Protocol Address     Age(min) Hardware Addr   Type   Interface
Internet 10.1.10.2   -        0014.a855.1788  ARPA   Vlan10
Internet 10.1.10.3   4        0014.a866.2898  ARPA   Vlan10
Internet 10.1.10.1   -        0000.0c07.ac0a  ARPA   Vlan10
```

Figure 5-40   *HSRP Virtual MAC Address*

Table 5-7   *HSRP Debug Commands*

Command	Description
Switch# **debug standby [errors] [events] [packets]**	Displays all state changes to HSRP, including all hello packets. Arguments minimize output.
Switch# **debug standby terse**	Displays all HSRP errors, events, and packets, except hello and advertisement packets.

Virtual Router Redundancy Protocol

Virtual Router Redundancy Protocol (VRRP) provides router interface failover in a manner similar to HSRP but with added features and IEEE compatibility. Like HSRP, VRRP enables a group of routers to form a single virtual router. In an HSRP or VRRP group, one router is elected to handle all requests sent to the virtual IP address. With Hot Standby Router Protocol (HSRP), this is the active router. A HSRP group has one active router, one standby router, and perhaps many listening routers. A VRRP group has one master router and one or more backup routers.

Table 5-8 compares HSRP and VRRP.

HSRP and VRRP are similar in their features and behaviors. The main difference is that HSRP is a Cisco proprietary implementation, whereas VRRP is an open standard. The consequence is that HSRP is usually found in Cisco networks. VRRP is used in multivendor implementations.

Table 5-8 *Comparison Between HSRP and VRRP*

HSRP	VRRP
HSRP is a Cisco proprietary protocol, created in 1994, and formalized with the RCF RCF 2281 in March 1998.	VRRP is an IEEE standard (RFC 2338 in 1998; then RFC 3768 in 2005) for router redundancy.
16 groups max.	255 groups max.
1 active, 1 standby, several candidates.	1 active, several backups.
Virtual IP is different from Active and Standby real IP addresses.	Virtual IP can be the same as one of the group members real IP address.
Uses 224.0.0.2 for hello packets.	Uses 224.0.0.18 for hello packets.
Default timers: hello 3 s, holdtime 10 s.	The default timers are shorter in VRRP than HSRP. This often gave VRRP the reputation of being faster than HSRP.
Can track interfaces or objects.	Can track only objects.
Uses authentication within each group by default. When authentication is not configured, a default authentication, using "cisco" as the password.	Support plaintext and HMAC/MD5 authentication methods (RFC 2338). The new VRRP RFC (RFC 3768) removes support for these methods. The consequence is that VRRP does not support authentication anymore. Nevertheless, current Cisco IOS still supports the RFC 2338 authentications mechanisms.

VRRP offers these redundancy features:

■ VRRP provides redundancy for the real IP address of a router or for a virtual IP address shared among the VRRP group members.

■ If a real IP address is used, the router with that address becomes the master. If a virtual IP address is used, the master is the router with the highest priority.

■ A VRRP group has one master router and one or more backup routers. The master router uses VRRP messages to inform group members that it is the master.

In Figure 5-41, Routers A, B, and C are members of a VRRP group. The IP address of the virtual router is the same as that of the LAN interface of Router A (10.0.0.1). Router A is responsible for forwarding packets sent to this IP address.

The clients have a gateway address of 10.0.0.1. Routers B and C are backup routers. If the master router fails, the backup router with the highest priority becomes the master router. When Router A recovers, it resumes the role of master router.

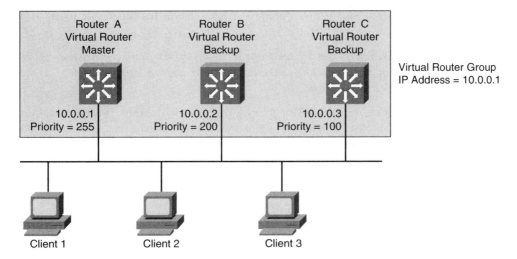

Figure 5-41   *VRRP Configuration with Three Routers*

VRRP Operation

Figure 5-42 shows a LAN topology in which VRRP is configured so that Routers A and B share the load of being the default gateway for Clients 1 through 4. Routers A and B act as backup virtual routers to one another should either one fail.

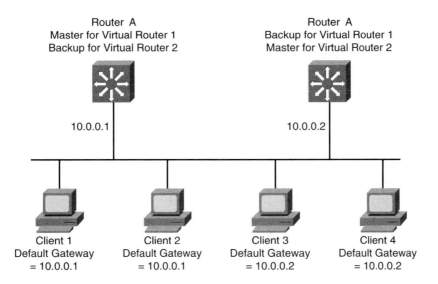

Figure 5-42   *VRRP Operation*

In Figure 5-42, two virtual router groups are configured. For virtual Router 1, Router A is the owner of IP address 10.0.0.1 and is therefore the master virtual router for clients configured with that default gateway address. Router B is the backup virtual router to Router A.

For virtual Router 2, Router B is the owner of IP address 10.0.0.2 and is the master virtual router for clients configured with the default gateway IP address 10.0.0.2. Router A is the backup virtual router to Router B.

Given that the IP address of the VRRP group is that of a physical interface on one of the group members, the router owning that address will be the master in the group. Its priority is set to 255. Backup router priority values can range from 1 to 254; the default value is 100. The priority value zero has special meaning, indicating that the current master has stopped participating in VRRP. This setting is used to trigger backup routers to quickly transition to the master without having to wait for the current master to time out.

With VRRP, only the master sends advertisements (the equivalent of HSRP hellos). The master sends the advertisement on multicast 224.0.0.18 protocol number 112 on a default interval of 1 second.

VRRP Transition Process

The dynamic failover, when the active (master) becomes unavailable, uses three timers within VRRP: the advertisement interval, the master down interval, and the skew time:

- The advertisement interval is the time interval between advertisements (in seconds). The default interval is 1 second.

- The master down interval is the time interval for backup to declare the master down (in seconds). The default is 3 x advertisement interval + skew time.

- The skew time (256 – priority / 256) ms ensures that the backup router with the highest priority becomes the new master.

Table 5-9 lists the steps involved in the VRRP transition for the scenario in Figure 5-42.

Note   In the case of an orderly shutdown of the VRRP master, it sends an advertisement with a priority of 0. This priority setting then triggers the backup router to take over quicker by waiting only the skew time instead of the master down interval. Therefore, in the previous example, Router B would have waited only 0.2 seconds to transition to the master state.

Configuring VRRP

Table 5-10 shows the steps needed to configure VRRP.

Example 5-20 illustrates a user configuring and verifying VRRP on Router A and Router B for the scenario, as shown in Figure 5-43.

Table 5-9   *VRRP Transition Process*

Step	Description	Notes
1.	Router A is currently the master, so it sends advertisements by default every 1 second.	Router A is the only device sending advertisements.
2.	Router A fails.	Advertisements stop.
3.	Router B and Router C stop receiving advertisements and wait for their respective master down interval to expire before transitioning to the master state.	By default, the master down interval is 3 seconds plus the skew time.
4.	Because the skew time is inversely proportional to priority, the master down interval of Router B is less than that of Router C. Router B has a master down interval of approximately 3.2 seconds. Router C has a master down interval of approximately 3.6 seconds.	The skew time for Router B equals (256 – 200) / 256, which is approximately equal to 0.2 seconds. The skew time for Router C equals (256 – 100) / 256, which is approximately equal to 0.6 seconds.
5.	Router B transitions to the master state after 3.2 seconds and starts sending advertisements.	—
6.	Router C receives the advertisement from the new master, so it resets its master down interval and remains in the backup state.	—

Table 5-10   *VRRP Configuration Steps*

Step	Description
1.	To enable VRRP on an interface. This makes the interface a member of the virtual group identified with the IP virtual address: `Switch(config-if)#vrrp group-number ip virtual-gateway-address`
2.	To set a VRRP priority for this router for this VRRP group: Highest value wins election as active router. Default is 100. If routers have the same VRRP priority, the gateway with the highest real IP address is elected to become the master virtual router: `Switch(config-if)# vrrp group-number priority priority-value`

3.	To change timer and indicate if it should advertise for master or just learn for backup routers:
	`Switch(config-if)#vrrp group-number timers advertise timer-value`
	`Switch(config-if)#vrrp group-number timers learn`

Example 5-20 *Configuring and Verifying VRRP*

```
RouterA# configure terminal
Enter configuration commands, one per line. End with CNTL/Z.
RouterA(config)# interface vlan 1
RouterA(config-if)# ip address 10.0.2.1 255.255.255.0
RouterA(config-if)# vrrp 1 ip 10.0.2.254
RouterA(config-if)# vrrp 1 timers advertise msec 500
RouterA(config-if)# end
RouterB# configure terminal
Enter configuration commands, one per line. End with CNTL/Z.
RouterB(config)# interface vlan 1
RouterB(config-if)# ip address 10.0.2.2 255.255.255.0
RouterB(config-if)# vrrp 1 ip 10.0.2.254
RouterB(config-if)# vrrp 1 priority 90
RouterB(config-if)# vrrp 1 timers learn
RouterB(config-if)# end
RouterA# show vrrp interface vlan 1
Vlan1 - Group 1
  State is Master
  Virtual IP address is 10.0.2.254
  Virtual MAC address is 0000.5e00.0101
  Advertisement interval is 0.500 sec
  Preemption is enabled
    min delay is 0.000 sec
 Priority is 100
  Master Router is 10.0.2.1 (local), priority is 100
  Master Advertisement interval is 0.500 sec
  Master Down interval is 2.109 sec
RouterB# show vrrp interface vlan 1
Vlan1 - Group 1
  State is Backup
  Virtual IP address is 10.0.2.254
  Virtual MAC address is 0000.5e00.0101
  Advertisement interval is 0.500 sec
  Preemption is enabled
    min delay is 0.000 sec
  Priority is 90
  Authentication is enabled
  Master Router is 10.0.2.1, priority is 100
  Master Advertisement interval is 0.500 sec
  Master Down interval is 2.109 sec (expires in 1.745 sec)
```

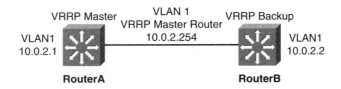

Figure 5-43   *VRRP Configuration*

A main difference between HSRP and VRRP is that in VRRP, the backup router does not send advertisements. Therefore, as shown in Example 5-20, the VRRP master is not aware of the current backup router.

Gateway Load Balancing Protocol

Although HSRP and VRRP provide gateway resiliency, for the standby members of the redundancy group, the upstream bandwidth is not used while the device is in standby mode.

Only the active router for HSRP and VRRP groups forwards traffic for the virtual MAC. Resources associated with the standby router are not fully utilized. Some load balancing can be accomplished with these protocols through the creation of multiple groups and through the assignment of multiple default gateways, but this configuration creates an administrative burden.

GLBP is a Cisco-proprietary solution created to enable automatic selection and simultaneous use of multiple available gateways in addition to automatic failover between those gateways. Multiple routers share the load of frames that, from a client perspective, are sent to a single default gateway address.

With GLBP, resources can be fully utilized without the administrative burden of configuring multiple groups and managing multiple default gateway configurations, as is required with HSRP and VRRP. Table 5-11 compares HSRP and GLBP protocols.

Table 5-11 *Comparison Between HSRP and GLBP*

HSRP	GLBP
Cisco Proprietary, 1994	Cisco Proprietary, 2005
16 groups max	1024 groups max
1 active, 1 standby, several candidates	1 AVG, several AVF, AVG load balances traffic among AVF and AVGs
Virtual IP is different from Active and Standby real IP addresses	Virtual IP is different from AVG and AVF real IP addresses
1 Virtual MAC address for each group	1 Virtual MAC address per AVF/AVG in each group
Uses 224.0.0.2 for hello packets	Uses 224.0.0.102 for hello packets
Can track interfaces or objects	Can only track objects
Default timers: hello 3 s, holdtime 10 s	Default timers: hello 3 s, holdtime 10 s
Authentication supported	Authentication supported

HSRP is typically used in Cisco networks as usually there are only two gateways for any subnet. GLBP can be used if more than two gateways exist for subnets to load share across the gateways.

GLBP Functions

The following are the GLBP functions:

- **GLBP active virtual gateway (AVG):** Members of a GLBP group elect one gateway to be the AVG for that group. Other group members provide backup for the AVG if the AVG becomes unavailable. The AVG assigns a virtual MAC address to each member of the GLBP group.

- **GLBP active virtual forwarder (AVF):** Each gateway assumes responsibility for forwarding packets that are sent to the virtual MAC address assigned to that gateway by the AVG. These gateways are known as AVFs for their virtual MAC address.

- **GLBP communication:** GLBP members communicate between each other through hello messages sent every 3 seconds to the multicast address 224.0.0.102, User Datagram Protocol (UDP) port 3222.

In Figure 5-44, Router A is acting as the AVG. Router A has assigned virtual MAC 0007.b400.0101 to itself and Router B is acting as AVF for the virtual Mac 0007.b400.0102 assigned to it by Router A. Client 1 default gateway is Router A and Client 2 default gateway is Router B based on the virtual MAC assignment.

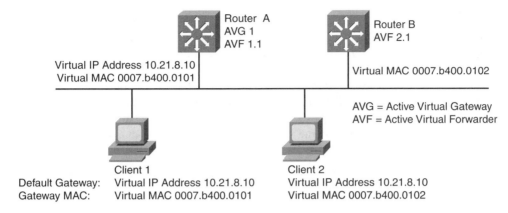

Figure 5-44 *GLB-Enabled Network*

GLBP Features

The following are the features of GLBP:

- **Load sharing:** You can configure GLBP in such a way that multiple routers can share traffic from LAN clients, thereby sharing the traffic load more equitably among available routers.

- **Multiple virtual routers:** GLBP supports up to 1024 virtual routers (GLBP groups) on each physical interface of a router and up to four virtual forwarders per group.

- **Preemption:** The redundancy scheme of GLBP enables you to preempt an AVG with a higher priority backup virtual gateway that has become available. Forwarder preemption works in a similar way, except that forwarder preemption uses weighting instead of priority and is enabled by default.

- **Efficient resource utilization:** GLBP makes it possible for any router in a group to serve as a backup, which eliminates the need for a dedicated backup router because all available routers can support network traffic.

GLBP provides upstream load sharing by utilizing the redundant uplinks simultaneously. It uses link capacity efficiently, thus providing peak-load traffic coverage. By making use of multiple available paths upstream from the routers or Layer 3 switches running GLBP, output queues may also be reduced.

Only a single path is used with HSRP or VRRP, while others are idle, unless multiple groups and gateways are configured. The single path may encounter higher output queue rates during peak times, which leads to lower performance from higher jitter rates. The impact of jitter is lessened and overall performance is increased because more upstream bandwidth is available, and additional upstream paths are used.

GLBP Operations

GLBP allows automatic selection and simultaneous use of all available gateways in the group. The members of a GLBP group elect one gateway to be the AVG for that group. Other members of the group provide backup for the AVG if it becomes unavailable. The AVG assigns a virtual MAC address to each member of the GLBP group. All routers become AVFs for frames addressed to that virtual MAC address. As clients send Address Resolution Protocol (ARP) requests for the address of the default gateway, the AVG sends these virtual MAC addresses in the ARP replies. A GLBP group can have up to four group members.

GLBP supports these operational modes for load balancing traffic across multiple default routers servicing the same default gateway IP address:

■ **Weighted load-balancing algorithm:** The amount of load directed to a router is dependent upon the weighting value advertised by that router.

■ **Host-dependent load-balancing algorithm:** A host is guaranteed use of the same virtual MAC address as long as that virtual MAC address is participating in the GLBP group.

■ **Round-robin load-balancing algorithm:** As clients send ARP requests to resolve the MAC address of the default gateway, the reply to each client contains the MAC address of the next possible router in round-robin fashion. All routers' MAC addresses take turns being included in address resolution replies for the default gateway IP address.

GLBP automatically manages the virtual MAC address assignment, determines who handles the forwarding, and ensures that each station has a forwarding path if failures to gateways or tracked interfaces occur. If failures occur, the load-balancing ratio is adjusted among the remaining AVFs so that resources are used in the most efficient way.

As shown in Figure 5-45, by default, GLBP attempts to balance traffic on a per-host basis using the round-robin algorithm. When a client sends an ARP message for the gateway IP address, the AVG returns the virtual MAC address of one of the AVFs. When a second client sends an ARP message, the AVG returns the next virtual MAC address from the list.

Having each resolved a different MAC address for the default gateway, Clients A and B send their routed traffic to separate routers, as shown in Figure 5-46, although they both have the same default gateway address configured. Each GLBP router is an AVF for the virtual MAC address to which it has been assigned.

GLBP Interface Tracking

Like HSRP, GLBP can be configured to track interfaces. In Figure 5-47, the WAN link from Router R1 is lost. GLBP detects the failure. Just like HSRP, GLBP decrements the gateway priority when a tracked interface fails. The second gateway then becomes primary. This transition is transparent for the LAN client.

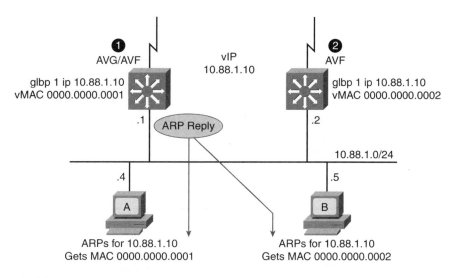

Figure 5-45   *GLBP AVG Operation*

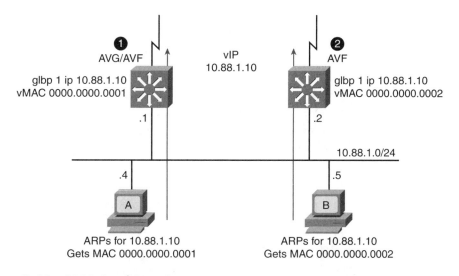

Figure 5-46   *GLBP Stead State Operation*

Because interface tracking was configured on R1, the job of forwarding packets for virtual MAC address 0000.0000.0001 will be taken over by the secondary virtual forwarder for the MAC, Router R2. Therefore, the client sees no disruption of service nor does the client need to resolve a new MAC address for the default gateway, as shown in Figure 5-48.

GLBP weighting determines whether a router can act as a virtual forwarder. Initial weighting values can be set and optional thresholds specified. Interface states can be tracked and a decrement value set to reduce the weighting value if the interface goes down. When the GLBP router weighting drops below a specified value, the router will no longer be an active virtual forwarder. When the weighting rises above a specified value, the router can resume its role as an active virtual forwarder.

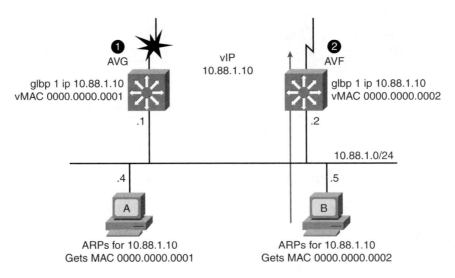

Figure 5-47   *GLBP Interface Tracking Detects Interface Failure*

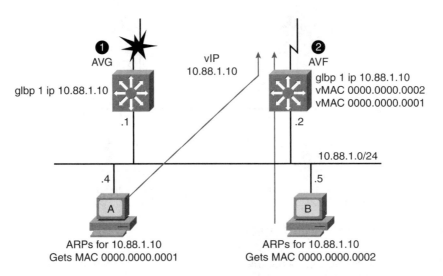

Figure 5-48   *GLBP Interface Tracking Enables Network Recovery*

The GLBP weighting mechanism is different from HSRP or VRRP. With HSRP and VRRP, one single threshold is defined. If the router priority (or weight) falls below the threshold, the router loses its active state. As soon as the router weight (or priority) exceeds the threshold, the router regains its active state. With GLBP, two thresholds are defined: one lower threshold that applies when the router loses weight, and one upper threshold that applies when the router regains weight. This double threshold mechanism enables more flexibility than the single threshold system.

In Figure 5-49, SW4 is forwarding. Its initial weight (or priority) is 110. SW4 tracks both fa0/23 and fa0/24 interfaces. Fa0/23 is the active interface. Losing fa0/23 decrements SW4 by 20 points, thus bringing SW4 weight down (from 110) to 90. Fa0/24 is a backup interface. Losing fa0/24 decrements SW4 by 10 points, thus bringing SW4 weight down (from 110) to 100, which is the default weight of the other routers. Losing both fa0/23 and fa0/24 brings SW4 weight down (from 110) to 80.

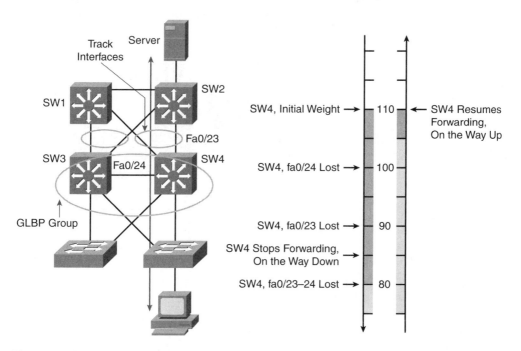

Figure 5-49   *GLBP Weighting Mechanism*

In Figure 5-49, losing fa0/24 brings SW4 weight to the same level as the other. If an election occurs, SW4 might or might not be the AVG but would still forward. Losing fa0/23 brings SW4 weight below the other routers weight. If an election occurs, SW4 would not be elected as AVG but would still be an AVF. The lower threshold is set to 85, which can be reached only by losing either fa0/23 or fa0/24. In other words, losing fa0/23 or fa0/24 decreases SW4 weight, and might change its status from AVG to AVF, but will not prevent SW4 from being a forwarder. It is only when both interfaces are lost that SW4 stops forwarding.

Losing one interface is an issue but does not prevent SW4 from forwarding. Losing both interfaces is the sign of a major connectivity problem in the network. For that reason, the network administrator decided that if SW4 lost both interfaces, it would not resume forwarding until both interfaces are back up. To implement this mechanism, the second threshold, the upper threshold, is set to 105. As long as SW4 weight does not go below the lower threshold (85), the upper threshold is not called. As soon as SW4 goes below the lower threshold, SW4 stops forwarding and the upper threshold is called. It is only then when SW4 weight will become higher than the upper threshold that SW4 will resume forwarding packets.

In this scenario, when both interfaces are lost, SW4 goes below the lower threshold (85) to reach 80. Recovering fa0/23 or fa0/24 would add 20 or 10 points to the weight, but each interface weight is not enough to have SW4 exceed the upper threshold, 105. It is only when both interfaces get reenabled that the weight exceeds the upper threshold and that SW4 resumes forwarding packets. The configuration for this scenario is shown in Figure 5-50.

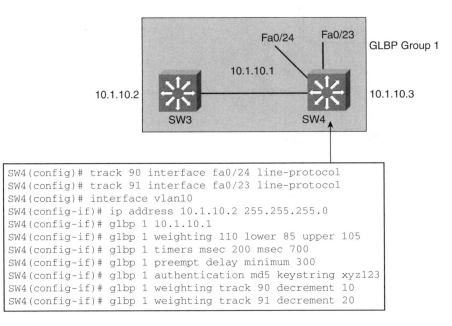

Figure 5-50 *GLBP Sample Configuration*

GLBP Configuration

Table 5-12 describes the steps needed to configure GLBP, and Figure 5-50 shows a sample configuration for the scenario presented in Figure 5-49.

GLBP with VLAN Spanning Across Access Layer Switches

Figure 5-51 depicts a topology in which STP has blocked one of the access uplinks, and this might result in a two-hop path at Layer 2 for upstream traffic when GLBP is configured at the distribution layer. In the example in Figure 5-51, Distribution A switch has a direct connection to the core and a redundant link to Distribution B. Because of spanning-tree operations, the interface directly linking to the core is in blocking state.

Table 5-12 *GLBP Configuration Steps*

Step	Description
1.	Enable GLBP on an interface. This command makes the interface a member of the virtual group identified with the IP virtual address: `Switch(config-if)#glbp` *group-number* `ip` *virtual-gateway-address*
2.	Set a GLBP priority for this router for this GLBP group. The highest value wins election as active router. The default is 100. If routers have the same GLBP priority, the gateway with the highest real IP address becomes the AVG: `Switch(config-if)#glbp` *group-number* `priority` *priority-value*
3.	Change timer values for hello interval and holdtime. Place the argument msec before the values to enter subsecond values: `Switch(config-if)#glbp` *group-number* `timers` *hello holdtime*

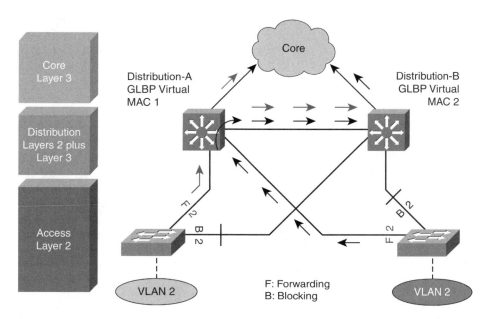

Figure 5-51 *GLBP and Spanning Tree*

Although invisible and transparent to VLAN 2 clients, this state results in the frames coming from VLAN 2 to transit through Distribution A and then actually go through Distribution B before being sent to the core.

In environments in which VLANs span across switches, HSRP is the recommended first hop redundancy protocol implementation. In all cases, the active gateway should be configured to also be the root bridge for the VLAN in which first hop redundancy is configured.

Cisco IOS Server Load Balancing

Cisco IOS Server Load Balancing (SLB) intelligently load balances TCP/IP traffic across multiple servers, as illustrated in Figure 5-52. Cisco IOS SLB is a Layer 4 or Layer 7 switching feature, depending on configuration. Currently, the only Catalyst switch that supports Cisco IOS SLB is the Catalyst 6500 switch. Cisco IOS SLB is a software-based feature. For high-performance, hardware-based server load balancing, Cisco recommends the Cisco Application Control Engine (ACE) service module for the Catalyst 6500 switches. The ACE service module can help to achieve performance up to 16 Gbps. Also, the ACE service module provides security via SSL encryption/decryption and bidirectional support for content inspection.

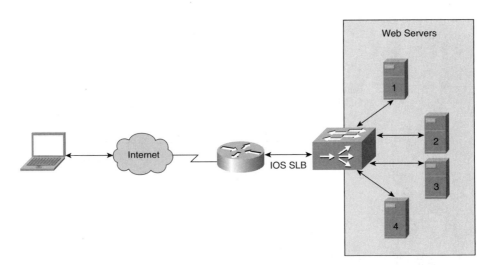

Figure 5-52 *Server Load Balancing*

Cisco IOS SLB presents a single virtual server IP address to requesting clients. For example, clients make IP requests, such as HTTP Get, to this virtual IP address. The switch then distributes (load balances) these requests across a series of servers (real servers). The switch load-balancing request is based on numerous factors, such as TCP and UDP protocol, load, and other load-balancing characteristics. Furthermore, the switch forwards requests from clients to the same server when necessary, such as with FTP when a client must communicate with the same server throughout the entire sequence or flow. Generally, client devices resolve the virtual server IP address through DNS.

Using Cisco IOS SLB for redundancy, scalability, and performance (load balancing) provides the following benefits:

- High performance is achieved through the distribution of client requests across a cluster of servers.

- Administration of server applications is easier. Clients know only about virtual servers; no administration is required for real server changes, making Cisco IOS SLB highly scalable.

- Security of the real server is provided because its address is never announced to the external network. Users are familiar only with the virtual IP address. Additionally, filtering of unwanted traffic can be based on both IP address and IP port numbers.

- Ease of maintenance with no downtime is achieved by allowing physical (real) servers to be transparently placed in or out of service while other servers handle client requests.

- Switches detect servers that are not responding and do not forward further requests to those servers until they begin to respond to polls from the switch.

In summary, Cisco IOS SLB enables users to represent a group of network servers (a server farm in a data center) as a single server instance, balance the traffic to the servers, and limit traffic to individual servers. The single server instance that represents a server farm is referred to as a virtual server. Figure 5-53 illustrates a Cisco IOS SLB applied to a server farm in a data center. The virtual web server IP address is 192.168.1.200 on port 80, and the real web servers are 192.168.1.1 and 192.168.1.2. Any request to the virtual web server address is served by the two real servers.

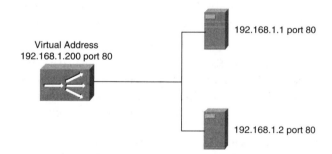

Figure 5-53   *SLB Virtual Server and Server Farm*

Cisco IOS SLB Modes of Operation

In an SLB environment, clients connect to the IP address of the virtual server. When a client initiates a connection to the virtual server, the SLB function chooses a real server for the connection based on a configured load-balancing algorithm.

Cisco IOS SLB supports the following redirection modes:

- **Dispatched mode:** Each of the real servers is configured with the virtual server address as a loopback address or secondary IP address. Cisco IOS SLB redirects packets to the real servers at the MAC layer. Because the virtual server IP address is not modified in dispatched mode, the real servers must be Layer 2–adjacent to Cisco IOS SLB, or intervening routers might not route to the chosen real server.

- **Directed mode:** The virtual server can be assigned an IP address that is not known to any of the real servers in a data center. Cisco IOS SLB translates packets exchanged between a client and a real server, translating the virtual server IP address to a real server address via Network Address Translation (NAT). For more information about Cisco IOS SLB support of different NAT types, refer to the Cisco IOS SLB configuration section of the Cisco product documentation for the Catalyst 6500 switches.

Configuring Cisco IOS SLB involves identifying server farms, configuring groups of real servers in data centers, and configuring the virtual servers that represent the real servers to the clients. The following sections provide a sample configuration of Cisco IOS SLB.

Configuring the Server Farm in a Data Center with Real Servers

The following steps describe how to configure Cisco IOS SLB in a server farm in a data center with real servers:

Step 1. Define the server farm:

```
Switch<config)# ip slb serverfarm serverfarm-name
```

Step 2. Associate the real server with the server farm:

```
Switch(config-slb-sfarm)# real ip-address-of-the-real-server
```

Step 3. Enable the real server defined to be used for the Cisco IOS server farm:

```
Switch(config-slb-real)# inservice
```

Example 5-21 shows a user configuring two server farms in a data center, PUBLIC and RESTRICTED. The PUBLIC server farm has associated with it three real servers: 10.1.1.1, 10.1.1.2, and 10.1.1.3. The RESTRICTED server farm has two real servers associated with it: 10.1.1.20 and 10.1.1.21. Figure 5-54 visually depicts the configuration.

Example 5-21 *Configuring Server Farm with Real Servers*

```
Switch# configure terminal
Enter configuration commands, one per line. End with CNTL/Z.
Switch(config)# ip slb serverfarm PUBLIC
Switch(config-slb-sfarm)# real 10.1.1.1
Switch(config-slb-real)# inservice
Switch(config-slb-real)# exit
Switch(config-slb-sfarm)# real 10.1.1.2
```

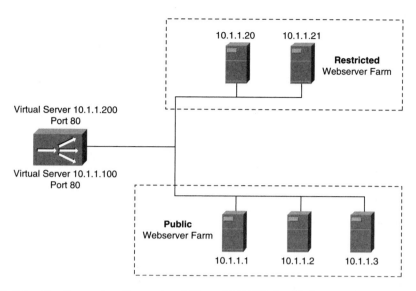

Figure 5-54 *Configuration Scenario of Cisco IOS SLB for Webserver Farms in a Data Center*

```
Switch(config-slb-real)# inservice
Switch(config-slb-real)# exit
Switch(config-slb-sfarm)# real 10.1.1.3
Switch(config-slb-real)# inservice
Switch(config-slb-real)# exit
Switch(config-slb-sfarm)# exit
Switch(config)# ip slb serverfarm RESTRICTED
Switch(config-slb-sfarm)# real 10.1.1.20
Switch(config-slb-real)# inservice
Switch(config-slb-real)# exit
Switch(config-slb-sfarm)# real 10.1.1.21
Switch(config-slb-real)# inservice
Switch(config-slb-real)# end
Switch#
```

Example 5-22 shows a user displaying the status of the server farms PUBLIC and RESTRICTED, the associated real servers, and their status, respectively.

Example 5-22 *Displaying SLB Real Servers*

```
Switch# show ip slb real

real                      farm name        weight    state        cons
- - - - - - - - - - - - - - - - - - - - - - - - - - - - - - - - - -
```

```
10.1.1.1              PUBLIC           8       OPERATIONAL        0
10.1.1.2              PUBLIC           8       OPERATIONAL        0
10.1.1.3              PUBLIC           8       OPERATIONAL        0
10.1.1.20             RESTRICTED       8       OPERATIONAL        0
10.1.1.21             RESTRICTED       8       OPERATIONAL        0
```

Example 5-23 shows a user displaying the configuration and status of server farms PUBLIC and RESTRICTED, respectively.

Example 5-23   *Displaying SLB Server Farm*

```
Switch# show ip slb serverfarm

server farm       predictor    nat   reals   bind id
- - - - - - - - - - - - - - - - - - - - - - - - - -
PUBLIC            ROUNDROBIN   none  3        0
RESTRICTED        ROUNDROBIN   none  2        0
```

Configuring Virtual Servers

The following steps describe how to configure virtual servers in Cisco IOS SLB:

Step 1.   Define the virtual server:

ip slb vserver *vserver-name*

Step 2.   Configure the IP address of the virtual server:

virtual *ip-address* [*network-mask*] {**tcp** | **udp**} [*port-number* | **wsp** |
wsp-wtp | **wsp-wtls** | **wsp-wtp-wtls**] [**service** *service-name*]

Step 3.   Associate the primary and secondary server farm to the virtual server:

serverfarm *primary-serverfarm-name* [**backup** *backup-serverfarm-name*
[**sticky**]]

Step 4.   Enable the virtual server:

inservice

Step 5.   Specify the clients allowed to access the virtual server:

client *ip-address* *network-mask*

Example 5-24 shows a user configuring the virtual servers PUBLIC_HTTP and RESTRICTED_HTTP, respectively, with the latter configuration showing how to restrict access to clients in the network 10.4.4.0.

Example 5-24   *Configuring Virtual Servers*

```
Switch# configure terminal
Enter configuration commands, one per line. End with CNTL/Z.
Switch(config)# ip slb vserver PUBLIC_HTTP
```

```
Switch(config-slb-vserver)# virtual 10.1.1.100 tcp www
Switch(config-slb-vserver)# serverfarm PUBLIC
Switch(config-slb-vserver)# inservice
Switch(config-slb-vserver)# exit
Switch(config)# ip slb vserver RESTRICTED_HTTP
Switch(config-slb-vserver)# virtual 10.1.1.200 tcp www
Switch(config-slb-vserver)# client 10.4.4.0 255.255.255.0
Switch(config-slb-vserver)# serverfarm RESTRICTED
Switch(config-slb-vserver)# inservice
Switch(config-slb-vserver)# end
Switch#
```

Example 5-25 shows a user verifying the configuration of the virtual servers
PUBLIC_HTTP and RESTRICTED_HTTP, respectively.

Example 5-25 *Displaying SLB Virtual Servers*

```
Switch# show ip slb vserver
slb vserver      prot  virtual              state         cons
- - - - - - - - - - - - - - - - - - - - - - - - - - - - - - -
PUBLIC_HTTP      TCP   10.1.1.100:80        OPERATIONAL     0
RESTRICTED_HTTP  TCP   10.1.1.200:80        OPERATIONAL     0
```

Example 5-26 shows a user verifying the restricted client access and status, respectively.

Example 5-26 *Displaying the Current SLB Connections*

```
Switch# show ip slb connections
vserver          prot client            real           state    nat
- - - - - - - - - - - - - - - - - - - - - - - - - - - - - - -
RESTRICTED_HTTP  TCP 10.4.4.0:80         10.1.1.20      CLOSING  none
```

Example 5-27 shows a user displaying detailed information about the restricted client
access status.

Example 5-27 *Displaying Detailed Information for an SLB Client*

```
Switch# show ip slb connections client 10.4.4.0 detail
VSTEST_UDP, client = 10.4.4.0:80
  state = CLOSING, real = 10.1.1.20, nat = none
  v_ip = 10.1.1.200:80, TCP, service = NONE
  client_syns = 0, sticky = FALSE, flows attached = 0
```

Example 5-28 shows a user displaying detailed information about the Cisco IOS SLB network status.

Example 5-28   *Displaying SLB Statistics*

```
Switch# show ip slb stats
Pkts via normal switching:    0
Pkts via special switching:   6
Connections Created:          1
Connections Established:      1
Connections Destroyed:        0
Connections Reassigned:       0
Zombie Count:                 0
Connections Reused:           0
```

Summary

Building a resilient and high available network is paramount as most organizations depend on the network for the business operations.

High availability involves several elements: redundancy, technology, people, processes and tools. At the network level, high availability involves making sure that there is always a possible path between two endpoints. High availability minimizes link and node failures to minimize downtime, by implementing link and node redundancy, providing alternate paths for traffic, and avoiding single points of failure.

Redundancy is a balance between too much redundancy, which increases complexity the network structure, and too little redundancy, which creates single points of failure. When uplinks fail, convergence path and convergence time have to be taken into account to evaluate the impact of the failure on the network infrastructure.

On Cisco IOS–based Catalyst switches, RPR, RPR+, SSO, and NSF with SSO are the various modes of Supervisor redundancy available. The preferred mode is the NSF with SSO because it provides both Layer 2 and Layer 3 protocol state syncing between active and standby Supervisors, therefore guaranteeing the least amount of network impact due to failover, if any at all.

Various first hop redundancy protocols exist including HSRP, VRRP, and GLBP. Currently, HSRP is the most popular choice.

HSRP operates with one router acting as active and the other backup router as a standby router. The active, standby, and other HSRP routers use a virtual IP address for redundancy to hosts. If the active router fails, the standby router becomes the active router and takes responsibility of the destination MAC and IP of the virtual IP address. In this manner, HSRP failover is transparent to the host. Routers running HSRP can be configured for preemption such that if a higher-priority HSRP peer comes online, the higher-priority router takes over the active router role. Otherwise, the latest active router remains the active router when new HSRP peers come online.

VRRP is similar to HSRP except that VRRP is an industry standard, whereas HSRP is a Cisco proprietary protocol. GLBP is another Cisco feature in which multiple routers not only act as backup default gateway routers but also share load in forwarding traffic, unlike HSRP and VRRP, where only the active router forwards traffic. Note that HSPR and VRRP can be distributed across VLANs, achieving load balancing using VLANs.

The Cisco IOS SLB features enable load balancing of connections to a group of real servers and therefore provide fault tolerance for the group of real servers. With this feature, hosts connect to a single virtual server, which in turn is supported by many real servers that are transparent to the host. IOS SLB also supports many forms of load balancing and redundancy.

Monitoring the network using SNMP, Syslog, and IP SLA are key element to ensure the high availability of the network and take corrective action to ensure increased availability.

Review Questions

Use the questions here to review what you learned in this chapter. The correct answers are found in Appendix A, "Answers to Chapter Review Questions."

1. True or False: Redundancy within network devices is enough to guarantee no single point of failure.

2. True or False: VRRP enables the use of multiple master routers for a VRRP group.

3. How long does a standby router take to detect the loss of the active router in HSRP with default timer values?

    a. 15 seconds

    b. 3 seconds

    c. 10 seconds

    d. 9 seconds

    e. <1 second

4. What is the default advertisement of the VRRP master router?

    a. 3 seconds

    b. 1 second

    c. 10 seconds

    d. 2 seconds

    e. None of the above

5. Which of the following is one of the SLB redirection modes?

    a. Hybrid mode

    b. Native mode

    c. Indirect mode

    d. Directed mode

6. What is the default GLBP load-balancing method?

    a. Round-robin

    b. Weighted

    c. Host-dependent

    d. Dispatched

    e. Directed

7. How many member routers can be forwarding in a GLBP group?

    a. 4

    b. 1

    c. 2

    d. 3

    e. No limit

8. Which of the following routing protocols is not supported as part of NSF?

    a. BGP

    b. OSPF

    c. IS-IS

    d. EIGRP

    e. RIP

9. What is the expected failover time for SSO mode for Layer 2 switching on the Catalyst 4500 family of switches?

    a. 2 to 4 minutes

    b. 30 to 60 seconds

    c. Less than 3 seconds

    d. Subsecond

    e. None of the above

## Chapter 6

Securing the Campus Infrastructure

This chapter covers the following topics:

- Switch Security Fundamentals

- Understanding and Protecting Against MAC Layer Attack

- Understanding and Protecting Against VLAN Attacks

- Understanding and Protecting Against Spoofing Attacks

- Securing Network Switches

- Switch Security Considerations

- Troubleshooting Performance and Connectivity

Securing the campus infrastructure is as important as designing a highly available network. If security is compromised, serious impact to business can occur.

This chapter defines the potential vulnerabilities related to VLANs that can occur within a network. After the vulnerabilities are identified, solutions for each vulnerability are discussed, and configuration commands are defined.

This chapter also discusses port security for denial of MAC spoofing and MAC flooding, and using private VLANs (PVLAN) and VLAN access control lists (VACL) to control VLAN traffic. VLAN hopping, Dynamic Host Control Protocol (DHCP) spoofing, Address Resolution Protocol (ARP) spoofing, and Spanning Tree Protocol (STP) attacks are also explained. This chapter also discusses potential problems, resulting solutions, and the method to secure the switch access with use of vty access control lists (ACL), and implementing Secure Shell Protocol (SSH) for secure Telnet access.

This chapter concludes with a description of tools used to monitor, analyze, and troubleshoot switch performance, connectivity, and security issues.

Switch Security Fundamentals

Much industry attention surrounds security attacks from outside the walls of an organization and at the upper Open Systems Interconnection (OSI) layers. Network security often focuses on edge routing devices and the filtering of packets based on Layer 3 and Layer 4 headers, ports, stateful packet inspection, and so forth. This includes all issues surrounding Layer 3 and above, as traffic makes its way into the campus network from the Internet. Campus access devices and Layer 2 communication are left largely unconsidered in most security discussions, and there is lack of security at this layer.

The default state of networking equipment highlights this focus on external protection and internal open communication. Firewalls, placed at the organizational borders, arrive in a secure operational mode and do not enable communication until configured to do so. Routers and switches that are internal to an organization and designed to accommodate communication, delivering needful campus traffic, have a default operational mode that forwards all traffic unless configured otherwise. Their function as devices that facilitate communication often results in minimal security configuration and renders them targets for malicious attacks. If an attack is launched at Layer 2 on an internal campus device, the rest of the network can be quickly compromised, often without detection. Also, non-malicious user intentions can also result in network disruption. Although activities such as a user plugging in a switch or a hub to a data port or configuring his or her laptop as a DHCP server are not intended to be malicious, nevertheless they can still result in network disruptions.

Many security features are available for switches and routers, but they must be enabled to be effective. As with Layer 3, where security had to be tightened on devices within the campus as malicious activity that compromised this layer increased; now security measures must be taken to guard against malicious activity at Layer 2. A new security focus centers on attacks launched by maliciously leveraging normal Layer 2 switch operations. Security features exist to protect switches and Layer 2 operations. However, as with access control lists (ACL) for upper-layer security, a policy must be established and appropriate features configured to protect against potential malicious acts while maintaining daily network operations.

Security Infrastructure Services

Security is an infrastructure service that increases the integrity of the network by protecting network resources and users from internal and external threats. Without a full understanding of the threats involved, network security deployments tend to be incorrectly configured, too focused on security devices, or lacking appropriate threat-response options.

You can evaluate and apply security on a module-by-module basis within the Cisco Enterprise Architecture, as shown in Figure 6-1.

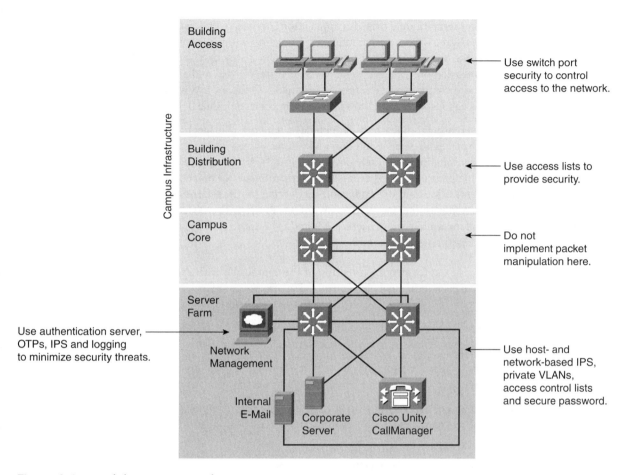

Figure 6-1 *Modularizing Internal Security*

The following are some recommended-practice security considerations for each module:

- The campus core layer in the campus infrastructure module switches packets as quickly as possible. It should not perform any security functions because these would slow down packet switching.

- The building distribution layer performs packet filtering to keep unnecessary traffic from the campus core layer. Packet filtering at the building distribution layer is a security function because it prevents some unwanted access to other modules. Given that switches in this layer are usually Layer 3-aware multilayer switches, the building distribution layer is often the first location that can filter based on network layer information.

- At the building access layer, access can be controlled at the port level with respect to the data link layer information (for example, MAC addresses).

- The server farm module provides application services to end users and devices. Given the high degree of access that most employees have to these servers, they often become the primary target of internally originated attacks. Use host- and network-based intrusion prevention systems (IPS), private VLANs, and access control to provide a more comprehensive response to attacks. Onboard IDS within multilayer switches can inspect traffic flows on the server farm module.

- The server farm module typically includes a network management system that securely manages all devices and hosts within the enterprise architecture. Syslog provides important information regarding security violations and configuration changes by logging security-related events (authentication and so on). Other servers, including an authentication, authorization, and accounting (AAA) security server, can work in combination with the one-time password (OTP) server to provide a high level of security to all local and remote users. AAA and OTP authentication reduce the likelihood of a successful password attack.

Several reasons exist for strong protection of the campus infrastructure, including security functions in each individual element of the enterprise campus:

Relying on the security that has been established at the enterprise edge fails as soon as security there is compromised. Several layers of security increase the protection of the enterprise campus, where usually the most strategic assets reside.

If the enterprise allows visitors into its buildings, potentially an attacker can gain physical access to devices in the enterprise campus. Relying on physical security is not enough.

Often, external access does not stop at the enterprise edge. Applications require at least an indirect access to the enterprise campus resources, requiring strong security.

Unauthorized Access by Rogue Devices

Rogue access comes in several forms, as shown in Figure 6-2. For example, because unauthorized rogue access points are inexpensive and readily available, employees sometimes plug them into existing LANs and build ad hoc wireless networks without IT department knowledge or consent. These rogue access points can be a serious breach of network security because they can be plugged into a network port behind the corporate firewall. Because employees generally do not enable any security settings on the rogue access point, it is easy for unauthorized users to use the access point to intercept network traffic and hijack client sessions.

Malicious rogue access points, although much less common than employee-installed rogue access points, are also a security concern. These rogue access points create an unsecured wireless LAN connection that puts the entire wired network at risk. Malicious rogues present an even greater risk and challenge because they are intentionally hidden from physical and network view by not broadcasting the SSID.

To mitigate Spanning Tree Protocol (STP) manipulation, use the root guard and the BPDU guard enhancement commands to enforce the placement of the root bridge in the network and to enforce the STP domain borders. The root guard feature is designed to provide a way to enforce the root bridge placement in the network. The STP bridge protocol data unit (BPDU) guard is designed to enable network designers to keep the active network topology predictable. Although the BPDU guard might seem unnecessary, given that the administrator can set the bridge priority to zero, there is still no guarantee that it will be elected as the root bridge because there might be a bridge with priority zero and a lower bridge ID. A BPDU guard is best deployed toward user-facing ports to prevent unauthorized switches from being attached to the network by an attacker.

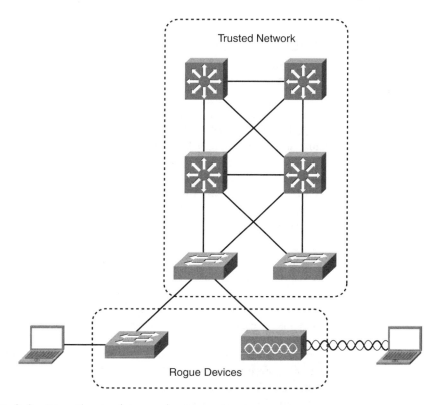

Figure 6-2   *Unauthorized Access by Rogue Devices*

Layer 2 Attack Categories

Layer 2 malicious attacks are typically initiated by devices directly connected to the campus network infrastructure. The attacks can originate from a physical rogue device placed on the network for malicious purposes. The attack also can come from an external intrusion that takes control of and launches attacks from a trusted device. In either case, the network sees all traffic as originating from a legitimate connected device.

Attacks launched against switches and at Layer 2 can be grouped as follows:

■   MAC layer attacks

■   VLAN attacks

- Spoofing attacks

- Attacks on switch devices

These attack methods and steps to mitigate these threats are discussed in more detail in this chapter.

Table 6-1 describes attack methods and the steps to mitigation.

Table 6-1   *Switch Security Attacks and Mitigation Steps*

Attack Method	Description	Steps to Mitigation
MAC Layer Attacks		
MAC address flooding	Frames with unique, invalid source MAC addresses flood the switch, exhausting content addressable memory (CAM) table space, disallowing new entries from valid hosts. Traffic to valid hosts is subsequently flooded out all ports.	Port security. MAC address VLAN access maps.
VLAN Attacks		
VLAN hopping	By altering the VLAN ID on packets encapsulated for trunking, an attacking device can send or receive packets on various VLANs, bypassing Layer 3 security measures.	Tighten up trunk configurations and the negotiation state of unused ports. Place unused ports in a common VLAN.
Attacks between devices on a common VLAN	Devices might need protection from one another, even though they are on a common VLAN. This is especially true on service-provider segments that support devices from multiple customers.	Implement private VLANs (PVLAN).
Spoofing Attacks		
DHCP starvation and DHCP spoofing	An attacking device can exhaust the address space available to the DHCP servers for a period of time or establish itself as a DHCP server in man-in-the-middle attacks.	Use DHCP snooping.

Attack Method	Description	Steps to Mitigation
Spanning-tree compromises	Attacking device spoofs the root bridge in the STP topology. If successful, the network attacker can see a variety of frames.	Proactively configure the primary and backup root devices. Enable root guard.
MAC spoofing	Attacking device spoofs the MAC address of a valid host currently in the CAM table. The switch then forwards frames destined for the valid host to the attacking device.	Use DHCP snooping, port security.
Address Resolution Protocol (ARP) spoofing	Attacking device crafts ARP replies intended for valid hosts. The attacking device's MAC address then becomes the destination address found in the Layer 2 frames sent by the valid network device.	Use Dynamic ARP Inspection. DHCP snooping, port security.
Switch Device Attacks		
Cisco Discovery Protocol (CDP) manipulation	Information sent through CDP is transmitted in clear text and unauthenticated, allowing it to be captured and divulge network topology information.	Disable CDP on all ports where it is not intentionally used.
Secure Shell Protocol (SSH) and Telnet attacks	Telnet packets can be read in clear text. SSH is an option but has security issues in version 1.	Use SSH version 2. Use Telnet with vty ACLs.

Understanding and Protecting Against MAC Layer Attack

A common Layer 2 or switch attack is MAC flooding, resulting in a switch's CAM table overflow, which causes flooding of regular data frames out all switch ports. This attack can be launched for the malicious purpose of collecting a broad sample of traffic or as a denial of service (DoS) attack.

A switch's CAM tables are limited in size and therefore can contain only a limited number of entries at any one time. A network intruder can maliciously flood a switch with a large number of frames from a range of invalid source MAC addresses. If enough new entries are made before old ones expire, new valid entries will not be accepted. Then, when traffic arrives at the switch for a legitimate device located on one of the switch ports that could not create a CAM table entry, the switch must flood frames to that address out all ports. This has two adverse effects:

■ The switch traffic forwarding is inefficient and voluminous and could potentially slow down the network for all users.

■ An intruding device can be connected to any switch port and capture traffic not normally seen on that port.

If the attack is launched before the beginning of the day, the MAC address table (also referred to as Content Addressable Memory [CAM] table) would be full when the majority of devices are powered on. Then frames from those legitimate devices cannot create MAC address table entries as they power on. If this represents a large number of network devices, the number of MAC addresses flooded with traffic will be high, and any switch port will carry flooded frames from a large number of devices.

If the initial flood of invalid MAC address table entries is a one-time event, the switch eventually ages out older, invalid MAC address table entries, allowing new, legitimate devices to create entries. Traffic flooding ceases and might never be detected, even though the intruder might have captured a significant amount of data from the network.

As Figure 6-3 shows, MAC flooding occurs in this progression; the following describes MAC flooding attack progression.

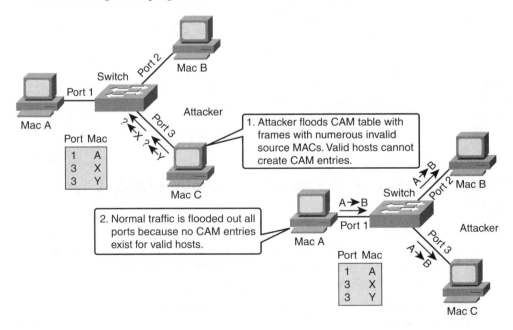

Figure 6-3 *MAC Address Flooding Attack*

Step 1.   Switch forwards traffic based on valid MAC address table entries.

Step 2.   Attacker (MAC address C) sends out multiple packets with various source MAC addresses.

Step 3.   Over a short time period, the CAM table in the switch fills up until it cannot accept new entries. As long as the attack is running, the MAC address table on the switch remains full.

Step 4.   Switch begins to flood all packets that it receives out of every port so that frames sent from Host A to Host B are also flooded out of Port 3 on the switch.

Suggested Mitigation for MAC Flooding Attacks

To prevent MAC Address flooding, port security can be used. Configure port security to define the number of MAC addresses allowed on a given port. Port security can also specify what MAC address is allowed on a given port. Port security is described in the following section.

Port Security

Port security is a feature supported on Cisco Catalyst switches that restricts a switch port to a specific set or number of MAC addresses. Those addresses can be learned dynamically or configured statically. The port then provides access to frames from only those addresses. If, however, the number of addresses is limited to four but no specific MAC addresses are configured, the port enables any four MAC addresses to be learned dynamically, and port access is limited to those four dynamically learned addresses.

A port security feature called *sticky learning*, available on some switch platforms, combines the features of dynamically learned and statically configured addresses. When this feature is configured on an interface, the interface converts dynamically learned addresses to *sticky secure* addresses. This adds them to the running configuration as if they were configured using the **switchport port-security** *mac-address* interface command.

Port Security Scenario 1

Imagine five individuals whose laptops are allowed to connect to a specific switch port when they visit an area of the building. You want to restrict switch port access to the MAC addresses of those five laptops and allow no addresses to be learned dynamically on that port.

Table 6-2 describes the process that can achieve the desired results for this scenario.

Table 6-2   *Implementing Port Security*

Step	Action	Notes
1	Configure port security.	Configure port security to allow only five connections on that port. Configure an entry for each of the five allowed MAC addresses. This, in effect, populates the MAC address table with five entries for that port and allows no additional entries to be learned dynamically.
2	Allowed frames are processed.	When frames arrive on the switch port, their source MAC address is checked against the MAC address table. If the frame source MAC address matches an entry in the table for that port, the frames are forwarded to the switch to be processed like any other frames on the switch.
3	New addresses are not allowed to create new MAC address table entries.	When frames with a nonallowed MAC address arrive on the port, the switch determines that the address is not in the current MAC address table and does not create a dynamic entry for that new MAC address because the number of allowed addresses has been limited.
4	Switch takes action in response to nonallowed frames.	The switch disallows access to the port and takes one of these configuration-dependent actions: (a) the entire switch port can be shut down; (b) access can be denied for that MAC address only and a log error can be generated; (c) access can be denied for that MAC address but without generating a log message.

Port Security Scenario 2

In this scenario, an attacker enables a hacking tool leading to the attacker's rogue device to flood switch CAM tables with bogus MACs, which fills up the MAC address table, as shown in Figure 6-4. When the MAC address table is full, it turns the VLAN into a hub and floods all unicast frames.

To prevent this attack, Figure 6-5 shows that port security is configured on the untrusted user ports. Enabling port security limits MAC flooding attacks and locks down the port. Port security also sets an SNMP trap for alerting to any violation. Port security allows the frames from already secured MAC address below the maximum number of MAC addresses enabled on that port, and any frame with new MAC address over the limit are dropped.

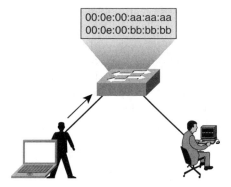

Figure 6-4 *MAC Flood Attack on a Switch Port*

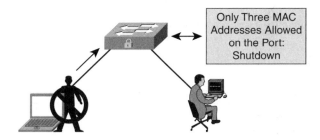

Figure 6-5 *Port Security Prevents MAC Flood Attack*

Configuring Port Security

Here are the steps to set up port security to limit switch port access to a finite number and a specific set of end-device MAC addresses.

To configure port security, follow these steps:

Step 1.   Enable port security:

```
Switch(config-if)#switchport port-security
```

Step 2.   Set a maximum number of MAC addresses that will be allowed on this port. Default is one:

```
Switch(config-if)#switchport port-security maximum value
```

Step 3.   Specify which MAC addresses will be allowed on this port (optional):

```
Switch(config-if)#switchport port-security mac-address mac-address
```

Step 4.   Define what action an interface will take if a nonallowed MAC address attempts access:

```
Switch(config-if)#switchport port-security violation {shutdown | restrict |
  protect}
```

Figure 6-6 depicts an access layer Catalyst 4500 switch scenario. A real-time media server plugs in to switch port 3/47. The switch port needs port security to prevent any unauthorized devices from plugging into the same port. The administrator has configured preferential QoS policies based on all traffic received on the port and other security ACLs. The network administrator requirement is not to shut down the port of the server but rather to restrict the port to only the authorized MAC address. In addition, the network administrator configures the switch to shut down port 2/2 in the guest lobby if any unauthorized workstation plugs into that port.

Access Layer Catalyst

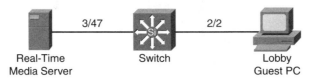

Real-Time
Media Server

3/47

Switch

2/2

Lobby
Guest PC

Figure 6-6 *Port Security Configuration*

Example 6-1 shows the configuration for this scenario.

Example 6-1 *Configuration of Port Security on Cisco IOS–Based Catalyst Switches*

```
4503(config)# interface FastEthernet 3/47
4503(config-if)# switchport
4503(config-if)# switchport mode access
4503(config-if)# switchport port-security
4503(config-if)# switchport port-security mac-address 0000.0000.0008
4503(config-if)# switchport port-security maximum 1
4503(config-if)# switchport port-security aging static
4503(config-if)# switchport port-security violation restrict
4503(config)# interface FastEthernet 2/2
4503(config-if)# switchport
4503(config-if)# switchport mode access
4503(config-if)# switchport port-security
4503(config-if)# switchport port-security mac-address 0000.0000.1118
4503(config-if)# switchport port-security maximum 1
4503(config-if)# switchport port-security aging static
4503(config-if)# switchport port-security violation shutdown
```

Caveats to Port Security Configuration Steps

Step 1.   Port security is enabled on a port-by-port basis using the **switchport port-security** command.

Step 2.   By default, only one MAC address is allowed access through a given switch port when port security is enabled. This parameter increases that number. It implies no restriction on specific MAC addresses, just on the total number of addresses that can be learned by the port. Learned addresses are not aged out by default but can be configured to do so after a specified time using the **switchport port-security aging** command. The value parameter can be any number from 1 to 1024, with some restrictions having to do with the number of ports on a given switch with port security enabled. The **switchport port-security aging static** command enables aging for statically configured secure addresses on the port.

Step 3.   Access to the switch port can be restricted to one or more specific MAC addresses. If the number of specific MAC addresses assigned using this command is lower than the value parameter set in Step 2, the remaining allowed addresses can be learned dynamically. If you specify a set of MAC addresses that is equal to the maximum number allowed, access is limited to that set of MAC addresses.

Step 4.   By default, if the maximum number of connections is achieved and a new MAC address attempts to access the port, the switch must take one of these actions:

- **Protect:** Frames from the nonallowed address are dropped, but there is no log of the violation.

- **Restrict:** Frames from the nonallowed address are dropped, a log message is created, and a Simple Network Management Protocol (SNMP) trap is sent.

- **Shut down:** If any frames are seen from a nonallowed address, the interface is errdisabled, a log entry is made, an SNMP trap is sent, and manual intervention or errdisable recovery must be used to make the interface usable. Shutdown mode is the default mode for violation.

Verifying Port Security

The **show port-security** command can be used to verify the ports on which port security has been enabled, as shown in Example 6-2. It also displays count information and security actions to be taken per interface.

The full command syntax is as follows:

```
show port-security [interface intf_id] [address]
```

Example 6-2   *Verifying Port Security Operation*

```
switch# show port-security
Secure Port MaxSecureAddr CurrentAddr SecurityViolation Security Action
            (Count)       (Count)     (Count)
----------------------------------------------------------------------
    Fa0/1        2             1              0            Restrict
----------------------------------------------------------------------
```

```
Total Addresses in System (excluding one mac per port)    : 0
Max Addresses limit in System (excluding one mac per port) : 6144
```

Arguments are provided to view port security status by interface or view the addresses associated with port security on all interfaces.

Use the **interface** argument to provide output for a specific interface, as shown in Example 6-3.

Example 6-3 *Verifying Port Security Configuration*

```
switch# show port-security interface fastethernet0/1
Port Security                 : Enabled
Port Status                   : Secure-up
Violation Mode                : Restrict
Aging Time                    : 60 mins
Aging Type                    : Inactivity
SecureStatic Address Aging    : Enabled
Maximum MAC Addresses         : 2
Total MAC Addresses           : 1
Configured MAC Addresses      : 0
Sticky MAC Addresses          : 0
Last Source Address:Vlan      : 001b.d513.2ad2:5
Security Violation Count      : 0
```

Use the **address** argument to display MAC address table security information, as shown in Example 6-4. The remaining age column is populated only when specifically configured for a given interface.

Example 6-4 *Verifying Port Security Using Address Argument*

```
switch# show port-security address
          Secure Mac Address Table
-------------------------------------------------------------------------
Vlan    Mac Address      Type                    Ports    Remaining Age
                                                            (mins)
----    -----------      ----                    -----    -------------
  2     001b.d513.2ad2   SecureDynamic           Fa0/1     60 (I)
-------------------------------------------------------------------------
Total Addresses in System (excluding one mac per port)    : 0
Max Addresses limit in System (excluding one mac per port) : 6144
```

Port Security with Sticky MAC Addresses

Port security can mitigate spoofing attacks by limiting access through each switch port to a single MAC address. This prevents intruders from using multiple MAC addresses over a short time period but does not limit port access to a specific MAC address. The most restrictive port security implementation would specify the exact MAC address of the single device that is to gain access through each port. Implementing this level of security, however, requires considerable administrative overhead.

Port security has a *sticky MAC addresses* feature that can limit switch port access to a single, specific MAC address without the network administrator having to gather the MAC address of every legitimate device and manually associate it with a particular switch port.

When sticky MAC addresses are used, the switch port converts dynamically learned MAC addresses to sticky MAC addresses and subsequently adds them to the running configuration as if they were static entries for a single MAC address to be allowed by port security. Sticky secure MAC addresses will be added to the running configuration but will not become part of the startup configuration file unless the running configuration is copied to the startup configuration after addresses have been learned. If they are saved in the startup configuration, they will not have to be relearned upon switch reboot, and this provides a higher level of network security.

Note   The interface converts all the dynamic secure MAC addresses, including those that were dynamically learned before sticky learning was enabled, to sticky secure MAC addresses.

The interface level configuration command that follows converts all dynamic port-security learned MAC addresses to sticky secure MAC addresses.

```
switchport port-security mac-address sticky
```

This command cannot be used on ports where voice VLANs are configured. Example 6-5 shows the configuration and verification of the sticky MAC address feature of port security.

Example 6-5   *Configuring and Verifying Port Security Sticky MAC-Address*

```
switch# show running-config fastethernet 0/1
interface FastEthernet0/1
 switchport access vlan 2
 switchport mode access
 switchport port-security maximum 2
 switchport port-security
 switchport port-security violation restrict
 switchport port-security mac-address sticky
 switchport port-security mac-address sticky 001b.d513.2ad2
```

```
switch# show port-security address
Secure Mac Address Table

-----------------------------------------------------------------

Vlan      Mac Address      Type                  Ports      Remaining Age
                                                            (mins)

----      -----------      ----                  -----      -------------

   2      001b.d513.2ad2   SecureSticky          Fa0/1      -
```

Blocking Unicast Flooding on Desired Ports

By default, switches flood packets with unknown destination MAC addresses to all ports in the same VLAN as the received port's VLAN. Some ports do not require flooding. For example, a port that has only manually assigned MAC addresses and that does not have a network device connected to that port other than the configured MAC address does not need to receive flooded packets. In addition, a port security–enabled port with a configured secure MAC address or port does not need to receive unknown unicast flooding if the port has already learned the maximum number of MAC addresses. If the network exhibits asymmetrical routing, excessive unicast flooding can occur and might cause all the devices in that VLAN to suffer as they receive the unneeded traffic. With asymmetrical routing, transmit and receive packets follow different paths between a host and the destination device. For more information about asymmetrical routing, see the following technical document at Cisco.com: "Unicast Flooding in Switched Campus Networks," Document ID: 23563:

www.cisco.com/en/US/products/hw/switches/ps700/products_tech_note09186a00801d0808.shtml

The unicast flood-blocking feature prevents the forwarding of unicast flood traffic on unnecessary ports. Restricting the amount of traffic on a per-port basis adds a level of security to the network and prevents network devices from unnecessarily processing nondirected packets.

Cisco Catalyst switches can restrict flooding of unknown multicast MAC-addressed traffic on a per-port basis, in addition to restricting flooding of unknown unicast destination MAC addresses. Use the following interface-level command:

`switchport block {unicast | multicast}`

Example 6-6 shows a user configuring unicast and multicast flood blocking on an access layer switch.

Example 6-6 *Configuration of Unicast and Multicast Flood Filtering on a Catalyst Switch*

```
4503# configure terminal
Enter configuration commands, one per line. End with CNTL/Z.
4503(config)# interface FastEthernet 3/22
4503(config-if)# switchport block unicast
4503(config-if)# switchport block multicast
```

Understanding and Protecting Against VLAN Attacks

On networks using trunking protocols, there is a possibility of rogue traffic "hopping" from one VLAN to another, thereby creating security vulnerabilities.

VLAN Hopping

VLAN hopping is a network attack whereby an end system sends packets to, or collects packets from, a VLAN that should not be accessible to that end system. This is accomplished by tagging the invasive traffic with a specific VLAN ID (VID) or by negotiating a trunk link to send or receive traffic on penetrated VLANs. VLAN hopping can be accomplished by switch spoofing or double tagging.

VLAN hopping attacks refer to a malicious device attempting to access VLANs for which it is not configured. There are two forms of VLAN hopping attacks.

The first form is due to the default configuration of the Catalyst switch port. Cisco Catalyst switches enable trunking in auto mode by default. As a result, the interface becomes a trunk upon receiving a DTP frame. An attacker can use this default behavior to access VLANs configured on the switch through one of the following methods:

■ An attacker can send a malicious DTP frame. Upon receiving the frame, the switch would form a trunk port, which would then give the attacker access to all the VLANs on the trunk. In Figure 6-7, the attacker port becomes a trunk port, and the attacker can attack a victim in any VLAN carried on the trunk.

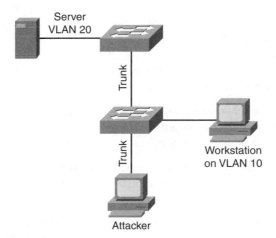

Figure 6-7 *VLAN Hopping*

■ In a switch spoofing attack, the network attacker configures a system to spoof itself as a switch. Typically, this is achieved by connecting an unauthorized Cisco switch to the switch port. The authorized switch can send DTP frames and form a trunk. The attacker again has access to all the VLANs through the trunk. In Figure 6-8, an unauthorized switch can form a trunk with the Cisco switch. The attacker device connects to the unauthorized switch and can attack a victim in another VLAN.

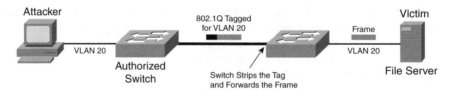

Figure 6-8   *VLAN Hopping via Switch Spoofing*

The following list describes the switch spoofing sequence of events:

1. Attacker gains access to a switch port and sends DTP negotiation frames toward a switch with DTP running and auto negotiation turned on (often, the default settings).

2. Attacker and switch negotiate trunking over the port.

3. Switch enables all VLANs (default) to traverse the trunk link.

4. Attacker sends data to, or collects it from, all VLANs carried on that trunk.

VLAN Hopping with Double Tagging

The second form of VLAN hopping attack is possible even if the trunking feature is turned off on the switch port. The attack involves sending frames with a double 802.1Q tag, as shown in Figure 6-9. This attack requires the client to be on a switch other than the attacking switch. Another requirement is that these two switches must be connected in the same VLAN as the attacking switch port or native VLAN of the trunk between the switch and the attacked VLAN.

In this method of VLAN hopping, any workstation can generate frames with two 802.1Q headers to cause the switch to forward the frames onto a VLAN that would be inaccessible to the attacker through legitimate means.

The first switch to encounter the double-tagged frame strips the first tag off the frame, because the first tag (VLAN 10) matches the trunk port native VLAN, and then forwards the frame out.

The result is that the frame is forwarded, with the inner 802.1Q tag, out all the switch ports as the switch does not have the MAC address in the table because the switch does not recognize that there is a second tag., including trunk ports configured with the native VLAN of the network attacker. The second switch then forwards the packet to the destination based on the VLAN ID in the second 802.1Q header. If the trunk does not match the native VLAN of the attacker, the frame would be untagged and flooded to only the original VLAN.

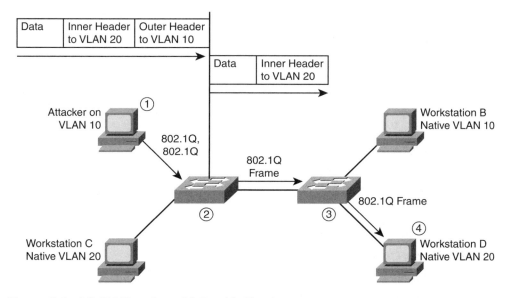

Figure 6-9 *VLAN Hopping with Double Tagging*

The following steps describe the double-tagging method of VLAN hopping:

Step 1.   Attacker (native VLAN 10) sends a frame with two 802.1Q headers to Switch 1.

Step 2.   Switch 1 strips the outer tag and forwards the frame to all ports within same native VLAN.

Step 3.   Switch 2 interprets frame according to information in the inner tag marked with VLAN ID 20.

Step 4.   Switch 2 forwards the frame out all ports associated with VLAN 20, including trunk ports.

Mitigating VLAN Hopping

The measures to defend the network from VLAN hopping are a series of best practices for all switch ports and parameters to follow when establishing a trunk port:

- Configure all unused ports as access ports so that trunking cannot be negotiated across those links.

- Place all unused ports in the shutdown state and associate them with a VLAN designed for only unused ports, carrying no user data traffic.

- When establishing a trunk link, purposefully configure arguments to achieve the following results:
  - The native VLAN is different from any data VLANs.
  - Trunking is set up as On or Nonegotiate rather than negotiated.
  - The specific VLAN range is carried on the trunk. This ensures that native VLAN will be pruned along with any other VLANs not explicitly allowed on the trunk.

Other methods to ensure VLAN security is using private VLAN to segregate users and using VLAN ACL to filter traffic within the same VLAN. Private VLAN is explained more in Chapter 2, "Implementing VLANs in Campus Networks."

For more information about best practice for configuring Catalyst switches, refer to the following URL on Cisco.com:

www.cisco.com/en/US/products/hw/switches/ps700/products_white_paper09186a00801b49a4.shtml

VLAN Access Control Lists

Access control lists (ACL) are useful for controlling access in a multilayer switched network. This topic describes VACLs and their purpose as part of VLAN security.

Cisco multilayer switches support three types of ACLs, as shown in Figure 6-10.

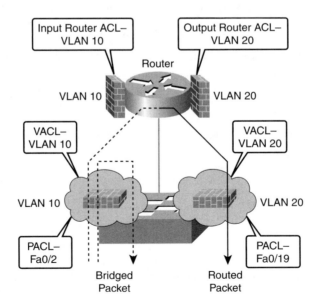

Figure 6-10 *Types of ACL Supported on Catalyst Switches*

- **Router access control lists (RACL):** Supported in the TCAM hardware on Cisco multilayer switches. In Catalyst switches, RACL can be applied to any routed interface, such as a switch virtual interface (SVI) or Layer 3 routed port.

- **Port access control list (PACL):** Filters traffic at the port level. PACLs can be applied on a Layer 2 switch port, trunk port, or EtherChannel port. PACLs act at the Layer 2 port level but can filter based on Layer 3/Layer 4 information.

- **VACLs:** Also known as VLAN access-maps, apply to all traffic in a VLAN. VACLs support filtering based on Ethertype and MAC addresses. VACLs are order-sensitive, similar to Cisco IOS–based route maps. VACLs can control traffic flowing within the VLAN or control switched traffic, whereas RACLs control only routed traffic.

Catalyst switches support four ACL lookups per packet: input and output security ACL and input and output quality of service (QoS) ACL.

The process of combining the ACEs from multiple feature ACLs is known as the *ACL merge*. Catalyst switches use two methods of performing a merge: order independent and order dependent. With order-independent merge, ACLs are transformed from a series of order-dependent actions to a set of order-independent masks and patterns. The resulting access control entry (ACE) can be large. The merge is processor- and memory-intensive.

Order-dependent merge is a recent improvement on some Catalyst switches in which ACLs retain their order-dependent aspect. The computation is much faster and is less processor-intensive.

For more information on order-dependent merge, refer to the following URL on Cisco.com:

www.cisco.com/warp/public/cc/pd/si/casi/ca6000/tech/65acl_wp.pdf

ACLs are supported in hardware through IP standard ACLs and IP extended ACLs, with permit and deny actions. ACL processing is an intrinsic part of the packet forwarding process. ACL entries are programmed in hardware. Lookups occur in the pipeline, whether ACLs are configured. This enables ACLs to effectively provide filtering at line-rate on a Catalyst switch and therefore can be used for security.

Configuring VACL

VACLs (also called VLAN access maps in Cisco IOS Software) apply to all traffic on the VLAN. You can configure VACLs for IP- and MAC-layer traffic.

VACLs follow **route-map** conventions, in which map sequences are checked in order.

When a matching permit ACE is encountered, the switch takes the action. When a matching deny ACE is encountered, the switch checks the next ACL in the sequence or checks the next sequence.

Three VACL actions are permitted:

■ **Permit** (with capture, Catalyst 6500 only)

■ **Redirect** (Catalyst 6500 only)

■ **Deny** (with logging, Catalyst 6500 only)

The VACL capture option copies traffic to specified capture ports. VACL ACEs installed in hardware are merged with RACLs and other features.

Two features are supported on only the Cisco Catalyst 6500:

■ **VACL capture:** Forwarded packets are captured on capture ports. The capture option is only on permit ACEs. The capture port can be an IDS monitor port or any Ethernet port. The capture port must be in an output VLAN for Layer 3 switched traffic.

■ **VACL redirect:** Matching packets are redirected to specified ports. You can configure up to five redirect ports. Redirect ports must be in a VLAN where a VACL is applied.

To configure VACLs, complete these steps:

Step 1.   Define a VLAN access map:

```
Switch(config)# vlan access-map map_name [seq#]
```

Step 2.   Configure a match clause:

```
Switch(config-access-map)# match {drop [log]} | {forward [capture]} |
    {redirect {{fastethernet | gigabitethernet | tengigabitethernet}
    slot/port} | {port-channel channel_id}}
```

Step 3.   Configure an action clause:

```
Switch(config-access-map)# action {drop [log]} | {forward [capture]} |
    {redirect {{fastethernet | gigabitethernet | tengigabitethernet}
    slot/port} | {port-channel channel_id}}
```

Step 4.   Apply a map to VLANs:

```
Switch(config)# vlan filter map_name vlan_list list
```

Step 5.   Verify the VACL configuration:

```
Switch# show vlan access-map map_name
Switch# show vlan filter [ access-map map_name | vlan_id ]
```

Example 6-7 shows configuration of VACL to drop all traffic from network 10.1.9.0/24 on VLAN 10 and 20 and drop all traffic to Backup Server 0000.1111.4444.

Example 6-7   *VACL Configuration*

```
switch(config)# access-list 100 permit ip 10.1.9.0 0.0.0.255 any
Switch(config)# mac access-list extended BACKUP_SERVER
Switch(config-ext-mac)# permit any host 0000.1111.4444
switch(config)# vlan access-map XYZ 10
```

```
switch(config-map)# match ip address 100
switch(config-map)# action drop
switch(config-map)# vlan access-map XYZ 20
switch(config-map)# match mac address BACKUP_SERVER
Switch(config-map)# action drop
switch(config-map)# vlan access-map XYZ 30
switch(config-map)# action forward
switch(config)# vlan filter XYZ vlan-list 10,20
```

Understanding and Protecting Against Spoofing Attacks

Spoofing attacks can occur because several protocols allow a reply from a host even if a request was not received. By spoofing, or pretending to be another machine, the attacker can redirect part or all the traffic coming from, or going to, a predefined target. After the attack, all traffic from the device under attack flows through the attacker's computer and then to the router, switch, or host.

A spoofing attack can affect hosts, switches, and routers connected to your Layer 2 network by sending false information to the devices connected to the subnet. Spoofing attacks can also intercept traffic intended for other hosts on the subnet. This section describes how to mitigate these attacks and how to configure switches to guard against Dynamic Host Control Protocol (DHCP), MAC, and Address Resolution Protocol (ARP) threats.

Catalyst Integrated Security Features

The Cisco Catalyst Integrated Security capabilities provide campus security on the Cisco Catalyst switches using integrated tools, as shown in Figure 6-11.

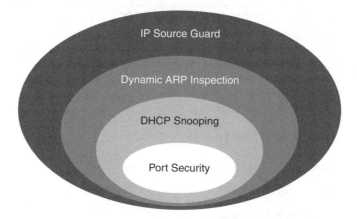

Figure 6-11 *Cisco Integrated Security Features*

- Port security prevents MAC flooding attacks.

- DHCP snooping prevents client attacks on the DHCP server and switch.

- Dynamic Address Resolution Protocol (ARP) inspection adds security to ARP using the DHCP snooping table to minimize the impact of ARP poisoning and spoofing attacks.

- IP Source Guard (IPSG) prevents IP spoofing addresses using the DHCP snooping table.

Port Security is covered in the MAC-based attack section of this chapter. DHCP snooping, DAI, and IP source guard can be used to prevent spoof attacks and are covered in depth in this section.

DHCP Spoofing Attack

DHCP is a protocol used to dynamically assign an IP address and default gateway among other configurations to a client in a network. DHCP is achieved through an exchange of protocol packets between the client and the DHCP server, as shown in Figure 6-12.

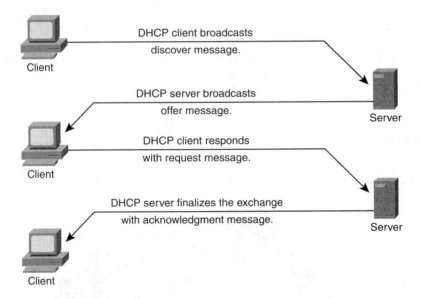

Figure 6-12   *DCHP*

DHCP uses four messages to provide an IP address to a client:

- DHCP discover broadcast from client

- DHCP offer broadcast to client

- DHCP unicast request from client

- DHCP unicast acknowledge to client

One of the ways that an attacker can gain access to network traffic is to spoof responses that would be sent by a valid DHCP server. The DHCP spoofing device replies to client DHCP requests. The legitimate server can reply also, but if the spoofing device is on the same segment as the client, its reply to the client might arrive first.

The intruder's DHCP reply offers an IP address and supporting information that designates the intruder as the default gateway or Domain Name System (DNS) server. For a gateway, the clients then forward packets to the attacking device, which in turn sends them to the desired destination. This is referred to as a man-in-the-middle attack, and it can go entirely undetected as the intruder intercepts the data flow through the network.

The following describes the DHCP spoof attack sequence:

1.   Attacker hosts a rogue DHCP server off a switch port.

2.   Client broadcasts a request for DHCP configuration information.

3.   The rogue DHCP server responds before the legitimate DHCP server, assigning attacker-defined IP configuration information.

4.   Host packets are redirected to the attacker's address as it emulates a default gateway for the erroneous DHCP address provided to the client.

A couple of scenarios can occur in a DHCP-enabled network. Attacker can cause a DoS attack by sending thousands of DHCP requests, as shown in Figure 6-13. The DHCP server does not have the capability to determine whether the request is genuine and therefore might end up exhausting all the available IP addresses. This results in a legitimate client not getting a IP address via DHCP.

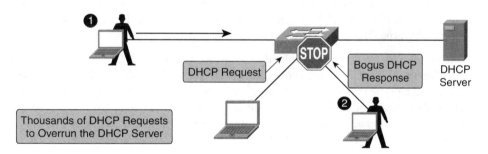

Figure 6-13   *DHCP Spoofing Attacks*

A second scenario can happen when the attacker attaches a DCHP server to the network and has it assume the role of the DHCP server for that segment. This enables the intruder to give out false DHCP information for the default gateway and domain name servers, which points clients to the hacker's machine. This misdirection enables the hacker to become a man-in-the-middle and to gain access to confidential information, such as user-name and password pairs, while the end user is unaware of the attack.

The following describes the DHCP spoof attack sequence, as shown in Figure 6-13:

1. Attacker hosts a rogue DHCP server off a switch port.

2. Client broadcasts a request for DHCP configuration information.

3. The rogue DHCP server responds before the legitimate DHCP server, assigning attacker-defined IP configuration information.

4. Host packets are redirected to the attacker's address as it emulates a default gateway for the erroneous DHCP address provided to the client.

DHCP snooping can prevent these two types of attacks. DHCP snooping is a per-port security mechanism used to differentiate an untrusted switch port connected to an end user from a trusted switch port connected to a DHCP server or another switch. It can be enabled on a per-VLAN basis. DHCP snooping enables only authorized DHCP servers to respond to DHCP requests and to distribute network information to clients.

DHCP Snooping

DHCP snooping is a Cisco Catalyst feature that determines which switch ports can respond to DHCP requests. Ports are identified as trusted and untrusted. Trusted ports can source all DHCP messages, whereas untrusted ports can source requests only. Trusted ports host a DHCP server or can be an uplink toward the DHCP server, as shown in Figure 6-14. If a rogue device on an untrusted port attempts to send a DHCP response packet into the network, the port is shut down. This feature can be coupled with DHCP Option 82, in which switch information, such as the port ID of the DHCP request, can be inserted into the DHCP request packet.

Untrusted ports are those not explicitly configured as trusted. A DHCP binding table is built for untrusted ports. Each entry contains the client MAC address, IP address, lease time, binding type, VLAN number, and port ID recorded as clients make DHCP requests. The table is then used to filter subsequent DHCP traffic. From a DHCP snooping perspective, untrusted access ports should not send any DHCP server responses, such as DHCPOFFER, DHCPACK, or DHCPNAK.

To enable DHCP snooping, use the commands listed in Table 6-3.

Example 6-8 illustrates sample DHCP snooping configuration for a simple topology of an access layer switch in Figure 6-15.

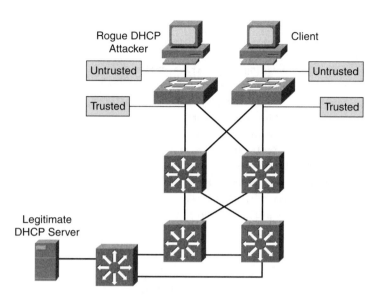

Figure 6-14 *DHCP Snooping Configuration*

Table 6-3 *Steps for Enabling DHCP Snooping*

Step	Comments
1. Enable DHCP snooping globally: `Switch(config)# ip dhcp snooping`	By default, the feature is not enabled.

2. Enable DHCP Option 82:
`Switch(config)# ip dhcp snooping`
`information option`
	This is optional for the forwarded DHCP request packet to contain information on the switch port where it originated.

3. Configure DHCP server interfaces or uplink ports as trusted:
`Switch(config-if)# ip dhcp snooping`
`trust`
	At least one trusted port must be configured. Use the no keyword to revert to untrusted.
	By default, all ports are untrusted.

4. Configure the number of DHCP packets per second (pps) that are acceptable on the port: `Switch(config-if)# ip dhcp snooping limit` `rate` *rate*	Configure the number of DHCP pps that an interface can receive. Normally, the rate limit applies to untrusted interfaces. This is used to prevent DHCP starvation attacks by limiting the rate of the DHCP requests on untrusted ports.
5. Enable DHCP snooping on specific VLANs: `Switch(config)# ip dhcp snooping vlan` *number* `[`*number*`]`	This is required to identify those VLANs that will be subject to DHCP snooping. Default is no VLANs are enabled for DHCP snooping.
6. Verify the configuration: `Switch# show ip dhcp snooping`	Verify the configuration.

Example 6-8   *DCHP Snooping Configuration*

```
switch(config)# ip dhcp snooping
switch(config)# ip dhcp snooping information option
switch(config)# ip dhcp snooping vlan 10,20
switch(config)# interface fastethernet 0/1
switch(config-if)# description Access Port
switch(config-if)# ip dhcp limit rate 5
switch(config)# interface fastethernet 0/24
switch(config-if)# description Uplink
switch(config-if)# switchport mode trunk
switch(config-if)# switchport trunk allowed vlan 10,20
switch(config-if)# ip dhcp snooping trust
```

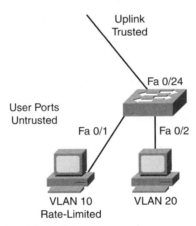

Figure 6-15   *DHCP Snooping Configuration*

The **show ip dhcp snooping** family of commands is used to display information about the DHCP snooping configuration, as shown in Example 6-9.

In Example 6-9, DHCP snooping is configured for VLANs 10 and 20 and operational on both of them. Only ports that are trusted or that have a rate limit applied will be shown in the output. Interface f0/1 has its rate limited and is not trusted, whereas interface f0/24 does not have any rate limitation and is trusted. All the other ports are untrusted and do not have a rate limit. They are not displayed.

Example 6-9   *Displaying DHCP Snooping Information*

```
switch# show ip dhcp snooping
Switch DHCP snooping is enabled
```

```
DHCP snooping is configured on following VLANs:
10,20
DHCP snooping is operational on following VLANs:
10,20
DHCP snooping is configured on the following L3 Interfaces:
Insertion of option 82 is enabled
   circuit-id default format: vlan-mod-port
   remote-id: 001a.e372.ab00 (MAC)
Option 82 on untrusted port is not allowed
Verification of hwaddr field is enabled
Verification of giaddr field is enabled
DHCP snooping trust/rate is configured on the following Interfaces:
Interface               Trusted    Allow option    Rate limit (pps)
----------------------  -------    ------------    ----------------
FastEthernet0/1         no         no              5
FastEthernet0/24        yes        yes             unlimited
```

ARP Spoofing Attack

In a normal ARP operation, a host sends a broadcast to determine the MAC address of a host with a particular IP address. The device at that IP address replies with its MAC address. The originating host caches the ARP response, using it to populate the destination Layer 2 header of packets sent to that IP address.

By spoofing an ARP reply from a legitimate device with a gratuitous ARP, an attacking device appears to be the destination host sought by the senders. The ARP reply from the attacker causes the sender to store the MAC address of the attacking system in its ARP cache. All packets destined for those IP addresses are forwarded through the attacker system.

An ARP spoofing attack follows the sequence shown in Table 6-4, as illustrated in Figure 6-16.

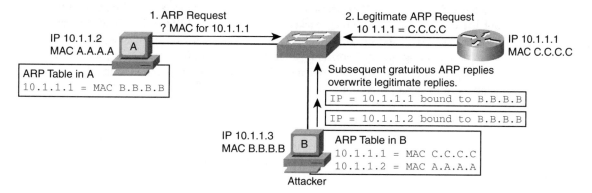

Figure 6-16 *ARP Poisoning*

Table 6-4 *ARP Spoofing Attack*

Sequence Number	Description
1.	Host A sends an ARP request for C's MAC address.
2.	Router C replies with its MAC and IP addresses. C also updates its ARP cache.
3.	Host A binds C's MAC address to its IP address in its ARP cache.
4.	Host B (attacker) sends ARP binding B's MAC address to C's IP address.
5.	Host A updates ARP cache with B's MAC address bound to C's IP address.
6.	Host B sends ARP binding B's MAC address to A's IP address.
7.	Router C updates ARP cache with B's MAC address bound to A's IP address.
8.	Packets are diverted through attacker (B).

Preventing ARP Spoofing Through Dynamic ARP Inspection

ARP does not have any authentication. It is quite simple for a malicious user to spoof addresses by using tools such as ettercap, dsniff, and arpspoof to poison the ARP tables of other hosts on the same VLAN. In a typical attack, a malicious user can send unsolicited ARP replies (gratuitous ARP packets) to other hosts on the subnet with the attacker's MAC address and the default gateway's IP address. Frames intended for default gateways sent from hosts with poisoned ARP tables are sent to the hacker's machine (enabling the packets to be sniffed) or an unreachable host as a DoS attack. ARP poisoning leads to various man-in-the-middle attacks, posing a security threat in the network.

Dynamic ARP inspection helps prevent the man-in-the-middle attacks by not relaying invalid or gratuitous ARP replies out to other ports in the same VLAN, as shown in Figure 6-17. Dynamic ARP inspection intercepts all ARP requests and all replies on the untrusted ports. Each intercepted packet is verified for valid IP-to-MAC bindings that are gathered via DHCP snooping. Denied ARP packets are either dropped or logged by the switch for auditing, so ARP poisoning attacks are stopped. Incoming ARP packets on the trusted ports are not inspected. Dynamic ARP inspection can also rate-limit ARP requests from client ports to minimize port scanning mechanisms.

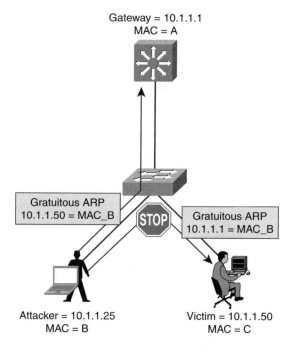

Figure 6-17 *Dynamic ARP Inspection*

To prevent ARP spoofing or "poisoning," a switch must ensure that only valid ARP requests and responses are relayed. DAI prevents these attacks by intercepting and validating all ARP requests and responses. Each intercepted ARP reply is verified for valid MAC-address-to-IP-address bindings before it is forwarded to a PC to update the ARP cache. ARP replies coming from invalid devices are dropped.

DAI determines the validity of an ARP packet based on a valid MAC-address-to-IP-address bindings database built by DHCP snooping. In addition, to handle hosts that use statically configured IP addresses, DAI can also validate ARP packets against user-configured ARP ACLs.

To ensure that only valid ARP requests and responses are relayed, DAI takes these actions:

■ Forwards ARP packets received on a trusted interface without any checks

■ Intercepts all ARP packets on untrusted ports

■ Verifies that each intercepted packet has a valid IP-to-MAC address binding before forwarding packets that can update the local ARP cache

■ Drops and logs ARP packets with invalid IP-to-MAC address bindings

Configure all access switch ports as untrusted and all switch ports connected to other switches as trusted. In this case, all ARP packets entering the network would be from an upstream distribution or core switch, bypassing the security check and requiring no further validation.

DAI can also be used to rate limit the ARP packets and then errdisable the interface if the rate is exceeded. Figure 6-18 shows the DAI recommended configuration.

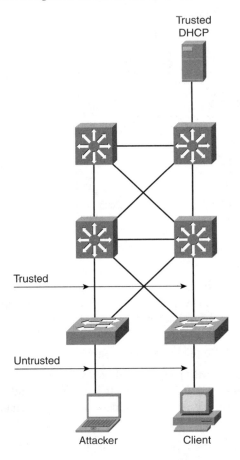

Figure 6-18 *DAI Recommended Configuration*

To illustrate DAI operation in a multilayer switched network, consider the network shown in Figure 6-19 with two switches, Switches A and B. Host 1 is connected to Switch A, and Host 2 is connected to Switch B. The DHCP server is connected to Switch A. DHCP snooping is enabled on both Switch A and Switch B as a prerequisite for DAI. The inter-switch links are configured as DAI trusted ports, and the user ports are left in the default untrusted state.

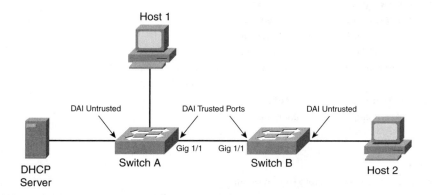

Figure 6-19   *DAI Enabled Catalyst Switches*

Example 6-10 shows the configuration and verification of the switches for DAI for the scenario in Figure 6-19. Assume that all the devices are in VLAN 10 in this scenario. (The switches connect to each other via uplink ports GigabitEthernet 1/1.)

Example 6-10   *Configuration and Verification of DAI on Catalyst Switch*

```
SwitchA# configure terminal
Enter configuration commands, one per line. End with CNTL/Z.
SwitchA(config)# ip arp inspection vlan 10
SwitchA(config)# interface gigabitEthernet 1/1
SwitchA(config-if)# ip arp inspection trust
SwitchA(config-if)# end
SwitchA#
SwitchB# configure terminal
Enter configuration commands, one per line. End with CNTL/Z.
 SwitchB(config)# ip arp inspection vlan 10
SwitchB(config)# interface gigabitEthernet 1/1
SwitchB(config-if)# ip arp inspection trust
SwitchB(config-if)# end
SwitchB#
SwitchA# show ip arp inspection interfaces
Interface         Trust State     Rate (pps)     Burst Interval
---------------   -----------     -----------    --------------
 Gi1/1             Trusted           None              N/A
 Gi1/2             Untrusted          15               1
 Fa2/1             Untrusted          15               1
 Fa2/2             Untrusted          15               1
```

```
  Fa2/3              Untrusted              15                  1
  Fa2/4              Untrusted              15                  1
<output skipped>
SwitchA# show ip arp inspection vlan 10
Source Mac Validation      : Disabled
Destination Mac Validation : Disabled
IP Address Validation      : Disabled
Vlan    Configuration    Operation    ACL Match         Static ACL
----    -------------    ---------    ---------         ----------
  10    Enabled          Active
Vlan    ACL Logging      DHCP Logging
----    -----------      ------------
  10    Deny             Deny
SwitchA#
SwitchA# show ip dhcp snooping binding
MacAddress          IpAddress        Lease(sec) Type          VLAN Interface
-----------------   ---------------  ---------- -------------  ---- --------------
00:01:00:01:00:01   10.10.10.1       4995       dhcp-snooping  10
FastEthernet2/1
SwitchB# show ip arp inspection interfaces
Interface         Trust State     Rate (pps)    Burst Interval
---------------   -----------     ----------    --------------
 Gi1/1            Trusted               None           N/A
 Gi1/2            Untrusted               15             1
 Fa2/1            Untrusted               15             1
 Fa2/2            Untrusted               15             1
 Fa2/3            Untrusted               15             1
 Fa2/4            Untrusted               15             1
<output skipped>
SwitchB# show ip arp inspection vlan 10
Source Mac Validation      : Disabled
Destination Mac Validation : Disabled
IP Address Validation      : Disabled
Vlan    Configuration    Operation    ACL Match         Static ACL
----    -------------    ---------    ---------         ----------
  10    Enabled          Active
Vlan    ACL Logging      DHCP Logging
----    -----------      ------------
  10    Deny             Deny
SwitchB#
SwitchB# show ip dhcp snooping binding
MacAddress          IpAddress      Lease(sec) Type          VLAN   Interface
-----------------   -------------  ---------- -------------  ----   --------------
00:02:00:02:00:02   10.10.10.2     4995       dhcp-snooping  10     FastEthernet2/2
```

Now if an attacker connects to Switch B, as shown in Figure 6-20, and tries to send a bogus ARP request, Switch B will detect it and drop the ARP request packet. The switch can also err-disable or shut down the port and send a log message to alert the administrator. DAI discards any ARP packets with invalid MAC address-to-IP address bindings.

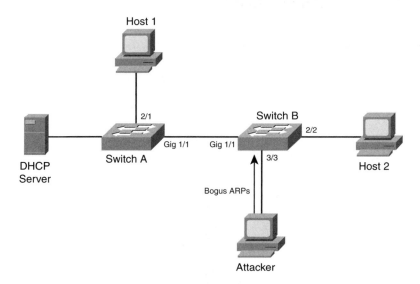

Figure 6-20   *DAI Prevents Attacker's Bogus ARP Request*

The error message displayed on the switch when such a security violation occurs is

```
02:46:49: %SW_DAI-4-DHCP_SNOOPING_DENY: 1 Invalid ARPs (Req) on Fa3/3, vlan
10.([0001.0001.0001/10.10.10.1/0000.0000.0000/0.0.0.0/09:23:24 UTC Thu Nov 27
2003])
```

Table 6-5 describes the commands used to configure DAI on Cisco Catalyst switch.

Table 6-5   *DAI Commands*

Command	Description
Switch(config)# **ip arp inspection vlan** *vlan_id [,vlan_id]*	Enables DAI on a VLAN or range of VLANs
Switch(config-if)# **ip arp inspection trust**	Enables DAI on an interface and sets the interface as a trusted interface
Switch(config)# **ip arp inspection validate** {[src-mac] [dst-mac] [ip]}	Configures DAI to drop ARP packets when the IP addresses are invalid, or when the MAC addresses in the body of the ARP packets do not match the addresses specified in the Ethernet header

It is generally advisable to configure all access switch ports as untrusted and to configure all uplink ports connected to other switches as trusted.

IP Spoofing and IP Source Guard

IP spoofing can occur when the attack is impersonating as a legitimate host on the network, as shown in Figure 6-21. IP spoofing can result in unauthorized access or DoS attacks initiated by the attacker.

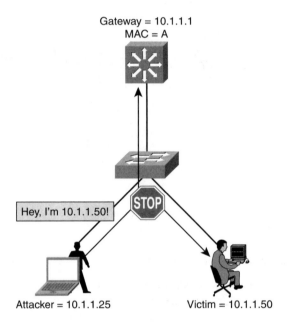

Figure 6-21 *IP Spoofing Attack*

IP Source Guard prevents a malicious host from attacking the network by hijacking its neighbor's IP address. IP Source Guard provides per-port IP traffic filtering of the assigned source IP addresses at wire speed. It dynamically maintains per-port VLAN ACLs based on IP-to-MAC-to-switch port bindings. The binding table is populated either by the DHCP snooping feature or through static configuration of entries. IP Source Guard is typically deployed for untrusted switch ports in the access layer.

IP Source Guard works closely with DHCP snooping. This feature can be enabled on a DHCP snooping untrusted Layer 2 port to prevent IP address spoofing, as shown in Figure 6-22. To start, all IP traffic on the port is blocked except for DHCP packets captured by the DHCP snooping process.

When a client receives a valid IP address from the DHCP server, or when a static IP source binding is configured by the user, a per-port and VLAN Access Control List (PVACL) is installed on the port.

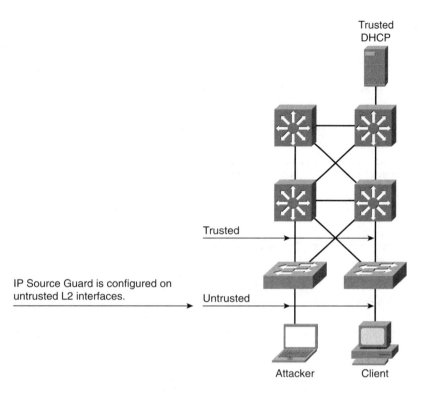

Figure 6-22 *IP Source Guard*

This process restricts the client IP traffic to those source IP addresses configured in the binding; any IP traffic with a source IP address other than that in the IP source binding is filtered out. This filtering limits a host's capability to attack the network by claiming a neighbor host's IP address.

IP Source Guard supports only the Layer 2 port, including both access and trunk. For each untrusted Layer 2 port, two levels of IP traffic security filtering exist:

■ **Source IP address filter:** IP traffic is filtered based on its source IP address. Only IP traffic with a source IP address that matches the IP source binding entry is permitted.

   An IP source address filter is changed when a new IP source entry binding is created or deleted on the port. The PVACL will be recalculated and reapplied in the hardware to reflect the IP source binding change. By default, if the IP filter is enabled without any IP source binding on the port, a default PVACL that denies all IP traffic is installed on the port. Similarly, when the IP filter is disabled, any IP source filter PVACL is removed from the interface.

■ **Source IP and MAC address filter:** IP traffic is filtered based on its source IP address in addition to its MAC address; only IP traffic with source IP and MAC addresses that match the IP source binding entry are permitted.

Configuring IPSG

IPSG requires that DHCP snooping be enabled on the required VLAN to enable automated IP source bindings.

Table 6-6 describes the procedure for enabling IP Source Guard.

Table 6-6   *IP Source Guard Configuration Commands*

	Command	Purpose
Step 1	Switch(config)# **ip dhcp snooping**	Enables DHCP snooping, globally. You can use the no keyword to disable DHCP snooping.
Step 2	Switch(config)# **ip dhcp snooping vlan** *number* [*number*]	Enables DHCP snooping on your VLANs.
Step 3	Switch(config-if)# **ip verify source vlan dhcp-snooping** Or Switch(config-if)# **ip verify source vlan dhcp-snooping port-security**	Enables IP Source Guard with source IP filtering. Enables IP Source Guard with source IP and source MAC address filtering.
Step 4	Switch(config-if)# **switchport port-security limit rate** *invalid-source-mac N*	(Optional) Sets the rate limit for bad packets. This rate limit also applies to the port where DHCP snooping security mode is enabled as filtering the IP and MAC address.
Step 5	Switch(config)# **ip source binding** *ip-addr* **ip vlan** *number* **interface** *interface-id*	Configures a static IP binding on the port.

For more information on how to configure IPSG on CatOS-based Catalyst 6500 switches, refer to the "Configuring DHCP Snooping and IP Source Guard" section in the software configuration guide on Cisco.com.

Figure 6-23 shows a scenario in which a workstation using DHCP for acquiring IP addresses and a server that uses a static IP address connect to a Catalyst switch. Example 6-11 shows configuration and verification of IPSG for the scenario in Figure 6-23.

Example 6-11   *Configuration and Verification of IPSG on Catalyst Switch*

```
Switch# configure terminal
Enter configuration commands, one per line. End with CNTL/Z.
Switch(config)# ip dhcp snooping
```

```
Switch(config)# ip dhcp snooping vlan 1,10
Switch(config)# ip dhcp snooping verify mac-address
Switch(config)# ip source binding 0000.000a.000b vlan 10 10.1.10.11 interface
  Fa2/18
Switch(config)# interface fastethernet 2/1
Switch(config-if)# switchport
Switch(config-if)# switchport mode access
Switch(config-if)# switchport port-security
Switch(config-if)# ip verify source vlan dhcp-snooping port-security
Switch(config)# interface fastethernet 2/18
Switch(config-if)# switchport
Switch(config-if)# switchport mode access
Switch(config-if)# switchport port-security
Switch(config-if)# ip verify source vlan dhcp-snooping port-security
Switch(config-if)# end
Switch# show ip source binding
MacAddress           IpAddress     Lease(sec)   Type            VLAN   Interface
-----------------    -----------   ----------   -------------   ----   ----------
00:02:B3:3F:3B:99    10.1.1.11     6522         dhcp-snooping   1      FastEthernet2/1
00:00:00:0A:00:0B    10.1.10.11    infinite     static          10     FastEthernet2/18
Switch# show ip verify source
Interface  Filter-type  Filter-mode  IP-address        Mac-address         Vlan
---------  -----------  -----------  ---------------   -----------------   ----------
Fa2/1      ip-mac       active       10.1.1.11         00:02:B3:3F:3B:99   1
Fa2/18     ip-mac       active       10.1.10.11        00:00:00:0a:00:0b   10
```

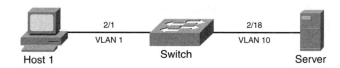

Figure 6-23 *IP Source Guard on Catalyst IOS-Based Switches*

Figure 6-24 shows that an attacker is connected to interface 2/10 and is trying to spoof the IP address of the server. The Catalyst switch detects and drops the packets in the hardware path. The Catalyst switch also provides an error message to indicate the violation.

IPSG is an essential security feature to prevent IP address spoof attacks at the Layer 2 level. Recommended practice is to enable IPSG on access layer switches in a multilayer switched network.

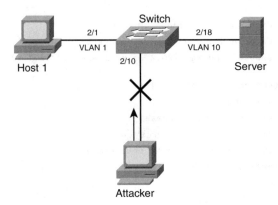

Figure 6-24 *IPSG Protecting Against an Attacker on Catalyst Switch*

Note The static IP source binding can be configured on a switch port only. If you issue the **IP source binding VLAN interface** command on a Layer 3 port, you will receive this error message:

Static IP source binding can be configured on the switch port only.

Securing Network Switches

Each switch in the network provides a variety of services that span beyond frame switching. These services range from management web interface, Cisco Discovery Protocol (CDP) neighbor discovery, to Telnet and preconfigured ports. Several of these services can be enabled by default to facilitate the switch initial integration into the network infrastructure. Some services might need to stay enabled, whereas others should be disabled when the integration is complete and if they are not needed. This section describes how to secure Layer 2 devices by protecting physical and virtual ports, disabling unneeded services, forcing the encryption of sessions, and enabling logging at the device level.

Neighbor Discovery Protocols

Neighbor Discovery Protocols (NDP) provide a summary of directly connected switches, routers, and other Cisco devices, as shown in Figure 6-25. CDP is the more commonly deployed NDP Layer 2 protocol enabled by default. The Link Layer Discovery Protocol (LLDP) is a vendor-neutral Layer 2 protocol equivalent to Cisco Discovery Protocol (CDP) that enables a network device to advertise its identity and capabilities on the local network. The protocol has been formally ratified as IEEE standard 802.1AB in 2005 and is also supported on Cisco devices. LLDP is disabled by default on Cisco devices.

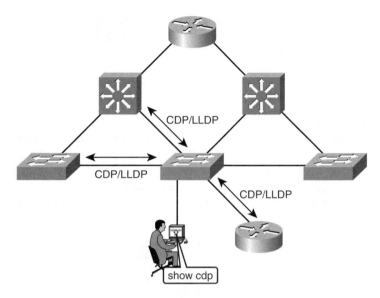

Figure 6-25 *Neighbor Discovery Protocol*

Cisco Discovery Protocol

Cisco Discovery Protocol (CDP) is a hello-based protocol, and all Cisco devices that run CDP periodically advertise their attributes to their neighbors by using a multicast address. CDP packets advertise a Time-To-Live (TTL) value in seconds, which indicates the length of time to retain the packet before discarding it. Cisco devices send CDP packets with a TTL value that is not 0 after an interface is enabled. A TTL value of 0 is sent immediately before an interface is idled. Sending a CDP packet with a TTL value of 0 enables a network device to quickly discover a lost neighbor.

By default, all Cisco devices receive CDP packets and cache the information in the packet. The cached information is then available to an NMS using SNMP.

If any information changes from the last received packet, the device caches the new information and discards the previous information even if its TTL value has not yet expired.

For security reasons, you should block SNMP access to CDP data (or any other data) from outside your network and from subnets other than your management station subnet.

Configuring CDP

CDP is enabled by default:

■ **no cdp run** disables CDP globally.

■ **no cdp enable** disables CDP on an interface.

When CDP is enabled the command **show cdp neighbor** displays a summary of which devices are seen on which ports, as shown in Example 6-12. You can get more detailed information about all neighbors with the command **show cdp neighbor detail**, as shown in Example 6-13.

Example 6-12 *Displaying CDP Information*

```
switch# show cdp neighbor
Capability Codes: R - Router, T - Trans Bridge, B - Source Route Bridge
                  S - Switch, H - Host, I - IGMP, r - Repeater, P - Phone,
                  D - Remote, C - CVTA, M - Two-port Mac Relay
Device ID        Local Intrfce     Holdtme Capability Platform Port ID
c2960-8          Fas 0/8           168              S I WS-C2960-Fas 0/8
```

Example 6-13 *Displaying Detailed CDP Information About Neighboring Cisco Devices*

```
4506# show cdp neighbor detail
- - - - - - - - - - - - - - - - - - - - -
Device ID: TBA03501074(SwitchA-6500)
Entry address(es):
 IP address: 10.18.2.137
Platform: WS-C6506, Capabilities: Trans-Bridge Switch IGMP
Interface: FastEthernet3/21, Port ID (outgoing port): 3/36
Holdtime : 170 sec


Version :
WS-C6506 Software, Version McpSW: 7.6(1) NmpSW: 7.6(1)
Copyright © 1995-2003 by Cisco Systems
advertisement version: 2
VTP Management Domain: '0'
Native VLAN: 1
Duplex: full


- - - - - - - - - - - - - - - - - - - - -
Device ID: SwitchC-4503
Entry address(es):
 IP address: 10.18.2.132
Platform: cisco WS-C4503, Capabilities: Router Switch IGMP
Interface: FastEthernet3/27, Port ID (outgoing port): FastEthernet3/14
Holdtime : 130 sec


Version :
Cisco Internetwork Operating System Software
IOS (tm) Catalyst 4000 L3 Switch Software (cat4000-I5S-M), Version 12.1(19)EW,
  CISCO ENHANCED PRODUCTION VERSION
```

```
Copyright © 1986-2003 by cisco Systems, Inc.
Compiled Tue 27-May-03 04:31 by prothero


advertisement version: 2
VTP Management Domain: 'cisco'
Native VLAN: 1
Duplex: full
```

Configuring LLDP

LLDP is disabled by default:

- **lldp run** enables LLDP globally.

- **lldp enable** enables LLDP on an interface.

Just like CDP, when LLDP is enabled the command **show lldp neighbor** displays a summary of which devices are seen on which ports, as shown in Example 6-14. You can get more detailed information about all neighbors with the command **show lldp neighbor detail**. If you need detailed information about only one neighbor on one link, you can also use (for example) **show lldp neighbor interface f0/8 detail**.

Example 6-14 *Configuring and Displaying LLDP Neighbors*

```
switch(config)# lldp run
switch(config)# end
switch# show lldp neighbor
Capability codes:
    (R) Router, (B) Bridge, (T) Telephone, (C) DOCSIS Cable Device
    (W) WLAN Access Point, (P) Repeater, (S) Station, (O) Other
Device ID           Local Intf    Hold-time   Capability      Port ID
c2960-8             Fa0/8         120         B               Fa0/8
Total entries displayed: 1
```

CDP Vulnerabilities

Attackers with knowledge of how CDP works could find ways to take advantage of the clear-text CDP packets to gain knowledge of the network, as shown in Figure 6-26. The CDP runs at Layer 2 and enables Cisco devices to identify themselves to other Cisco devices. However, the information sent through CDP is transmitted in clear text and is unauthenticated. Utilizing a packet analyzer, attackers could glean information about the network device from CDP advertisements.

CDP is necessary for management applications such as the Cisco Works-LAN Management Suite (LMS) and cannot be disabled without impairing some network-management applications. However, CDP can be selectively disabled on interfaces where management is not being performed.

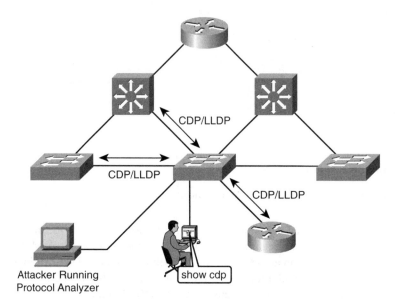

Figure 6-26   *CDP Vulnerabilities*

Table 6-7 describes how CDP can be used maliciously.

Table 6-7   *Using CDP Maliciously*

Sequence of Events	Description
1.	System administrator uses CDP to view neighbor information.
2.	Attacker uses a packet analyzer to intercept CDP traffic.
3.	Attacker analyzes information in CDP packets to gain knowledge of network address and device information.
4.	Attacker formulates attacks based on known vulnerabilities of network platforms.

Securing Switch Access

Network administrators typically use telnet to access switches. But nowadays, SSH is becoming standard in enterprises due to stricter requirements for security. Similarly, accessing devices via HTTP is being replaced with secure HTTPS.

Telnet Vulnerabilities

Telnet is not a secure protocol and has vulnerabilities as follows:

- All usernames, passwords, and data sent over the public network in clear text are vulnerable, as shown in Figure 6-27.

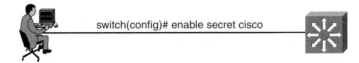

switch(config)# enable secret cisco

Figure 6-27 *Telnet Vulnerabilities*

- A user with an account on the system could gain elevated privileges.

- A remote attacker could crash the Telnet service, preventing legitimate use of that service by performing a DoS attack such as opening too many bogus Telnet sessions.

- A remote attacker could find an enabled guest account that might be present anywhere within the trusted domains of the server.

Telnet is being replaced by SSH, which is more secure, and ACL should be configured to restrict access only to authorized users accessing the device through VTY line ACL. Both of these topics are explained in the following sections.

Secure Shell

SSH is a client and server protocol used to log in to another computer over a network to execute commands in a remote machine and to move files from one machine to another. It provides strong authentication and secure communications over insecure channels. It is a replacement for rlogin, rsh, rcp, and rdist in addition to Telnet.

When using the SSH login (instead of Telnet), the entire login session, including transmission of password, is encrypted, as shown in Figure 6-28; therefore, it is almost impossible for an outsider to collect passwords.

64njgvboenflewkt5hnsf38sgporegkm

Figure 6-28 *SSH*

Although SSH is secure, vendors' implementations of SSH might contain vulnerabilities that could enable a remote attacker to execute arbitrary code with the privileges of the SSH process or to cause a DoS. Most of the SSH vulnerabilities have been addressed in the latest Cisco IOS Software.

Note   SHS version 1 implementations are vulnerable to various security compromises. Whenever possible, use SSH version 2 instead of SSH version 1.

To activate SSH on a vty interface, use the **transport input ssh** command.

SSH configuration on an IOS switch is done with the following steps:

Step 1.   Configure a user with a password.

Step 2.   Configure the hostname and domain name.

Step 3.   Generate RSA keys.

Step 4.   Allow SSH transport on the vty lines.

Example 6-15 shows a configuration commands required for configuring SSH.

Example 6-15   *SSH Configuration*

```
switch(config)# username xyz password abc123
switch(config)# ip domain-name xyz.com
switch(config)# crypto key generate rsa
switch(config)# ip ssh version 2
switch(config)# line vty 0 15
switch(config-line)# login local
switch(config-line)# transport input ssh
```

VTY ACLs

Cisco provides ACLs to permit or deny Telnet/SSH access to the vty ports of a switch. Cisco devices vary in the number of vty ports available by default. When configuring vty ACLs, ensure that all default ports are removed or have a specific vty ACL applied.

Telnet/SSH filtering is normally considered an extended IP ACL function because it is filtering a higher-level protocol. However, because the **access-class** command is used to filter incoming Telnet/SSH sessions by source address and to apply filtering to vty lines, standard IP ACL statements can be used to control vty access. The **access-class** command also applies standard IP ACL filtering to vty lines for outgoing Telnet/SSH sessions that originate from the switch.

You can apply vty ACLs to any combination of vty lines. The same ACL can be applied globally to all vty lines or separately to each vty line. The most common practice is to apply the same ACL to all vty lines.

To configure vty ACLs on a Cisco switch, create a standard IP ACL and apply the ACL on the vty interfaces. Rather than applying the ACL to a data interface, apply it to a vty line or range of lines with the **access-class** command, as shown in Figure 6-29.

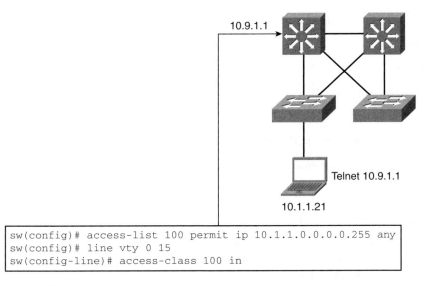

```
sw(config)# access-list 100 permit ip 10.1.1.0.0.0.0.255 any
sw(config)# line vty 0 15
sw(config-line)# access-class 100 in
```

Figure 6-29 *VTY ACL Configuration*

HTTP Secure Server

A web interface is available to configure most switches. The main weakness of the web interface is that it is not encrypted, and part of it does not offer any filtering. By default, it can be viewed by any user entering the switch IP address in a web browser address bar.

To protect the web service, you can take several steps:

- Use HTTPS instead of unprotected HTTP by using the command **ip http secure-server** instead of the **ip http server** command.

- To use HTTPS, the web server residing on the switch needs to send a certificate. This certificate can be downloaded to the switch if the network uses a Public Key Infrastructure (PKI), a key management infrastructure, or is generated on the switch locally with the command **crypto key generate rsa**. A domain name must be defined to generate a certificate.

- Access to the web service should be filtered so that only the administrator machine or subnet can gain access to the web interface. This is done by creating an access list. In this example, machines on subnet 10.1.9.0/24 have the right to access any IP address of the Layer 3 switch. The access list filter is then applied to the web service with the command **http access-class**.

- Users accessing the web service might use it to configure the switch. These users should be authenticated. The **http authentication local** command decides that the switch contains a local list of user credentials. The **username** *xyz* **password** *abc123* creates a local user.

Following are the configurations steps for enabling HTTP access:

Step 1.   Configure username and password.

Step 2.   Configure domain name.

Step 3.   Generate RSA keys.

Step 4.   Enable HTTPS (SSL) server.

Step 5.   Configure HTTP authentication.

Step 6.   Configure an access list to limit access.

Example 6-16 shows configuration of HTTPS on a switch.

Example 6-16   *HTTPS Configuration*

```
sw(config)# access-list 100 permit ip 10.1.9.0 0.0.0.255 any
sw(config)# username xyz password abc123
sw(config)# ip domain-name xyz.com
sw(config)# crypto key generate rsa
sw(config)# no ip http server
sw(config)# ip http secure-server
sw(config)# http access-class 100 in
sw(config)# http authentication local
```

Authentication Authorization Accounting (AAA)

The AAA network-security services provide the primary framework through which you set up access control on a Cisco IOS switch, as shown in Figure 6-30. AAA is an architectural framework for configuring a set of three independent security functions in a consistent manner.

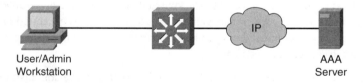

User/Admin
Workstation

IP

AAA
Server

Figure 6-30   *Authentication Authorization Accounting*

AAA provides a modular way of performing the following services:

■   Authentication

■   Authorization

■   Accounting

Note Be extremely careful when configuring AAA because you might accidentally lock yourself out of the router or switch, in which case you might need to initiate password recovery to return to the original state.

Authentication

Authentication provides a method for handling the following:

- User identification

- Login and password dialog

- Challenge and response

- Messaging

- Encryption

Authentication identifies users prior to accessing the network and network services. AAA configures authentication by defining a named list of authentication methods and then applying that list to various interfaces. The method list defines the types of authentication performed and their sequence. These methods are applicable on a per-interface basis. However, all interfaces on Cisco routers and switches adhere to a default method list named Default when no other authentication methods are defined. A defined method list always overrides the default method list.

All authentication methods, except for local, line password, and enable authentication, require the use of AAA.

Authorization

Authorization provides the method for remote access control. This remote access control includes one-time authorization or authorization for each service on a per-user account list or a user group basis.

The AAA authorization process on switches or routers works by contacting a common, centralized database of a set of attributes that describe the network user's authorized services, such as access to different parts of the network. The centralized server returns a result of allowed services to the switch or router in question to execute the user's actual capabilities and restrictions. This database is generally a centrally located server, such as a RADIUS or TACACS+ security server. However, using a local database is possible. The remote security servers, such as RADIUS and TACACS+, authorize users for specific rights by associating their attribute-value pairs (AVP). TACACS+ and RADIUS use these AVPs for configurations that are applied to users or a group of users. Each AVP consists of a type identifier associated with one or more assignable values. AVPs specified in user and group profiles define the authentication and authorization characteristics for their respective users and groups.

For example, with TACACS+ authorization, an AVP of Outacl=10 applies the out ACL 10 to a user; the AVP of Idletime=30 sets an idle timeout value for a user to 30 minutes.

AVPs are usually in the form a=b or a*b, in which a is the attribute and b is the value. The = separator indicates that the AVP is mandatory. The * separator indicates that the AV pair is optional. Table 6-8 and Table 6-9 illustrate examples of RADIUS AVPs and TACACS+ AVPs, respectively.

Table 6-8   *Examples of RADIUS AVPs*

Attribute	Type of Value
User-Name	String
Password	String
CHAP-Password	String
Client-Id	IP address
Login-Host	IP address
Login-Service	Integer
Login-TCP-Port	Integer

All authorization methods require the use of AAA. As with authentication, AAA authorization is applicable on a per-interface basis.

Table 6-9   *Examples of TACACS+ AVPs*

Attribute	Type of Value
Inacl	Integer
Addr-pool	String
Addr	IP address
Idletime	Integer
Protocol	Keyword
Timeout	Integer
Outacl	Integer

Accounting

Accounting provides the method for collecting and sending security server information used for billing, auditing, and reporting. This type of information includes user identities, network access start and stop times, executed commands (such as PPP), number of packets, and number of bytes. This information is useful for auditing and improving security as each switch or router monitors each user.

In many circumstances, AAA uses protocols such as RADIUS, TACACS+, or 802.1X to administer its security functions. If your switch is acting as a network access server, AAA is the means through which a switch establishes communication between your network access server and your RADIUS, TACACS+, or 802.1X security server.

AAA is dynamic in that it enables configuration of authentication and authorization on a per-line (per-user) or per-service (for example, IP, IPX, or virtual private dial-up network [VPDN]) basis. Creating method lists and then applying those method lists to specific services or interfaces achieves the per-line or per-user application.

Configuring AAA Authentication

The AAA security services facilitate a variety of login authentication methods. Before configuring any AAA security, use the **aaa new-model** command to initialize a AAA access control model on Cisco IOS switches or routers. Furthermore, use the **aaa authentication login** command to enable AAA login authentication in Cisco IOS. With the **aaa authentication login** command, configure one or more lists of authentication methods that each switch or router tries per user during login. These lists are configurable using the following Cisco IOS configuration commands:

```
login authentication line {default | list-name} method1 [method2...]
```

list-name defines the list name, whereas *method1* [*method2*...] defines the authentication methods in order, such as TACACS+ or RADIUS. list-name is case-sensitive, as with any other Cisco named lists.

To apply the authentication list to an input line, use the following line command:

```
login authentication {default | list-name}
```

Example 6-17 illustrates configuring of the VTY terminals in Cisco IOS for TACACS+ authentication as the first method. The second method, local login, occurs when the TACACS+ server is unreachable.

Example 6-17 *Example of Configuring AAA Authentication in Cisco IOS*

```
Switch(config)# aaa new-model
Switch(config)# aaa authentication login TEST tacacs+
Switch(config)# tacacs-server host 192.168.100.100
Switch(config)# line vty 0 4
Switch(config-line)# login authentication TEST
```

First-time users of AAA might find the configuration daunting. With some practice, though, configuring AAA becomes fairly simple. When configuring AAA, always use a console connection to avoid locking yourself out of the router or switch through misconfiguration. To illustrate the simplicity of configuring AAA, the following example presents a step approach to configuring AAA for authentication using TACACS+ on a Catalyst 3750 running Cisco IOS:

Step 1.   Configure the TACACS+ server for a test user:

When using Cisco ACS for Microsoft Windows, create a new test user without a specific options.

Step 2.   Configure a new network device on the TACACS+ server:

When using Cisco ACS for Microsoft Windows, create a new network device by specifying the DNS name and IP address, and specify a key to be used for TACACS+.

Step 3.   Access the switch using the Console (out-of-band) connection.

Step 4.   Enable AAA globally:

```
svs-san-3550-1(config)# aaa new-model
```

Step 5.   Configure the TACACS+ server and key:

```
svs-san-3550-1(config)# tacacs-server host 172.18.114.33
svs-san-3550-1(config)# tacacs-server key bcmsn
```

Step 6.   Configure the default login access:

```
svs-san-3550-1(config)# aaa authentication login default group tacacs+
enable
```

Step 7.   Test the login using a separate connection:

This enables you to troubleshoot and make changes in real time while testing the configuration.

For more information on Authentication, Authorization and Accounting, refer to the following URL on Cisco.com:

www.cisco.com/en/US/docs/ios/12_2/security/configuration/guide/scfaaa.html

For more information about RADIUS, TACACS+, refer to the following URL:

www.cisco.com/en/US/tech/tk59/technologies_tech_note09186a0080094e99.shtml

For more information about 802.1x, refer to the following URL:

www.cisco.com/en/US/products/ps6662/products_ios_protocol_option_home.html

Configuring AAA Authorization

Switches and routers use AAA authorization to limit the services that are available to specific users. AAA authorization uses information retrieved from the user's profile, which is located either in the local user database on the switch or on the security server, to configure the user's session. Afterward, the switch or router grants access to services requested by the user only if the information in the user profile allows for it. These services include the ability to execute commands, use network access such as PPP, or enter configuration options.

In addition, you should create method lists, which are similar to the AAA authentication configuration, to define authorizations. Method lists are specific to the authorization type requested. The following options are available for AAA authorization:

- **Auth-proxy:** Applies security policies on a per-user basis. With the use of auth-proxy, each user brings up a web browser to authenticate to a TACACS+ or RADIUS server before accessing the network. Upon successful authentication, the authentication server passes additional ACL entries and profile information to the router or switch to enable the users into the network.

- **Commands:** Applies authorization to all EXEC commands, including configuration commands associated with a specific privilege level. An example is limiting network operation users to only show commands when accessing switches and routers in the enterprise network for normal operations.

- **EXEC:** Refers to the attributes associated with a user EXEC terminal session.

- **Network:** Applies to the types of network connections. An example of using network authorization is authorization granting remote users access to network protocols such as PPP, SLIP, or ARAP during login for remote access.

- **Reverse access:** Refers to reverse Telnet sessions commonly used on console servers for access to different lines.

Similar to the configuration of AAA authentication, AAA authorization uses named method lists in its configuration. AAA supports the following five different methods of authorization:

- **TACACS+:** A client/server method that stores specific rights for users by associating AVPs for each user. The AAA authorization daemon on the Cisco switch or router communicates with the TACACS+ server to determine correct authorization for different options, such as EXEC and network access.

- **RADIUS:** Similar to TACACS+ in that RADIUS is also a server/client model for a Cisco router or switch to request authorization about a specific user. RADIUS servers store specific rights about users by associating specific attributes.

- **If-authenticated:** Enables a user to access any requested function as long as the AAA daemon previously and successfully authenticated the user.

- **None:** Effectively disables authorization for the respective interface.

- **Local:** Uses a database of usernames and passwords configured on the respective switch or router. Local databases on Cisco IOS routers and switches configure using the **username** command and enable only a subset of feature-controlled functions.

To configure AAA authorization using named method lists, use the following commands in the global and interface configuration modes, respectively:

```
aaa authorization {auth-proxy | network | exec | commands level | reverse-
access | configuration | ipmobile} {default | list-name} [method1
```

```
[method2...]] authorization {arap | commands level | exec | reverse-access}
{de fault | list-name}
```

To have the multilayer switch request authorization information via a TACACS+ security server, use the **aaa authorization** command with the **group tacacs+** method keyword. The **group tacacs+** method instructs the switch to use a list of all TACACS+ servers for authentication; refer to the Cisco IOS command reference for AAA on the Cisco.com website for additional methods. To allow users to access the functions they request as long as they have been authenticated, use the **aaa authorization** command with the **if-authenticated** method keyword. If you select this method, all requested functions are automatically granted to authenticated users.

To select local authorization, which means that the router or access server consults its local user database to determine which functions a user is permitted to use, use the **aaa authorization** command with the **local** method keyword. The functions associated with local authorization are defined by using the **username** global configuration command. To have the network access server request authorization via a list of RADIUS security servers, use the **aaa authorization** command with the **group radius** method keyword. Example 6-18 illustrates configuring AAA authorization for users via VTY access for shell commands.

Example 6-18   *Configuring AAA Authorization in Cisco IOS*

```
Switch(config)# aaa new-model
Switch(config)# aaa authorization commands 0 default if-authenticated group tacacs+
Switch(config)# line vty 0 4
Switch(config-line)# authorization commands 0 default
```

Configuring AAA Accounting

AAA supports the following six different accounting types:

- **Network accounting:** Provides information for all PPP, SLIP, or ARAP sessions, including packet and byte counts.

- **Connection accounting:** Provides information about all outbound connections made from the network, such as Telnet and rlogin.

- **EXEC accounting:** Provides information about user EXEC terminal sessions (user shells) on the network access server, including username, date, start and stop times, the access server IP address, and (for dial-in users) the telephone number from which the call originated.

- **System accounting:** Provides information about all system-level events (for example, when the system reboots and when accounting is turned on or off).

- **Command accounting:** Provides information about the EXEC shell commands for a specified privilege level executed on a network access server.

■ **Resource accounting:** Provides start and stop record support for calls that have passed user authentication.

To configure AAA accounting in Cisco IOS, first configure the global accounting method list and enable accounting using the following command:

```
aaa accounting {system | network | exec | connection | commands level}
{default | list-name} {start-stop | stop-only | none} [method1    [method2...]]
```

Second, apply the accounting method to an interface or line using the following command:

```
accounting {arap | commands level | connection | exec} {default | list-name}
```

Example 6-19 illustrates configuring accounting on the vty lines.

Example 6-19 *Configuring EXEC Accounting on vty Lines*

```
Switch(config)# aaa new-model
Switch(config)# aaa accounting exec default start-stop group tacacs+
Switch(config)# line vty 0 4
Switch(config-line)# accounting exec default
```

Security Using IEEE 802.1X Port-Based Authentication

The IEEE 802.1X standard defines a port-based access control and authentication protocol that restricts unauthorized workstations from connecting to a LAN through publicly accessible switch ports, as shown in Figure 6-31. The authentication server authenticates each workstation that is connected to a switch port before making available any services offered by the switch or the LAN.

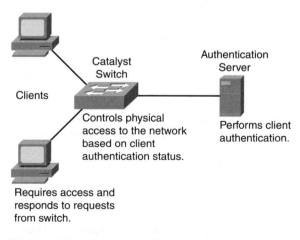

Figure 6-31 *802.1X-Based Port Authentication*

Until the workstation is authenticated, 802.1X access control enable only Extensible Authentication Protocol over LAN (EAPOL) traffic through the port to which the workstation is connected. After authentication succeeds, normal traffic can pass through the port.

With 802.1X port-based authentication, the devices in the network have specific roles, as follows:

- **Client:** The device (workstation) that requests access to LAN and switch services and then responds to requests from the switch. The workstation must be running 802.1X-compliant client software, such as what is offered in the Microsoft Windows XP operating system. (The port that the client is attached to is the supplicant [client] in the IEEE 802.1X specification.)

- **Authentication server:** Performs the actual authentication of the client. The authentication server validates the identity of the client and notifies the switch whether the client is authorized to access the LAN and switch services. Because the switch acts as the proxy, the authentication service is transparent to the client. The RADIUS security system with Extensible Authentication Protocol (EAP) extensions is the only supported authentication server.

- **Switch (also called the authenticator):** Controls physical access to the network based on the authentication status of the client. The switch acts as an intermediary (proxy) between the client (supplicant) and the authentication server, requesting identifying information from the client, verifying that information with the authentication server, and relaying a response to the client. The switch uses a RADIUS software agent, which is responsible for encapsulating and decapsulating the EAP frames and interacting with the authentication server.

The switch port state determines whether the client is granted access to the network. When configured for 802.1X port-based authentication, the port starts in the unauthorized state. While in this state, the port disallows all ingress and egress traffic except for 802.1X protocol packets. When a client is successfully authenticated, the port transitions to the authorized state, allowing all traffic for the client to flow normally.

If the switch requests the client identity (authenticator initiation) and the client does not support 802.1X, the port remains in the unauthorized state, and the client is not granted access to the network.

In contrast, when an 802.1X-enabled client connects to a port and the client initiates the authentication process (supplicant initiation) by sending the EAPOL-start frame to a switch that is not running the 802.1X protocol, no response is received, and the client begins sending frames as if the port is in the authorized state.

You control the port authorization state by using the **dot1x port-control** interface configuration command:

```
dot1x port-control {auto | force-authorized | force-unauthorized}
```

The following is an explanation of the keywords:

- **force-authorized:** Disables 802.1X port-based authentication and causes the port to transition to the authorized state without any authentication exchange required. The port transmits and receives normal traffic without 802.1X-based authentication of the client. This is the default setting. This configuration mode supports any non-dot1x-enabled client.

- **force-unauthorized:** Causes the port to remain in the unauthorized state, ignoring all attempts by the client to authenticate. The switch cannot provide authentication services to the client through the interface. This configuration mode can be enabled to prevent connections from any users from unauthorized ports.

- **auto:** Enables 802.1X port-based authentication and causes the port to begin in the unauthorized state, enabling only EAPOL frames to be sent and received through the port. The authentication process begins when the link state of the port transitions from down to up (authenticator initiation) or when an EAPOL-start frame is received (supplicant initiation). The switch requests the identity of the client and begins relaying authentication messages between the client and the authentication server. The switch uniquely identifies each client attempting to access the network by using the client MAC address. This configuration mode can be used on ports that connect to a 802.1X client.

If the client is successfully authenticated (receives an "accept" frame from the authentication server), the port state changes to authorized, and all frames from the authenticated client are enabled through the port.

If the authentication fails, the port remains in the unauthorized state, but authentication can be retried. If the authentication server cannot be reached, the switch can retransmit the request. If no response is received from the server after the specified number of attempts, authentication fails, and network access is not granted.

When a client logs out, it sends an EAPOL-logout message, causing the switch port to transition to the unauthorized state.

Configuring 802.1X

To implement 802.1X port-based authentication, follow these steps:

Step 1.   Enable AAA:

```
Switch(config)# aaa new-model
```

Step 2.   Create an 802.1X port-based authentication method list:

```
Switch(config)# aaa authentication dot1x {default} method1 [method2...]
```

Step 3.   Globally enable 802.1X port-based authentication:

```
Switch(config)# dot1x system-auth-control
```

Step 4.   Enter interface configuration mode and specify the interface to be enabled for 802.1X port-based authentication:

```
Switch(config)# interface type slot/port
```

Step 5.   Enable 802.1X port-based authentication on the interface:

```
Switch(config-if)# dot1x port-control auto
```

Step 6.   Return to privileged EXEC mode:

```
Switch(config)# end
```

Figure 6-32 shows a scenario where a PC is attached to FA0/1 on the switch and the device is getting authenticated via 802.1X with a Radius server. Example 6-20 shows the configuration for the scenario in Figure 6-32.

Figure 6-32   *802.1X Configuration*

Example 6-20   *802.1X Configuration*

```
sw(config)# aaa new-model
sw(config)# radius-server host 10.1.1.50 auth-port 1812 key xyz123
sw(config)# aaa authentication dot1x default group radius
sw(config)# dot1x system-auth-control
sw(config)# interface fa0/1
sw(config-if)# description Access Port
sw(config-if)# switchport mode access
sw(config-if)# dot1x port-control auto
```

Switch Security Considerations

Network security vulnerabilities include loss of privacy, data theft, impersonation, and loss of integrity. Basic security measures should be taken on every network to mitigate adverse effects of user negligence or acts of malicious intent.

Best practices following these general steps are required whenever placing new equipment in service.

Step 1.   Consider or establish organizational security policies.

Step 2.   Secure switch device and protocols

Step 3.   Mitigate compromises launched through a switch.

Organizational Security Policies

You should consider the policies of an organization when determining what level of security and what type of security should be implemented. You must balance the goal of reasonable network security against the administrative overhead that is clearly associated with extremely restrictive security measures.

A well-established security policy has these characteristics:

- Provides a process for auditing existing network security

- Provides a general security framework for implementing network security

- Defines disallowed behaviors toward electronic data

- Determines which tools and procedures are needed for the organization

- Communicates consensus among a group of key decision makers and defines responsibilities of users and administrators

- Defines a process for handling network security incidents

- Enables an enterprisewide, all-site security implementation and enforcement plan

Securing Switch Devices and Protocols

Implementation of a basic security configuration on every installed Cisco device is a requirement for preventing network vulnerabilities. Cisco recommends the following security measures on every Cisco device in your network to aid in network-security protection:

- Configure strong system passwords.

- Restrict management access using ACLs.

- Secure physical access to the console.

- Secure access to vty lines.

- Configure system warning banners.

- Disable unneeded or unused services.

- Trim and minimize the use of CDP/LLDP.

- Disable the integrated HTTP daemon (where appropriate).

- Configure basic system logging (syslog).

- Secure SNMP.

- Limit trunking connections and propagated VLANs.

- Secure the spanning-tree topology.

The techniques listed here are simple and easy to understand for those interested in implementing a minimum level of security on Cisco switches. This list is not a complete list, and you should review additional product security configurations per platform. Furthermore, these security principles are applicable to other Cisco products, including routers, SAN switches, and network appliances. The following sections discuss each item in the previous list in more detail.

Configuring Strong System Passwords

Use the **enable secret** command to set a password that grants enabled access to the Cisco IOS system, instead of using the **enable password** command. Because the **enable secret** command simply implements an MD5 hash on the configured password, that password remains vulnerable to dictionary attacks. Therefore, standard practices in selecting a feasible password apply. Try to pick passwords that contain letters, numbers, and special characters. An example of a feasible password is "$pecia1$"—that is, the word "specials," where each "s" has been replaced by "$" and the letter "l" has been replaced with the numeral "1."

Restricting Management Access Using ACLs

Creating ACLs to limit management and remote access traffic aids in prevention of unauthorized access and DoS attacks against management interfaces. Example 6-21 illustrates a sample ACL configuration that limits traffic to the management VLAN (in this case, VLAN 601) to only system administrators in the 10.1.3.0/24 subnet.

In Example 6-21, the subnet 10.1.2.0/24 is used for accessing all network devices for management purposes. This subnet does not pass user data traffic. Limiting access to this subnet for system administrators in another specific subnet, 10.1.3.0/24, prevents typical enterprise users from accessing the management subnet. As a result, ACLs that limit management traffic reduce vulnerability of the network devices and limit unauthorized access to the management subnet.

Example 6-21   *Sample ACL for Restricting Access to Management Subnet*

```
(text deleted)
!
interface Vlan600
 description User LAN
 ip address 10.1.1.1 255.255.255.0
!
interface Vlan601
 description Management VLAN
 ip address 10.1.2.1 255.255.255.0
 ip access-group 100 in
!
interface Vlan602
```

```
 description IT LAN
ip address 10.1.3.1 255.255.255.0
!
(text delete)
!
!
access-list 100 permit ip 10.1.3.0 0.0.0.255 10.1.2.0 0.0.0.255
access-list 100 deny   ip any any log
!
```

For more details on configuring ACLs, consult Cisco.com.

Securing Physical Access to the Console

Physical security of switches or routers is often overlooked but is a valuable security precaution. Console access requires a minimum level of security both physically and logically. An individual who gains console access to a system gains the ability to recover or reset the passwords or to reload the system, thereby enabling that individual to bypass all other security measures implemented on that system. Consequently, it is imperative to physically secure access to the console by using security personnel, closed circuit television, card-key entry systems, locking cabinets, access logging, or other means to control physical access as standard practice.

Securing Access to vty Lines

The minimum recommended security practices for securing access to vty lines are

- Apply ACLs on all vty lines to limit in-band access only to management stations from specific subnets.

- Configure strong passwords for all configured vty lines.

- Use Secure Shell Protocol (SSH) instead of Telnet to access the device remotely.

Configuring System Warning Banners

For both legal and administrative purposes, configuring a system warning banner to display prior to login is a convenient and effective way of reinforcing security and general usage policies. Clearly stating the ownership, usage, access, and protection policies prior to a login aids in stronger prosecution if unauthorized access occurs. Use the global configuration **banner** command to configure system banner messages. For more information about configuring banners, refer to the following URL:

www.cisco.com/en/US/docs/ios/fundamentals/configuration/guide/cf_connections_ps6350_
TSD_Products_Configuration_Guide_Chapter.html.

Disabling Unneeded or Unused Services

By default, in Cisco IOS versions 11.2 and earlier, Cisco routers implement multiple TCP and UDP servers to facilitate management and integration into existing environments. However, in Cisco IOS versions 11.3 and later, most TCP and UDP servers are disabled by default. In addition, most installations do not require these services, and disabling them reduces overall security exposure. Multilayer switched networks typically do not use the following services:

■   TCP Small Servers (Echo, Chargen, Discard, Daytime)

■   UDP Small Servers (Echo, Discard, Chargen)

■   Finger

■   Auto config

■   Packet Assembler and Disassembler (PAD)

■   BOOTP server

■   Identification service

■   NTP without authentication

■   Source routing

■   IP Proxy-ARP

■   ICMP unreachables

■   ICMP redirects

■   Directed broadcast forwarding

■   Maintenance Operation Protocol (MOP)

For a description and the associated commands to disable these services, consult Cisco.com.

For a secure network, you should carefully evaluate every device configuration before applying it. For example, only appropriate VLANs should be allowed on the trunk to other devices, instead of allowing all VLANs. Another example is disabling Dynamic Trunk Protocol (DTP) and Port Aggregation Protocol (PAgP) protocols on end user ports where those features are not needed. Some of these features are enabled by default on Catalyst switches, so you need to make careful considerations for the default configuration and for additional configuration by the user. Avoiding unneeded services and making the configuration deterministic makes the network less susceptible to attack. The premise of plug-n-play might bode well for ease of installation, but it tremendously increases vulnerability of your network. Cisco customers generally want plug-n-play for ease of use, and as the products evolve, more and more security features become plug-n-play. Nevertheless, using a default security configuration on any device, Cisco or not, is a security risk.

Keep in mind that this chapter focuses on the discussion of Cisco devices. Securing your network includes securing not only your Cisco devices but also your hosts, servers, and any other network device.

Trimming and Minimizing Use of CDP/LLDP

Security with CDP/LLDP remains fairly controversial. Although CDP/LLDP propagates detailed information about respective network devices, correct planning and configuration of CDP/LLDP enables it to be a fairly safe protocol. This is a great advantage because auxiliary VLANs and specific solutions in many multilayer switched networks require CDP/LLDP. For a practical and secure deployment of CDP/LLDP, adhere to the following CDP/LLDP configuration guidelines:

- Disable CDP/LLDP on a per-interface basis. Run CDP/LLDP only for administrative purposes, such as on interswitch connections and interfaces where IP Phones reside.

- Confine CDP/LLDP deployment to run between devices under your control. Because CDP/LLDP is a link-level (Layer 2) protocol, it does not propagate end-to-end over a MAN or WAN unless a Layer 2 tunneling mechanism is in place. As a result, for MAN and WAN connections, CDP tables might include the service provider's next-hop router or switch and not the far-end router under your control.

- Do not run CDP/LLDP to any unsecured connection, such as Internet connections.

Disabling the Integrated HTTP Daemon

Although Cisco IOS provides an integrated HTTP server for ease of management, the recommendation is to disable this feature, especially in multilayer switched networks that do not use this method for management. Otherwise, any unauthorized user might gain access via the web interface and make configuration changes. A user might also send numerous HTTP requests to the switch or router, which might cause high CPU utilization, resulting in a DoS-type attack on the system. In Cisco IOS, the integrated HTTP server is disabled by default. If HTTP access is necessary, use a different HTTP port, and use ACLs to isolate access from only trusted subnets or workstations. Use the following command in Cisco IOS to disable HTTP server access on a switch:

```
no ip http server
```

Example 6-22 illustrates disabling HTTP server access.

Example 6-22   *Disabling IP HTTP Server Access*

```
svs-san-msfc# configure terminal
Enter configuration commands, one per line. End with CNTL/Z.
svs-san-msfc(config)# no ip http server
svs-san-msfc(config)# end
```

If HTTP access is needed, it is recommended to change the default TCP port number (80) using the **ip http port** *port-no* command. Secure HTTP is recommended over http access. Secure HTTP can be enabled via the **ip http secure-server** command.

Configuring Basic System Logging

To assist and simplify both problem troubleshooting and security investigations, monitor switch subsystem information received from the logging facility. To render the on-system logging useful, increase the default buffer size; generally, the default buffer size is not adequate for logging most events.

For more information about system logging, refer to the "System Logging" section in Chapter 5, "Implementing High Availability and Redundancy in a Campus Network."

Securing SNMP

Whenever possible, avoid using SNMP read-write features. SNMPv2c authentication consists of simple text strings that are communicated between devices in clear, unencrypted text. In most cases, a read-only community string is sufficient. To use SNMP in a secure method, use SNMPv3 with an encrypted password and use ACL to limit SNMP from only trusted workstations and subnets. SNMP is covered in more detail in Chapter 5.

For additional information on how to secure SNMP, refer to the following document on Cisco.com: "Securing Simple Network Management Protocol," Document ID: 20370, www.cisco.com/en/US/tech/tk648/tk362/technologies_tech_note09186a0080094 489.shtml.

Limiting Trunking Connections and Propagated VLANs

By default, specific models of Catalyst switches that are running Cisco IOS automatically negotiate trunking capabilities. This poses a security risk because the negotiation enables the introduction of an unauthorized trunk port into the network. If an unauthorized trunk port is used for traffic interception and to generate DoS attacks, the consequences can be far more serious than if only an access port is used. (A DoS attack on a trunk port might affect multiple VLANs, whereas a DoS attack on an access port affects only a single VLAN.) To prevent unauthorized trunks, disable automatic negotiation of trunking on host and access ports. In addition, remove unused VLANs from trunks manually or by using VTP. Refer to Chapter 2 for more information on how to disable automatic negotiation of trunking and other VLAN configurations such as VTP.

Securing the Spanning-Tree Topology

It is important to protect the Spanning Tree Protocol (STP) process of the switches that compose the infrastructure. Inadvertent or malicious introduction of STP BPDUs potentially overwhelms a device or creates a DoS. The first step in stabilizing a spanning-tree installation is to positively identify the intended root and designated bridge in the design and to hard-set that bridge's STP bridge priority to an acceptable root value. Configuring specific bridge priorities aids in prevention of inadvertent shifts in the STP root due to an uncontrolled introduction of a new switch. Enable the STP root-guard feature to prevent authorized bridges with lower priorities from taking over the legitimate one.

In addition, use the STP BPDU Guard feature to prevent host devices from maliciously sending BPDUs to a port. This feature, when enabled, works with the STP PortFast feature to protect the network from unwanted BPDU traffic injection. Upon receipt of an unauthorized STP BPDU, the feature automatically disables the port until user intervention occurs or a time-out value is reached.

Mitigating Compromises Launched Through a Switch

Follow these best practices to mitigate compromises through a switch:

■ Proactively configure unused router and switch ports.

■ Execute the **shutdown** command on all unused ports and interfaces.

■ Place all unused ports in a "parking-lot" VLAN used specifically to group unused ports until they are proactively placed into service.

■ Configure all unused ports as access ports, disallowing automatic trunk negotiation.

  ■ **Physical device access:** Physical access to the switch should be closely monitored to avoid rogue device placement in wiring closets with direct access to switch ports.

  ■ **Access port–based security:** Specific measures should be taken on every access port of any switch placed into service. Ensure that a policy is in place outlining the configuration of unused switch ports in addition to those that are in use.

For ports enabled for end-device access, there is a macro called **switchport host**, which when executed on a specific switch port, takes these actions: sets the switch port mode to access, enables spanning tree PortFast, and disables channel grouping.

Note   The **switchport host** macro disables EtherChannel, disables trunking, and enables STP PortFast.

The command is a macro that executes several configuration commands. There is no command such as **no switchport host** to revoke the effect of the **switchport host** command. To return an interface to its default configuration, use the **default interface** *interface-id* global configuration command. This command returns all interface configurations to the default.

Troubleshooting Performance and Connectivity

Cisco provides software and hardware tools to help perform complex troubleshooting and performance analyses. The ability to monitor and analyze the traffic on your network is the first step to optimizing performance. Traffic monitoring enables you to identify bottlenecks, underused resources, and places where you might implement improvements such as port aggregation (increasing link bandwidth by combining several physical ports into a single virtual link). Optimizing the performance of your Cisco multilayer switched network helps to maximize use of existing resources and reduces unnecessary duplication of network components. This ensures that the network runs efficiently and supports multiple solutions. The troubleshooting and monitoring tools also play a critical part in preventing or thwarting any security attacks. This section explains some of the most commonly used features to monitor and understand performance and aid in troubleshooting Cisco multilayer switched networks.

Techniques to Enhance Performance

Performance management includes maintaining internetwork performance at acceptable levels by measuring and managing various network performance variables. This section covers some of the techniques used to enhance network performance.

Critical performance-management issues are as follows:

- **User/application performance:** For most users, response time is the critical performance success factor. This variable might shape the perception of network success by both your users and application administrators.

- **Capacity planning:** The process of determining future network resource requirements to prevent a performance or availability impact on business-critical applications.

- **Proactive fault management:** Involves both responding to faults as they occur and implementing solutions that prevent faults from affecting performance.

The critical success tasks that need to be performed for performance management are

- **Gather a baseline for both network and application data.**

  This step aids in troubleshooting performance issues during network operations. A typical router or switch baseline report would include capacity issues related to CPU, memory, buffer management, link utilization, and throughput. In addition, other types of baseline data need to be included depending on your defined objectives. For instance, an availability baseline would demonstrate increased stability and availability of the network environment. Perform a baseline comparison between old and new environments to verify solution requirements. Develop a good network topology diagram as part of this step.

- **Perform a what-if analysis on your network and applications.**

A what-if analysis involves modeling and verifying solutions. Before adding a new solution to the network, document some of the alternatives. The documentation for this analysis includes major questions, methodology, data sets, and configuration files. The essential what-if analysis should contain enough information for someone other than the author to re-create the solution.

■ **Perform exception reporting for capacity issues.**

If capacity requirements outstrip available resources, a mechanism should be in place to notify network administrators of that fact. This could include setting up periodical SNMP polling on some key parameters of the network devices, such as CPU and memory, and having the network management station alert the administrator if anomalous behavior occurs.

■ **Determine the network management overhead for all proposed or potential network management services.**

Network management services affect network and application performance. Make sure that the network measurement planning takes into account the additional resources required to perform measurement and management. For instance, SNMP polling of devices needs CPU cycles from the switch or router. If the device is already running at an above-average CPU utilization, the management services might further strain the device. In addition, the bandwidth required for these management functions should be considered if the links are heavily utilized to avoid oversubscription.

■ **Analyze the capacity information.**

Examine all the data you have gathered to determine capacity and management requirements. This is the most important task, forming the basis for the next step.

■ **Periodically review capacity information, baseline, and exceptions for the network and applications.**

Periodically repeat your analysis to identify changes in network use and growth patterns. The time interval chosen for measurement depends on the nature of the network measured and can vary over weekdays versus weekends and also on a monthly or yearly basis. Reviewing the capacity periodically is critical to avoid unexpected network or application downtime and to plan for future growth.

■ **Maintain upgrade or tuning procedures set up to handle capacity issues on both a reactive and longer-term basis.**

Set up procedures to handle future capacity requirements. For instance, if you think that your network might need another link addition to a port channel based on certain thresholds, make sure that you plan for this change. Having the cabling and configuration procedure in place in advance minimizes the time required to make the change and ensures that the network runs smoothly without major downtime.

The remainder of this section focuses on the various Cisco Catalyst switches and modules that assist in performance management and troubleshooting network exceptions to ensure optimal performance through monitoring and preventing any security attacks.

Monitoring Performance with SPAN and VSPAN

The Switched Port Analyzer (SPAN) feature is an important aid in performance management and troubleshooting. SPAN copies network traffic from a VLAN or group of ports to a selected port. This port is usually connected to a network analyzer, such as a SwitchProbe device, a workstation running a packet-capturing application, or a remote monitoring (RMON) probe. SPAN does not affect the switching of network traffic on source ports or VLANs.

Local SPAN involves configuring source ports, source VLANs, and destination ports on the same Catalyst switch. Local SPAN, which involves configuring one or more VLANs as the source of the SPAN session, is also called VSPAN. All ports in the source VLANs become source ports in a VSPAN. Local SPAN copies traffic from one or more source ports in any VLAN or from one or more VLANs to a destination port for analysis. For example, as shown in Figure 6-33, the switch copies all traffic transmitted to and from Port 3/1 (the source port) to Port 3/5 (the destination port). A workstation running a packet-capturing application on Port 3/5 thus receives all network traffic received and transmitted on port 3/1.

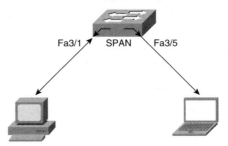

Fa3/1   SPAN   Fa3/5

Figure 6-33   *Switched Port Analyzer*

SPAN sessions support the monitoring of only ingress network traffic (ingress SPAN), only egress network traffic (egress SPAN), or traffic flowing in both directions. Ingress SPAN copies network traffic received by the source ports and VLANs for analysis to the destination port. Egress SPAN copies network traffic transmitted from the source ports and VLANs to the destination port. When the *both* keyword is used, SPAN copies the network traffic received and transmitted by the source ports and VLANs to the destination port.

By default, local SPAN monitors all network traffic, including multicast and bridge protocol data unit (BPDU) frames.

SPAN supports the configuration of both switched and routed ports as SPAN source ports. SPAN can monitor one or more source ports in a single SPAN session. Configuring source ports in any VLAN is allowed. Trunk ports are valid source ports mixed with non-trunk source ports. However, trunk encapsulation (dot1q or ISL) configuration of the destination port determines the encapsulation of the packets forwarded to the destination port. If the destination port is not configured for trunk encapsulation, the ISL or dot1q is removed from the frame before egress transmission.

Note   An intrusion prevention system (IPS) typically uses the ingress feature on the destination port to thwart attacks in the network by sending TCP resets to the attacker TCP session or sending alarms to network management stations. Catalyst switches can be configured to dynamically learn MAC addresses on the destination SPAN port using the **learning** keyword.

The following additional guidelines or restrictions apply to local SPAN:

- Both Layer 2 switched ports (LAN ports configured with the **switchport** command) and Layer 3 ports (LAN ports configured with the **no switchport** command) can be configured as source or destination ports in Cisco IOS–based switches.

- A port can act as the destination port for only one SPAN session.

- A port cannot be configured as a destination port if it is a source port of a span session.

- Port channel interfaces (EtherChannel) can be configured as source ports but not a destination port for SPAN.

- SPAN supports configuration of source ports belonging to different VLANs.

- Traffic direction is "both" by default for SPAN sources.

- Destination ports never participate in a spanning-tree instance. Local SPAN includes BPDUs in the monitored traffic, so any BPDUs seen on the destination port are from the source port. As a result, SPAN destination ports should not be connected to another switch because this might cause a network loop.

- Destination ports get a copy of all packets switched through the switch regardless of whether the packets actually leave the switch due to STP blocking state on an egress port.

The following additional guidelines or restrictions apply to VSPAN:

- VSPAN sessions, with both ingress and egress options configured, forward duplicate packets from the source port only if the packets get switched in the same VLAN. One copy of the packet is from the ingress traffic on the ingress port, and the other copy of the packet is from the egress traffic on the egress port.

- VSPAN monitors only traffic that leaves or enters Layer 2 ports in the VLAN:

  - Routed traffic that enters a monitored VLAN is not captured if the SPAN session is configured with that VLAN as an ingress source because traffic never appears as ingress traffic entering a Layer 2 port in the VLAN.

  - Traffic that is routed out of a monitored VLAN, which is configured as an egress source in a SPAN session, is not captured because the traffic never appears as egress traffic leaving a Layer 2 port in that VLAN.

On Cisco IOS-based switches, use the following commands in configuration mode to configure local SPAN.

```
monitor session session-id source {interface interface-id | vlan vlan-id [,][-]
  {rx | tx | both}
monitor session session-id destination interface interface-id [encapsulation
  {dot1q | isl}] [ingress vlan vlan-id]
```

Example 6-23 shows the configuration and verification of a local SPAN session on a Cisco IOS–based switch for the topology in Figure 6-33. The source interface is FastEthernet 3/1, and the destination interface is FastEthernet 3/5.

Example 6-23 *Local SPAN Configuration and Verification on Cisco IOS–Based Catalyst Switches*

```
4506(config)# monitor session 1 source interface FastEthernet 3/1
4506(config)# monitor session 1 destination interface FastEthernet 3/5
4506(config)# end
4506# show monitor session 1
Session 1
- - - - -
Type               : Local Session
Source Ports       :
   Both            : Fa3/1
Destination Ports  : Fa3/5
 Encapsulation     : Native
         Ingress   : Disable
```

Figure 6-34 shows a scenario in which the administrator needs to troubleshoot the traffic flow between a client in VLAN 10 and server in VLAN 20. Example 6-24 shows the configuration of a VSPAN session on a Cisco IOS–based Catalyst switch with rx-only traffic for VLAN 10 and tx-only traffic for VLAN 20 and destination port interface FastEthernet 3/4.

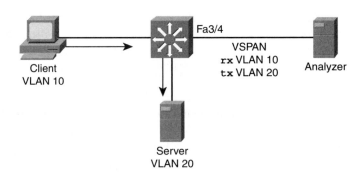

Figure 6-34 *VSPAN Scenario*

Example 6-24 *VSPAN Configuration and Verification on Cisco IOS–Based Catalyst Switches*

```
cat4k(config)# monitor session 1 source vlan 10 rx
cat4k(config)# monitor session 1 source vlan 20 tx
cat4k(config)# monitor session 1 destination interface FastEthernet 3 /4
cat4k# show monitor session 1
Session 1
-----
Type               : Local Session
Source VLANs       :
    RX Only        : 10
    TX Only        : 20
Destination Ports  : Fa3/4
    Encapsulation  : Native
          Ingress  : Disabled
```

Using SPAN to Monitor the CPU Interface of Switches

The ability to span the CPU comes in handy when you are trying to troubleshoot traffic destined to the CPU of the Supervisor Engine. Traffic destined to the Supervisor Engine includes the control traffic, such as BPDUs, SNMP traffic, and so on. Normal switch traffic is not forwarded to the CPU and is handled via hardware switching. Captured traffic also includes Telnet traffic and broadcast traffic seen in the same subnet as the Supervisor Engine. It could help to identify any DoS attack on the Switch CPU.

To configure a SPAN to monitor the CPU traffic on the Catalyst 4500 switches, use the keyword **cpu** in the **monitor session source** configuration, as shown in Example 6-25.

Example 6-25 *Configuration and Verification of SPAN to Monitor the CPU Port on Catalyst 4500 Switches*

```
4506(config)# monitor session 1 source cpu ?
  both    Monitor received and transmitted traffic
  queue   SPAN source CPU queue
  rx      Monitor received traffic only
  tx      Monitor transmitted traffic only
  <cr>
4506(config)# monitor session 1 destination interface fastEthernet 3/21
4506(config)# end
4506# show monitor session 1
Session 1
-----
```

```
Type                   : - Source Ports     :
    Both               : CPU Destination Ports : Fa3/21
    Encapsulation  : Native
          Ingress : Disabled
```

Tip   It is recommended to configure the capture filter in the network analyzer to narrow the capture only to traffic destined to a particular source or destination or a type of traffic. This greatly reduces the time required to analyze the captured data for interesting traffic and reduces the amount of buffer space required to capture the frames. In addition, using display filters in the analyzer helps to better analyze the captured frames.

Monitoring Performance with RSPAN

Remote SPAN (RSPAN) is similar to SPAN, but it supports source ports, source VLANs, and destination ports on different switches, which provide remote monitoring of multiple switches across a switched network. Each RSPAN session carries the SPAN traffic over a user-specified RSPAN VLAN. This VLAN is dedicated for that RSPAN session in all participating switches.

The RSPAN source ports can be trunks carrying the RSPAN VLAN. Local SPAN and RSPAN do not monitor the RSPAN traffic in the RSPAN VLAN seen on a source trunk. For example, if the source port carries VLAN 1 through 10, with 10 being the RSPAN VLAN, the local span of that port does not mirror the RSPAN traffic to the destination port. However, the local SPAN correctly monitors traffic for the other VLANs 1 through 9. To receive the RSPAN traffic on a destination port, the port must be configured as the RSPAN destination port for that RSPAN VLAN.

The destination ports in the RSPAN VLAN receive RSPAN traffic from the source ports or source VLANs. The source ports or VLANs in an RSPAN session may be different on different source switches, but they must be the same for all sources on each RSPAN source switch. Each RSPAN source switch must have either ports or VLANs as RSPAN sources.

Figure 6-35 shows an RSPAN configuration across multiple switches. Access Switches A and B act as the RSPAN source, distribution Switch C acts as the intermediate switch, and data center Switch D acts as the RSPAN destination switch where the probe is connected. Without RSPAN, the user must go to each of the closet switches and manually configure local SPAN to monitor the traffic. For example, the administrator charged with monitoring Ports A1 and A2 needs to configure a local SPAN session on Switch A and then configure a separate local SPAN session to monitor /ports B1, B2, and B3. This type of configuration is obviously not scalable for geographically separated switch closets; RSPAN enables the administrator to monitor these remote ports from the data center switch. In this case, the trunks between the switches carry RSPAN VLAN traffic for the RSPAN to work correctly.

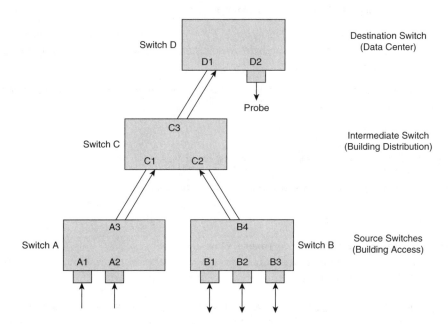

Figure 6-35 *Remote RSPAN Example*

RSPAN consists of an RSPAN source session, an RSPAN VLAN, and an RSPAN destination session. It is advisable to configure separate RSPAN source sessions and destination sessions on different network devices. To configure an RSPAN source session on one network device, associate a set of source ports and VLANs with an RSPAN VLAN. To configure an RSPAN destination session on another device, associate the destination port with the RSPAN VLAN.

In addition to the guidelines and restrictions that apply to SPAN, these guidelines apply to RSPAN:

- Configure the RSPAN VLANs in all source, intermediate, and destination network devices. If enabled, the VLAN Trunking Protocol (VTP) can propagate configurations of VLANs numbered 1 through 1024 as RSPAN VLANs. Manually configure VLANs numbered higher than 1024 as RSPAN VLANs on all source, intermediate, and destination network devices.

- Switches impose no limit on the number of RSPAN VLANs configured.

- Configure any VLAN as an RSPAN VLAN as long as all participating network devices support configuration of RSPAN VLANs, and use the same RSPAN VLAN for each RSPAN session.

RSPAN configuration involves the following two steps:

Step 1. Configure the RSPAN VLAN in the VTP server. This VLAN is then dedicated for RSPAN. If VTP transparent mode is used, configure RSPAN in all the devices in the domain consistently.

Step 2. Configure the RSPAN session in the source and destination switches and ensure that the intermediate switches carry the RSPAN VLAN across respective VLAN trunks.

On Cisco IOS–based Catalyst switches, use the following commands in configuration mode to configure RSPAN.

On the source switch:

```
monitor session session source {interface interface-id | vlan vlan-id} [,][-] {rx |
  tx | both}
monitor session session destination remote vlan vlan-id
```

On the destination switch:

```
monitor session session source remote vlan vlan-id
monitor session session destination interface interface-id [encapsulation {dot1q
  | isl}] [ingress vlan vlan-id]
```

Example 6-26 shows the configuration and verification of an RSPAN session between two Catalyst 2950 switches. Switch 2950-1 is the source switch for the RSPAN session, and 2950-2 is the destination switch with the network analyzer. Only the Catalyst 2950 and Catalyst 2955 series switches require an additional port to be designated as the reflector port. The reflector should be left unconnected and is used internally by the Catalyst 2950 for implementing RSPAN. In Example 6-26, the reflector port is interface FastEthernet 0/24. The reflector port is used on the Catalyst 2950 switches as a way to overcome the limitation of that switch architecture for SPAN. Figure 6-36 depicts the network scenario for this example.

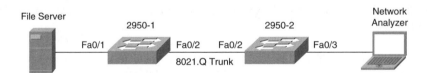

Figure 6-36 *RSPAN Using Cisco IOS–Based Catalyst 2950 Switches*

Example 6-26 *RSPAN Configuration and Verification on Cisco IOS–Based Catalyst Switches*

```
2950-1(config)# vlan 100
2950-1(config-vlan)# remote-span
```

```
2950-1(config-vlan)# exit
2950-1(config)# monitor session 1 source interface FastEthernet 0/1
2950-1(config)# monitor session 1 destination remote vlan 100 reflector-port
  FastEthernet 0/24
2950-1(config)# in FastEthernet 0/2
2950-1(config-if)# switchport mode trunk
2950-1(config-vlan)# end
2950-1#
2950-2(config)# monitor session 2 source remote vlan 100
2950-2(config)# monitor session 2 destination interface FastEthernet 0/3
2950-2(config)# in FastEthernet 0/2
2950-2(config-if)# switchport mode trunk
2950-2(config-vlan)# end
2950-2#
2950-1# show monitor
Session 1
-----
Type                    : Remote Source Session
Source Ports            :
     Both               : Fa0/1
Reflector Port          : fa0/24
Dest RSPAN VLAN         : 100
2950-1# show interfaces trunk
Port         Mode            Encapsulation   Status          Native vlan
Fa0/2        on              802.1q          trunking        1
Port         Vlans allowed on trunk
Fa0/2        1-4094
Port         Vlans allowed and active in management domain
Fa0/2        1-30,100
Port         Vlans in spanning tree forwarding state and not pruned
Fa0/2        1-30,100
2950-2# show interfaces trunk
Port         Mode            Encapsulation   Status          Native vlan
Fa0/2        on              802.1q          trunking        1
Port         Vlans allowed on trunk
Fa0/2        1-4094
Port         Vlans allowed and active in management domain
Fa0/2        1-30,100
Port         Vlans in spanning tree forwarding state and not pruned
Fa0/2        1-30,100
2950-2# show monitor session 2
Session 2
-----
Type                    : Remote Destination Session
```

```
Source RSPAN VLAN : 100
Destination Ports : Fa0/3
    Encapsulation: Native
          Ingress: Disabled
```

Monitoring Performance with ERSPAN

Enhanced Remote SPAN (ERSPAN) is similar to RSPAN, but it supports source ports, source VLANs, and destination ports on different switches, even across the Layer 3 boundary, which provides remote monitoring of multiple switches across a switched or routed network. Each ERSPAN session carries the SPAN traffic over a GRE tunnel. The source and destination switches must support GRE in hardware. Currently, the ERSPAN feature is supported only on the Catalyst 6500 family of switches.

To configure an ERSPAN source session on one switch, you associate a set of source ports or VLANs with a destination IP address, ERSPAN ID number, and, optionally, a VRF name. To configure an ERSPAN destination session on another switch, you associate the destination ports with the source IP address, ERSPAN ID number, and, optionally, a VRF name.

ERSPAN source sessions do not copy locally sourced RSPAN VLAN traffic from source trunk ports that carry RSPAN VLANs. ERSPAN source sessions do not copy locally sourced ERSPAN GRE-encapsulated traffic from source ports.

Each ERSPAN source session can have either ports or VLANs as sources, but not both.

The ERSPAN source session copies traffic from the source ports or source VLANs and forwards the traffic using routable GRE-encapsulated packets to the ERSPAN destination session. The ERSPAN destination session switches the traffic to the destination ports, as shown in Figure 6-37.

The following guidelines and restrictions apply to ERSPAN:

- The payload of a Layer 3 ERSPAN packet is a copied Layer 2 Ethernet frame, excluding any ISL or 802.1Q tags.

- ERSPAN adds a 50-byte header to each copied Layer 2 Ethernet frame and replaces the 4-byte cyclic redundancy check (CRC) trailer.

- ERSPAN supports jumbo frames that contain Layer 3 packets of up to 9202 bytes. If the length of the copied Layer 2 Ethernet frame is greater than 9170 bytes (9152-byte Layer 3 packet), ERSPAN truncates the copied Layer 2 Ethernet frame to create a 9202-byte ERSPAN Layer 3 packet.

ERSPAN configuration involves the following two steps:

Step 1.   Configure the source ERSPAN session.

Step 2.   Configure the destination ERSPAN session on a different switch.

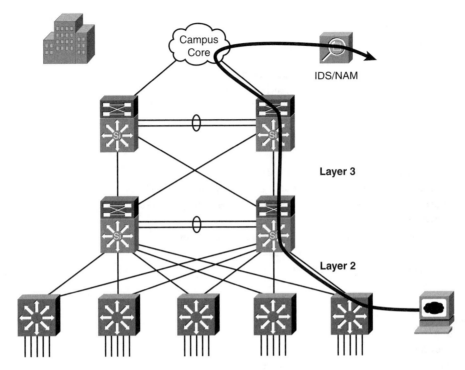

Figure 6-37 *ERSPAN Using Cisco Catalyst 6500 Switches*

Example 6-27 shows the configuration and verification of ERSPAN on the source and destination switches for the scenario shown in Figure 6-38, where the IDS/NAM is connected to a switch that is separated from the source switch through a Layer 3 network.

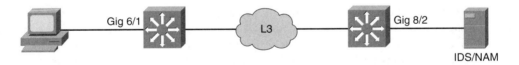

Figure 6-38 *ERSPAN Across Layer 3 Boundary*

Example 6-27 *ERSPAN Configuration and Verification on a Catalyst 6500 Switch*

```
Switch1(config)# monitor session 66 type erspan-source
Switch1(config-mon-erspan-src)# source interface gigabitethernet 6/1
Switch1(config-mon-erspan-src)# destination
Switch1(config-mon-erspan-src-dst)# ip address 10.10.10.10
Switch1(config-mon-erspan-src-dst)# origin ip address 20.20.20.200
Switch1(config-mon-erspan-src-dst)# erspan-id 111
```

```
Switch1# show monitor session 66
Session 66
- - - - -
Type                    : ERSPAN Source Session
Status                  : Admin Enabled
Source Ports            :
   Both                 : Gi6/1
Destination IP Address  : 10.10.10.10
Destination ERSPAN ID   : 111
Origin IP Address       : 20.20.20.200
Switch2(config)# monitor session 60 type erspan-destination
Switch2(config-erspan-dst)# destination interface gigabitethernet 8/2
Switch2(config-erspan-dst)# source
Switch2(config-erspan-dst-src)# ip address 10.10.10.10
Switch2(config-erspan-dst-src)# erspan-id 111
Switch2# show monitor session 60
Session 60
- - - - - - - - - -
Type                    : ERSPAN Destination Session
Status                  : Admin Enabled
Destination Ports       : Gi8/2
Source IP Address       : 10.10.10.10
Source ERSPAN ID        : 111
```

Monitoring Performance Using VACLs with the Capture Option

The Catalyst 6500 family of switches offers an additional feature to monitor traffic flows through the switch. SPAN, VSPAN, and RSPAN configuration applies to all traffic on the source port or source VLAN in one or both directions. Using VACLs with the capture option, the network analyzer receives only a copy of traffic matching the configured ACL. Because the ACL might match Layers 2, 3, or 4 information, the VACL with the capture option offers a useful and powerful complementary value to the SPAN and RSPAN features.

The VACL with the capture option on the Catalyst 6500 family of switches also overcomes the session number limit. The VACL with the capture option works by a user setting up a VACL to match the interesting traffic and then configuring the capture port, which receives the copy of the matched traffic.

The following configuration guidelines apply to using the capture option in VACL:

■   The capture port needs to be in the spanning-tree forwarding state for the VLAN.

■   The switch has no restriction on the number of capture ports.

- The capture port captures only packets permitted by the configured ACL.

- Capture ports transmit only traffic belonging to the capture port VLAN. To capture traffic going to many VLANs, configure the capture port as a trunk carrying the required VLANs.

In Figure 6-39, a user is troubleshooting a session timeout between a server with IP address 10.1.1.1 and client with IP address 10.1.1.2.

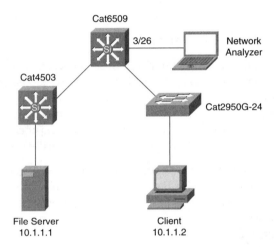

Figure 6-39 *Capturing Using a VACL*

Example 6-28 shows the VACL with the capture option configuration and verification for the troubleshooting scenario presented in Figure 6-39 on the Cisco IOS–based Catalyst 6500 family of switches. In Example 6-28, the *bcmsnvacl* defined by the **access-map** command is applied on VLAN 1. Example 6-28 also shows configuring the network analyzer port, GigabitEthernet 3/26, to receive the captured frames on VLAN 1 using the **switchport capture** command.

Example 6-28 *Configuration and Verification of VACL with the Capture Option*

```
cat6k(config)# access-list 101 permit ip host 10.1.1.1 host 10.1.1.2
cat6k(config)# access-list 101 permit ip host 10.1.1.2 host 10.1.1.1
cat6k(config)# vlan access-map bcmsnvacl
cat6k(config-access-map)# match ip address 101
cat6k(config-access-map)# action forward capture
cat6k(config-access-map)# exit
cat6k(config)# vlan filter bcmsnvacl vlan-list 1
cat6k(config)# in GigabitEthernet 3/26
cat6k(config-if)# switchport
cat6k(config-if)# switchport capture allowed vlan 1
cat6k(config-if)# switchport capture
```

```
cat6k(config-if)# end
cat6k# show vlan access-map
Vlan access-map "bcmsnvacl" 10
        match: ip address 101
        action: forward capture
cat6k# show vlan filter
VLAN Map bcmsnvacl:
```

Troubleshooting Using L2 Traceroute

Layer 2 (L2) traceroute is equivalent to the IP traceroute command except that this trace is for Layer 2 connectivity troubleshooting based on MAC addresses. L2 traceroute is a powerful tool for determining the path of a frame through the Layer 2 topology. The administrator needs to know only the source and destination MAC addresses of the devices in question. L2 traceroute also identifies the physical connection of any device in the network, freeing the administrator from having to manually check each switch.

To illustrate a typical troubleshooting scenario, consider a situation in which the connection between a server and client is slow. To troubleshoot this problem, identify the source and destination IP addresses of this session. When the IP addresses are determined, you can easily find the MAC address of these devices by consulting the ARP tables of the workstation, client, and adjacent routers. Next, you need to locate the ports where the actual client and server are connected in the Layer 2 infrastructure. If, however, the L2 topology is large, it might be difficult to find out where these two devices connect with just their IP addresses and MAC addresses unless the ports are clearly labeled and the network is clearly organized.

L2 traceroute is useful in these situations to trace the device connection into the network using just the MAC addresses. The L2 traceroute command also works with IP addresses specified as part of the command for directly connected subnet devices.

L2 traceroute requires the following conditions to function properly:

- All the switches and interfaces in the network require CDP to be running and functioning properly.

- All intermediate switches between the source and device in question must support the L2 traceroute feature.

In Figure 6-40, a user needs to identify the performance and path on a hop-by-hop basis for a specific server and client exhibiting slow file-transfer performance. Example 6-29 shows a user using the L2 traceroute feature with the source MAC address of the server, 0000.0000.0007, to the destination MAC address of the client, 0000.0000.0011. To perform L2 tracerouting, the user can choose any switch in the network as long as that switch has both the source and destination MAC addresses in the MAC address table. In this example, the user performed the L2 traceroute command on the Catalyst 2950 of Figure 6-40.

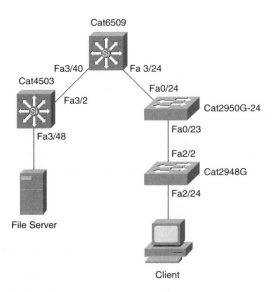

Figure 6-40 *L2 Traceroute*

Example 6-29 *L2 traceroute Output from Cisco IOS–Based Switches*

```
2950G# traceroute mac 0000.0000.0007 0000.0000.0011
Source 0000.0000.0007 found on 4503
4503 (14.18.2.132) : Fa3/48 => Fa3/2
6500 (14.18.2.145) :  3/40 => 3/24
2950G (14.18.2.176) : Fa0/24 => Fa0/23
2948G (14.18.2.91) :  2/2 => 2/24
Destination 0000.0000.0011 found on 2948G Layer 2 trace completed
```

Enhancing Troubleshooting and Recovery Using Cisco IOS Embedded Event Manager

The Embedded Event Manager (EEM) feature has the capability to monitor events happening in the switch using embedded event collectors. The events tracked could be a generation of a syslog message, incrementing of a certain counter, or the result of a Generic Online Diagnostic (GOLD) test. Based on the detection of these events, custom actions could be performed, including configuration changes, email notification, or paging the system administrator.

EEM greatly improves troubleshooting and recovery of network failures by providing the capability not only to detect a great variety of events in the switch but also to take immediate actions without user invention.

Table 6-10 shows a sample set of events and typical actions that can be automated with EEM. It is important to remember that actions based on an event are fully user configurable.

Table 6-10 *Sample EEM Scenarios*

Event (User Configurable)	Action (User Defined)
A specific interface error crosses a user-defined threshold.	Disable the interface and bring up a backup interface.
Configuration changes are made during production hours.	Deny the configuration changes and send an email alert.
A GOLD diagnostic test fails.	Generate a custom syslog message indicating the action to take for Level 1 network operators.
A user logs into the system.	Generate a custom login message based on the user ID.
Unauthorized hardware is removed or added from the switch.	Send a page to the administrator.
It is necessary to collect data for capacity planning.	Run a user-defined set of commands to collect the capacity information at regular intervals.

The EEM feature is configurable in the following two ways:

■ **EEM using applet CLI:** Cisco IOS CLI–based configuration that provides a limited set of actions and detection

■ **EEM using Tool Command Language (TCL) script:** Provides full flexibility in defining the events and the subsequent actions

EEM enables customers to define their own custom TCL script that can be executed on the Catalyst switch. For more information about EEM, refer to the following documentation on Cisco.com (requires a Cisco.com username and password): "Embedded Event Manager 2.0," www.cisco.com/en/US/partner/products/sw/iosswrel/ps1838/products_feature_guide091 86a008025951e.html.

Performance Monitoring Using the Network Analysis Module in the Catalyst 6500 Family of Switches

The Network Analysis Module (NAM) for the Cisco Catalyst 6500 family of switches is part of the end-to-end network management and monitoring solution. Network administrators need to collect statistics about voice, video, and data applications. The NAM gathers multilayer information about voice, video, and data flows up through the application layer, helping to simplify the task of managing multiservice switched LANs that support a variety of data, voice, and video applications.

The NAM monitors and analyzes network traffic using Remote Network MONitoring (RMON) Management Information Base (MIB). RMON MIB was developed by IETF to support monitoring and protocol analysis of LANs. The original version (sometimes referred to as RMON1) focused on OSI Layer 1 and Layer 2 information in Ethernet and Token Ring networks. It has been extended by RMON2, which adds support for network- and application layer monitoring and by SMON, which adds support for switched networks.

The embedded NAM Traffic Analyzer Software in the NAM gives any web browser access to the RMON1 (RFC 1757), RMON2 (RFC 2021), SMON (RFC 2613), DSMON (RFC 3287), and voice-monitoring features of the NAM. Furthermore, the NAM Software provides the ability to troubleshoot and monitor network availability and health.

In addition to extensive MIB support, the NAM can also monitor individual Ethernet VLANs, which enables the NAM to serve as an extension to the basic RMON support provided by the Catalyst Supervisor Engine.

The TrafficDirector application, or any other IETF-compliant RMON application, can access link, host, protocol, and response-time statistics for capacity planning and real-time application protocol monitoring. Filters and capture buffers are also available for troubleshooting the network.

The NAM supports having multiple data sources simultaneously. The NAM can use the following data sources for traffic analyses:

- Ethernet, Fast Ethernet, Gigabit Ethernet, trunk port, or Fast EtherChannel; SPAN or RSPAN source port; and VSPAN and VACL with the capture option.

- Locally generated NetFlow Data Export (NDE) records. The NDE feature collects individual flow statistics of the traffic switched through the switch. NDE can also export the collected information to external flow collectors such as the NetFlow FlowCollector application. The NAM is another example of such a flow collector.

Summary

Security is a primary concern in maintaining a secure, stable, and uninterrupted network. Network security goes far beyond the information in this chapter and includes topics such as intrusion detection, firewalls, virus protection, and operating system patching. Unless you recognize and understand the importance of network security, your network is at risk. The following list summarizes the aspects and recommended practices for avoiding, limiting, and minimizing network vulnerabilities strictly related to Catalyst switches as a single network entity:

- Layer 2 attacks vary in nature and include spoofing attacks, VLAN attacks, MAC flood attacks, and switch device attacks, among others.

- Use strong passwords with SSH access instead of Telnet exclusively to Cisco network devices.

- Disable unused services such as TCP and UDP small services where appropriate.

- Use AAA for centralized authentication, authorization, and accounting of network devices and remote access.

- Use an access control feature such as 802.1X or port security to restrict workstation access to Catalyst switches.

- Use DHCP snooping to prevent rogue DHCP servers on the network.

- Use IPSG and DAI with DHCP snooping to prevent IP address and ARP spoofing attacks.

- Apply management ACLs to limit remote access to Cisco network devices.

- Apply data plane security ACLs to filter unwarranted traffic in the network.

- Use private VLANs where appropriate to limit communication in specific VLANs.

- Use troubleshooting and monitoring tools such as SPAN, VSPAN, RSPAN, ERSPAN, L2 Traceroute, EEM, and NAM to ensure proper network performance.

Review Questions

Use the questions here to review what you learned in this chapter. The correct answers are found in Appendix A, "Answers to Chapter Review Questions."

1. True or False: When configuring SNMP on Cisco routers and switches, use SNMPv2c because SNMP version 2c supports the use of encrypted passwords for authentication rather than the use of simple text or unencrypted passwords, as in version 1.

2. True or False: Using the 802.1X access control feature is preferable to using port security because the 802.1X protocol is a standards-based feature that supports centralized management.

3. True or False: The DHCP snooping trust interface is enabled only on ports with DHCP clients.

4. Which of the following is not a recommended management security configuration on Catalyst switches?

   a. Using SSH and disabling Telnet service

   b. Disabling unnecessary or unused services, such as MOP or Proxy-ARP

   c. Configuring ACLs to restrict specific users to manage the network devices

   d. Policing to limit specific types of traffic to specific bandwidth parameters

   e. Disabling remote access to switches

   f. Physically preventing access to console ports

5. Which command correctly enables Catalyst switches to enact AAA security configurations?

  a. ppp authentication chap

  b. aaa new-model

  c. aaa authentication login default group RADIUS

  d. username name password password

6. Which of the following is not a supported 802.1X port authorization state?

  a. Force-authorized

  b. Force-unauthorized

  c. Auto

  d. Desirable

7. Which of the following features is a requirement for configuring DAI?

  a. IPSG

  b. DHCP snooping

  c. IGMP snooping

  d. Proxy ARP

8. Which of the following methods can prevent a single 802.1Q tag VLAN hopping attack?

  a. Turn off auto-negotiation of speed/duplex.

  b. Turn off trunk negotiation.

  c. Turn off PAgP.

  d. Turn on PAgP.

9. Which of the following prevents MAC address spoofing?

  a. Port security

  b. DHCP snooping

  c. IGMP snooping

  d. MAC notification

10. Which of the following types of ACLs can be applied to a Layer 2 port? (Choose all that apply.)

  a.   Router ACL

  b.   QACL

  c.   PACL

  d.   VACL

  e.   All of the above

11. True or False: Sticky port security allows for easier configuration of MAC addresses that need to be secured.

Chapter 7

Preparing the Campus Infrastructure for Advanced Services

This chapter covers the following topics:

- Planning for Wireless, Voice, and Video Application in the Campus Network

- Understanding QoS

- Implementing IP Multicast in the Campus Network

- Preparing the Campus Infrastructure to Support Wireless

- Preparing the Campus Infrastructure to Support Voice

- Preparing the Campus Infrastructure to Support Video

Advanced services in the campus network are driving a new era of mobility, collaboration, and virtual business. Consider a campus network that supports connectivity for any mobile device. Consider the cost-savings associated with high-definition video conferencing. Consider the business advantage of reducing travel costs associated with training and participating in virtual training. Consider attending a meeting in Asia from your desk? Consider using a single converged network for voice communications? Advanced services such as wireless, voice, and video in the campus network are delivering the mentioned applications to the campus network today.

This chapter focuses on advanced services in the network to include wireless, voice, and video. The chapter is organized into sections where planning information is presented for wireless, voice, and video, followed by introductions to QoS and multicast, and ending with information on preparing and implementing wireless, voice, and video. QoS and multicast are introduced because QoS is a requirement for voice and video in the campus network, while multicast is used by several video applications.

Planning for Wireless, Voice, and Video Application in the Campus Network

As noted in the introduction, Cisco documentation considers wireless, voice, and video applications as advanced technologies. As time progresses, these advanced technologies are trending toward becoming a standard deployment technology. Each of these advanced technologies—wireless, voice, and video—stretches the technology breadth of most network engineers as the typical Layer 2 and 3 network technologies are broad enough by themselves. Of the three advance technologies, the wireless technology requires the most extra effort for application to the campus network.

Note   Because this book is about switching, this chapter focuses only on wireless from the application in the enterprise. The term *wireless* in the context of this book is strictly limited to Wi-Fi in the campus and does not represent any cellular or other wireless technologies, such as Bluetooth.

It is interesting to note that during the evolution of this title, Voice over IP (VoIP), a voice application built to use TCP/IP, has transitioned from a new sleek feature to an enterprise-class voice application in widespread use today. In addition, VoIP application in the network has been eased as well because the Cisco switches now support intelligent features that ease configuration of voice.

Note   In the context of this chapter, the terms voice, IP telephony, and VoIP are used interchangeably to describe the application of telephony and its additional features and applications in the enterprise network.

Video as an application is used in several enterprises for training, internal TV, and so on; however, most enterprises also use web-based video such as flash video to deliver enterprise video-on-demand training, and such. As with VoIP, video has transitioned from a nice feature to a standard feature found in campus networks. The next three subsections focus on the motivation behind deploying wireless, voice, and video in the campus network starting with wireless.

The Purpose of Wireless Network Implementations in the Campus Network

The motivation behind implementing wireless in the campus network is straightforward: productivity. End users who can access network resources without a physical connection in a meeting, conference room, at lunch, and so on are more productive than end users who do not have such access. Moreover, in today's world of collaboration, end users of the campus network need to access resources from within meetings, trainings, water cooler talks, and so on. In the next few years, the wireless implementation in the campus network will be as standard as cellular phones. In brief, the following list highlights the motivation behind deploying wireless networks in the campus network:

- **Productivity:** Users gain productivity through the ability to access resources while in meetings, training, presentations, at lunch, and so on.

- **Mobility:** Users on the go within the campus can be mobile with access to campus resource, such as e-mail.

- **Enhanced collaboration:** Wireless networks enable enhanced user collaboration through the benefit of a network without wires.

- **Campus interconnectivity:** Wireless networks have the capability to interconnect remote offices, offsite networks, and so on that cannot interconnect to the campus network over traditional physical network cable.

Note Wireless network access points usually connect to the access layer of the campus network. However, certain cable plant or physical requirements might require these devices to be connected to the distribution or core layers. Nevertheless, an access point is considered an edge device from a campus networking point of view.

Note The motivation behind deploying wireless in the campus network is to provide mobility to end users and the associated productivity gains.

Wireless free users from requiring a physical cable to access network resources. The next section discusses the advantages of converging voice with data in the campus network.

The Purpose of Voice in the Campus Network

The overlying purposes for using voice in a campus network is simple: cost-savings and increased productivity. Most enterprises have jumped onto the VoIP bandwagon and are successfully deploying this technology. Each of these enterprises has enjoyed success with these deployments as they have bought cost-savings and increased user productivity. In detail, the following list captures the motivations behind deploying voice in the campus network:

- **More efficient use of bandwidth and equipment:** For example, traditional telephony networks use a 64-kbps channel for every voice call. Packet telephony shares bandwidth among multiple logical connections and offloads traffic volumes from existing voice switches.

- **Lower costs for telephony network transmission:** A substantial amount of equipment is needed to combine 64-kbps channels into high-speed links for transport across the network. Packet telephony multiplexes voice traffic alongside data traffic. In other words, voice traffic and data traffic coexist on the same network infrastructure.

This consolidation represents substantial savings on capital equipment and operations costs.

- **Consolidation of voice and data network expense:** Data networks that function as separate networks from voice networks become major traffic carriers. The underlying voice networks are converted to use the packet-switched architecture to create a single integrated communications network with a common switching and transmission system. The benefit is significant cost-savings on network equipment and operations.

- **Increased revenue from new service:** For instance, packet telephony enables new integrated services, such as broadcast-quality audio, unified messaging, and real-time voice and data collaboration. These services increase employee productivity and profit margins well above those of basic voice services. In addition, these services enable companies and service providers to differentiate themselves and improve their market position.

- **Capability to leverage access to new communications devices:** Using packet technology enables companies and service providers to reach devices that are largely inaccessible to the time-division multiplexing (TDM) infrastructures of today. Examples of such devices are computers, wireless devices, household appliances, personal digital assistants, and cable set-top boxes. Intelligent access to such devices enable companies and service providers to increase the volume of communications they deliver, the breadth of services they offer, and the number of subscribers they serve. Packet technology, therefore, enables companies to market new devices, including videophones, multimedia terminals, and advanced IP phones.

- **Flexible pricing structure:** Companies and service providers with packet-switched networks can transform their service and pricing models. Because network bandwidth can be dynamically allocated, network usage no longer needs to be measured in minutes or distance. Dynamic allocation gives service providers the flexibility to meet the needs of their customers in ways that bring them the greatest benefits.

- **Emphasis on greater innovation in service:** Unified communications use the IP infrastructure to consolidate communication methods that were previously independent; for example, fax, voice mail, e-mail, landline telephones, cellular telephones, call centers, and the web. The IP infrastructure provides users with a common method to access messages and initiate real-time communications—independent of time, location, or device.

Note   The key motivations behind deploying voice in the campus network are cost-savings, increased efficiency of the network, and productivity gains from voice services.

In summary, it is easy to understand why enterprises have and continue to deploy VoIP in the campus network. The next section details the purposes behind deploying wireless in the campus network.

From a deployment perspective, all voice devices and software applications for use by end users or customers connect to the access layer of the campus network. The processing and computing functions of voice are generally found in the data center. The "Planning for Wireless" section goes into further detail about planning for voice in the campus network.

The Purpose of Video Deployments in the Campus Network

Video has a unique purpose in the campus network as previously discussed. Its purpose is certain around collaboration. Perhaps the most interesting and practical use of video lately is TelePresence. If you have not experienced TelePresence, you need to. It is absolutely amazing how real it feels. Nonetheless, TelePresence requires a tremendous amount of bandwidth requirements that drive enterprise network bandwidth requirements not only in the campus but also among campus networks. The best application of TelePresence is communication across multiple campus and remote sites. In summary, the motivation behind deploying video in the campus network is as follows:

- **Collaboration:** Video conferencing technologies such as TelePresence and the video support in WebEx support enhanced collaboration.

- **Cost-savings:** Video technologies reduce travel costs by enabling remote users to attend meetings, trainings, and so on without being physically present.

Note   The main motivation for deploying video in the campus network is enhanced collaboration and cost-savings associated with virtual trainings and meetings.

Now that the motivation behind each advanced technology is understood, the next three sections dive into the background information about the technology necessary to understand the planning and preparation behind each technology.

Planning for the Campus Network to Support Wireless Technologies

Wireless LANs are often compared to standard LANs and viewed as "LANs without cables." WLANs actually integrate into the LAN infrastructure to extend it. It does have similarities with wired LANs. Nevertheless, it also presents important differences that you need to appreciate to perform a successful integration in the campus network. The next section provides some background information before discussing wireless LANs to campus LANs and the associated preparation.

Introduction to Wireless LANs (WLAN)

Wireless networks solve the data exchange problem without wires. Following are different types of wireless data communication methods, each of which has its advantages and drawbacks:

- **Infrared (III):** High data rates, lower cost, and short distance

- **Narrowband:** Low data rates, medium cost, license required, limited distance

- **Spread spectrum:** Limited to campus coverage, medium cost, high data rates

- **Personal Communications Service (PCS):** Low data rates, medium cost, citywide coverage

- **Cellular:** Low to medium cost, national and worldwide coverage (typical cell phone carrier)

- **Ultra-wideband (UWB):** Short-range high-bandwidth coverage

As implied in the list of communications method, wireless in the campus uses the spread spectrum methodology. The spread spectrum wireless focus is on the three unlicensed bands: 900 MHz, 2.4 GHz, and 5 GHz. The 900-MHz and 2.4-GHz bands are referred to as the Industrial, Scientific, and Medical (ISM) bands, and the 5-GHz band is commonly referred to as the Unlicensed National Information Infrastructure (UNII) band.

Figure 7-1 refers to the frequencies for these bands. They are as follows:

- **900-MHz band:** 902 MHz to 928 MHz

- **2.4-GHz band:** 2.4 GHz to 2.483 GHz

- **5-GHz band:** 5.150 MHz to 5.350 MHz, 5.725 MHz to 5.825 MHz, with some countries supporting middle bands between 5.350 MHz and 5.825 MHz

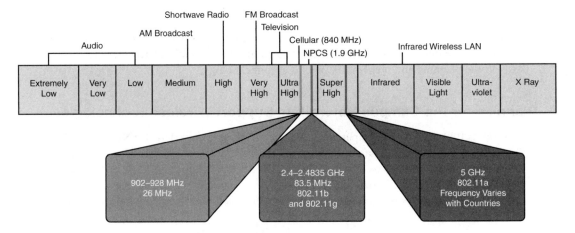

Figure 7-1 *Unlicensed Frequency Bands*

There are many different types of networks offered. Each unique network provides some defined coverage area. Figure 7-2 lists each wireless technology and illustrates the corresponding coverage areas.

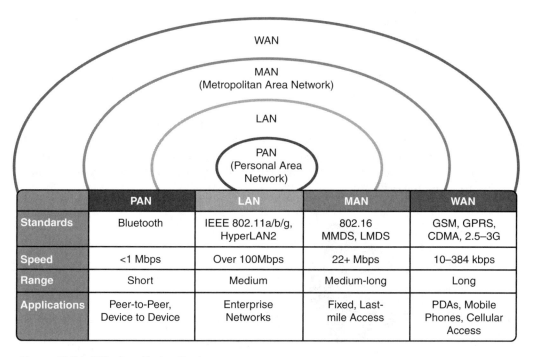

	PAN	LAN	MAN	WAN
Standards	Bluetooth	IEEE 802.11a/b/g, HyperLAN2	802.16 MMDS, LMDS	GSM, GPRS, CDMA, 2.5–3G
Speed	<1 Mbps	Over 100Mbps	22+ Mbps	10–384 kbps
Range	Short	Medium	Medium-long	Long
Applications	Peer-to-Peer, Device to Device	Enterprise Networks	Fixed, Last-mile Access	PDAs, Mobile Phones, Cellular Access

Figure 7-2 *Wireless Technologies*

The following is a brief list of the different applications of wireless networks, starting with the smallest area:

■ **Personal-area network (PAN):** Typically designed to cover your personal workspace. Radios are typically low-powered, do not offer options in antenna selection, and limit the size of the coverage area to approximately 15 to 20 feet radially. One such PAN network is Bluetooth. Good examples of this technology are communications between PCs and peripherals or between wireless phones and headsets. In the PAN wireless network, the customer owns 100 percent of the network; therefore, no airtime charges are incurred.

■ **LAN:** Designed to be an enterprise-based network that enables for complete suites of enterprise applications to be used without wires. A LAN typically delivers Ethernet-capable speeds (up to 10 Gbps). In the LAN wireless network, the customer owns 100 percent of the network; therefore, no airtime charges are incurred.

■ **Metropolitan-area network (MAN):** Deployed inside a metropolitan area, allowing wireless connectivity throughout an urban area. A MAN typically delivers up to broadband speeds (similar to digital subscriber line [DSL]) but is not capable of Ethernet speeds. In the wireless MAN, the wireless network might be from a licensed carrier, requiring the customer to purchase airtime, or it might be built out and supported by one entity, such as a police department. A new standard coming of age in the MAN is WiMAX. Information is available on the Internet with regard to WiMAX.

- **WAN:** Typically slower in speed but offers more coverage, sometimes including rural areas. Because of their vast deployment, all wireless WANs require that a customer purchase airtime for data transmission.

Campus networks, of course, apply LAN-based wireless networks (WLAN). Cisco offers a wide range of wireless products for the LAN and other applications such the MAN and WAN. WLAN products have limited range but relatively high-speeds in excess of 108 Mbps. Figure 7-3 illustrates the coverage areas and data rates of various wireless data networks in use today for WLANs.

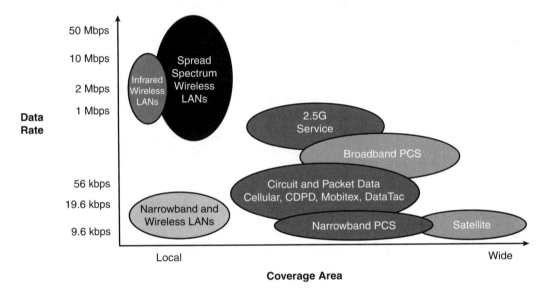

Figure 7-3 *Wireless Data Networks*

For the purpose of applying WLANs to the campus network, note the speeds and range of WLAN products discussed at a high-level in this section. Because there are entire books dedicated to WLANs, it would be too much material to cover the technology in detail from a switching perspective. As such, the remainder of information on WLANs in this chapter focuses on planning and preparation in the campus network. Consult Cisco.com or other texts for additional information on how WLANs operate.

Cisco WLAN Solutions as Applied to Campus Networks

Cisco classifies its campus network WLAN solutions and products into a framework denoted as the Cisco Unified Wireless Network, which is broken down into the following subelements:

■ **Client devices:** Cisco Compatible or Cisco Aironet 802.11a/b/g/ client adapters are strongly recommended for the Cisco Unified Wireless Network. However, with more than 90 percent of shipping client devices certified as Cisco-compatible, almost any client device that you select should be Cisco-compatible certified. In addition, Cisco-compatible client devices interoperate with and support innovative and unique Cisco Unified Wireless Network features, such as fast secure roaming, integrated IPS, location services, and a variety of extensible authentication types.

■ **Mobility platform:** Cisco offers access points and bridges for the carpeted enterprise, ruggedized environments, and challenging environments, such as the outdoors. Cisco Aironet lightweight access points are dynamically configured and managed through Lightweight Access Point Protocol (LWAPP), which is discussed later in this section. In addition, Cisco Aironet autonomous access points have the option to be converted to operate as lightweight access points running the LWAPP are supported. Note that not all Cisco Aironet autonomous AP models can be converted to LWAPP APs; see Cisco.com for more information.

Note   Cisco offers a wide range of wireless AP models. For a complete and current reference of AP models, consult references to wireless AP models on Cisco.com.

■ **Network unification:** The Cisco Unified Wireless Network leverages the customer's existing wired network and investment in Cisco products. It supports a seamless network infrastructure across a range of platforms by unification with Cisco WLAN controllers.

■ **World-class network management:** Cisco delivers a world-class network management system (NMS) that visualizes and helps secure your air space. The Cisco Wireless Control Systems (WCS) supports WLAN planning and design, radio frequency management, location tracking, and IPS, in addition to WLAN systems configuration, monitoring, and management. This platform easily manages multiple controllers and their associated lightweight access points.

■ **Unified advanced services:** Cisco provides unified support of leading-edge applications. Cisco offers advanced services that are industry leading, innovative, and comprehensive. Wireless lightweight access points, location appliances, and wireless IP phones deliver the Cisco Unified Wireless Network advanced services.

Although detailed information and configuration of these elements is not necessary for switching, they can be referenced in voice deployments. The next section discusses similarities and differences of LANs and WLANs.

Comparing and Contrasting WLANs and LANs

As previously noted, wired LANs require that users locate in one place and stay there. Because WLANs are an extension to the wired LAN network, they enable users to be mobile while using the mobile devices in different places without a wired network connection. A WLAN can be an overlay to, or substitute for, a traditional wired LAN network.

With Cisco WLANs, mobile users can

■   Move freely around a facility

■   Enjoy real-time access to the wired LAN at wired Ethernet speeds

■   Access all the resources of wired LANs

WLANs are essentially 802.11 LANs; recall the 802 nomenclature of 802 from CCNA switching. Fundamentally, the data in WLANs is sent over radio waves. In wired LANs, the data is sent over wires. However, the network interface of WLANs looks similar to wired LANs for the user.

The following list summarizes similarities and differences between wired and wireless LANs:

■   Both WLANs and wired LANs define the physical and data link layers and use MAC addresses. The same protocols and applications can be used over LANs and WLANs. Examples of such protocols are the IP and IP Security (IPsec) protocol for virtual private networks (VPN). Examples of applications are web, FTP, and Simple Network Management Protocol (SNMP) management.

■   In WLANs, radio frequencies are used as the physical layer of the network.

■   WLANs use carrier sense multiple access collision avoidance (CSMA/CA) instead of carrier sense multiple access collision detection (CSMA/CD), which is used by Ethernet LANs. Collision detection is not possible because a sending station cannot receive at the same time that it is transmitting and, therefore, cannot detect a collision. Instead, the Request To Send (RTS) and Clear To Send (CTS) protocols are used to avoid collisions.

■   WLANs use a different frame format than wired Ethernet LANs. Additional information for WLANs is required in the Layer 2 header of the frame.

■   Radio waves used by WLANs have problems not found in wires.

■   Connectivity issues in WLANs can be caused by coverage problems, RF transmission, multipath distortion, and interference from other wireless services or other WLANs.

■   Privacy issues are possible because radio frequencies can reach outside the facility and physical cable plan.

■   In WLANs, mobile clients are used to connect to the network.

■   Mobile devices are often battery-powered.

■   WLANs are available worldwide; however, because WLANs use radio frequencies, they must follow country-specific regulations for RF power and frequencies. This requirement does not apply to wired LANs.

WLANs obviously present challenges beyond wire LANs. Discussion of the problems, possible solutions, and further technical information about WLAN operations is outside the scope of this text. Consult Cisco.com for more information. The next section of the chapter introduces the standalone versus controller-based approaches to WLAN deployments, a topic critical to planning WLAN deployments in the campus.

Standalone Versus Controller-Based Approaches to WLAN Deployments in the Campus Network

For a deployment of a Cisco Unified Wireless Network into a campus network, two deployment strategies exist for WLAN solutions. These deployment solutions are the standalone WLAN solution and the controller-based WLAN solution.

Synonymous with its naming, the standalone WLAN solution uses independent access points as a deployment strategy. For scaled WLAN deployments that use the standalone solution, Cisco recommends the use of Cisco Wireless LAN Solution Engine (WLSE) for centralized management and monitoring. Standalone WLAN solutions may be referred to as autonomous WLAN solutions in other documents and texts.

Conversely, the controller-based WLAN solution uses centralized management systems to not only manage and monitor the access point, but also control, configure, and operate each access point. Controller-based WLAN solutions might be referred to as lightweight WLAN solutions in other documents and texts.

In brief, standalone WLAN Solutions (Autonomous WLAN Solutions) are deployed using independent access points and optionally use a WLSE for centralized management. Controller-based WLAN solutions are deployed with a centralized controller, whereas the controller not only manages and monitors the access, but also controls, configures, and operates each access point.

The following two subsections dive further into each WLAN solution to provide background information necessary to plan a campus network deployment.

Standalone WLAN Solution

Figure 7-4 highlights a typical model for deploying the standalone WLAN solution in a campus network.

As previously noted, the standalone WLAN solution uses an independent (standalone) access point with centralized management and monitoring through a WLSE. Moreover, this solution also uses access control servers (ACS) in either a RADIUS or TACACS+ configuration for access control. Wireless domain services might be provided for radio frequency management and secure roaming. The Cisco switches deployed in the campus might support power of Ethernet (POE) to power the access points. PoE is discussed in further detail later in this chapter.

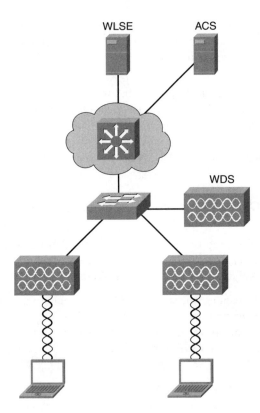

Figure 7-4   *Standalone WLAN Solution*

Because each access point operates independently of each other in a standalone solution, the access points simply translate the wireless media (denoted 802.11) to Ethernet media (802.3.) and send the frames to the Cisco switch. The Cisco switch interprets the frames from the access point as any other Ethernet and switches the frames accordingly. In other words, the access point is relatively transparent to the switch from a traffic perspective.

Controller-Based WLAN Solution

As previously discussed, the controller-based solution provides for centralized operation compared to a standalone solution. Figure 7-5 illustrates the components of a controller-based WLAN solution.

The definition of the devices shown in Figure 7-5 as part of a controller-based solution are described as follows:

- Controller-based access points.

- Network infrastructure with router and switches. Switches can be used to supply power to the access points (PoE).

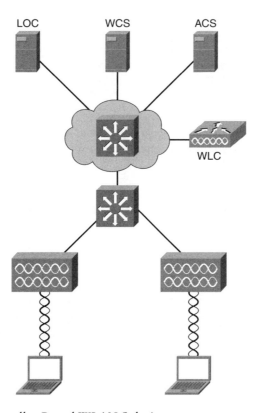

Figure 7-5   *Controller-Based WLAN Solution*

- Cisco Wireless LAN Controller (WLC) for the control, configuration, and monitoring of the access points.

- Cisco Wireless Control System (WCS) for WLAN management (recommended).

- Cisco Wireless Location Appliance for location tracking (optional application server).

- Cisco Secure Access Control Server (ACS) for wireless security and authentication using RADIUS and TACACS+ protocol.

The controller-based solution divides the processing of the 802.11 wireless protocols between the access points and a centralized Cisco Wireless LAN Controller (WLC). The processing of the 802.11 data and management protocols and the access point functionality is also split between the access points and the WLC. Even though this process sounds confusing, the designation between what the access points manages and what the WLC manages is simple. Most of the time, the access point manages critical functions, whereas the controller manages all the other functions.

> **Note**   In the controller-based WLAN solution, the process of the 802.11 wireless proto-
> cols is split between the access points and a centralized Cisco Wireless LAN controller.
> The access point manages the time-critical functions, whereas the controller manages all
> the other functions.

> **Note**   Within the wireless architecture design guides, the concept of dividing the frame
> and management processing functions between the access point and the WLC is referred
> to as a split MAC.

Figure 7-6 illustrates the behavior of the split processing between the access point and
the WLC.

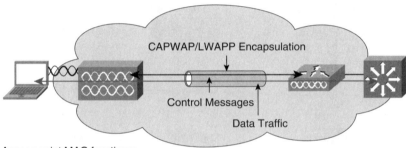

Access point MAC functions:

- 802.11: Beacons, probe responses.
- 802.11 control: Packet acknowledgment
  and transmission.
- 802.11e: Frame queuing and packet
  prioritization.
- 802.11i: MAC layer data encryption and
  decryption.

Controller MAC functions:

- 802.11 MAC management: Association
  requests and actions.
- 802.11e: Resource reservation.
- 802.11i: Authentication and key
  management.

Figure 7-6   *Split MAC of Controller-Based Solution*

As noted in Figure 7-6, the access point handles the portions of the protocol that have
real-time requirements to include the following:

■   Frame exchanges handshake between a client and access point when transferring a
    frame over the air

■   Transmission of beacon frames

■   Buffering and transmission of frames for clients in power save operation

■   Response to probe request frames from clients

■   Forwarding notification of received probe requests to the controller

- Providing real-time signal quality information to the controller with every received frame

- Monitoring each radio channel for noise, interference, and presence of other WLANs

- Monitoring for the presence of other access points

All remaining functionality is handled in the Cisco WLC, where time-sensitivity is not a concern and controllerwide visibility is required. The WLC functions include the following:

- 802.11 authentication and de-authentication

- 802.11 association and reassociation (mobility)

- 802.11 frame translation and bridging

The next two subsections focus on traffic handling and traffic flow of the controller-based solutions.

Traffic Handling in Controller-Based Solutions

Traffic handling in controller-based solutions is different than standalone solutions. Consider the following notes when planning for a wireless deployment in a campus network:

- Data and control messages are encapsulated between the access point and the WLAN controller using the Control and Provisioning of Wireless Access Points (CAPWAP) method or the Lightweight Access Point Protocol (LWAPP). Although both are standards-based, LWAPP was never adopted by any other vendor other than Cisco.

- Control traffic between the access point and the controller is encapsulated with the LWAPP or CAPWAP and encrypted.

- The data traffic between the access point and controller is also encapsulated with LWAPP or CAPWAP. The data traffic is not encrypted. It is switched at the WLAN controller, where VLAN tagging and quality of service (QoS) are also applied.

- The access point accomplishes real-time frame exchange and certain real-time portions of MAC management. All client data traffic is sent via the WLAN controller.

- WLAN controller and access point can be in the same or different broadcast domains and IP subnets. Access points obtain an IP address via DHCP, and then join a controller via a CAPWAP or LWAPP discovery mechanism.

The next subsection discusses the traffic flow in a controller-based solution.

Traffic Flow in a Controller-Based Solution

As previously noted, all traffic in a controller-based solution flows throw the WLC. For example, Figure 7-7 illustrates two clients communicating over a wireless network in a controller-based solution. As alluded to previously in Figure 7-6, the WLC is generally deployed in the distribution layer.

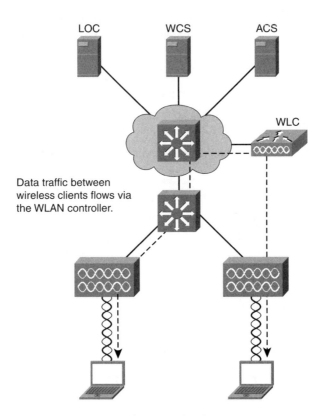

Figure 7-7   *Traffic Flow in a Controller-Based Solution*

The traffic between the two wireless mobile stations is forwarded from the access points to the controller and then sent to wireless mobile stations, respectively. Denote the traffic flows to the WLC and not between the mobile stations directly. The campus network switch simply switches Ethernet frames and is not aware that the frames ultimately end at a wireless client.

Note   In review, traffic flow for wireless clients in a controller-based solution is via the WLC, which differs significantly from a standalone solution in which the access points send traffic natively.

Controllers (WLC) in the controller-based solution are generally deployed in the distribution layer. As previously noted, access points are generally deployed in the access layer except where physical boundaries might require additional access points in other locations.

Hybrid Remote Edge Access Points (HREAP)

HREAP are useful for providing high-availability of controller-based wireless solutions in remote offices. The purpose of these access points is to still offer wireless client connectivity when their connection to the controller (WLC) is lost. A typical controller-based access point always needs connectivity to its controller. When this connectivity is lost, the access point stops offering wireless services and starts looking for another controller. It restores wireless services only when it has regained connectivity to a controller.

HREAPs are controller-based access points. The main difference with standard controller-based access points is that the HREAP can survive the loss of connectivity to its controller. The HREAP reverts to a mode close to a standalone access point and remains to offer wireless access to its wireless clients.

Figure 7-8 illustrates sample behavior of a HREAP solution.

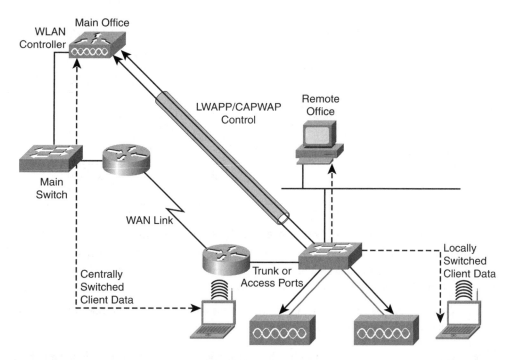

Figure 7-8 *Example of a HREAP Deployment*

The HREAP is usually adapted to remote offices where only one or two access points are deployed; generally remote offices use wireless deployments for only a few access points because the size is usually small. Moreover, in a remote office situation, the controller is not local but accessed through a WAN connection. The HREAP might also be adapted to small offices with only one controller and no backup controller. Figure 7-8 illustrates an example of HREAP.

Note Of note, plan for deployment of HREAP for remote sites where redundant access points are limited.

Review of Standalone and Controller-Based WLAN Solutions

The two WLAN solutions have different characteristics and advantages. Obviously for scaled wireless deployments, the controller-based solution offers significant advantages in terms of centralizing resources. Per the Cisco wireless design guides, any campus network with more than 200 users should utilize a controller-based solution for wireless deployments.

Table 7-1 highlights and reviews the main differences to consider when planning for wireless network deployment in the campus network.

Table 7-1 *Comparison of Standalone and Controller-Based Wireless Solutions*

	Standalone	**Controller-Based**
Access point	Standalone IOS	Controller-based delivered IOS
Configuration	Via access point	Via controller
Operation	Independent	Dependent on WLC
Management and monitoring	Via WLSE	Via WCS
Redundancy	Via multiple access points	Via multiple WLAN controllers

Gathering Requirements for Planning a Wireless Deployment

Wireless technology spans the scope of the topics covered in this text. Any comprehensive plan for a wireless deployment in a campus network should include advice from a trained specialist or consultant as a best practice.

In review, you can use the following list of wireless requirements as a guide when working with specialists or consultants when planning a wireless deployment:

■ Collect requirements to determine how many ports of what type are needed and how they should be configured.

■ Check the existing network to verify how the requirements can integrate into the existing deployment. You will often find that, beyond the pure port count issue, the impact on bandwidth might imply additional connections.

- Plan additional equipment needed to fulfill the requirements.

- Plan implementation.

- Implement new network components.

Moreover, due to the nature of access point behavior, consider building a test plan to verify acceptable wireless implementation. In review of the behavior of an initial connection of a wireless client, it first detects the wireless network and tries to connect at Layer 2 (using 802.11). This connection might imply an 802.1X dialog between the access point (in autonomous mode) or the controller and a AAA server. When this step is complete, the wireless client tries to move to Layer 3 and obtains an IP address. The wireless client then has IP reachability to the network. Knowing these steps can help you troubleshoot wireless connectivity issues. For example, if the controller cannot communicate with the RADIUS server, the client might not associate to the wireless network.

The following list illustrates a sample test for verifying a wireless deployment that can be used as a guide for creating your own test plan:

- Can you reach the AP or WLC from management stations?

- Can the AP reach the DHCP server?

- Does the AP get an IP address from the DHCP server?

- Can the WLC reach the Radius or TACACS+ server?

- Does the client get an IP address?

- Can the client access network, server, or Internet services?

Planning for the Campus Network to Support Voice

Voice services running alongside the data network in the campus are becoming a standard of enterprise networks over traditional telephony networks for many reasons. As previously discussed, cost-savings is a major reason for voice deployments in the campus. Voice deployments in the campus are often referred to as VoIP deployments because from a technology perspective, voice in the campus network runs on top of TCP/IP. Nevertheless, the Return on Investment (ROI) associated with VoIP is significant as VoIP does require an initial start-up cost. However, the initial start-up cost will be returned in cost-savings over the life of the VoIP installation.

From a planning point-of-view, because the telephony services associated with VoIP runs over the campus network, data and voice application traffic must harmoniously coexist. As such, mechanisms must be set in place to differentiate traffic and to offer priority processing to delay sensitive voice traffic. We have all experienced the situation of poor audio quality, echo, jitter, and drop audio on our cell phones. Without careful planning, VoIP in the campus network might experience similar behaviors.

To solve the differentiation problem, Cisco switches use QoS policies to mark and qualify traffic. In addition, Cisco switches can utilize a specific VLAN to keep voice traffic separate from other data to ensure that it is carried through the network with special handling and with minimal delay. Despite the specific configuration or implementation, design and implementation considerations need to be made for all campus switches supporting VoIP.

> **Note** As a best practice, Voice deployment designs should include QoS, a separate VLAN for Voice Traffic, and Power over Ethernet (PoE).

Introduction to Unified Communications

For reference when planning VoIP integration into the campus network, you need to review the entire VoIP architecture. Cisco refers to its architecture and suite of VoIP products and related services as Unified Communications. Unified Communications include more products and services than just the Cisco IP Phone. Figure 7-9 illustrates the products of the Cisco Unified Communications suite.

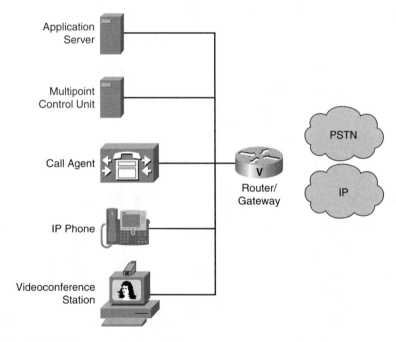

Figure 7-9 *Unified Communications Components*

The devices in Figure 7-9 are summarized as follows:

- **IP Phone:** Provides IP voice to the desktop.

- **Gatekeeper:** Provides connection admission control (CAC), bandwidth control and management, and address translation.

- **Gateway:** Provides translation between VoIP and non-VoIP networks, such as the public switched telephone network (PSTN). It also provides physical access for local analog and digital voice devices, such as telephones, fax machines, key sets, and PBXs.

- **Multipoint control unit:** Provides real-time connectivity for participants in multiple locations to attend the same videoconference or meeting.

- **Call agent:** Provides call control for IP phones, CAC, bandwidth control and management, and telephony address translation for IP addresses or telephone numbers.

- **Application server:** Provides services such as voice mail, unified messaging, and Cisco Unified Communications Manager Attendant Console.

- **Videoconference station:** Provides access for end-user participation in videoconferencing. The videoconference station contains a video capture device for video input and a microphone for audio input. The user can view video streams and hear the audio that originates at a remote user station.

The deployment of Unified Communications may include either components, such as software voice applications, interactive voice response (IVR) systems, and softphones, provide additional services to meet the communications needs of your specific enterprise deployment. For planning purposes, a Unified Communications deployment may require assistance from other specialists or consultants.

Campus Network Design Requirements for Deploying VoIP

Voice traffic has extremely stringent QoS requirements. Voice traffic generally generates a smooth demand on bandwidth and has a minimal impact on other traffic, as long as voice traffic is managed.

When planning for a VoIP deployment, consider the following traffic requirements:

- Voice packets are small, typically between 60 bytes and 120 bytes in size.

- VoIP cannot tolerate drop or delay because it can lead to poor voice quality.

- VoIP uses UDP because TCP retransmit capabilities are useless for voice.

- Specifically, for optimal voice quality, delay should be less than 150 ms one way.

- Although no packet loss is ideal, acceptable packet loss is 1 percent.

The QoS requirements for data traffic vary greatly. Different applications, such as a human resources application versus an ATM application, have different demands on the network. Even different versions of the same application can have varying network traffic characteristics.

Data traffic can demonstrate either a smooth or bursty characteristic, depending on the application, but it differs from voice and video in terms of delay and drop sensitivity. Almost all data applications can tolerate some delay and generally can tolerate high drop rates. Figure 7-10 illustrates typical traffic rates of voice traffic versus application traffic.

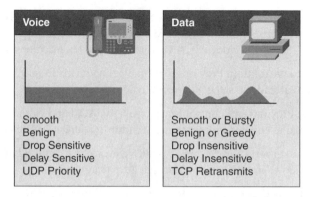

Figure 7-10   *Comparing Voice and Data Traffic*

> **Note**   In review, user data traffic generally uses a variable amount and is immune to average frame drops and latency. Conversely, voice traffic is generally low bandwidth but sensitive to frame drops and latency.

Because data traffic can tolerate drops, the retransmit capabilities of TCP become important and, as a result, many data applications use TCP. Voice traffic uses UDP because there is no need to retransmit drop frames as the voice is real time.

In enterprise networks, important (business-critical) applications are usually easy to identify. Most applications can be identified based on TCP or UDP port numbers. Some applications use dynamic port numbers that, to some extent, make classifications more difficult. Cisco IOS Software supports network-based application recognition (NBAR), which can be used to recognize dynamic port applications.

Consequently, it is important to plan for QoS in the campus for voice traffic to minimize traffic drops and latency in the campus network. Voice traffic is generally low-bandwidth compared to available bandwidth in the campus network.

> **Note**   When designing campus networks with voice, plan for QoS to minimize latency and frame drops of voice traffic.

The application of QoS occurs throughout the campus based on specific QoS configuration. The "Understanding QoS" section goes into detail about preparing and implementing QoS. The next section discusses planning for video in the campus network.

Planning for the Campus Network to Support Video

For networking professionals, video is often seen as just a Layer 7 application. Under this generic term, many different types of applications may be grouped, each of them having its own set of usage and technical specifications. Video applications are usually seen as bandwidth-intensive. Bandwidth-intensive applications are so named because they send a large number of frames onto the network. The content of the frame plays an important role in the overall bandwidth consumption. The content of the frame depends on the type of application for which video is used.

Some video applications are real time, such as video conferencing or TelePresence. The main concern for this type of video is real time. Frames must transit without delay, and QoS is a critical element. Voice might be contained in the video flow or sent as a distinct flow.

Some other video applications are not as sensitive to real-time issues. They usually are one-way streams, where a client station is playing a video stream that is sent from a source. The client station might buffer part of the video flow. The main concern is often quality, and quality depends on several factors such as resolution, number of frames per second, type of codec, and so on, which is not dependent on the design of the campus network. A practical application of one-way streams is on-demand video used for training purposes.

Because multiple persons might receive one-way video streams simultaneously, as in the case of watching a live video feed, the video feed might use multicast to send the traffic to multiple users simultaneously instead of sending traffic to each user autonomously. The "Understanding IP Multicast" section discusses this concept more. In brief, consider planning for deploying multicast for any application that sends traffic to multiple users concerning especially live video feeds.

Note   In summary, real-time video applications such as TelePresence require the amble bandwidth for video traffic, QoS, and high-availability to ensure 99.9 percent uptime. Keep in mind, one-way video applications such as on-demand training are not as sensitive to latency and jitter as real-time video.

Note that real-time video applications are often peer-to-peer. Moreover, when planning for deployments, video applications deploy in the access layer just like a voice or data endpoint.

Voice and Video Traffic

You need to understand the voice and video traffic profiles associated with video applications in the campus network. These traffic profiles ultimately drive the design of the campus network for a voice or video application.

As illustrated in Figure 7-11, a video flow has different characteristics from a voice flow. Voice traffic is usually not bandwidth-intensive but requires steady bandwidth. Commonly, 50 voice packets would need to be sent per second for voice, each packet representing a few hundred bytes worth of voice data.

Because of the nature of the algorithm used to encode the flow, video traffic has a different pattern. Traffic is often bursty, as each image or group of images needs several packets to be transmitted. Depending on the changes from one image to the next, there might be short time intervals without any network activity or sudden bursts when the whole image needs to be changed.

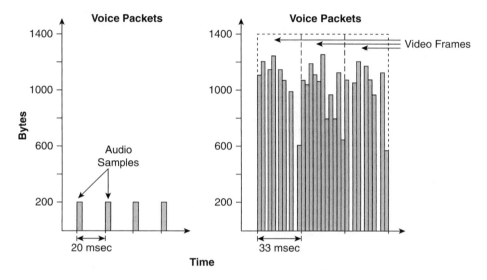

Figure 7-11   *Voice Versus Video Traffic*

Overall, real-time video streams typically consume a lot of bandwidth and are often bursty, although they usually do not consume all the available bandwidth. Consider these characteristics when preparing the campus network for video and voice.

Video Traffic Flow in the Campus Network

Traffic flow for video applications, in the case of peer-to-peer interactive video, is close to the voice flow. In Figure 7-12, two TelePresence (high-definition video conferencing) stations are communicating. The flow goes from one station to the access switch, then to the distribution switch, then to the core switch before reaching the distribution layer of the second building, and then to the access switch and the second station. This pattern is close to the voice flow between two phones. Just like a voice call, TelePresence stations may rely on a central server from where information about the session can be obtained. A detailed discussion of TelePresence is outside the scope of this book; consult Cisco.com for more details.

Data traffic does not often transit from one station to the other. Data clients usually communicate with data centers to upload or download data. Video streaming applications have the same behavior as data: They retrieve information from data centers and have little if no peer-to-peer interaction.

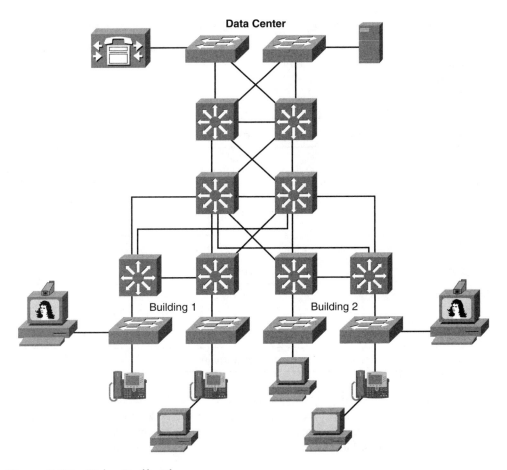

Figure 7-12 *Video Traffic Flow*

As a result, when planning video integration into the campus network, denote whether the following applications will be deployed:

- Peer-to-peer applications, such as TelePresence

- Video streaming applications, such as video-on-demand training

- Video TV-type applications, such as Cisco IP TV

- IP surveillance applications for security

Denoting these applications and referencing the material in this section can determine campus network design and configuration requirements.

Design Requirements for Voice, Data, and Video in the Campus Network

Table 7-2 details the bandwidth, delay, jitter, packet loss, availability, power, security, and management requirements for planning voice, data, and video application in the campus network.

Table 7-2 *Design Requirements Review for Voice, Data, and Video*

Requirement	Data	Voice	Video
Bandwidth	High	Low	High
Delay	If less than a few msec, not applicable	Less than 150 msec	Less than 150 msec for real-time video
Jitter	Not applicable	Low	Low
Packet Loss	Less than 5%	Less than 1%	Less than 1%
Availability	High	High	High
Inline Power	No	Optional	Optional for select devices
Security	High	Medium	Low or Medium
Provisioning	Medium Effort	Significant Effort	Medium Effort

In review, the tolerance to delay and jitter of video traffic depends on the type of video flow: Real time video, such as video conferencing with embedded voice, has the same delay and jitter constraints as voice traffic. One-way video streams are less sensitive to delay and jitter issues. Most video playing devices can buffer 5 seconds or more worth of video flow.

Video traffic also has little tolerance to packet loss. If too many frames are lost, the image does not refresh properly and the user experience degrades. Here again, the quality depends on the type of application used. Tolerance to packet loss is often higher for slow rate and low-definition real-time interactive video flows than for one-way video streams.

The next section discusses QoS, a requirement of most campus network designs, especially those that integrate voice and video.

Understanding QoS

Cisco switches provide a wide range of QoS features that address the needs of voice, video, and data applications sharing a single campus network. Cisco QoS technology enables you to implement complex networks that predictably manage services to a variety of networked applications and traffic types including voice and video.

Using QoS features and services, you can design and implement networks that conform to either the Internet Engineering Task Force (IETF) integrated services (IntServ) model or the differentiated services (DiffServ) model. Cisco switches provide for differentiated services using QoS features, such as classification and marking, traffic conditioning, congestion avoidance, and congestion management.

For a campus network design, the role of QoS in the campus network is to provide the following characteristics:

- **Control over resources:** You have control over which network resources (bandwidth, equipment, wide-area facilities, and so on) are used. For example, critical traffic, such as voice, video, and data, might consume a link with each type of traffic competing for link bandwidth. QoS helps to control the use of the resources (for example, dropping low-priority packets), thereby preventing low-priority traffic from monopolizing link bandwidth and affecting high-priority traffic, such as voice traffic.

- **More efficient use of network resources:** By using network analysis management and accounting tools, you can determine how traffic is handled and which traffic experiences delivery issues. If traffic is not handled optimally, you can use QoS features to adjust the switch behavior for specific traffic flows.

- **Tailored services:** The control and visibility provided by QoS enables Internet service providers to offer carefully tailored grades of service differentiation to their customers. For example, an internal enterprise network application can offer different service for an ordering website that receives 3000 to 4000 hits per day, compared to a human resources website that receives only 200 to 300 hits per day.

- **Coexistence of mission-critical applications:** QoS technologies make certain that mission-critical applications that are most important to a business receive the most efficient use of the network. Time-sensitive voice and video applications require bandwidth and minimized delays, whereas other applications on a link receive fair service without interfering with mission-critical traffic.

QoS provides solutions for its defined roles by managing network congestion. Congestion greatly affects the network availability and stability problem areas, but congestion is not the sole factor for these problem areas. All networks, including those without congestion, might experience the following three network availability and stability problems:

- **Delay (or latency):** The amount of time it takes for a packet to reach a destination

- **Delay variation (or jitter):** The change in inter-packet latency within a stream over time

- **Packet loss:** The measure of lost packets between any given source and destination

Latency, jitter, and packet loss can occur even in multilayer switched networks with adequate bandwidth. As a result, each multilayer switched network design needs to plan for QoS. A well-designed QoS implementation aids in preventing packet loss while minimizing latency and jitter.

QoS Service Models

As discussed in the previous section, the two QoS architectures used in IP networks when designing a QoS solution are the IntServ and DiffServ models. The QoS service models differ by two characteristics: how the models enable applications to send data, and how networks attempt to deliver the respective data with a specified level of service.

A third method of service is the best-effort service, which is essentially the default behavior of the network device without QoS. In summary, the following list restates these three basic levels of service for QoS:

- **Best-effort service:** The standard form of connectivity without guarantees. This type of service, in reference to Catalyst switches, uses first-in, first-out (FIFO) queues, which simply transmit packets as they arrive in a queue with no preferential treatment.

- **Integrated services:** IntServ, also known as hard QoS, is a reservation of services. In other words, the IntServ model implies that traffic flows are reserved explicitly by all intermediate systems and resources.

- **Differentiated services:** DiffServ, also known as soft QoS, is class-based, in which some classes of traffic receive preferential handling over other traffic classes. Differentiated services use statistical preferences, not a hard guarantee such as integrated services. In other words, DiffServ categorizes traffic and then sorts it into queues of various efficiencies.

From the perspective of campus network design, differentiated service is the method used, because most switches support DiffServ and not IntServ.

Figure 7-13 illustrates the queuing components of a Cisco switch. These components match to the building blocks of QoS in a campus network. The figure illustrates the classification that occurs on ingress packets. After the switch classifies a packet, it determines whether to place the packet into a queue or drop the packet. Queuing mechanisms drop packets only if the corresponding queue is full without the use of congestion avoidance.

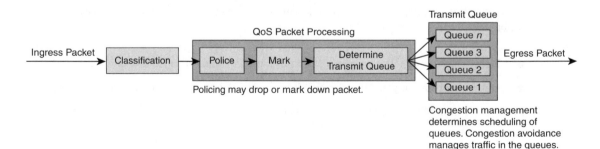

Figure 7-13 *Cisco QoS Model*

As illustrated in Figure 7-13, QoS in the campus network has the following main components:

- Traffic classification and marking

- Traffic shaping and policing

- Congestion management

- Congestion avoidance

Later sections in this chapter discuss these QoS components and how they apply to the campus network. The next section discusses a side topic related to configuring QoS that needs planning consideration.

AutoQoS

As a side note to the QoS components, Cisco AutoQoS is a product feature that enables customers to deploy QoS features for converged IP telephony and data networks much more quickly and efficiently. Cisco AutoQoS generates traffic classes and policy map CLI templates. Cisco AutoQoS simplifies the definition of traffic classes and the creation and configuration of traffic policies. As a result, in-depth knowledge of the underlying technologies, service policies, link efficiency mechanisms, and Cisco QoS best-practice recommendations for voice requirements is not required to configure Cisco AutoQoS.

Cisco AutoQoS can be extremely beneficial for these planning scenarios:

- Small to medium-sized businesses that must deploy IP telephony quickly but lack the experience and staffing to plan and deploy IP QoS services

- Large customer enterprises that need to deploy Cisco telephony solutions on a large scale, while reducing the costs, complexity, and time frame for deployment, and ensuring that the appropriate QoS for voice applications is set in a consistent fashion

- International enterprises or service providers requiring QoS for VoIP where little expertise exists in different regions of the world and where provisioning QoS remotely and across different time zones is difficult

Moreover, Cisco AutoQoS simplifies and shortens the QoS deployment cycle. Cisco AutoQoS aids in the following five major aspects of a successful QoS deployment:

- Application classification

- Policy generation

- Configuration

- Monitoring and reporting

- Consistency

Auto-QoS is mentioned in this section because it's helpful to know that Cisco switches provide a feature to ease planning, preparing, and implementing QoS by abstracting the in-depth technical details of QoS. For a sample configuration of auto-QoS, consult Cisco.com.

The next section begins the discussion of traffic classification and marking.

Traffic Classification and Marking

Traffic classification and marking ultimately determine the QoS applied to a frame. Special bits are used in frames to classify and mark for QoS. There are QoS bits in the frame for both Layer 2 and Layer 3 applications. The next subsection goes into the definition of these bits for classification and marking in more detail.

DSCP, ToS, and CoS

Figure 7-14 illustrates the bits used in Ethernet packets for classification. Network devices use either Layer 2 class of service (CoS) bits of a frame or Layer 3 IP Precedence and Differentiated Services Code Point (DSCP) bits of a packet for classification. At Layer 2, 3 bits are available in 802.1Q frames for classification for up to eight distinct values (levels of service): 0 through 7. These Layer 2 classification bits are referred to as the CoS values. At Layer 3, QoS uses the six most significant ToS bits in the IP header for a DSCP field definition. This DSCP field definition allows for up to 64 distinct values (levels of service)—0 through 63—of classification on IP frames. The last 2 bits represent the Early Congestion Notification (ECN) bits. IP Precedence is only the three most significant bits of the ToS field. As a result, IP Precedence maps to DSCP by using IP Precedence as the three high-order bits and padding the lower-order bits with 0.

A practical example of the interoperation between DSCP and IP Precedence is with Cisco IP Phones. Cisco IP Phones mark voice traffic at Layer 3 with a DSCP value of 46 and, consequently, an IP Precedence of 5. Because the first 3 bits of DSCP value 46 in binary is 101 (5), the IP Precedence is 5. As a result, a network device that is only aware of IP Precedence understands the packet priority similarly to a network device that can interpret DSCP. Moreover, Cisco IP Phones mark frames at Layer 2 with a CoS value of 5.

Figure 7-15 illustrates the ToS byte. P2, P1, and P0 make up IP Precedence. T3, T2, T1, and T0 are the ToS bits. When viewing the ToS byte as DSCP, DS5 through DS0 are the DSCP bits. For more information about bits in the IP header that determine classification, refer to RFCs 791, 795, and 1349.

Note Using DSCP values for classification of packets is the leading method for classification in all enterprise switching networks.

Typical Ethernet Packet

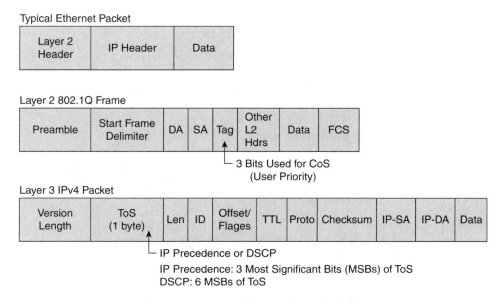

Figure 7-14 *Bits Used in Ethernet packets for Classification*

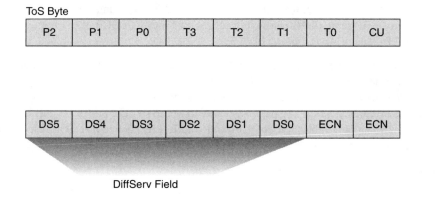

Figure 7-15 *DiffServ Field in IP Header*

Classification

Classification distinguishes a frame or packet with a specific priority or predetermined criteria. In the case of Catalyst switches, classification determines the internal DSCP value on frames. Catalyst switches use this internal DSCP value for QoS packet handling, including policing and scheduling as frames traverse the switch.

The first task of any QoS policy is to identify traffic that requires classification. With QoS enabled and no other QoS configurations, all Cisco routers and switches treat traffic with a default classification. With respect to DSCP values, the default classification for ingress frames is a DSCP value of 0. The terminology used to describe an interface configured for treating all ingress frames with a DSCP of 0 is untrusted. In review, the following methods of packet classification are available on Cisco switches:

- Per-interface trust modes

- Per-interface manual classification using specific DSCP, IP Precedence, or CoS values

- Per-packet based on access lists

- Network-Based Application Recognition (NBAR)

When planning QoS deployments in campus networks, always apply QoS classification as close to the edge as possible, preferable in the access layer. This methodology allows for end-to-end QoS with ease of management.

Note   Apply QoS classification and marking configurations as close to the edge as possible, preferably in the access layer.

Trust Boundaries and Configurations

Trust configurations on Catalyst switches quantify how a frame is handled as it arrives in on a switch. For example, when a switch configured for "trusting DSCP" receives a packet with a DSCP value of 46, the switch accepts the ingress DSCP of the frame and uses the DSCP value of 46 for internal DSCP.

Cisco switches support trusting via DSCP, IP Precedence, or CoS values on ingress frames. When trusting CoS or IP Precedence, Cisco switches map an ingress packet's CoS or IP Precedence to an internal DSCP value. The internal DSCP concept is important because it represents how the packet is handled in the switch. Tables 7-3 and 7-4 illustrate the default mapping tables for CoS-to-DSCP and IP Precedence-to-DSCP, respectively. These mapping tables are configurable.

Table 7-3   *Default CoS-to-DSCP Mapping Table*

CoS	0	1	2	3	4	5	6	7
DSCP	0	8	16	24	32	40	48	56

Table 7-4   *Default IP Precedence-to-DSCP Mapping Table*

IP Precedence	0	1	2	3	4	5	6	7
DSCP	0	8	16	24	32	40	48	56

Figure 7-16 illustrates the Catalyst QoS trust concept using port trusting. When the Catalyst switch trusts CoS on ingress packets on a port basis, the switch maps the ingress value to the respective DSCP value. When the ingress interface QoS configuration is untrusted, the switch uses 0 for the internal DSCP value for all ingress packets.

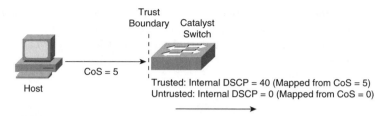

Figure 7-16   *QoS Trust Concept*

Marking

Marking in reference to QoS on Catalyst switches refers to changing the DSCP, CoS, or IP Precedence bits on ingress frames. Marking is configurable on a per-interface basis or via a policy map. Marking alters the DSCP value of packets, which in turn affects the internal DSCP. For instance, an example of marking would be to configure a policy map to mark all frames from a video server on a per-interface basis to a DSCP value of 40, resulting in an internal DSCP value of 40 as well.

Traffic Shaping and Policing

Both shaping and policing mechanisms control the rate at which traffic flows through a switch. Both mechanisms use classification to differentiate traffic. Nevertheless, there is a fundamental and significant difference between shaping and policing.

Shaping meters traffic rates and delays (buffers) excessive traffic so that the traffic rates stay within a desired rate limit. As a result, shaping smoothes excessive bursts to produce a steady flow of data. Reducing bursts decreases congestion in downstream routers and switches and, consequently, reduces the number of frames dropped by downstream routers and switches. Because shaping delays traffic, it is not useful for delay-sensitive traffic flows such as voice, video, or storage, but it is useful for typical, bursty TCP flows. Figure 7-17 illustrates an example of traffic shaping applied to TCP data traffic.

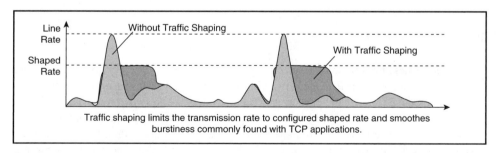

Figure 7-17   *Traffic Shaping as Applied to TCP Traffic*

For more information on which Cisco switches support shaping and configuration guidelines for shaping, consult the Cisco.com website. In campus networks, policing is more commonly used and is widely supported across the Cisco platforms when compared to shaping.

Policing

In contrast to shaping, policing takes a specific action for out-of-profile traffic above a specified rate. Policing does not delay or buffer traffic. The action for traffic that exceeds a specified rate is usually drop; however, other actions are permissible, such as trusting and marking.

Policing on Cisco switches follows the leaky token bucket algorithm, which allows for bursts of traffic compared to rate limiting. The leaky token bucket algorithm is as effective at handling TCP as it is at handling bursts of UDP flows. Figure 7-18 illustrates the leaky token bucket algorithm.

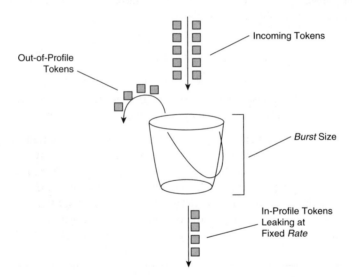

Figure 7-18   *Leaky Token Bucket*

When switches apply policing to incoming traffic, they place a number of tokens proportional to the incoming traffic packet sizes into a token bucket in which the number of tokens equals the size of the packet. At a regular interval, the switch removes a defined number of tokens, determined by the configured rate, from the bucket. If the bucket is full and cannot accommodate an ingress packet, the switch determines that the packet is out of profile. The switch subsequently drops or marks out-of-profile packets according to the configured policing action, but notice that the number of packets leaving the queue is proportional to the number of tokens in the bucket.

Note that the leaky bucket is only a model to explain the differences between policing and shaping.

A complete discussion of the leaky token bucket algorithm is outside the scope of this book.

The next sections discuss congestion management and congestion avoidance. Congestion management is the key feature of QoS.

Congestion Management

Cisco switches use multiple egress queues for application of the congestion-management and congestion-avoidance QoS features. Both congestion management and congestion avoidance are a per-queue feature. For example, congestion-avoidance threshold configurations are per queue, and each queue might have its own configuration for congestion management and avoidance.

Moreover, classification and marking have little meaning without congestion management. Switches use congestion-management configurations to schedule packets appropriately from output queues when congestion occurs. Cisco switches support a variety of scheduling and queuing algorithms. Each queuing algorithm solves a specific type of network traffic condition.

Congestion management comprises several queuing mechanisms, including the following:

- FIFO queuing

- Weighted round robin (WRR) queuing

- Priority queuing

- Custom queuing

The following subsections discuss these queuing mechanisms in more detail.

FIFO Queuing

The default method of queuing frames is FIFO queuing, in which the switch places all egress frames into the same queue, regardless of classification. Essentially, FIFO queuing does not use classification, and all packets are treated as if they belong to the same class. The switch schedules packets from the queue for transmission in the order in which they are received. This behavior is the default behavior of Cisco switches without QoS enabled. Figure 7-19 illustrates the behavior of FIFO queuing.

Weighted Round Robin Queuing

Scheduling packets from egress queues using WRR is a popular and simple method of differentiating service among traffic classes. With WRR, the switch uses a configured weight value for each egress queue. This weight value determines the implied bandwidth of each queue. The higher the weight value, the higher the priority that the switch applies to the egress queue. For example, consider the case of a Cisco switch configured for QoS and WRR. In this example, the Cisco switches use four egress queues. If Queues 1 through 4 are configured with weights 50, 10, 25, and 15, respectively, Queue 1 can utilize 50 percent of the bandwidth when there is congestion. Queues 2 through 4 can utilize 10, 25, and 15 percent of the bandwidth, respectively, when congestion exists. Figure 7-20 illustrates WRR behavior with eight egress queues. Figure 7-20 also illustrates tail-drop and WRED properties, which are explained in later sections.

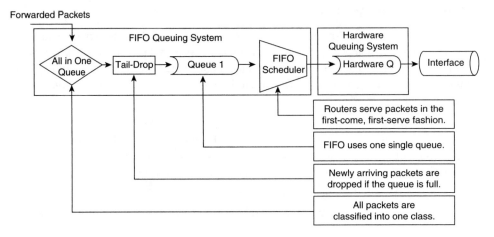

Figure 7-19 *FIFO Queuing*

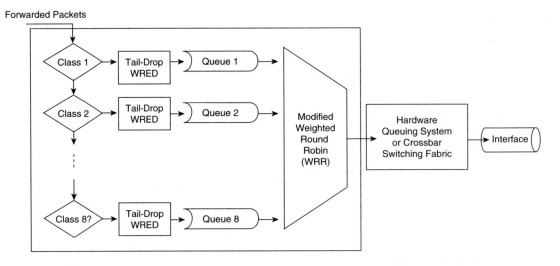

Figure 7-20 *Weighted Round Robin*

The transmit queue ratio determines the way that the buffers are split among the different queues. If you have multiple queues with a priority queue, the configuration requires the same weight on the high-priority WRR queues and for the strict-priority queue. Generally, high-priority queues do not require a large amount of memory for queuing because traffic destined for high-priority queues is delay-sensitive and often low volume. As a result, large queue sizes for high- and strict-priority queues are not necessary. The recommendation is to use memory space for the low-priority queues that generally contain data traffic that is not sensitive to queuing delays. The next section discusses strict-priority queuing with WRR.

Although the queues utilize a percentage of bandwidth, the switch does not actually assign specific bandwidth to each queue when using WRR. The switch uses WRR to schedule packets from egress queues only under congestion. Another noteworthy aspect of WRR is that it does not starve lower-priority queues because the switch services all queues during a finite time period.

Priority Queuing

One method of prioritizing and scheduling frames from egress queues is to use priority queuing. When applying strict priority to one of these queues, the switch schedules frames from that queue if there are frames in that queue before servicing any other queue. Cisco switches ignore WRR scheduling weights for queues configured as priority queues; most Catalyst switches support the designation of a single egress queue as a priority queue.

Priority queuing is useful for voice applications in which voice traffic occupies the priority queue. However, since this type of scheduling can result in queue starvation in the non-priority queues, the remaining queues are subject to the WRR queuing to avoid this issue.

Custom Queuing

Another method of queuing available on Cisco switches strictly for WAN interfaces is Custom Queuing (CQ), which reserves a percentage of available bandwidth for an interface for each selected traffic type. If a particular type of traffic is not using the reserved bandwidth, other queues and types of traffic might use the remaining bandwidth.

CQ is statically configured and does not provide for automatic adaptation for changing network conditions. In addition, CQ is not recommended on high-speed WAN interfaces; refer to the configuration guides for CQ support on LAN interfaces and configuration details. See the configuration guide for each Cisco switch for supported CQ configurations.

Congestion Avoidance

Congestion-avoidance techniques monitor network traffic loads in an effort to anticipate and avoid congestion at common network bottleneck points. Switches and routers achieve congestion avoidance through packet dropping using complex algorithms (versus the simple tail-drop algorithm). Campus networks more commonly use congestion-avoidance techniques on WAN interfaces (versus Ethernet interfaces) because of the limited bandwidth of WAN interfaces. However, for Ethernet interfaces of considerable congestion, congestion avoidance is useful.

Tail Drop

When an interface of a router or switch cannot transmit a packet immediately because of congestion, the router or switch queues the packet. The router or switch eventually transmits the packet from the queue. If the arrival rate of packets for transmission on an interface exceeds the router's or switch's capability to buffer the traffic, the router or switch simply drops the packets. This behavior is called tail drop because all packets for transmission attempting to enter an egress queue are dropped until there is space in the queue for another packet. Tail drop is the default behavior on Cisco switch interfaces.

For environments with a large number of TCP flows or flows where arbitrary packet drops are detrimental, tail drop is not the best approach to dropping frames. Moreover, tail drop has these shortcomings with respect to TCP flows:

- The dropping of frames usually affects ongoing TCP sessions. Arbitrary dropping of frames with a TCP session results in concurrent TCP sessions simultaneously backing off and restarting, yielding a "saw-tooth" effect. As a result, inefficient link utilization occurs at the congestion point (TCP global synchronization).

- Aggressive TCP flows might seize all space in output queues over normal TCP flow as a result of tail drop.

- Excessive queuing of packets in the output queues at the point of congestion results in delay and jitter as packets await transmission.

- No differentiated drop mechanism exists; premium traffic is dropped in the same manner as best-effort traffic.

- Even in the event of a single TCP stream across an interface, the presence of other non-TCP traffic might congest the interface. In this scenario, the feedback to the TCP protocol is poor; as a result, TCP cannot adapt properly to the congested network.

Weighted Random Early Detection

WRED is a congestion-avoidance mechanism that is useful for backbone speeds. WRED attempts to avoid congestion by randomly dropping packets with a certain classification when output buffers reach a specific threshold.

Figure 7-21 illustrates the behavior of TCP with and without RED. As illustrated in the diagram, RED smoothes TCP sessions because it randomly drops packets, which ultimately reduces TCP windows. Without RED, TCP flows go through a slow start simultaneously. The end result of RED is better link utilization.

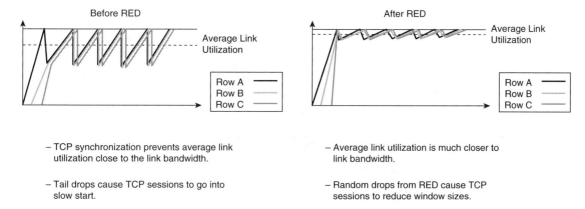

- TCP synchronization prevents average link
  utilization close to the link bandwidth.

- Tail drops cause TCP sessions to go into
  slow start.

- Average link utilization is much closer to
  link bandwidth.

- Random drops from RED cause TCP
  sessions to reduce window sizes.

Figure 7-21   *Link Utilization Optimizations with Congestion Avoidance*

RED randomly drops packets at configured threshold values (percentage full) of output buffers. As more packets fill the output queues, the switch randomly drops frames in an attempt to avoid congestion without the saw-tooth TCP problem. RED works only when the output queue is not full; when the output queue is full, the switch tail-drops any additional packets that attempt to occupy the output queue. However, the probability of dropping a packet rises as the output queue begins to fill above the RED threshold.

RED works well for TCP flows but not for other types of traffic, such as UDP flows and voice traffic. WRED is similar to RED except that WRED takes into account classification of frames. For example, for a single output queue, a switch configuration might consist of a WRED threshold of 50 percent for all best-effort traffic for DSCP values up to 20, and 80 percent for all traffic with a DSCP value between 20 and 31. In this example, the switch drops existing packets in the output queue with a DSCP of 0 to 20 when the queue's threshold reaches 50 percent. If the queue continues to fill to the 80 percent threshold, the switch then begins to drop existing packets with DSCP values above 20. If the output queue is full even with WRED configured, the switch tail-drops any additional packets that attempt to occupy the output queue. The end result of the WRED configuration is that the switch is less likely to drop packets with higher priorities (higher DSCP value). Figure 7-22 illustrates the WRED algorithm pictorially.

On most Cisco switches, WRED is configurable per queue. Nevertheless, it is possible to use WRR and WRED together. A best-practice recommendation is to designate a strict-priority queue for high-priority traffic using WRR and use WRED for congestion avoidance with the remaining queues designated for data traffic.

For planning for the campus network, consider using WRED on highly congested interfaces, particularly WAN interfaces that interconnect data centers.

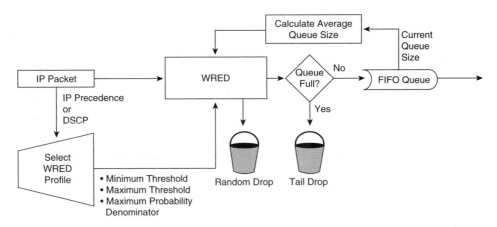

Figure 7-22 *Weighted Random Early Detection*

Implementing IP Multicast in the Campus Network

The demand is increasing for Internet, intranet, and multimedia applications in which one sender transmits to a group of receivers simultaneously. Examples of these applications include the following:

■ Transmitting a corporate message to all employees

■ Broadcasting video and audio, including interactive video for distance learning and IPTV

■ Transmitting data from a centralized data warehouse to multiple departments

■ Communicating stock quotes to brokers

■ Computing collaboratively

■ Algorithmic trading floor applications using cloud computing

Subsequently, using IP multicast instead of unicast to distribute this information reduces the overall network load and bandwidth consumption. This is a result of IP multicast's simultaneous distribution of an IP data frame to a host group that is defined by a single multicast IP address, or flow. To accomplish this same distribution with unicast would require the source to send a unicast frame to each host independently.

Note Multicast reduces overall network load and bandwidth by distributing traffic to multiple end users simultaneously.

This section discusses IP multicast routing and its inherent advantages, functionality, and configuration in campus network. This chapter begins with an introduction to multicast and then discusses the fundamentals of the IP multicast. This chapter also discusses the important Layer 3 and Layer 2 multicast protocols and the design recommendation for deploying multicast in multilayer switched networks.

Introduction to IP Multicast

Multimedia applications offer the integration of sound, graphics, animation, text, and video. As the ways of conducting business have become more complex, these types of applications have become increasingly popular in the enterprise networks. However, applying several multimedia applications onto a multilayer switched network and sending the multimedia streams over a campus data network is a complicated process due to bandwidth consumption on the network.

Multimedia traffic uses one of the following methods of transmission, each of which has a different effect on network bandwidth:

- **Unicast:** With a unicast design, an application sends one copy of each packet to every client's unicast address. As a result, unicast transmission has significant scaling restrictions. If the group is large, the same information must be carried multiple times, even on shared links.

- **Broadcast:** In a broadcast design, an application sends only one copy of each packet using a broadcast address. Broadcasting a packet to all devices is inefficient, except in the case where only a small subset of the network actually needs to see the packet. Broadcast multimedia is dispersed throughout the network similarly to normal broadcast traffic in that every host device must process the broadcast multimedia data frame. However, unlike standard broadcast frames, which are generally small, multimedia broadcasts can reach data rates as high as 13 Mbps or more. Even if an end station is not using multimedia applications, the device still processes the broadcast traffic. This requirement might use most, if not all, of the allocated bandwidth for each device. For this reason, Cisco highly discourages broadcast implementation for applications delivering data, voice, or video to multiple receivers.

- **Multicast:** The most efficient solution to transmit multimedia applications is multicast, which falls between unicast and broadcast. In multicast transmission, a multimedia server sends one copy of each packet to a special address that represents multiple clients. Unlike the unicast environment, a multicast server sends out a single data stream to multiple clients. Unlike the broadcast environment, the client device decides whether to listen to the multicast address. Multicasting saves bandwidth and controls network traffic by forcing the network to forward packets only when necessary. By eliminating traffic redundancy, multicasting reduces network bandwidth consumption and host processing. Furthermore, Catalyst switches can process IP multicast packets and deliver those packets only to receivers that request receipt of those packets at both Layer 2 and Layer 3.

IP multicast is the transmission of an IP data packet to a host group that is defined by a single IP address called a multicast IP address. A host can join or leave the multicast IP group dynamically regardless of the location or number of members. An important characteristic of the multicast is its capability to limit variation in delivery time (jitter) of IP multicast frames along the complete server-to-client path.

In Figure 7-23, the video server transmits a single video stream for each multicast group. A multicast, or host, group is defined as a set of host devices listening to a specific multicast address. Cisco routers and switches replicate the video stream as required to the host groups that arc in the path. This technique enables an arbitrary number of clients to subscribe to the multicast address and receive the stream. One host can be a part of one or more multicast groups for multiple applications. In addition, routers can transmit multiple data streams for different applications for a single group address.

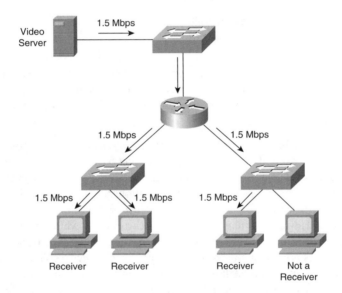

Figure 7-23 *Multicast Traffic*

In the multicast scenario shown in Figure 7-23 only 1.5 Mbps of server-to-network bandwidth is utilized, leaving the remaining bandwidth free for other uses.

Note In a unicast scenario, the server sequences through a transmission of multiple copies of the data, so variability in delivery time is large, especially for large transmissions or large distribution lists.

IP multicast relies on the concept of a virtual group address called the multicast IP address. In IP unicast routing, a packet is routed from a source address to a destination address, traversing the IP network on a hop-by-hop basis. In IP multicast, the packet's destination address is not assigned to a single destination. Instead, receivers join a group; when they do, packets addressed to that group begin flowing to them. All members of the group receive the packet; a host must be a member of the group to receive the packet. Multicast sources do not need to be members of that group. In Figure 7-24, packets sent by group member 3 (represented by the solid arrows) are received by group members 1 and 2 but not by the nonmember of the group. The nonmember host can also send packets (represented by the dotted arrows) to the multicast group that are received by all three group members because all the new hosts are members of the multicast group. Group members 1 and 2 do not send multicast packets; they are just the receivers.

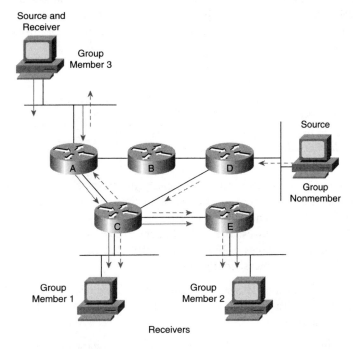

Figure 7-24 *Multicast Group Membership*

IP multicast traffic uses UDP as the transport layer protocol. Unlike TCP, UDP adds no reliability, flow control, or error-recovery functions to IP. Because of the simplicity of UDP, data packet headers contain fewer bytes and consume less network overhead than TCP.

Because the location of hosts in the group is widely spread in the network, the multicast router sends the packets to respective multiple interfaces to reach all the hosts. This makes the multicast forwarding more complex. To avoid duplication, several multicast routing protocols use reverse path forwarding (RPF), discussed in the section "Reverse Path Forwarding," later in this chapter.

This section discusses the following fundamentals of IP multicast in more detail:

■ Multicast IP address structure

■ Multicast MAC address structure

- Reverse path forwarding

- Multicast forwarding tree

Multicast IP Address Structure

The range of IP addresses is divided into classes based on the high-order bits of a 32-bit IP address. IP multicast uses the Class D addresses, which range from 224.0.0.0 to 239.255.255.255. These addresses consist of binary 1110 as the most significant bits (MSB) in the first octet, followed by a 28-bit group address, as shown in Figure 7-25. Unlike with Class A, B, and C IP addresses, the last 28 bits of a Class D address are unstructured.

Figure 7-25 *Multicast IP Address Structure*

These remaining 28 bits of the IP address identify the multicast group ID, which is a single address that is typically written as decimal numbers in the range 224.0.0.0 to 239.255.255.255. The Internet Assigned Numbers Authority (IANA) controls the assignment of IP multicast addresses. The Class D address range is used only for the group address or destination address of IP multicast traffic. The source address for multicast datagrams is always the unicast source address.

IP multicast addresses specify a set of IP hosts that have joined a group and are interested in receiving multicast traffic designated for that particular group. Table 7-5 outlines the IP multicast address conventions.

Applications allocate multicast addresses dynamically or statically. Dynamic multicast addressing provides applications with a group address on demand. Because dynamic multicast addresses have a specific lifetime, applications must request this type of address only for as long as the address is needed.

Table 7-5 *Multicast IP Address Ranges*

Description	Range
Reserved link local addresses	224.0.0.0 to 224.0.0.255
Globally scoped addresses	224.0.1.0 to 238.255.255.255
Source-specific multicast addresses	232.0.0.0 to 232.255.255.255
GLOP addresses	233.0.0.0 to 233.255.255.255
Limited-scope addresses	239.0.0.0 to 239.255.255.255

Statically allocated multicast addresses are reserved for specific protocols that require well-known addresses, such as Open Shortest Path First (OSPF). IANA assigns these well-known addresses, which are called permanent host groups and are similar in concept to the well-known TCP and UDP port numbers.

The following sections discuss the details of the multicast addresses listed in Table 7-5.

Reserved Link Local Addresses

IANA has reserved addresses in the range 224.0.0.0 to 224.0.0.255 (link local destination addresses) to be used by network protocols on a local network segment. Routers do not forward packets in this address range, because these packets are typically sent with a Time-To-Live (TTL) value of 1. Network protocols use these addresses for automatic router discovery and to communicate important routing information. For example, OSPF uses the IP addresses 224.0.0.5 and 224.0.0.6 to exchange link-state information.

Address 224.0.0.1 identifies the all-hosts group. Every multicast-capable host must join this group when initializing its IP stack. If you send an ICMP echo request to this address, all multicast-capable hosts on the network answer the request with an ICMP echo reply.

Address 224.0.0.2 identifies the all-routers group. Multicast routers join this group on all multicast-enabled interfaces.

Globally Scoped Addresses

Addresses in the range 224.0.1.0 to 238.255.255.255 are called globally scoped addresses. Companies use these addresses to multicast data between organizations and across the Internet. Multicast applications reserve some of these addresses for use through IANA. For example, IANA reserves the IP address 224.0.1.1 for the Network Time Protocol (NTP).

Source-Specific Multicast Addresses

Addresses in the 232.0.0.0 to 232.255.255.255 range are reserved for Source-Specific Multicast (SSM), an extension of the Protocol Independent Multicast (PIM) protocol that allows for an efficient data-delivery mechanism in one-to-many communications. In SSM, forwarding decisions are based on both group and source addresses, which is referred to as (S,G). The special notation of (S,G), pronounced "S comma G," uses S as the IP address of the source and G as the multicast group address. This unique (S,G) is known within SSM as a channel. SSM also removes address allocation problems because the source address makes each channel unique. SSM requires that the host be aware of the source and the group it wants data from and a method to signal this (S,G) requirement to the router.

GLOP Addresses

RFC 3180, "GLOP Addressing in 233/8," proposes that the 233.0.0.0 to 233.255.255.255 address range be reserved for statically defined addresses by organizations that already have an autonomous system number reserved. This practice is called GLOP addressing and the term is not an acronym. The autonomous system number of the domain is embedded into the second and third octets of the 233.0.0.0 to 233.255.255.255 address range. For example, the autonomous system 62010 is written in hexadecimal format as F23A. Separating the two octets F2 and 3A results in 242 and 58 in decimal format, respectively. These values result in a subnet of 233.242.58.0/24 that is globally reserved for autonomous system 62010 to use.

Limited-Scope Addresses

Addresses in the 239.0.0.0 to 239.255.255.255 range are called limited-scope addresses or administratively scoped addresses. These addresses are described in RFC 2365, "Administratively Scoped IP Multicast," to be constrained to a local group or organization. Companies, universities, or other organizations use limited-scope addresses to have local multicast applications where edge routers to the Internet do not forward the multicast frames outside their intranet domain.

Multicast MAC Address Structure

Similar to the manner in which an IP address maps to a unique MAP address, an IP multicast address also maps to a unique multicast MAC address. The multicast MAC address is derived from the IP multicast address.

Multicast MAC addresses start with the 25-bit prefix 0x01-00-5E (which in binary is 00000001.00000000.01011110.0xxxxxxx.xxxxxxxx.xxxxxxxx), where x represents a wildcard) with the 25th bit set to 0. Because all the IP multicast addresses have the first 4 bits set to 1110, the remaining 28 least significant bits (LSB) of multicast IP addresses must map into the 23 LSBs of the MAC address. As a result, the MAC address loses 5 bits of uniqueness in the IP-to-MAC address mapping process. The 5 bits that are not used are the 5 MSBs of the 28 remaining LSBs after 4-bit, 1110, MSBs. This method for mapping multicast IP addresses to MAC addresses results in a 32:1 mapping, where each multicast MAC address represents a possible 32 distinct IP multicast addresses. Figure 7-26 shows an example of the multicast IP-to-MAC address mapping.

A host that joins one multicast group programs its network interface card to listen to the IP-mapped MAC address. If the same MAC address maps to a second MAC multicast address already in use, the host CPU processes both sets of IP multicast frames. Furthermore, because switches forward frames based on the multicast MAC address if configured for Layer 2 multicast snooping, they forward frames to all the members corresponding to other IP multicast addresses of the same MAC address mapping, even if the frames belong to a different IP multicast group. For example, multicast IP addresses 238.1.1.2 and 238.129.1.2 both map to the same multicast MAC address 01:00:5E:01:01:02. As a result, a host that registered to group 238.1.1.2 also receives the traffic from 238:129:1.2 because the same MAC multicast address is used by both IP multicast flows. It is recommended to avoid overlapping when implementing multicast applications in the multilayer switched network by tuning the destination IP multicast addresses at the application level.

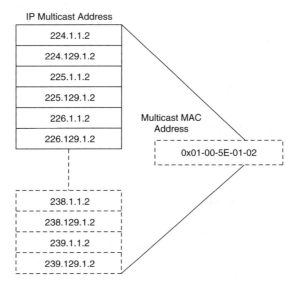

Figure 7-26   *Sample Multicast IP-to-MAC Mapping*

Reverse Path Forwarding

Multicast-capable routers and multilayer switches create distribution trees that control the path that IP multicast traffic takes through the network to achieve loop-free forwarding. Reverse Path Forwarding (RPF) is the mechanism that performs an incoming interface check to determine whether to forward or drop an incoming multicast frame. RPF is a key concept in multicast forwarding. This RPF check helps to guarantee that the distribution tree for multicast is loop-free. In addition, RPF enables routers to correctly forward multicast traffic down the distribution tree.

In unicast routing, traffic is routed through the network along the path from the single source to the single destination host. A router that is forwarding unicast packets does not consider the source address, by default; the router considers only the destination address and how to forward the traffic toward the destination with the exception of specialized CEF features. Upon receipt of unicast packets, the router scans through its routing table for the destination address and then forwards a single copy of the unicast packet out the correct interface to the destination.

In multicast forwarding, the source is sending traffic to an arbitrary group of hosts that is represented by a single multicast group address. When a multicast router receives a multicast packet, it determines which direction is the upstream direction (toward the source) and which one is the downstream direction (toward the receivers). A router forwards a multicast packet only if the packet is received on the correct upstream interface determined by the RPF process.

Note, although routers build a separate IP multicast routing table, the RFP check is dependent on the unicast IP routing table for determining the correct upstream and downstream interfaces.

For traffic flowing down a source tree, the RPF check procedure works as follows:

■ The router looks up the source address in the unicast routing table to determine whether it arrived on the interface that is on the reverse path (lowest-cost path) back to the source.

■ If the packet has arrived on the interface leading back to the source, the RPF check is successful, and the router replicates and forwards the packet to the outgoing interfaces.

■ If the RPF check in the previous step fails, the router drops the packet and records the drop as an RPF failed drop.

The top portion of Figure 7-27 illustrates an example where the RPF check fails. The router in the figure receives a multicast packet from source 151.10.3.21 on Interface S0. A check of the unicast route table shows that this router uses Interface S1 as the egress interface for forwarding unicast data to 151.10.3.21. Because the packet instead arrived on Interface S0, the packet fails the RPF check, and the router drops the packet. In the bottom portion of Figure 7-27, the RPF check succeeds. With this example, the multicast packet arrives on Interface S1. The router checks the unicast routing table and finds that Interface S1 is the correct ingress interface. The RPF check passes, and the router forwards the packet.

In multilayer switched networks where multiple routers connect to the same LAN segment, only one router forwards the multicast traffic from the source to the receivers on the outgoing interfaces. This router is denoted as the Protocol Independent Multicast Designated Router (PIM DR) and is illustrated in Figure 7-28. Router A, the PIM-designated router (PIM DR), forwards data to VLAN 1 and VLAN 2. Router B receives the forwarded multicast traffic on VLAN 1 and VLAN 2, and it drops this traffic because the multicast traffic fails the RPF check. Traffic that fails the RPF check is called non-RPF traffic.

Multicast Forwarding Tree

Multicast-capable routers create multicast distribution trees that control the path that IP multicast traffic takes through the network to deliver traffic to all receivers.

The following are the two types of distribution trees:

■ Source trees

■ Shared trees

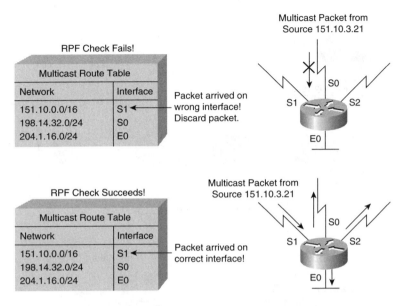

Figure 7-27 *Reverse Path Forwarding*

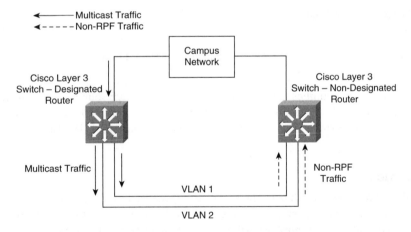

Figure 7-28 *Non-RPF Multicast Traffic*

Source Trees

The simplest form of a multicast distribution tree is a source tree with its root at the source and its branches forming a tree through the network to the receivers. Because this tree uses the shortest path through the network, it is also referred to as a shortest path tree (SPT).

Figure 7-29 shows an example of an SPT for group 224.1.1.1 rooted at the source, Host A, and connecting two receivers, Hosts B and C.

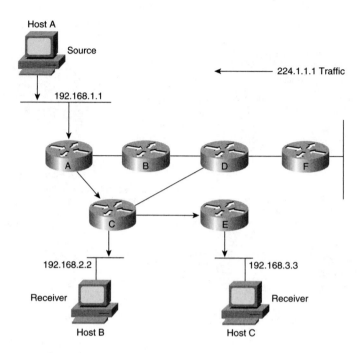

Figure 7-29 *IP Multicast Source Distribution Tree*

Using the (S,G) notation, the SPT for the example shown in Figure 7-29 is (192.168.1.1, 224.1.1.1).

The (S,G) notation implies that a separate SPT exists for each source sending to each group. For example, if host B is also sending traffic to group 224.1.1.1 and Hosts A and C are receivers, a separate (S,G) SPT would exist with a notation of (192.168.2.2, 224.1.1.1).

Shared Trees

Unlike source trees, which have their root at the source, shared trees use a single common root placed at some chosen point in the network. This shared root is called a rendezvous point (RP). Figure 7-30 shows a shared unidirectional tree for the group 224.1.1.1 with the root located at Router D. Source traffic is sent toward the RP on a shared tree. The traffic is then forwarded down the shared tree from the RP to reach all the receivers unless the receiver is located between the source and the RP, in which case the multicast traffic is serviced directly.

In Figure 7-30 multicast traffic from the sources, Hosts A and D, travels to the root (Router D) and then down the shared tree to the two receivers, Hosts B and C. Because all sources in the multicast group use a common shared tree, a wildcard notation written as (*,G), pronounced "star comma G," represents the tree. In this case, * means all sources, and G represents the multicast group. Therefore, the shared tree shown in the figure is written as (*, 224.1.1.1).

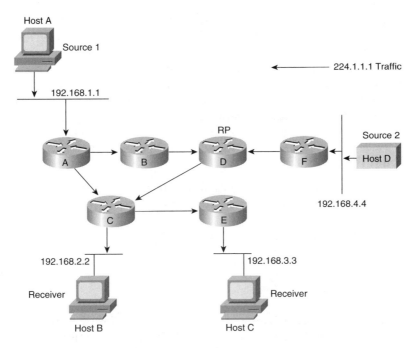

Figure 7-30 *IP Multicast Shared Tree Distribution*

Comparing Source Trees and Shared Trees

Both source trees and shared trees avoid multicast traffic loops. Routing devices replicate the multicast packets only where the tree branches.

Members of multicast groups join or leave at any time; as a result, the distribution trees update dynamically. When all the active receivers on a particular branch stop requesting traffic for a particular multicast group, the routers prune that branch from the tree and stop forwarding traffic down it. If one receiver on that branch becomes active and requests the multicast traffic, the router dynamically modifies the distribution tree and starts forwarding traffic again.

Source trees have the advantage of creating the optimal path between the source and the receivers. This advantage guarantees the minimum amount of network latency for forwarding multicast traffic. However, this optimization requires additional overhead because the routers maintain path information for each source. In a network that has thousands of sources and thousands of groups, this overhead quickly becomes a resource issue on routers or multilayer switches. Memory consumption and troubleshooting complexity from the size of the multicast routing table are factors that network designers need to take into consideration when designing multicast networks.

Shared trees have the advantage of requiring the minimum amount of state information in each router. This advantage lowers the overall memory requirements and complexity for a network that allows only shared trees. The disadvantage of shared trees is that, under certain circumstances, the paths between the source and receivers might not be the optimal paths, which can introduce additional latency in packet delivery. As a result, shared trees might overuse some links and leave others unused, whereas source-based trees (where sources are distributed) usually distribute traffic across a set of links. For example, in Figure 7-30, the shortest path between Host A (Source 1) and Host B (a receiver) is between Router A and Router C. Because Router D is the root for a shared tree, the traffic traverses Routers A, B, D, and then C. Network designers need to carefully consider the placement of the RP when implementing a shared tree–only environment.

IP Multicast Protocols

Similar to IP unicast, IP multicast uses its own routing, management, and Layer 2 protocols. The following are two important multicast protocols:

- Protocol Independent Multicast (PIM)
- Internet Group Management Protocol (IGMP)

PIM

A multicast routing protocol is responsible for the construction of multicast delivery trees and enabling multicast packet forwarding. Different IP multicast routing protocols use different techniques to construct multicast trees and to forward packets. The PIM routing protocol leverages whichever unicast routing protocols are used to populate the unicast routing table to make multicast forwarding decisions.

Furthermore, routers use the PIM neighbor discovery mechanism to establish PIM neighbors using hello messages to the ALL-PIM-Routers (224.0.0.13) multicast address for building and maintaining PIM multicast distribution trees. In addition, routers use PIM hello messages to elect the designated router (DR) for a multicast LAN network.

PIM encompasses two distinct versions: PIM version 1 and PIM version 2. This chapter compares the two in the section "Comparison and Compatibility of PIM Version 1 and Version 2," later in this chapter.

PIM has the following four modes of operation, which are discussed in the following sections:

- PIM dense mode
- PIM sparse mode
- PIM sparse-dense mode
- PIM bidirectional

Sparse-dense mode is most common in large enterprise networks. There is a small movement toward bidirectional PIM in large enterprise networks; however, as of early 2010, few large enterprise adopters exist.

PIM Dense Mode

PIM dense mode (PIM-DM) multicast routing protocols rely on periodic flooding of the network with multicast traffic to set up and maintain the distribution tree. PIM relies on its neighbor information to form the distribution tree. PIM-DM uses a source distribution tree to forward multicast traffic, which is built by respective routers as soon as any multicast source begins transmitting. Figure 7-31 illustrates an example of PIM-DM.

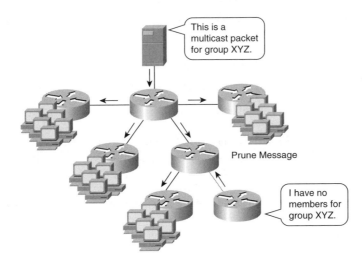

Figure 7-31   *PIM Dense Mode*

PIM Dense Mode is obsolete and no longer deployed in campus networks. This section still exists for the purpose of completeness.

PIM-DM assumes that the multicast group members are densely distributed throughout the network and that bandwidth is plentiful, meaning that almost all hosts on the network belong to the group. When a router configured for PIM-DM receives a multicast packet, the router performs the RPF check to validate the correct interface for the source and then forwards the packet to all the interfaces configured for multicasting until pruning and truncating occurs. All downstream routers receive the multicast packet until the multicast traffic times out. PIM-DM sends a pruning message upstream only under the following conditions:

- Traffic arrives on a non-RPF, point-to-point interface; this is the next-hop router interface that does not have a best route toward the multicast source.

- A leaf router without receivers sends a prune message, as shown in Figure 7-31, and the router, which does not have members or receivers, sends the prune message to the upstream router.

- A nonleaf router receives a prune message from all of its neighbors.

In summary, PIM-DM works best when numerous members belong to each multimedia group. PIM floods the multimedia packet to all routers in the network and then prunes routers that do not service members of that particular multicast group.

Consider when planning multicast in the campus network that PIM-DM is most useful in the following cases:

- Senders and receivers are in close proximity to one another.

- PIM-SM goes through a dense-mode flooding phase before fully relying on the RP for multicast forwarding.

- There are few senders and many receivers.

- The volume of multicast traffic is high.

- The stream of multicast traffic is constant.

Nevertheless, PIM-DM is not the method of choice for most campus networks enterprise because of its scalability limitations and flooding properties.

PIM Sparse Mode

The second approach to multicast routing, PIM sparse mode (PIM-SM), is based on the assumptions that the multicast group members are sparsely distributed throughout the network and that bandwidth is limited.

It is important to note that PIM-SM does not imply that the group has few members, just that they are widely dispersed. In this case, flooding would unnecessarily waste network bandwidth and could cause serious performance problems. Therefore, PIM-SM multicast routing protocols rely on more selective techniques to set up and maintain multicast trees.

PIM-SM protocols begin with an empty distribution tree and add branches only as the result of explicit requests to join the distribution. Figure 7-32 illustrates a sample of PIM sparse mode.

With PIM-SM, each data stream goes to a relatively small number of segments in the campus network. Instead of flooding the network to determine the status of multicast members, PIM-SM defines an RP. When a sender wants to send data, it first does so to the RP. When a receiver wants to receive data, it registers with the RP, as shown in Figure 7-32. When the data stream begins to flow from sender to RP to receiver, the routers in the path automatically optimize the path to remove unnecessary hops. PIM-SM assumes that no hosts want the multicast traffic unless they specifically ask for it. In PIM-SM, the shared tree mode can be switched to a source tree after a certain threshold to have the best route to the source. All Cisco IOS routers and switches, by default, have the SPT threshold set to 0, such that the last-hop router switches to SPT mode as soon as the host starts receiving the multicast, to take advantage of the best route for the multicast traffic.

Note   To clarify a common confusion, sparse-mode only uses the RP as a initial point to forward multicast by default; configuration options exist to foreword all traffic to the RP.

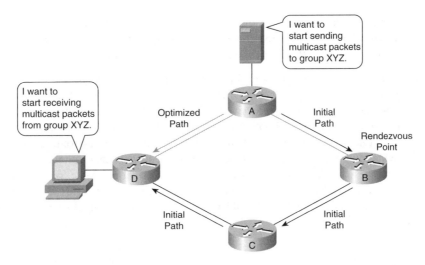

Figure 7-32   *Multicast PIM Sparse Mode*

PIM-SM is optimized for environments where there are many multipoint data streams. When planning for multicast deployments in the campus network, choose PIM-SM with IP under the following scenarios:

■   There are many multipoint data streams.

■   At any moment, there are few receivers in a group.

■   The type of traffic is intermittent or busty.

PIM Sparse-Dense Mode

PIM can simultaneously support dense mode operation for some multicast groups and sparse mode operation for others. Cisco has implemented an alternative to choosing just dense mode or just sparse mode on a router interface, however. This was necessitated by a change in the paradigm for forwarding multicast traffic via PIM that became apparent during its development. It turned out that it was more efficient to choose sparse or dense mode on a per-group basis rather than a per-router interface basis. Sparse-dense mode facilitates this ability.

PIM sparse-dense mode enables individual groups to use either sparse or dense mode depending on whether RP information is available for that group. If the router learns RP information for a particular group, sparse mode is used; otherwise, dense mode is used. Note, PIM spare-dense mode is seldom used in campus networks.

PIM Bidirectional

Bidirectional PIM (bidir-PIM) is an extension of the existing PIM-SM feature and shares many SPT operations. Bidir-PIM is suited for multicast with larger numbers of sources.

Bidir-PIM can unconditionally forward source traffic toward the RP upstream on the shared tree without registering for sources as in PIM-SM. This enables traffic to be passed up the shared tree toward the RP. To avoid multicast packet loops, bidir-PIM introduces a mechanism called designated forwarder (DF) election, which establishes a loop-free SPT rooted at the RP. The DF is responsible for forwarding multicast packets received on that network upstream to the RP. One DF exists for every RP of bidirectional groups.

A router creates only (*,G) entries for bidirectional groups. The outgoing interface list of multicast traffic (olist) of a (*,G) entry includes all the interfaces for which the router has been elected as DF and that have received either an IGMP or a PIM join message. If a packet is received from the RPF interface toward the RP, the packet is forwarded down-stream according to the olist of the (*,G) entry. Otherwise, when the router that is DF for the receiving interface forwards the packet toward the RP, all other routers must discard the packet. These modifications are necessary and sufficient to enable forwarding of traf-fic in all routers based solely on the (*, G) multicast routing entries. This feature elimi-nates any source-specific state and enables scaling capability to an arbitrary number of sources.

Automating Distribution of RP

PIM-SM and PIM sparse-dense modes use various methods, discussed in this section, to automate the distribution of the RP. This mechanism has the following benefits:

- It eliminates the need to manually configure RP information in every router and switch in the network.

- It is easy to use multiple RPs within a network to serve different group ranges.

- It enables load-splitting among different RPs and enables the arrangement of RPs according to the location of group participants.

- It avoids inconsistency; manual RP configurations may cause connectivity problems if not configured properly.

PIM uses the following mechanisms to automate the distribution of the RP:

- Auto-RP

- Bootstrap router (BSR)

- Anycast-RP

- MSDPAnycast-RP and MSDP are outside the context of SWITCH; more information about these mechanisms can be found on Cisco.com.

Auto-RP

Auto-RP automates the distribution of group-to-RP mappings in a PIM network. Group-to-RP mappings define which multicast groups use which RP for sparse mode or sparse-dense mode.

All routers and Layer 3 devices in the PIM network learn about the active group-to-RP mapping from the RP mapping agent by automatically joining the Cisco-RP-discovery (224.0.1.40) multicast group. The RP mapping agent is the router that sends the authoritative discovery packets that notify other routers which group-to-RP mapping to use, as shown in Figure 7-33. The RP mapping agent sends this information every 60 seconds. Such a role is necessary if conflicts occur (such as overlapping group-to-RP ranges).

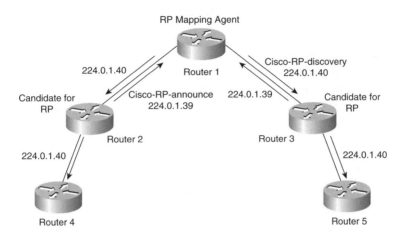

Figure 7-33   *Auto-RP Mechanism*

Mapping agents also use IP multicast to discover which routers in the network are possible candidate RPs by joining the Cisco-RP-announce (224.0.1.39) group to receive candidate RP announcements. Candidate RPs send RP-announce multicast messages for the particular groups every 60 seconds. The RP mapping agent uses the information contained in the announcement to create entries in group-to-RP cache. RP mapping agents create only one entry per group. If more than one RP candidate announces the same range, the RP mapping agent uses the IP address of the RP to break the tie.

It is recommended that an RP mapping agent be configured on the router with the best connectivity and stability. All routers within the TTL number of hops from the RP mapping router receive the Auto-RP discovery messages.

Sparse mode environments require a default RP to join the Auto-RP discovery group, but sparse-dense mode environments do not need a default RP for Auto-RP. It is recommended to use RP for the global groups. There is no need to reconfigure the group address range that the RP serves. RPs that are discovered dynamically through Auto-RP take precedence over statically configured RPs. Typically, campus networks use a second RP for the local groups.

Bootstrap Router

A bootstrap router (BSR) is a router or Layer 3 device that is responsible for distributing RP. Using a BSR is another way to distribute group-to-RP mapping information in the PIM multicast network. However, BSR works only with PIM version 2. A BSR uses hop-to-hop flooding of special BSR messages instead of multicast to distribute the group-to-RP mapping.

BSR uses an election mechanism to select the BSR router from a set of candidate routers and multilayer switches in the domain. The BSR election uses the BSR priority of the device contained in the BSR messages that flow hop-by-hop through the network. Each BSR device examines the message and forwards it out all interfaces only if the message has either a higher BSR priority than the router's own BSR priority or has the same BSR priority but with a higher BSR IP address.

The elected BSR sends BSR messages with a TTL of 1 with its IP address to enable candidate BSRs to learn automatically about the elected BSR. Neighboring PIM version 2 routers or multilayer switches receive the BSR message and multicast the message out all other interfaces (except the one on which it was received) with a TTL of 1 to distribute the BSR messages hop-by-hop, as shown in Figure 7-34.

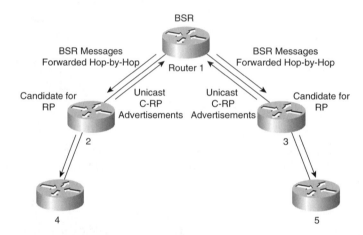

Figure 7-34   *BSR Mechanisms*

Candidate RPs send candidate RP advertisements showing the group range for which each is responsible to the BSR, which stores this information in its local candidate RP cache. The BSR includes this information in its bootstrap messages and disseminates it to all PIM routers using 224.0.0.13 with a TTL of 1 in the domain hop-by-hop. Based on this information, all routers can map multicast groups to specific RPs. As long as a router is receiving the bootstrap message, it has a current RP map. Routers and multilayer switches select the same RP for a given group because they all use a common RP hashing algorithm.

Comparison and Compatibility of PIM Version 1 and Version 2

PIM version 2 is a standards-based multicast protocol in the Internet Engineering Task Force (IETF). Cisco highly recommends using PIM version 2 in the entire multilayer switched network. The Cisco PIM version 2 implementation enables interoperability and transition between version 1 and version 2, although there are a few caveats. For example, if a PIM version 2 router detects a PIM version 1 router, the version 2 router downgrades itself to version 1 until all version 1 routers have been shut down or upgraded.

PIM version 2 uses the BSR to discover and announce RP-to-group mapping information for each group prefix to all the routers in a PIM domain. This is the same function accomplished by Auto-RP. However, the BSR feature is part of the PIM version 2 specifications because bootstrap messages are sent on a hop-by-hop basis, and a PIM version 1 router prevents these messages from reaching all routers in a network. Therefore, if a network has a PIM version 1 router with Cisco routers, it is best to use Auto-RP rather than the bootstrap mechanism. Nevertheless, Auto-RP is a standalone protocol, separate from PIM version 1, and is Cisco proprietary. The BSR mechanism interoperates with Auto-RP on Cisco routers.

A PIM version 2 BSR that is also an Auto-RP mapping agent automatically advertises the RP elected by Auto-RP. That is, Auto-RP prevails in its imposition of a single RP on every router in the group.

In summary, PIM version 2 includes the following improvements over PIM version 1:

- A single, active RP exists per multicast group, with multiple backup RPs. This single RP compares to multiple active RPs for the same group in PIM version 1.

- A BSR provides a fault-tolerant, automated RP discovery and distribution mechanism. Thus, routers dynamically learn the group-to-RP mappings.

- Sparse mode and dense mode are properties of a group, as opposed to an interface. Cisco strongly recommends sparse-dense mode configurations.

- PIM join and prune messages have more flexible encodings for multiple address families.

- A more flexible hello packet format replaces the query packet to encode current and future capability options.

- Register messages to an RP indicate whether they were sent by a border router or a designated router.

- PIM no longer uses the IGMP protocol for transport; PIM version 2 uses stand-alone packets.

When planning for PIM deployments in the campus network, prefer to use PIM version 2 over PIM version 1.

Note   Several newer versions of PIM sparse-mode protocols are gaining popularity in campus networks. These versions include the following:

- Any Source Multicast (ASM), which uses RPs with either shortest path tree or shared tree.

- Source Specific Multicast (SSM)), which does not use RP and is designed using only shortest path tree.

- Bidirectional PIM (Bi-dir PIM), which is based on shared trees only.

These versions are outside the scope of CCNP SWITCH; consult Cisco.com for additional information about these versions.

Configuring Internet Group Management Protocol

Hosts use IGMP to dynamically register themselves in a multicast group on a particular LAN. Hosts identify group memberships by sending IGMP messages to their local designated multicast router. Routers and multilayer switches, configured for IGMP, listen to IGMP messages and periodically send out queries to discover which groups are active or inactive on a particular subnet or VLAN.

The following list indicates the current versions of IGMP:

- IGMP version 1 (IGMPv1) RFC 1112

- IGMP version 2 (IGMPv2) RFC 2236

- IGMP version 3 (IGMPv3) RFC 3376

- IGMP version 3 lite (IGMPv3 lite)

IGMPv1

According to the IGMPv1 specification, one multicast router per LAN must periodically transmit host membership query messages to determine which host groups have members on the router's directly attached LAN networks. IGMP query messages are addressed to the all-host group (224.0.0.1) and have an IP TTL equal to 1. A TTL of 1 ensures that the corresponding router does not forward the query messages to any other multicast router.

When the end station receives an IGMP query message, the end station responds with a host membership report for each group to which the end station belongs.

IGMPv2

Version 2 of IGMP made several enhancements to the previous version, including the definition of a group-specific query. The group-specific query message enables a router to transmit a specific query to one particular group. IGMPv2 also defines a leave group message for the hosts, which results in lower leave latency.

There are four types of IGMP messages of concern to the host-router interaction:

- Membership query

- Version 2 membership report

- Leave report

- Version 1 membership report

IGMPv2 uses the IGMPv1 membership report for backward compatibility with IGMPv1. Newer versions of IGMP or multicast routing protocols use new message types. Any other or unrecognized message types are ignored.

IGMPv3

IGMPv3 is the next step in the evolution of IGMP. IGMPv3 adds support for source filtering that enables a multicast receiver to signal to a router the groups from which it wants to receive multicast traffic and from which sources to expect traffic. This membership information enables Cisco IOS Software to forward traffic from only those sources from which receivers requested the traffic.

In IGMPv3, the following types of IGMP messages exist:

- Version 3 membership query
- Version 3 membership report

IGMPv3 supports applications that explicitly signal sources from which they want to receive traffic. With IGMPv3, receivers signal membership to a multicast host group in one of the following two modes:

- **INCLUDE mode:** The receiver announces membership to a host group and provides a list of source addresses (the INCLUDE list) from which it wants to receive traffic.

- **EXCLUDE mode:** The receiver announces membership to a multicast group and provides a list of source addresses (the EXCLUDE list) from which it does not want to receive traffic. The host receives traffic only from sources whose IP addresses are not listed in the EXCLUDE list. To receive traffic from all sources, which is the behavior of IGMPv2, a host uses EXCLUDE mode membership with an empty EXCLUDE list.

IGMPv3 Lite

IGMPv3 lite is a Cisco-developed transitional solution for application developers to immediately start programming applications for SSM. Specifically, IGMPv3 lite enables application developers to write and run SSM applications on hosts that do not yet support IGMPv3 in their operating system kernel.

Applications require the Host Side IGMP Library (HSIL) for IGMPv3 lite. This software library provides applications with a subset of the IGMPv3 API required to write SSM applications. HSIL was developed for Cisco by Talarian.

One part of the HSIL is a client library linked to the SSM application. It provides the SSM subset of the IGMPv3 API to the SSM application. If possible, the library checks whether the operating system kernel supports IGMPv3. If it does, the API calls simply are passed through to the kernel. If the kernel does not support IGMPv3, the library uses the IGMPv3 lite mechanism.

When using the IGMPv3 lite mechanism, the library tells the operating system kernel to join to the whole multicast group, because joining to the whole group is the only method for the application to receive traffic for that multicast group for IGMPv1 or IGMPv2. In addition, the library signals the (S,G) channel subscriptions to an IGMPv3 lite server process. A server process is needed because multiple SSM applications might be on the same host. This server process then sends IGMPv3 lite-specific (S,G) channel subscriptions to the last-hop Cisco IOS router or multilayer switch.

This Cisco IOS router or multilayer switch then sees both the IGMPv1 or IGMPv2 group membership report from the operating system kernel and the (S,G) channel subscription from the HSIL daemon. If the router sees both of these messages, it interprets them as an SSM (S,G) channel subscription and joins the channel through PIM-SM. Refer to the documentation accompanying the HSIL software for more information on how to use IGMPv3 lite with your application.

IGMP Snooping

IGMP snooping is an IP multicast constraining mechanism that examines Layer 2 and Layer 3 IP multicast information to maintain a Layer 2 multicast forwarding table. This constrains multicast traffic at Layer 2 by configuring Layer 2 LAN ports dynamically to forward multicast traffic only to those ports that want to receive it.

IGMP snooping operates on multilayer switches, even switches that do not support Layer 3 routing. IGMP snooping requires the LAN switch to examine, or "snoop," the IGMP join and leave messages sent between hosts and the first-hop designated multicast router.

When the host joins multicast groups either by sending an unsolicited IGMP join message or by sending an IGMP join message in response to a general query from a multicast router, the switch sees an IGMP host report packet from a host for joining a particular multicast group. The switch snoops the IGMP packets and adds the host's interface from which the IGMP report packet originated to the associated multicast Layer 2 forwarding table entry. IGMP snooping forwards only the first host join message per multicast group to the multicast routers and suppresses the rest of the joining messages for that multicast group. The switch receives the multicast traffic from the multicast router for that group specified in the join message and forwards that multicast traffic to the interfaces where join messages were received.

When hosts want to leave a multicast group, either they ignore the periodic general IGMP queries sent by the multicast router (a process known as silent leave) or they send a group-specific IGMPv2 leave message. When the switch receives a group-specific IGMPv2 leave message from a host, the switch responds with a MAC-based group-specific query to determine whether any other devices connected on that VLAN are interested in receiving multicast traffic for the specific multicast group. If the switch does not receive an IGMP join message in response to the general query, the switch removes the table entry of the host. If the last leave message was from the only host in the group and the switch does not receive an IGMP join message in response to the general query, it removes the group entry and relays the IGMP leave message to the multicast router. The first-hop designated router then removes the group from that interface and stops forwarding multicast traffic on the interface for the group specified in the leave message.

IGMP snooping supports the fast-leave processing feature, which allows IGMP snooping to remove a Layer 2 interface from the multicast forwarding table without first responding with IGMP group-specific queries to the host port. Upon receiving a group-specific IGMP version 2 or 3 leave message, the switch immediately removes the interface from the Layer 2 forwarding table entry for that multicast group, unless a multicast router is detected on the respective interface. Fast-leave processing improves bandwidth management for all hosts in a VLAN on a multilayer switched network.

The IGMP protocol transmits messages as IP multicast packets; as a result, switches cannot distinguish IGMP packets from normal IP multicast data at Layer 2. Therefore, a switch running IGMP snooping must examine every multicast data packet to determine whether it contains pertinent IGMP control information. If IGMP snooping is implemented on a low-end switch with a slow CPU, this could have a severe performance impact when data is transmitted at high rates. The solution to this problem is to implement IGMP snooping with special ASICs that can perform IGMP snooping in hardware.

To configure IGMP snooping on a Cisco IOS switch, perform the following steps:

Step 1. Enable IGMP snooping globally. (By default, it is enabled globally.)

```
Switch(config)# ip igmp snooping
```

Step 2. (Optional.) Switches add multicast router ports to the forwarding table for every Layer 2 multicast entry. The switch learns of such ports through snooping IGMP queries, flowing PIM and DVMRP packets, or interpreting CGMP packets from other routers. Configure the IGMP snooping method. The default is PIM.

```
Switch(config)# ip igmp snooping vlan vlan-id mrouter learn [cgmp |
  pim-dvmrp]
```

Step 3. (Optional.) If needed, configure the router port statically. By default, IGMP snooping automatically detects the router ports.

```
Switch(config)# ip igmp snooping vlan vlan-id mrouter interface
  interface-num
```

Step 4. (Optional.) Configure IGMP fast leave if required.

```
Switch(config)# ip igmp snooping vlan vlan-id fast-leave
```
```
Switch(config)# ip igmp snooping vlan vlan-id immediate-leave
```

Step 5. (Optional.) By default, all hosts register and add the MAC address and port to the forwarding table automatically. If required, configure a host statically on an interface. Generally, static configurations are necessary when troubleshooting or working around IGMP problems.

```
Switch(config)# ip igmp snooping vlan vlan-id static mac-address
  interface interface-id
```

Note   The command syntax of some of the commands might be different for different switch platforms. Refer to the product documentation for more information.

To configure IP multicast on Catalyst switches running Cisco IOS, perform the following steps:

Step 1.   Enable multicast routing on Layer 3 globally.

```
Switch(config)# ip multicast-routing
```

Step 2.   Enable PIM on the interface that requires multicast.

```
Switch(config-if)# ip pim [dense-mode | sparse-mode | sparse-dense-mode]
```

Step 3.   (Optional.) Configure RP if you are running PIM sparse mode or PIM sparse-dense mode. The Cisco IOS Software can be configured so that packets for a single multicast group can use one or more RPs. It is important to configure the RP address on all routers (including the RP router). To configure the address of the RP, enter the following command in global configuration mode:

```
Switch(config)# ip pim rp-address ip-address [access-list-number] [override]
```

Step 4.   (Optional.) To designate a router as the candidate RP for all multicast groups or for a particular multicast group by using an access list, enter the following command in global configuration mode:

```
Switch(config)# ip pim send-rp-announce interface-type interface-number
scope ttl [group-list access-list-number] [interval seconds]
```

The TTL value defines the multicast boundaries by limiting the number of hops that the RP announcements can take.

Step 5.   (Optional.) To assign the role of RP mapping agent on the router configured in Step 4 for AutoRP, enter the following command in global configuration mode:

```
Switch(config)# ip pim send-rp-discovery scope ttl
```

Step 6.   (Optional.) All systems using Cisco IOS Release 11.3(2)T or later start in PIM version 2 mode by default. In case you need to reenable PIM version 2 or specify PIM version 1 for some reason, use the following command:

```
Switch(config-if)# ip pim version [1 | 2]
```

Step 7.   (Optional.) Configure a BSR border router for the PIM domain so that bootstrap messages do not cross this border in either direction. This ensures that different BSRs will be elected on the two sides of the PIM border. Configure this command on an interface such that no PIM version 2 BSR messages will be sent or received through the interface.

```
Switch(config-if)# ip pim bsr-border
```

Step 8. (Optional.) To configure an interface as a BSR candidate, issue the following command:

```
Switch(config)# ip pim bsr-candidate interface-type hash-mask-length [priority]
```

hash-mask-length is a 32-bit mask for the group address before the hash function is called. All groups with the same seed hash correspond to the same RP.

priority is configured as a number from 0 to 255. The BSR with the largest priority is preferred. If the priority values are the same, the device with the highest IP address is selected as the BSR. The default is 0.

Step 9. (Optional.) To configure an interface as an RP candidate for BSR router for particular multicast groups, issue the following command:

```
Switch(config)# ip pim rp-candidate interface-type interface-number ttl
 group-list access-list
```

Example 7-1 shows a sample configuration of PIM sparse mode in Cisco IOS with an RP address of 10.20.1.254.

Example 7-1 *Configuration of PIM Sparse Mode in Cisco IOS*

```
Router# conf t
Router(config)# ip multicast-routing
Router(config)# interface vlan 1
Router(config-if)# ip pim sparse-mode
Router(config-if)# interface vlan 3
Router(config-if)# ip pim sparse-mode
Router(config-if)# exit
Router(config)# ip pim rp-address 10.20.1.254
```

Example 7-2 shows a sample configuration of PIM sparse-dense mode in Cisco IOS with a candidate BSR.

Example 7-2 *Multicast Configuration of Sparse-Dense Mode with BSR*

```
Router(config)# ip multicast-routing
Router(config)# interface vlan 1
Router(config-if)# ip pim sparse-dense-mode
Router(config-if)# exit
Router(config)# ip pim bsr-candidate vlan 1 30 200
```

Example 7-3 shows a sample Cisco IOS configuration of the Auto-RP that is advertising the IP address of VLAN 1 as the RP.

Example 7-3 *IP Multicast Configuration of Sparse-Dense Mode with Auto-RP*

```
Router(config)# ip multicast-routing
Router(config)# interface vlan 1
Router(config-if)# ip pim sparse-dense-mode
Router(config-if)# exit
Router(config)# ip pim send-rp-announce vlan 1 scope 15 group-list 1
Router(config)# access-list 1 permit 225.25.25.0.0.0.0.255
Router(config)# exit
```

In addition to the preceding commands, every Cisco switch supports additional multicast tuning features such as rate limiting and altering the protocol timers. Refer to the product documentation for more information.

Preparing the Campus Infrastructure to Support Wireless

As previously noted, WLANs replace the Layer 1 transmission medium of a traditional wired network radio transmission over the air. This section focuses on the specific scenario's around a campus network deployment.

Wireless LAN Parameters

Supporting wireless requires additional WLAN preparation beyond the campus network implementation. Foremost, range, interference, performance, and security must be properly planned and prepared before campus network integration of the solution. This section focuses on deploying wireless in terms of its network connectivity to the Cisco switches. Planning for wireless range, interference, performance, and security are outside the scope of this book. The next section begins the discussion of preparing the campus network to support wireless with the standalone WLAN solution.

Configuring Switches to Support WLANs

The configuration for supporting WLANs in the campus is broken down into two sections focusing on the standalone and controller-based solution, respectively.

Preparing the Campus Network for Integration of a Standalone WLAN Solution

The access layer switch port configuration for standalone access points is straightforward. As a best practice, the switch and the access port interface are configured as a trunk port and carry at least a data and management VLAN. The management VLAN is used for administrative purposes and might or might not be the native VLAN. There can be one or more data VLANs. If there is more than one VLAN, each VLAN will be associated to different SSIDs. Upon associating to one of the available SSIDs, the wireless client becomes a station within the VLAN and associated IP subnet. For more information on SSIDs, consult basic WLAN information on Cisco.com.

Moreover, the switch might be configured to support Power over Ethernet (PoE); however, PoE is not a requirement, rather a feature to ease installations. PoE is covered more in the next section on voice in campus network as PoE is more commonly associated with voice installations. Lastly, as with any WLAN deployment, a DHCP server provides IP addresses, DNS, and so on for the access points and the wireless clients.

A model of this integration is illustrated in Figure 7-35.

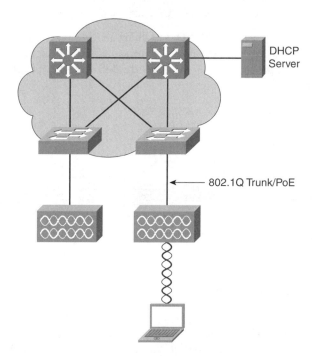

Figure 7-35   *Standalone WLAN Solution Integrated into Campus Network*

Preparing the Campus Network for Integration of a Controller-Based WLAN Solution

As with the standalone WLAN solution, the switch and the access port interface are configured as trunk port and carry at least a data and management VLAN. The management VLAN is used for administrative purposes and might or might not be the native VLAN. There can be one or more data VLANs.

Of note, the VLAN configured on the access points are not required to be the same VLANs configure on the controller. This is because the controller and the access points can be in different IP subnets.

Different than the standalone WLAN solution, the mapping of the SSID, VLAN, QoS, and IP subnet is done by the WLAN controller. When a client associates to an SSID on an access point, the client becomes a station within that VLAN and associated subnet connected to the WLAN controller. The wireless client then gets an IP address from the VLAN connected to the WLAN controller that is mapped to the SSID used by the client.

Any VLAN can be connected to the access point. All traffic arriving at the access point is encapsulated and sent to the controller. Therefore, a clear differentiation is made between the client VLAN and the access point VLAN. Therefore, the access point and the WLAN controller can be on same or different IP subnets, and there can be a Layer 3 IP router between access point and WLAN controller.

In this configuration, Layer 2 and Layer 3 roaming are supported by the WLAN controller, whether the access points connect to the same or to different controllers that are part of the same group. Figure 7-36 illustrates the behavior of the controller-based solution described.

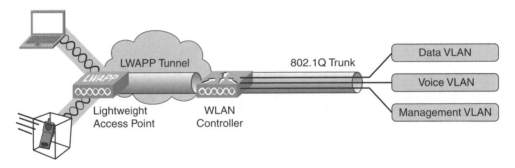

Figure 7-36   *Controller-Based WLAN Solution Integrated into Campus Network*

In the case of an HREAP, some WLANs are centrally switched, which means that data for these WLANs is encapsulated and sent to the controller, just like a standard controller-based access point. Some other WLANs are locally switched, which means that traffic is sent to the switch local to the HREAP and not sent to the controller.

The consequence of this behavior is that the port to an HREAP must be a 802.1Q trunk. The native VLAN is the HREAP VLAN that communicates with the controller.

Note   Access lists and firewalls on the network are required to enable the traffic between controllers, access points, and management stations for the successful operation of a wireless network. Consult Cisco.com for additional information on which TCP and UDP ports should be allowed through access-lists and firewalls for any WLAN solution.

In review, the configuration of Cisco switches connected to access points are simply trunk ports. Earlier chapters covered specific configuration of trunk ports; review the configuration details in those chapters for specific configuration outside. The next section goes over preparation details for voice.

Preparing the Campus Infrastructure to Support Voice

Implementing voice in a campus network requires close cooperation between network engineers and enterprise voice specialist. Voice integration needs to be planned thoroughly to integrate seamlessly into an existing campus network. When you reach the implementation phase, you need to configure the access switches for VoIP support. This section describes the step involved in the configuration required to support VoIP on campus switches. It also describes a simple test plan that can be used so that a phone properly communicates and integrates to the network infrastructure.

IP Telephony Components

The following list of IP telephony components reviews devices commonly found deployed in the campus networks:

- **IP Phones:** Support calls in an IP telephony network. They perform voice-to-IP (and vice versa) coding and compression using special hardware. IP Phones offer services such as user directory lookups and Internet access for stock quotes. The telephones are active network devices and require power for their operation. Typically, a network connection or an external power supply provides the power.

- **Switches with inline power:** Enable a modular wiring-closet infrastructure to provide centralized power for Cisco IP telephony networks. These switches are similar to traditional switches, with an option to provide power to the LAN ports where IP phones are connected. In addition, they perform some basic QoS mechanisms, such as packet classification, which is a baseline for prioritizing voice through the network.

- **Call-processing manager:** Cisco Unified Communications Manager provides central call control and configuration management for IP Phones. Cisco Unified Communications Manager provides the core functionality to initialize IP telephony devices and perform call setup and routing of calls throughout the network. Cisco Unified Communications Manager supports clustering, which provides a distributed scalable and highly available IP telephony model. In small or remote networks, Cisco offers a router-based solution for call-processing. This solution is referred to as Cisco Unified Communications Manager Express (CUCME).

- **Voice gateway:** Also called voice-enabled routers or switches, voice gateways provide voice services such as voice-to-IP coding and compression, PSTN access, IP packet routing, backup call processing, and voice services. Backup call processing enables voice gateways to take over call processing if the primary call-processing manager fails. Typically, voice gateways support a subset of the call-processing functionality supported by CUCM.

Recall from the voice planning section of this chapter that voice traffic has specific requirements. The voice flow needs steady pace and constant bandwidth to operate free of delay and jitter issues. Therefore, the first requirement for voice traffic integration is to implement QoS, which addresses bandwidth, delay, jitter, and packet loss requirements.

QoS does not solve bandwidth issues per se. QoS can prioritize only packets. When congestion is severe, QoS might not be sufficient anymore to guarantee voice traffic quality.

Configuring Switches to Support VoIP

From a switch perspective, Cisco switches generally apply three configuration options for supporting VoIP:

■ Voice VLANs

■ QoS

■ Power of Ethernet (PoE)

The next three sections discuss these features in more detail.

When this framework is implemented, voice-specific configuration can be added. At the access layer, PoE is configured if needed. Then, from the access ports and throughout the network, QoS is configured to encompass for the voice flow. AutoQoS can be used to configure QoS policies for VoIP on the access ports and the trunk links.

As delay is a permanent concern, ensure that high availability is configured throughout the network, and that the failover timers are set to a short value, to minimize the impact of a lost device on the ongoing voice conversations.

Voice VLANs

Cisco switches offer a unique feature called Voice VLANs, alternately named auxiliary VLAN. The voice VLAN feature enables you to overlay a voice topology onto a data network seamlessly. Voice VLANs provide for logical networks, even though the data and voice infrastructure are physically the same.

Note   Voice VLANs allow for logical separation of voice traffic from IP Phones or voice network devices on the same physical network as data traffic. Voice VLANs are optional but strongly recommended for any campus network deployment.

The voice VLAN feature places the phones into their own VLANs without any end-user intervention on the IP Phone. These VLAN assignments can be seamlessly maintained, even if the phone is moved to a new location. The user simply plugs the phone into the switch, and the switch provides the phone with the necessary VLAN information via the Cisco Discovery Protocol (CDP). By placing phones into their own VLANs, network administrators gain the advantages of network segmentation and control. Furthermore, network administrators can preserve their existing IP topology for the data end stations. IP Phones can be easily assigned to different IP subnets using standards-based DHCP operation.

With the phones in their own IP subnets and VLANs, network administrators can more easily identify and troubleshoot network problems. In addition, network administrators can create and enforce QoS or security policies.

With the Voice VLAN feature, Cisco enables network administrators to gain all the advantages of physical infrastructure convergence while maintaining separate logical topologies for voice and data terminals. This creates the most effective way to manage a multiservice network.

If an end-user workstation is attached to the Cisco IP Phone that connects to a Cisco switch with a Voice VLAN configuration, traffic from the user workstation is switched through the phone on the native VLAN, by default. The native VLAN is not tagged and is the actual switch port VLAN configuration . The Cisco IP Phone sends traffic with an 802.1q tag if a Voice VLAN is configured for a VLAN besides the native VLAN. Figure 7-37 illustrates this behavior.

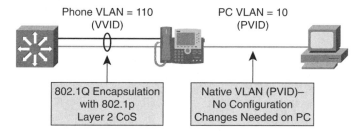

- The IP Phone is configured with a VVID during the initial Cisco Discovery Protocol exchange.
- The IP Phone is recognized uration via Cisco Discovery Protocol.

Figure 7-37   *Voice VLAN with Multiple VLANs*

The Voice VLAN feature on Cisco switches uses special nomenclature. The switch refers to the native VLAN for data traffic as the port VLAN ID (PVID) and the Voice VLAN for voice service as the voice VLAN ID (VVID). Moreover, the term Voice VLAN can be represented by the acronym VVLAN, and older Catalyst switches can refer to the Voice VLAN as the auxiliary especially those switches running Cisco CatOS.

The following steps highlight the commands to configure and to verify basic functionality of the Voice VLAN feature:

Step 1.   Ensure that QoS is globally enabled with the command **mls qos** and enter the configuration mode for the interface on which you want to configure Voice VLANs.

Step 2.   Enable the voice VLAN on the switch port and associate a VLAN ID using the interface command **switchport voice vlan** *vlan-id*.

Step 3.   Configure the port to trust CoS or trust DSCP as frames arrive on the switch port using the **mls qos trust cos** or **mls qos trust dscp** commands, respectively.

Recall that the **mls qos trust cos** trust ingress CoS where **mls qos trust dscp** trust ingress DSCP values. Do not confuse the two commands as each configures the switch to look at different bits in the frame for classification.

Step 4. Verify the voice VLAN configuration using the command **show interfaces** **interface-id** *switchport*.

Step 5. Verify the QoS interface configuration using the command **show mls qos** **interface** *interface-id*.

In Example 7-4, interface FastEthernet0/24 is configured to set data devices to VLAN 1 by default and VoIP devices to the voice VLAN 700. The switch uses CDP to inform an attached IP Phone of the VLAN. As the port leads to an end device, portfast is enabled. See earlier chapters for more on the Spanning Tree Protocol.

Example 7-4 *Sample Interface Configuration for Voice VLANs in Cisco IOS*

```
(text deleted)
!
mls qos
!
(text deleted)
!
interface FastEthernet0/24

 switchport mode dynamic desirable
 switchport voice vlan 700
 mls qos trust cos
 power inline auto
 spanning-tree portfast
!
(text deleted)
!
```

QoS for Voice Traffic from IP Phones

In a campus QoS implementation, boundaries are defined where the existing QoS values of frames can be accepted (trusted) or altered. Cisco switches apply configurations at these "trust boundaries" to enforce QoS classification and marking as traffic makes its way into the network. At these boundaries, traffic will be optionally allowed to retain its original QoS marking or will optionally have new marking ascribed because of policies associated with its entry point into the network.

Note When a switch that is configured for QoS receives a frame, the switch is either configured to accept the frames DSCP and CoS marking or alter the frames' DSCP or CoS marking.

The term trust from a switch port QoS configuration point-of-view, implies that the switch accepts any DSCP or CoS value received on its port.

Trust boundaries establish a border for traffic entering the campus network. As traffic traverses the switches of the campus network, it is handled and prioritized according to the marks received or trusted when the traffic originally entered the network at the trust boundary.

At the trust boundary device, QoS values are trusted if they are considered to accurately represent the type of traffic and precedence processing that the traffic should receive as it enters the campus network.

If untrusted, the traffic is marked with a new QoS value that is appropriate for the policy that is in place at the point where the traffic enters the campus network. Ideally, the trust boundary exists at the first switch that receives traffic from a device or IP Phone. It is also acceptable to establish the trust boundary as all the traffic from an access switch that enters a distribution layer switch port.

To enable QoS on a switch, some models of Cisco switches just require you to enter any QoS command; some others need to have QoS support globally enabled through the command **mls qos.** Refer to the Cisco configuration guide for your specific model of the Cisco switch for more information.

In the Example 7-4, QoS support is first enabled globally. The CoS values received from the phone are trusted and not altered.

You can use the **show mls qos** family of commands to display QoS configuration on specific models of Cisco switches. Check the product configuration guides for your specific switch.

Power over Ethernet

All VoIP-enabled devices need a source of power. When these devices are handheld or mobile devices, the source of energy is usually a battery. Desktop or wall-mount VoIP phones can be connected to an A/C adapter for power.

Although power is easily available in an office environment, using one AC/DC socket per VoIP device might be considered as a waste of physical resources. Because the phone has a cable connection to the Ethernet switch, a logical solution is to use this cable to provide power and connectivity.

This setting, called Power over Ethernet (PoE), implies that the power comes through the Ethernet cable. The source of this power can be the switch itself, if the switch supports the PoE feature.

If the switch cannot provide power, it is often possible to install an intermediate device between the switch and the VoIP phone. This device will receive power from a power outlet and will connect to the switch with another cable. It connects to the port to which the phone is supposed to connect. A third cable runs from this intermediate device to the phone, providing power along with data transmission to and from the switch. This device is called a power injector.

To decrease the cost and complexity of the installation, powering the devices directly from the switch is often seen as the best solution.

A great advantage of PoE is that no electrician is required. Anyone qualified to run Category 5e cable can install the cabling required to power PoE enabled devices. The standard Category 5e cable requirements still apply (maximum 328 feet or 100 meters).

Two common PoE methods exist: the Cisco inline power and the IEEE 802.3af standard. Cisco inline power is prestandard because the IEEE 802.3 standard did not include specifications for PoE. The 802.3af task force amended this omission and a standard was realized in 2003. Cisco was actively involved in the 802.3af taskforce and support of the IEEE inline power standard. One of the main differences is that 802.3af uses a power detection mechanism that detects if the connected device needs power. Standard ratification of 802.3af occurred on September 11, 2009.

New Cisco devices (switches, access points) support both methods for backward compatibility. No specific configuration is required to choose the Cisco prestandard or the 802.3af standard. The IEEE 803.2af standard will be enhanced with a new standard 802.3at, which will provide more power in future.

Note   Link Layer Discovery Protocol-Media Endpoint Discovery (LLDP) protocol is a new standards-based protocol currently implemented in the Cisco phone and switching products. This protocol provides capability for the switches to recognize and provide power to any vendor phone attached to the network.

An interim solution from Cisco called enhanced PoE provides up to 20W of power with the E-series switches. Although most devices can use power supplied by a standard 802.3af source, some new devices require more power.

Power requirements for access-points are specific. Cisco IP Phones use less than 15 Watts and can be powered from a standard 802.3af switch.

PoE support is done at the port level. The command **power inline auto** is sufficient to enable PoE and autodetection of power requirements. A device not needing any PoE can still be connected to that port: Power is supplied only if the device requires it. The amount of power supplied will be automatically detected. You still have to plan for the overall power consumed by all the devices connected to the PoE switch.

The command **show power inline**, as shown in Example 7-5, displays the configuration and statistics about the used power drawn by connected powered devices and the capacity of the power supply.

Example 7-5   *Inline Power Example*

```
Switch# show power inline fastethernet 4/1
Available:665(w)   Used:663(w)    Remaining:2(w)
Interface  Admin    Oper     Power          Device          Class
                             (Watts)

---- ---- ---- ---- ---- ---- ---- ---- ---- ---- ---- ----

Fa4/1      auto     on           5.0 Cisco IP Phone 7960 n/a
Interface  AdminPowerMax    AdminAllocation
           (milli-watts)    (milli-watts)

---- ---- ---- ---- ---- ---- ---- ---- ---- ---- ---- --

Fa4/1      15400            15400
Switch#
```

Every switch has a dedicated maximum amount of power available for PoE. The power used by each PoE port is deducted from the total available power. The power used by each device is dynamically learned from via CDP. This feature allows for optimization of the actual power consumption, as a PoE device does not always consume the maximum amount of power it needs. For example, an IP Phone classified as 15 Watts might use up to 15 Watts when fully utilized, but use only 6 or 7 Watts while it is on hook.

Note   Pay close attention to power budgeting and associated power supply requirements because many designers overlook PoE power requirements.

Nevertheless, if a phone is said to require up to 15 Watts, if the remaining power at the switch level is less than 15 Watts, the phone will not get power at all. Notice that not all switches have 15 Watts of power available for all ports. Some switches have all ports being PoE with 15 Watts each (which is the maximum possible power under the 802.3af protocol); some others have only a few ports supporting PoE, and not all of them offer 15 Watts.

When a VoIP device obtains power and accesses the network at Layer 2, it needs to obtain an IP address. Just like any other client device, it can obtain this IP address through a DHCP server.

Additional Network Requirements for VoIP

One additional requirement of Cisco IP phones is that they also need to download a specific configuration file that can provide them with specific voice information, such as Codec to use, location of the CUCM or CUCME. This configuration file is downloaded using TFTP. The TFTP server IP address can be configured manually into each Cisco IP Phone, or provided as a DHCP option 150 (TFTP server address).

The VoIP device then downloads its configuration file from the TFTP server and also verifies whether a newer firmware is available. It then tries to reach a CUCM or CUCME server. This server's IP address can be provided within the configuration file or can be provisioned through DNS. Many deployments tend to use the CUCM or CUCME as the

TFTP server to simplify the overall procedure, thus removing the need for an external TFTP server and DNS resolution.

When the phone contacts the CUCM or CUCME, it registers to it, obtains its line extension number, and is ready to place or receive calls.

To test voice implementation, it is recommended to work through the logical boot process of the phone.

Like any other networking device, a phone upon boot up needs to receive power. It will then receive an IP address. If the IP address is received via DHCP, the DHCP option should also provide the CUCM or CUCME IP address. The phone downloads its configuration and firmware from the voice server, before registering, obtaining a phone extension and is ready to place a call.

When testing a new VoIP implementation, a logical testing scheme is to check that the phone receives power; then an IP address actually tries to get to the CUCM or CUCME, and registers there. When all these steps are completed, the phone can place and receive calls.

Preparing the Campus Infrastructure to Support Video

As previously discussed, video is no longer in its infancy, but it's still a growing and evolving technology yielding tremendous benefits to the enterprise in forms of collaboration. When deploying this technology in the campus, several switch configurations need to be considered. This section reviews video components and applications and discusses a few best practices for storage.

Video Components

Video components were covered in the planning section on video in this chapter. As a short review, the following list highlights the most common video applications found deployed in campus networks:

■ Peer-to-peer video

■ TelePresence

■ IP surveillance

■ Digital media systems

IP surveillance and digital media systems were not covered as video applications in the planning section. IP surveillance systems record video for security purposes. Traditional surveillance security companies now offer IP solutions, and Cisco offers its own solution as well. IP surveillance solutions enable for features not typical with traditional video surveillance. These features include digital video archiving, on-demand viewing, and e-mail and web video updates.

Moreover, digital media systems offer video as a means of communication. Cisco currently offers a digital media system that offers a full set of features to include social video, digital signage, and IPTV systems. The Cisco digital media system is geared for learning, communication, and collaboration.

As with peer-to-peer video and TelePresence, IP surveillance and digital media systems bandwidth and availability requirements must be taken into account when designing a campus network.

Configuring Switches to Support Video

Cisco switches do not require any specific or standard configuration to support video. However, PoE is optional for some models of IP surveillance cameras, and QoS features might be necessary to guarantee bandwidth or solve traffic congestion issues caused by high-bandwidth applications such as TelePresence. The recommend best practice goals for jitter, latency, and packet loss of TelePresence or any real-time (interactive) video applications is as follows:

■   Packet loss of less than 0.5 percent

■   Jitter of less than 10 ms one-way

■   Latency of less than 150 ms one-way

As a best practice for achieving these goals for TelePresence or other high-bandwidth video applications, consider implementing the QoS configurations:

■   Classify and mark traffic by using DSCP as close to its edge as possible, preferably on the first-hop access layer switch. If a host is trusted, allow the trusted hosts to mark their own traffic.

■   Trust QoS on each inter-switch and switch to router links to preserve marking as frames travel through the network. See RFC4594 for more information.

■   Limit the amount of real-time voice and video traffic to 33 percent of link capacity; if higher than this, TelePresence data might starve out other applications resulting in slow or erratic performance of data applications.

■   Reserve at least 25 percent of link bandwidth for the best-effort data traffic.

■   Deploy a 1 percent Scavenger class to help ensure that unruly applications do not dominate the best-effort data class.

■   Use DSCP-based Weighted Random Early Detection (WRED) queuing on all TCP flows, wherever possible.

The preceding list is only a high-level synopsis of a few best-practice guidelines for TelePresence and other high-bandwidth applications. However, these applications require a detailed analysis end-to-end of the entire enterprise network for preparing any QoS implementation. As such, the context of QoS needed for TelePresence is outside the scope of this book. Review additional documentation on Cisco.com or consult with specialist prior to implementing TelePresence in a campus network.

Summary

This chapter presented topics pertaining to implementing wireless, voice, and video into the campus network. As evident by the amount of material presented and the brevity that some of the topics covered, you should consult specialist, experts, and persons experienced with these technologies before planning an implementation. Switching is a broad enough topic without the inclusion of these advance technologies.

Nevertheless, the follow list summarizes several key points for wireless, voice, and video from this chapter:

- When planning for a wireless deployment, carefully consider the standalone WLAN solution and the controller-based solution. For networks of more than a few access points, the best practice is to use a controller-based solution.

- When preparing for a wireless deployment, verify your switch port configuration as a truck port. Access points optionally support trunking and carry multiple VLANs. Wireless clients can map to different SSIDs, which it turn might be carried on different VLANs.

- When planning for a voice implementation in the campus network, best-practice guides recommend the use of QoS and the use of a separate VLAN for voice traffic. Power over Ethernet (PoE) is another option to power Cisco IP Phones without the use of an AC/DC adapter.

- When preparing for the voice implementation, ensure that you configure QoS as close to the edge port as possible. Best practice guides recommend trusting DSCP or CoS of frames entering the switch.

- When planning for a video implementation, denote whether the video application is real-time video or on-demand video. Real-time video requires low latency and send traffic in bursts at high bandwidth.

- When preparing for a video implementation such as TelePresence, consult with a specialist or expert to ensure the campus network meets all the requirements in terms of bandwidth, QoS, and such.

Review Questions

Use the questions here to review what you learned in this chapter. The correct answers are found in Appendix A, "Answers to Chapter Review Questions."

1. When planning for access point deployments in a wireless LAN of a campus network, what are the two Cisco best-practice solutions?

   a. Standalone WLAN solutions (autonomous solutions)

   b. Network-based WLAN solutions

   c. Controller-based WLAN solutions

   d. Internet router-based WLAN solutions

2. What video applications are driving video deployments in the campus network?

   a. TelePresence

   b. Remote training and learning

   c. Virtual classrooms

   d. Video-on-demand

3. In a controller-based WLAN solution, which device does all the traffic flow through when communicating between wireless nodes?

   a. WLSE

   b. RADIUS server

   c. WLC

   d. WCS

4. Which devices can support power through 802.3af?

   a. Access points

   b. WLCs

   c. IP surveillance cameras

   d. Cisco IP Phones

5. When planning for a wireless LAN deployment in a campus network, which factor generally determines whether to deploy a standalone solution or a controller-based solution?

   a. Variety of different wireless clients models in use, such as Dell, HP, Intel, and so on

   b. Number of access switches in the campus

   c. Scale and size of the Wireless LAN and then number of access points required

   d. Encryption requirements

6. When a Cisco switch is configured for a Voice VLANs, connected Cisco IP Phones learn of the Voice VLAN ID (VVID) through which mechanism?

   a. DHCP.

   b. ARP.

   c. CDP.

   d. DNS.

   e. None of the above. Cisco IP Phones must be statically configured for Voice VLANs.

7. When deploying voice (IP telephony) and video in the campus network, as a best practice where in the campus network should voice traffic be classified for QoS?

   a. Distribution layer

   b. Core layer

   c. Access layer

8. QoS has no affect on the behavior of traffic flows in the campus network unless one of the following conditions holds true?

   a. There is congestion in the network.

   b. There is excess available bandwidth in the network.

   c. The network uses port-channels.

   d. The network uses 802.1q trunks to interconnect switches.

9. When a Cisco switch assigns a CoS value to an incoming frame, what component of QoS does the procedure map to?

   a. Classification and marking

   b. Shaping and policing

   c. Congestion management

   d. Congestion avoidance

10. Which command overrides CoS values on ingress frames to 1?

   a. mls qos dscp 1

   b. mls qos trust cos

   c. mls cos 1

   d. mls qos cos 1

11. What is the purpose of trust boundaries?

   a. To determine the classification of a packet at a specific location in the network.

   b. To determine where in the network packets are dropped.

   c. To determine where in the network to reclassify packets.

   d. It is an administrative configuration in which Layer 2 or Layer 3 priority designations of frames or packets are either accepted or not.

12. Consider a network design in which a video server needs a higher class of service for video data compared to other regular data traffic. The server does not support 802.1q tagging or setting bits in the IP field for priority. Furthermore, the server transmits other management traffic besides the video. Which of the following QoS components and methods would correctly prioritize traffic from the video server?

   a. Port-based classification in which the configuration would set all ingress frames from the server to a DSCP value of 36

   b. Port-based classification using a policy map that uses a class map with an ACL that distinctively marks frames for video traffic with a DSCP value of 36

   c. Using a policer to mark all frames from the server above a certain rate with a DSCP value of 36

   d. Using an input ACL to classify all frames from the server with a DSCP value of 36

13. Which QoS model requires end-to-end configuration?

   a. LFI

   b. IntServ

   c. DiffServ

   d. Traffic conditioning

14. What are two benefits of the voice (auxiliary) VLAN feature of Catalyst switches? (Choose two.)

   a. Reduced bandwidth utilization

   b. Easier troubleshooting

   c. Data and voice segmentation

   d. Redundancy

15. Which of the following features is used to distinguish voice VLAN traffic from access (data) traffic in a packet? (Choose two.)

   a. ISL encapsulation

   b. DHCP

   c. HSRP

   d. 802.1Q tagging

   e. marking

16. By default, Cisco IP Phones mark traffic at the IP layer and at Layer 2. Which of the following fields is marked in the IP header by Cisco IP Phones to indicate priority at Layer 3?

   a. CoS

   b. TTL

   c. DSCP

   d. Checksum

   e. Identifier

17. What differentiates IP multicast from other transmission modes?

   a. IP multicast sends packets to a single host.

   b. IP multicast sends packets to groups of hosts where specific hosts process the packet.

   c. IP multicast sends packets to all hosts sequentially.

   d. IP multicast sends packets to all hosts simultaneously.

18. What is one potential drawback to source distribution trees compared to shared distribution trees?

   a. Increased latency

   b. Increased memory overhead

   c. Suboptimal path calculations

   d. Increased bandwidth utilization

19. Under which condition should you choose PIM sparse mode as opposed to PIM dense mode?

    a. Bandwidth is plentiful.

    b. The multicast group has many members.

    c. The hosts in the multicast group are widely dispersed.

    d. Almost all hosts on the network belong to the multicast group.

20. Which version of IGMP adds support for source filtering?

    a. IGMPv1

    b. IGMPv2

    c. IGMPv3

    d. IGMPv3 lite

21. Which command correctly displays the contents of the IP multicast routing table?

    a. show ip mfib

    b. show ip mroute

    c. show mroute table

    d. show ip pim interface

22. When preparing for a TelePresence deployment in the campus network, what is the max latency that traffic flow, one-way, should experience?

    a. 1 sec

    b. 150 msec

    c. 10 msec

    d. 1 msec

Answers to Chapter Review Questions

Chapter 1

1. A
2. B
3. B
4. A, B, C, and D
5. A
6. C
7. A
8. C
9. A and B
10. C
11. A, B, C, and E
12. A, B, and E
13. A, B, and E
14. A, B, and E
15. E
16. A, B, and C
17. D
18. C
19. C

20. C

21. D

22. B, C, and E

23. C

24. A

25. Prepare, Plan, Design, Implement, Operate, and Optimize

26. A, B, and D

27. A

Chapter 2

1. True

2. False

3. False

4. True

5. False

6. False

7. A

8. D

9. A

10. B

11. C

12. A

13. B

14. A and C

15. D

16. A

17. A

18. B

19. C

20. D

21. A and E

22. C

23. D

24. D

25. B, C, and D

26. A

27. D

28. VTP pruning uses VLAN advertisements to determine when a trunk connection is flooding traffic needlessly.

29. Private VLANs provide security and reduce the use of IP subnets by isolating traffic between the end stations even though they are in the same VLAN.

30. If Workstations A and B are members of the same community Private VLAN, they can communicate with each other, but they cannot communicate if each workstation is a member of a different community, Private VLAN, or a member of the same isolated Private VLAN. In any case, all ports that are members of either isolated or community Private VLAN can communicate with promiscuous ports.

31. True

32. A and B

Chapter 3

1. False

2. False

3. A

4. B

5. B

6. E

7. D

8. False

9. A

10. A

11. A

12. C

13. D

Chapter 4

1. False

2. True

3. True

4. A

5. B

6. C

7. B and F

8. The order is D, A, E, B, and C.

9. C and E

10. B

11. D

12. C

13. B and E

14. C and D

15. D

16. E

17. C

18. A

19. DHCP is a client-server application, in which the DHCP client contacts a DHCP server for configuration parameters using a broadcast request. If a client is in a different subnet than a server, the broadcast is forwarded using the DHCP relay agent feature by the local router or multilayer switch.

20. B and C

Chapter 5

1. False

2. False

3. D

4. A

5. D

6. A

7. E

8. E

9. D

Chapter 6

1. True

2. True

3. False

4. F

5. B

6. D

7. B

8. B

9. B

10. B, C, and D

11. True

Chapter 7

1. A and C

2. A

3. C

4. A, C, and D

5. C

6. C

7. C

8. A

9. A

10. D

11. A

12. B

13.   B

14.   B and C

15.   D and E

16.   C

17.   B

18.   D

19.   C

20.   C

21.   B

22.   B

Index

Numerics

J-K-L

M

S

W-X-Y-Z

FREE Online
Edition

Your purchase of **Implementing Cisco IP Switched Networks (SWITCH) Foundation Learning Guide** includes access to a free online edition for 45 days through the Safari Books Online subscription service. Nearly every Cisco Press book is available online through Safari Books Online, along with more than 5,000 other technical books and videos from publishers such as Addison-Wesley Professional, Exam Cram, IBM Press, O'Reilly, Prentice Hall, Que, and Sams.

SAFARI BOOKS ONLINE allows you to search for a specific answer, cut and paste code, download chapters, and stay current with emerging technologies.

Activate your FREE Online Edition at
www.informit.com/safarifree

> **STEP 1:** Enter the coupon code: OJPIZAA.

> **STEP 2:** New Safari users, complete the brief registration form.
> Safari subscribers, just log in.

If you have difficulty registering on Safari or accessing the online edition, please e-mail customer-service@safaribooksonline.com